Bartons Point

Copper
Works

Rope
Walk

Rope Walk

Charles River

Let's Ship Yard

Ferry to Charles Town

Eb.N. Mill Damm

Mill Pond.

N. Water Mill

Gees Ship Y:d

Hudsons Point

Hunt &
White's
Ship Yd

Ferry Way
Ferry

Burying
Place

Bakera

Rucks W.

Salem Street

more
ough's
Ship Y.

Bowling
green

Watermill

Baptist Meeting

Hanover

Treamount St.

School

Old Way

ack Street

Middle Street.

Union S.

Lyn Street

North Street

Thunt
Wharfe

Thorntons
Yard.

N. Battery.

Burroughs W.

Grant &
Greenwood
Ship Y & Wharfe

Clarks Ship
Yd

Clarks Ship Y.d & Wharfe

Scarletts Wharfe.

5th Street

Clarks W.

Galleys W.

Highwoods W.

Fidch

Cornhill

King St

G.

Clark Square

Ship Street

Hatchinstons W.

Lees Ship Yd

Borells W.

Wentworths Wharfe

Woodmans W.

Butlers Wharfe

Old Wharfe.

Clarks Wharfe.

Marshalls W.

Fools Whar

Olivers Dock

Parmers W.

Greenleafs Yd

Long Ware H.

Wings Sh Yd

Olivers Wharfe

Gales Sh Yd

Long Wharfe

Old Wharfe.

Fort Hill

S Battery.

HARBOUR

Gibbes W.

Hubbards W.

The Last American Puritan

Increase Mather. Oil painting by Jan van der Spriett, London, 1688.

MICHAEL G. HALL

The
Last American
Puritan

The Life of Increase Mather

1639–1723

WESLEYAN UNIVERSITY PRESS

Middletown, Connecticut

All inquiries and permissions requests should be addressed to the Publisher, Wesleyan University Press,
110 Mt. Vernon Street, Middletown, Connecticut 06457

Distributed by Harper & Row Publishers, Keystone Industrial Park, Scranton, Pennsylvania 18512

LIBRARY OF CONGRESS CATALOGING-IN-PUBLICATION DATA

Hall, Michael G. (Michael Garibaldi)
    The last American Puritan.

    Bibliography: p.
    Includes index.
    1. Mather, Increase, 1639–1723.   2. Puritans—
Massachusetts—Biography.   3. Massachusetts—History—
Colonial period, ca. 1600–1775.   I. Title.
F67.M468H35   1988   974.4′02′0924 [B]   87-7367
ISBN 0-8195-5128-7

Manufactured in the United States of America

FIRST EDITION

To

MARGARET NIXON HALL

for whom I herewith divest myself of the Mathers

and

ELIZABETH HOOD HALL

whose love and strength makes life a joy

Contents

List of Illustrations

Preface

On July 13, 1986, a story in the *New York Times* quoted Pope John Paul II on the subject of angels. "The angels are those creatures which are unseen," the pope told a large audience. "They are invisible, for they are purely spiritual beings." I was struck by the similarity to Increase Mather's book on angels, which he published in 1696, not long after the Salem witchcraft trials. Both religious leaders felt the need to reaffirm the traditional teachings of the church about an invisible spirit world to a society of, in the pope's words, "rationalists and materialists." The similarity reminded me of how, twenty years ago, I had read the autobiography of Pope John XXIII and found in it the same piety and awe of God's presence that Increase Mather had expressed in *his* autobiography. It is ironic that the Puritan leader of Massachusetts, to whom the pope was the Red Whore of Babylon, and these twentieth-century popes should have so much in common. The world views of seventeenth-century New England Puritans and twentieth-century Roman popes are closer to each other than either is to the secular and materialistic world view that dominates the industrialized countries of today.

I first became interested in Increase Mather when I was studying the American colonies from the point of view of English colonial policy. For four years, 1688–1691, Increase Mather was in London negotiating with kings and high ministers of state for a new charter for Massachusetts—not the usual setting of a Puritan minister. His autobiography, written in the rhetoric of Whig politics, dealt largely with the negotiations in England and had not before been published. I edited it for publication. Later, when I was interested in the history of science in early America, I studied his diaries, because Mather was an enthusiast of early modern science. He published a book on comets in 1683, the first of its kind in English, and organized a philosophical society in Boston modelled on the Royal Society of Isaac Newton and Robert Boyle. Hundreds of pages of his diaries have survived, in a next-to-illegible handwriting. Mather was a prodigious scholar who carefully noted in his diaries what he read from day to day. In the end I completed a typescript of the diaries. The time had come for me to choose between a published edition of the diaries or a biography. No comprehensive biography of Increase Mather had been written since the important studies of New England begun in the 1930s, and, therefore, I chose to write one.

A biography of Increase Mather inevitably led me into the intricacies of New England Puritanism. The history of religion had not been a major interest of mine. What made it palatable was Mather's universality of interest. Besides the well-publicized jeremiads, which are today exaggeratedly used to characterize American Puritan culture, Mather wrote history, doctrine, a small book on witches, widely credited with stopping the trials and executions of 1692, the first American biography, and scores of evangelical and proselytizing sermons that seem often to contradict prevailing views of what seventeenth-century New England Puritanism was all about.

It became apparent to me that the high point of New England Puritan culture came in the 1670s. That was the time when self-awareness was most fully articulated and before the social, political and intellectual forces that would erode Puritanism had taken effect. Increase Mather was the leading exponent of that Puritan culture; he was one of the men who "invented New England," and he was New England's leading defender in the ensuing fifty years. Paradoxically, he also became the sole New Englander responsible for Massachusetts's second royal charter, which wiped out the political basis for the Puritan state.

Mather's private life was, I discovered, as interesting as his public career. His life was dominated by an extraordinary Oedipal conflict with his father and an equally complex relationship with his famous son Cotton. For years Mather's church sought to ordain Cotton as an assistant to his father, but for years Increase put them off. When he could do so no longer, he preached an ambivalent sermon on Numbers 20.26, which suggested bitterly that his son would supplant him in the ministry. Increase was then at the height of his powers and on the threshold of political leadership.

Having studied Increase Mather inter alia for twenty-five years, I am in debt to more people than I can adequately thank. Walter Muir Whitehill, Stephen Riley, Clifford K. Shipton, Lester A. Cappon, and Leo and Helen Flaherty were among those who gave me generous help in those early years. I realize now how lucky I was. More recently, Marcus Mc-Corison at the American Antiquarian Society in Worcester, and Louis L. Tucker at the Massachusetts Historical Society have put the resources of those great research institutions at my disposal. The American Antiquarian Society is the major repository of Mather's books and papers, and it is to that staff that I am most indebted: Mary Brown and her successor, Keith Arbour; John Hench, Fred Bauer, and William Joyce, with whom I collaborated twice; and Nancy Burkett and Marie Lamoureux are among those who have made my work there easy and enjoyable.

My own university and department gave freely during these years in funds to make research trips possible, in released time, and in support for typing and related costs. I am particularly grateful to William S. Livingston, vice-president and dean of the graduate school, for his support, and to my colleagues in the department of history. I am indebted also to David Damerall and Kenneth Silverman, both of whom gave scholarly asistance noted in the appropriate places below. I wish to thank all those who worked on the final manuscript: Sally Weegar, Jill Bickers, David Nalle, and special thanks to Jeannette Hopkins of Wesleyan University Press for her editorial guidance. The inadequacies are mine.

The Last American Puritan

CHAPTER I

The Legacy, Birth, and Education of a Puritan

[1639-1661]

"P" FOR PURITAN

On the longest day of the year, June 21, 1639, Richard and Katherine Mather's last son was born. Two days later, Richard baptized his son in his own church in Dorchester, Massachusetts, naming him Increase because of the "never-to-be-forgotten *Increase, of every sort, wherewith* GOD favoured the Country, about the time of his Nativity."[1] It was four years after Richard and Katherine Mather had left England for this new and favored country.

Richard Mather and Katherine Holt had been born in the western midlands of England into a vigorous and creative time in England's history. In 1596, the year Richard was born, Queen Elizabeth had been on the throne for thirty-seven years. In poetry and prose, music, and the theatre, in schooling and literacy, English culture had reached a high water mark. Men of action and adventure were everywhere. It was an heroic age of seamen, the age of Drake and the repulse of the Armada. Richard Hakluyt's *Principal Navigations and Voyages of the English Nation* had appeared in 1589 to tell English men and women in their own tongue of English adventures overseas. It was also a time when the religious revival within the Church of England known as Puritanism had reached early maturity in the writings of John Preston, Richard Sibbes, and William Ames. Richard Mather's generation would demand political and religious change from the Elizabethan world and by the middle of the next century, when change was slow in coming, they would bring down both the monarchy and the church. A few of them would break away and carry that radical spirit for reform to the New World, to a New England.

Richard Mather and Katherine Holt were born into a class of substantial yeomen and lesser gentry in the western midlands not far from where Liverpool has since spread out across the old pastoral countryside. It was a slow-paced world of farms, small villages, and market towns, where, as in all parts of rural England, the Puritan religious fervor made steady headway amongst sober people.

Richard's father insisted that he go to grammar school, and so Richard walked the three miles each way in summer and boarded near the school in winter. By the time he was fourteen or fifteen he hoped to go on to the university, but his father either could not or would not pay for it. Instead, at fifteen Richard was told to take a job teaching school. He left his parents' home for good then, as did many another young man; it was a common pattern among certain social classes in the England of that day for children to leave their parents' homes in early adolescence. Richard began to teach English and Latin grammar to children some miles away in the town of Toxteth. He boarded in the family of a well-to-do gentleman who had several children in the school.[2]

The family in which he lived was a pious one and almost certainly practiced the regular devotional exercises that were a hallmark of English Puritan life, distinguishing the slow spread of Puritanism through English society. The entire household, servants as well as family, met morning and evening for prayers and scripture reading, and possibly also the singing of psalms. Meals began with prayers of thanksgiving. The older children were given responsibility in reading and leading prayers and for catechizing the younger children. In this atmosphere of systematic daily devotion, young men and women were inculcated with a piety that traced its roots back to St. Augustine's *Confessions.*

A continuum of experience linked English Puritans to the continental reformed churches and these in turn, to mystical and devotional traditions within the medieval Roman church—Loyola's *Spiritual Exercises;* Francis de Sale's *Introduction to the Devout Life;* St. Teresa de Avila's *The Interior Castle.*[3] English Puritanism brought a traditional and daily devotional regimen into the family and the household. While English Puritans did not believe that prayers and devotions would earn them any merit towards salvation, they did believe they could soften Calvin's severe doctrine of human inability. If a man believed in Christ, he would receive grace: "The federal theory," Perry Miller wrote, "freeing man from the absolute moral impotence of the strict doctrine, first made possible an enlargement of his innate capacities."[4]

Devotional exercises of Pauline or Augustinian piety were not the only influences leading Richard Mather towards Puritanism. Several Church of England priests in nearby parishes were Puritan in their conduct of services, no doubt dispensing with the elaborate vestments of their office, and, particularly, the simple, white surplice, a symbolic act in hundreds of cases of the Puritan clergy's resistance to a centralized church liturgy. That centralized liturgy, defined in minute detail by the Book of Common Prayer, ironically had played a critical role in England's earlier break from Rome, but under Elizabeth and now under James I in the early seventeenth century it represented the worst of an authoritarian and irreligious ecclesiastical establishment. Devout men and women across England found church services according to the Prayer Book void of spiritual meaning, "nothing more than empty ritual, a routine made up of external gestures without deep inner commitment."[5] Richard Mather's generation came to reserve its greatest disdain for such empty forms of worship: "This corrupt Service booke has stunk above ground twice forty yeares, in the nostrills of many godly, who breathed in the pure ayre of the holy Scriptures."[6] Presumably Mather studied the writings of Puritan religious writers like John Preston and Richard Sibbes, men who developed the theological and doctrinal positions of the movement, read and debated with leaders of the reformed churches on the continent, and defined the broad spectrum of ideas that came to characterize the Puritan movement in England. Mather left little exact evidence of his reading, and we do not know what specific influences led him on towards a life of scholarship, only that he was largely self-educated, a circumstance that set him apart from his peers in later years.

Essential to Puritan thought was belief in the utter, inescapable sinfulness of man. "Every man is born stark dead in sin," wrote Thomas Shepard. "He is born empty of every inward principle of life, void of all graces, and hath no more good in him (whatsoever he thinks) than a dead carrion hath. . . . Their bodies are living coffins to carry a dead soul up and down."[7] Puritan writers reserved their most pithy language for efforts to convey the worthlessness of human nature.

The corollary was that human ability had no role at all in a person's spiritual growth, all of which depended on the gift of God's grace, totally free, unconditioned, and unmerited. God, it was a Puritan belief, provided not only the content of belief and instruction for devotional exercise through scripture, but the will to believe itself. Without the unearned gift of grace no one could believe, so sinful was the natural person.

Awareness of this dependence on grace for all that is good and a sense of personal guilt and wickedness that for a moment shattered self-esteem both were characteristic of the Puritan experience of conversion, a new birth in Christ. This personal experience of a new birth was to become a focus of dissension in America. The climax of Richard Mather's experience of spiritual regeneration, to be passed on to his son and grandson as surely as if it were inheritance of property, occurred in his eighteenth year. His son, almost certainly relying on a written account among his father's papers, described Richard's anguished experience: "the pangs of the New Birth were exceedingly terrible to him, inasmuch as many times when they were at Meals in the Family where he sojourned, he would absent himself to retire under hedges and other secret places, there to lament his misery before God. But after some time, the Lord revived his broken heart by sending the holy Spirit in the Ministry of the Word to apply the *Precious Promises* of the Gospel to his Soul."[8]

Sometime in the next few years, Richard Mather, then about twenty, left the school and family where he had spent his adolescence and entered Brasenose College, Oxford. The experience was disappointing and before long he returned to Toxteth without taking a degree. Few clues remain of his university life. He was certainly older than most entering students, and more mature. His son later observed that going to university after already having experienced religious rebirth had set him aside from ordinary collegiate life—"removed him from temptations." Or perhaps Mather simply could not meet the costs. At any rate, the families at Toxteth asked him to return to them and he did, first resuming his post at the school and then seeking ordination in the church.[9]

Nothing is more typical of the spread of Puritanism in England than this process of selection at the grass roots of society. A community, whose religious life centered in family devotions, would encourage one of their own to become their minister. It was a process repeated a thousand times in the spread of English reformed religion to America, always in the form appropriate to the specific time and place. In Richard Mather's England, that meant ordination as a priest in the Church of England, and in his mid-twenties he applied for and received ordination from his bishops and began his ministry.[10]

Birthplace in Lancashire of Richard Mather, Increase Mather's father

In these years, too, he met and fell in love with Katherine Holt. Katherine was the daughter of Edmund Holt, one of England's small country gentry, a landowner and farmer who disapproved of his daughter's marriage to a village priest, and a Puritan at that. But Katherine also had become a Puritan, her commitment to a life in Christ no less devout than Richard's. After two years, her father relented, and in 1624 the two were married. With her dowry and his own resources they were able to purchase a home of their own in the village of Much-Wooton, Lancashire. For the next ten years they lived there and prospered. Richard Mather became increasingly popular in the region, reaching out further and further to preach the Word, not only in regular Sabbath services, but on weekdays and saints' days, by invitation from Puritan families elsewhere in a region so Puritan it was dubbed "the Holy Land."[11] Katherine directed the household and the ordering of their family. Every two years or so she gave birth to a son; one died in infancy, but by 1634 Richard and Katherine had three living sons, Samuel, Timothy and Nathaniel.

Richard Mather, suspended from Anglican ministry for nonconformity, came to Massachusetts in 1635 and settled in Dorchester. Oil painting by an unknown artist

Richard Mather, 1670. Woodcut by John Foster based on earlier oil painting, the first print known to have been made in the American colonies

In those ten years the Puritan movement within the Church of England had come to be opposed by another and more traditional faction at court, in the church, and across the country in an England that was deeply divided. James I had replied to the Millenary Petition twenty years before, "No Bishops, No King," and the royal court was hostile to Puritanism; it stuck firmly to the principle of absolute, hierarchical authority, no less in church than in state. When Charles I came to the throne in 1624, he appointed as Bishop of London his friend William Laud, a brilliant scholar and administrator, founder of educational institutions and international scholarships. Laud took on the leadership of the anti-Puritan wing of the church, and in his diocese of London compiled "O and P" lists, marking down against the name of every priest in the diocese an "O" for orthodox or "P" for Puritan. The "P"'s were summoned before him for a tongue-lashing and frequently a strict injunction against preaching further in London. [12]

In 1630 Charles I made Laud Archbishop of Canterbury, and Laud's attack on the Puritan clergy broadened. One after another the most celebrated Puritan preachers in England were brought before their bishops and silenced. Also in 1630 a handful of Puritan gentlemen, headed by John Winthrop, Lord of the Manor of Groton, led a large party of men and women to New England; the year before they had been granted a royal charter to establish a plantation in the name of the "Governor and Company of the Mattachusetts Bay in Newe England," but unknown to the crown, Winthrop and his party had no intention of creating a joint-stock trading company like the one that had settled Jamestown in Virginia twenty years before. They planned instead to emigrate with their families to start life afresh in America.

Winthrop and his closest colleagues were not priests escaping persecution by high-church bishops but, rather, lay gentlemen who had economic and political as well as religious motives for leaving England at a time of constitutional crisis. In 1629 Charles I prorogued Parliament and would not call it again until 1639; the outcome would be civil war. Gentry across the land had been scandalized at the licentiousness of the court, among them Winthrop, a devout Puritan layman, who held a position in the Court of Wards and experienced at first hand the corruption of government and the difficulty of maintaining a traditional household in a period of economic dislocation. When he and a handful of landed Puritan laymen organized the first settlement of Massachusetts, they did so with the blessing of some clergymen in the Church of England. Most notable among those sympathetic to the enterprise was the famous John Cotton, who had distinguished himself at Cambridge for wit and scholarship; he had become a Puritan during his ministry in the parish church at Boston, Lincolnshire. Cotton journeyed down to Southampton to preach a farewell sermon for Winthrop's departure.

In the next two years, Archbishop Laud extended his policy of routing Puritan clergy from the church—the policy of "Thorough"—and in 1632 John Cotton was silenced and went into hiding to avoid arrest. He fled to America in 1633. Laud, sensing that the plantation in New England would become an escape route for such Puritan clergy, began legal proceedings against the plantation, and in 1634 a writ of quo warranto was issued. It might have quashed the infant colony of Massachusetts before it was half-formed if the rising tide of rebellion in England had not soon diverted Laud with more immediate concerns. Meanwhile Cotton was invited into the church at Boston, from which vantage point he would become a great figure in the shaping of New England Congregationalism.

In 1634 Richard Mather himself was investigated by a commission of bishops. *"What!"* one of the bishops burst out, *"Preach Fifteen years and never wear a Surplice? It had been better for him that he had gotten Seven Bastards."* [13] This story, related by Mather in his autobiography and repeated by his son, is so stereotyped in its details that one doubts this exact exchange of words took place. No matter. The consequence was the same. Like scores of others, Mather was forbidden to preach in England. After agonized soul-searching, he and Katherine decided to leave the security of their home and families and flee to Massachusetts to join the Puritan settlement.

MIGRATION AS GOD'S WILL

Richard Mather wrote out the reasons for going to America in a long, studied document. He set forth twenty-four reasons, some of them elaborated into hypothetical objections and answers, an exercise in decision-making common to Puritan practice. Richard no doubt had seen the most famous among such public rationales, John Winthrop's "Reasons for Going to America," almost certainly circulated in manuscript throughout the English Puritan community. [14] Both men, John Winthrop, Lord of Groton Manor, gentleman, governor of the company, and Richard Mather, village priest, put the same question in a dozen different ways: what is God's will in this matter? Will I best serve my calling here, or there? The idea of calling, of vocation, permeated the

English understanding of the social order. It was not an exclusively Puritan concept, but the Puritans gave it great importance. For the Puritan the social order was an expression of God's will; everyone had his or her place in society. It was each person's responsibility to know what God wanted him to do, and then to devote himself in all humility to do it.

Each Puritan struggled to decide whether or not to leave all that was dear and secure and to cast his lot in a dangerous ocean voyage on an unknown future in a wild and uncivilized land. What does God call me to do? Can I do it here in England? Can I do it better there?[15] Richard Mather, silenced in his ministry in Engand, concluded, as had John Winthrop and John Cotton, that he and his wife should gamble their lives and their children's lives on this new undertaking. In the spring of 1635 they packed what they could, sold what they could not, and loaded their possessions on pack horses, the children riding in baskets slung across a gentle horse. They travelled across the west of England, down the Severn valley to Bristol, and from there they took passage to America.

Hundreds of other English families were leaving for Massachusetts every year during the 1630s. Since they usually brought with them all their possessions, furniture, clothing, tools, and what money they could get from selling their homes and farms, the settlements in Massachusetts experienced ten years of capital growth. When Richard and Katherine Mather arrived in Boston, they did indeed seem to find a heaven-sent increase. Never had a new land seemed more rich. The sea sparkled in the sun off rocky headlands and deep harbors. Clear streams flowed strong and deep through sweet-scented pine and broadleaf forests. And, unlike those of the old world, New England's riches were unspoken for. No great landlords owned the land, the forests, the rights to hunting and fishing. There were no royal forests or great houses. There are no poachers where all is free. With a climate not greatly different from old England, bountiful in fish and game birds, with timber and good land for the asking, New England was New Canaan, a land of milk and honey.

A GATHERING OF VISIBLE SAINTS

The religious leaders of the settlement—to distinguish them for the moment from the secular leaders—found themselves in the position of having to work out a new approach to reformed religion more pragmatic than had been the adaptation of continental reformed ideas to English Puritanism. Much was retained from continental theorists, and more from English writers, but in translating words into actions, the immigrants defined and invented their own unique religion. From the broad spectrum of English ideas and proposals was winnowed a rather narrow set of propositions that came gradually to be New England orthodoxy. One after another element of the English Puritan movement was rejected, and its advocates were forced to acquiesce to the new orthodoxy or get out of Massachusetts. The Puritanism of New England thus had a complex ancestry of continental Calvinism translated and altered by English churchmen before its rebirth in Massachusetts between 1630 and 1641.[16] Within fifty years it would itself begin to be transformed into the pietistic religion of the eighteenth century.

At first, without premeditation, these Puritans settled in clusters; often families from the same regions of England sought each other out and settled in together. In the beginning there were eight such clusters. From the very first, Massachusetts settlement was grouped into inward-focused towns. Salem was the oldest village, but Boston, on a narrow peninsula jutting northward into the bay, quickly became the political center because John Winthrop built his home there. He had articulated on shipboard earlier the powerful communal ethic of Puritanism that helped shape the tight settlement pattern: "We have a covenant with God. . . . Build a City on a Hill. . . . We will be bound together with ligaments of love. . . . The good of the whole overpasses any person's individual need."[17]

Winthrop was more responsible than anyone else for the rapid development of a social and political organization remarkable for its self-government. Every adult male church member would have equal power to vote for the governor, deputy-governor, and ruling magistrates. With surprising rapidity, settlers forced the creation of a representative form of republican government. The governor, his deputy, and the magistrates would be elected annually. Each town would elect deputies to represent it at the General Court, which met twice a year to pass legislation, and which was soon divided into two houses sitting separately, the magistrates in one, the deputies in the other, each with a veto over the other. The magistrates, elected at large and serving collectively as a Court of Assistants to the governor, as well as acting individually in small cases, were generally recognized to be superior to the deputies in wealth, education, social status, and authority. The deputies tended to reflect the opinions of the villagers who elected them; the magistrates were supposed to represent the best interest of the colony at large and thus had large powers of discretion. Most local governmental responsibilities, including the raising and expenditure of taxes, keeping the peace and ordering public improvements, devolved on the towns. A democratic "Town Meeting" evolved. Within fewer than twenty years after 1630, the Massachusetts Bay Colony had developed a full-blown republican government.

Richard and Katherine Mather arrived in the midst of these extraordinary developments. For them, as for other Puritans, the creation of a new religious order was even more important than the building of a political structure. Although the Puritans who came after 1630 emphasized that they were not separatists, they were in fact engaged in a revolution in English culture. As Charles Hambrick-Stowe put it, "The Puritan vanguard was dedicated to the destruction of an entire world view, a whole system of values and meaning woven from Roman liturgical forms and pagan religious traditions in their English manifestations. The clearest illustration of this 'purification' process was the Puritan renunciation of the ecclesiastical year according to saint's days and local agricultural legends."[18]

The full thrust of this change in world view was not apparent until Puritans actually controlled the society in which they lived. Neither Winthrop nor Mather had suggested in their reasons for going to America that this wholesale reform was part of their intent. Yet once there and in control, the Puritans quickly and steadily replaced the traditional English village culture with a new one. Sports, dances, music, and games, whether practiced by the common villagers or gentle classes, all went. Acceptable modes of interaction between all classes of people and between the sexes were changed. Dress, adornment, and hair styles for both sexes, the upbringing of children, the conduct of business, there was nothing that was not reformed. Marriage became a civil service, no longer performed in church as a sacrament. "Not a single saint's day survived the voyage to New England. Entirely new temporal patterns and rhythms emerged as Puritan spirituality developed and matured."[19] Christmas, Easter, and other high holy days disappeared from the calendar. For half a century, Boston shops and schools stayed open on December twenty-fifth. Even the names of months and days—either Roman or pagan in origin—were dropped, for antiseptic reasons. Monday, December 23 became 23d 10m. One small concession to tradition was to begin each year on March 25, Lady Day; hence March was numbered the first month, February the twelfth.

In place of the familiar calendar, life in Massachusetts was set around a regular seven-day weekly cycle culminating in the Sabbath. Sabbath began with family prayers on Saturday night and was kept sacrosanct, free from work, play, or travel all day Sunday. Attendance at public worship, whether for a communicating member of a church or not, was mandatory. During the course of the year as need arose the government set aside days of public prayer and fasting—Fast Days of Humiliation, or, more rarely, Days of Thanksgiving. Fast days, exulted John Eliot, were "so many Sabbaths more" in the year.[20]

Max Weber characterized English Puritanism in his essay *The Protestant Ethic and the Spirit of Capitalism* (1904–05) as an essentially ascetic movement, and indeed it was. Puritan asceticism took the form of opposition to all expression of human pride. In this sense Puritanism was anti-humanistic and its asceticism the natural corollary to the belief that man is by nature a sinful, evil creature. Pride, pleasure in one's humanity—expressed, for example, by long hair or fashionable dress—came to be considered a vice equal to and often linked together with the vices of drunkenness, gambling, idleness, and "worldliness." Puritan asceticism was, however, in Weber's phrase, "worldly asceticism." It required man to live in the world and not retreat from it. Monastic asceticism, hair shirts, meagre diets, and mortification of the flesh had no part to play in the Puritan lifestyle.[21] Wine and beer were drunk freely, men and women dressed sensibly and appropriately to their station in society; celibacy was frowned on.

The Puritan ministers who took the lead in developing this cultural revolution were far from being all alike as peas in a pod. Among them were such different men as John Cotton, the great scholar and preacher; John Wilson, an ordained clergyman who came with Winthrop's fleet and founded the church in Boston; Hugh Peters, a bellicose warrior of a Puritan who returned to England to be chaplain to Oliver Cromwell; and Roger Williams, charming, star-struck youth, a visionary who as a consequence of his Puritan excesses was exiled even from Massachusetts. The new form of church organization centered on a gathering of visible saints, that is to say, men and women who believed themselves chosen for salvation. These were the elect, people whose experience of a new birth gave them reasonable grounds to hope that they were the recipients of God's holy spirit, the beneficiaries of Christ's sacrifice, the redeemed who would at the Day of Judgment sit on the right hand of God. The company of the elect included both visible and invisible believers: "Invisible, in respect of their relation wherein they stand to

Christ. . . ; Visible, in respect of the profession of their faith, in their persons, & in particular Churches."[22] The churches of Massachusetts were composed of visible saints.

Although the idea that a pure church should consist only of visible saints was not a new one, the idea had not been put into practice before by English Puritans, at least not by those who stopped short of separatism. As early as 1590 John Barrow had organized a small group of extremist Puritans; they broke with the established church, teaching that it was hopelessly impure, and organized their own, separate worship. For most English Puritans this was an act of schism. The separatist churches were forced to go underground or into exile; the pilgrims of Scrooby, Leyden, and after 1620, of Plymouth in New England were such separatists. The overwhelming majority of English Puritans remained in the established Church of England, hoping to reform it from within. All the early religious leaders of Massachusetts had been ordained in the English church and came to New England as ordained clergymen. Once in New England, although still professing themselves non-separating Puritans in communion with the national English church, they invented a new kind of ordination. In Massachusetts there were no bishops to ordain, no ecclesiastical hierarchy to enforce conformity, no Book of Common Prayer to describe a uniform liturgy of worship. Everything about organized worship not only could but must now be invented. Even the traditional English ordinations were thought invalid, as Richard Mather discovered to his chagrin when he learned he was expected to be ordained a second time, according to New England's new rules.[23]

Not every arriving clergyman had identical ideas about how to do it. If churches were to be composed only of visible saints, as a practical matter one had to be able to distinguish the truly elect from the merely hopeful. A sharp disagreement occurred at once, with one group favoring a fairly broad approach to church membership and another a strict one. Two of New England's most admired theologians, Thomas Hooker and John Cotton, came to the fore as champions of these two differing points of view. The controversy contributed to a general dissatisfaction in the earliest settlements, and, as a result of this discontent, hundreds of Puritan families packed up and left Masschusetts Bay for the Connecticut River Valley, where they established a string of new settlements along that river. Thomas Hooker went with them as their principal religious guide, leaving John Cotton the principal influence in the settlements at the Bay.

Such was the situation when Richard and Katherine Mather arrived in 1635. Two other clergymen who were to play leading parts in creating the new church also arrived in that year, Thomas Shepard and John Norton, each ten years younger than Mather. Shepard and Norton had each spent seven years at Cambridge University and both held the degree of Master of Arts. In other ways these two were very different. Norton's strength lay in his classical scholarship, his mastery of languages, his analytical mind. He could have had a fellowship at Cambridge by conforming to the Church of England, but he chose to become a Puritan instead. When continental churchmen wrote to New England to learn what kinds of worship the Puritans were organizing, Norton was chosen to draft the reply. His book-length *The Answer,* written in Latin, the international language of scholarship in the West, was one of the first attempts to describe the new church evolving in Massachusetts.[24] Shepard's background was quite different from Norton's. His parents were poor and died young, leaving him a penniless orphan, though he managed to attend the university on a scholarship. He was a man of obsessive humility and at the same time a man whose direct and pungent language made him a brilliant spokesman for Puritanism. *The True Convert . . .,* his collection of sermons published posthumously in Boston in 1648, went through seventeen printings in the seventeenth century alone, and no Puritan is more often quoted today to illustrate what Puritan religion was all about.

When these three, Mather, Norton, and Shepard, arrived in Massachusetts, John Cotton was already ensconced with John Wilson at the church in Boston. The exodus to Connecticut had almost emptied several nearby communities. Shepard went to take Thomas Hooker's place at Newton, a village just inland from Boston later to change its name to Cambridge. Norton went up the coast to a thriving community at Ipswich. Richard Mather, on Cotton's advice, took his family to the town of Dorchester, across an arm of the sea south of Boston, where scores of farmsteads had been vacated by people moving off to the Connecticut River Valley. Thereafter these four, Cotton, Shepard, Norton, and Mather, were at the center of virtually every major development in the evolution of the New England church.

The Mathers' home in Dorchester was a farming and fishing village described in 1634 as "the greatest Towne in *New England* well wooded and watered; very good arable grounds, and Hay-ground, faire Cornefields, and pleasant Gardens, with Kitchin-gardens."[25] Now half-empty, the town would soon fill up again from the stream of new immigrants

John Winthrop, first governor of Massachusetts Bay Colony and governor when
Increase Mather was born in 1639

Portrait assumed to be of John Cotton, leader of Massachusetts Congregationalism. Richard Mather, Increase's father, married Cotton's widow, Sarah, in
1656, and Increase married his daughter, Maria, in 1661; no portraits exist of
women in the Mather family

arriving throughout the decade. Over the winter of 1635, Mather gathered together a half-dozen settlers he thought could make the nucleus of one of the new Congregational churches. By April of the next year he was ready. Several ministers from neighboring towns and several magistrates came for the formal opening; but the visiting ministers and magistrates found opinions and beliefs they distrusted. They warned Mather about them and suggested that he should wait. Governor John Winthrop wrote in his journal: "The reason was for that most of them (Mr. Mather and one more excepted) had builded their comfort of salvation upon unsound grounds, viz., some upon dreams and ravishes of the spirit by fits; others upon the reformation of their lives; others upon duties and performances, etc."[26] In other words, the ministers and magistrates already in New England concluded that the newcomers did not meet their standards of who was a visible saint and who was not. Mather was told he must winnow out those whose spiritual experience did not measure up.

This issue of definition of visible sainthood had divided John Cotton and Thomas Hooker, but now Hooker was gone to the Valley, and Cotton was undisputed leader in the Bay. Richard Mather accepted his judgment and over the ensuing months helped establish the rules of procedure Cotton had recommended for screening potential new church members. The new procedure was to require the candidate to provide a narrative of his or her spiritual life. William Perkins had long ago analyzed the stages of spiritual growth leading to a new birth in Christ. Cotton and his followers believed that by comparing a personal narrative to this theoretical morphology of conversion, they could judge whether or not an individual was indeed one of the visible saints. In general, the churches springing up in eastern Massachusetts accepted this test. Thus originated one of the most distinctive and controversial features of early New England Congregationalism.[27]

Far more revolutionary even than the testament of conversion was the basis of the new churches' legitimacy. Across Europe and in England churches were created by an ecclesiastical establishment. In England clergymen might be selected for a parish by whoever possessed the right of *advowson;* the priest so appointed held his spiritual authority by virtue of ordination by a bishop. Episcopal ordination was a key issue between Puritans in the English church (who argued it was unscriptural) and their bishops. Now, in America, the Puritans had the chance to try some other way. New England Puritans reversed the order of authority. The fellowship came first; the minister came later. Men and women came together in Christian fellowship and then, having created themselves into a church, sought out a person to function as their pastor. The church fellowship ordained this man, and in the early years, he was thought to have spiritual authority (to offer the sacraments with legitimacy) only in that one congregation. Many churches existed for years before they found suitable pastors. The minister owed his spiritual authority not to a ministry of peers to which he henceforth owed strong allegiance, but rather to a congregation of laymen, brothers, and sisters in Christ. The church—the body of visible saints—chose him and set out the terms of his contract. Thus was begun in America a reformed church without hierarchy, a religious structure deriving its spiritual authority as well as its worldly living directly from the people.

CHILDHOOD

When the townsmen of Dorchester distributed public land to settlers, they gave Richard and Katherine Mather more than a hundred acres to support themselves and their family. Richard Mather received much of his pay as minister in farm produce. Katherine Mather managed the complex household economy, and more than once her husband gave her credit for caring for the worldly needs of the family, thus leaving him free to spend his days in his study. She, it seems, made the decisions about hiring farmhands and domestic servants, buying and selling cattle or poultry, planting and harvesting—a role quite contrary to the submissive and subordinate role wives are usually thought to have played in seventeenth-century English society.

Although the Dorchester tówn meeting voted to support a free school, the position of schoolmaster was filled irregularly, and the burden of instruction of children fell on parents and in the Mather house at first on Katherine Mather. Increase recalled later in life how he had learned to read from his mother, and how she often repeated the wish that he become a scholar and a minister of the gospel.[28] Richard Mather took over the boys' education as soon as they had learned to read. Given the absolute authority of the father in seventeenth-century English families, Richard, probably more than Katherine, set the tone of the children's early life. The three older boys had finished their primary schooling in England. The fourth son, Eleazar, born in Dorchester in 1637, and Increase, born in 1639, were both taught at home. They hardly knew their older brothers: Samuel, the oldest, who went away to college when Increase was two; Timothy, who showed little aptitude for books and was apprenticed to farmwork; and Nathaniel, who left home for college in

1646, when Increase was seven. In the end, although separated for many years, these two, Increase and Nathaniel, would maintain the closest and longest relationship.[29] Their father spoke out plainly on his attitude towards child-raising and schooling. In his own childhood he had hated school because of the frequent beatings of a harsh schoolmaster. In his autobiography Richard wrote, "But Oh that all Schoolmasters would learn Wisdome, Moderation and Equity towards their Scholars, and seek rather to win the hearts of Children by righteous, loving, and courteous usage, than to alienate their minds by partiality and undue severity, which had been my utter undoing, had not the good Providence of God, and the Wisdome and Authority of my Father prevented."[30]

When, some years later, in 1657, Richard Mather spoke to his church about raising children, he also urged parents to love and teach their children. To feed and to clothe them was not enough. Turks and Indians did that; even bears cared for the physical needs of their young. A Christian must do more: "Unless therefore you love your own sorrow and shame, you must not leave your children to themselves, neglecting to instruct them in the ways of God, but as you love yourselves and your own comfort, you must be careful of this duty." The nurture of children was, wrote Mather, one of the central purposes of marriage: "Husbands and Wives must live in peace that their prayers (for their children) may not be hindered."[31]

Four of the five surviving sons of the Mathers would become ministers of the Gospel, all of them committed at an early age to carry out the reforms in religion begun by their father and his generation. Increase recalled standing at his father's elbow when the older man had torn across and thrown away an important-looking document. Asked by the boy what it was, Richard had answered that it was his certificate of ordination by the bishops. *"I tore it, because I took no pleasure in keeping a monument of my sin and folly in submitting to that Superstition, the very remembrance whereof is grievous to me."*[32] All the sons understood that the war their father waged was a political war as well as a revolution in belief and feeling. Civil war raged at home in England. In 1643 Massachusetts took the King's name from its oath of allegiance and the next year outlawed any public show of support for the crown. William Hooke urged his hearers to "lye in wait in the wilderness, to come upon the backs of God's enemies with deadly Fasting and Prayer, murtherers that will kill point blanke from one end of the world to the other."[33]

A

PLATFORM OF
CHURCH DISCIPLINE

GATHERED OUT OF THE WORD OF GOD:
AND AGREED UPON BY THE ELDERS:
AND MESSENGERS OF THE CHURCHES
ASSEMBLED IN THE SYNOD AT CAMBRIDGE
IN NEW ENGLAND

To be prefented to the Churches and Generall Court
for their confideration and acceptance,
in the Lord.

The Eight Moneth Anno 1649

Pfal: 84 1. *How amiable are thy Tabernacles O Lord of Hofts?*

Pfal: 26.8. *Lord I have loved the habitation of thy houfe & the place where thine honour dwelleth.*

Pfal: 27.4. *One thing have I defired of the Lord that will I feek after, that I may dwell in the houfe of the Lord all the dayes of my life to behold the Beauty of the Lord & to inquire in his Temple.*

Printed by *S G* at *Cambridge* in *New England*
and are to be fold at *Cambridge* and *Bofton*
Anno Dom: 1 6 4 9 .

Title page of "A Platform of Church Discipline," of the Synod of 1649, sole
published seventeenth-century standard of New England church discipline

Richard Mather's role in this war was that of theorist of the new church. From his exile in America he sent four books to be published in London to explain and to recommend the Congregational form of church organization: *An Apologie for Church Covenant* (1643), *Church Government and Church Government Discussed* (1643), *A Modest and Brotherly Answer to Mr. Charles Herle* (1644), and *A Reply to Mr. Rutherford* (1646).[34] The books soon earned him a reputation on both sides of the Atlantic, and Puritans in Massachusetts came to rely on the judgment of this man who alone of the early church leaders in the Bay had no university degree. Richard's preoccupation with scholarship and writing would be mirrored in the lives of all his four minister sons, Increase Mather most of all.

The struggle in England was between Anglican monarchists and Puritan parliamentarians. As the latter won, they fell out among themselves, Presbyterians in the majority arguing for one kind of church polity, a minority of Independents for another. There were Presbyterians in New England too, particularly at Newbury, where two respected Puritans, Thomas Parker and James Noyse, organized the congregation along Presbyterian lines.[35] Far more worrisome, across New England a distressing variety of more radical religious views appeared. In England the confusion that came with civil war opened the door to a multitude of radical sects: Anabaptists, Fifth Monarchy, Familist, Ranters, and many others. To keep such disorder and confusion from reaching America, the Massachusetts General Court, with the support of leading ministers, called a synod to meet and recommend ways of bringing some kind of uniformity to the practice of worship.

The General Court wanted guidelines about infant baptism, especially. The question of whose children were eligible for baptism in the new churches touched every parent and roused stronger feelings than any other church question. "In most churches," the General Court stated, "the ministers do baptize onely such children whose nearest parents, one or both of them, are settled members, in full communion with one or other of these churches, (but) there be some who do baptize the children if the grandfather or grandmother be such members, though the immediate parents be not. . . . On the other side there be some amongst us who do thinke that whatever be the state of the parents, baptisme ought not to be dispensed to any infants whatsoever."[36]

When representatives of the churches met at Cambridge in 1646 to write a general policy for New England churches, Richard Mather was one of several ministers asked to prepare suggestions for a "Platform of Church Discipline." His proposals became the working draft for the final document.[37] This "Cambridge Platform" more than any other document became an official description of the church in Massachusetts. It was approved by the synod, circulated to each congregation in Massachusetts for corrections, and finally adopted by the General Court. The congregational system permitted no central authority; the Platform was a recommendation only. It was the only published standard of church practice for the rest of the century.

Most of the text of the Cambridge Platform was taken without change from Richard Mather's working draft. He began with definitions of some basic terms in Puritan church polity.[38]

The Catholick Church, is the whole company of those that are elected, redeemed, & in time effectually called from the state of sin & death unto a state of Grace, and salvation in Iesus Christ. (II,1)

This church is either Triumphant, or Militant. Triumphant, the number of them who are Gloryfied in heaven: Militant, the number of them who are conflicting with their enemies upon earth. (II,2)

This Militant Church is to be considered as Invisible, & Visible. Invisible, in respect of their relation wherein they stand to Christ . . .: Visible, in respect of the profession of their faith, in their persons, and in particular Churches. . . . (II,3)

A Congregational-church is by the institution of Christ a part of the Militant-visible-church, consisting of a company of Saints by calling, united into one body, by a holy covenant, for the publick worship of God. . . . (II,6)

In New England each congregation would stand alone and not as part of a larger, national organization like the Church of England. Its independency set it apart from Presbyterian church structures. Each congregation would be created by a covenant among its members. The act of covenanting to worship together in Christ created a Congregational church. A limit on size would emphasize fellowship.

(Members of a church) ought not to be of greater number than may ordinarily meet together conveniently in one place. (III,4)

There is no greater Church than a Congregation, which may ordinarily meet in one place. (III,5)

Particular churches cannot be distinguished one from another but by their formes. . . . This *Form* is the *Visible Covenant,* Agreement or consent wherby they give themselves up to the Lord, . . . which is usually called the *Church-Covenant.* (IV,2-3)

The essence of the Congregational church was the fellowship of lay brethren, not a hierarchy of priests or bishops.

A Church being a company of people combined together by covenant for the worship of God, it appeareth therby, that there may be the essence and being of a church without any officers. . . . (VI,1)

The only officers for which Puritans found scriptural evidence were Pastors and Teachers, Ruling Elders and Deacons, and no other officers were recognized; these four received their office from the church fellowship itself and not from some higher authority as in Europe.

Officers are to be *called by such Churches,* whereunto they are to minister. . . . The *choyce* of such Church-officers belongeth not to the civil-magistrates, as such, or diocesan-bishops, or patrones. . . . Ordination therefore is not to go before, but to follow *election.* The essence & substance of the outward calling of an ordinary officer in the Church, doth not consist of his ordination, but in his voluntary & free election by the Church, and in his accepting of that election. (VIII,5,9; IX,2)

Never before in a Christian state had any religious community been so free to govern itself.

In respect of the body, or *Brotherhood* of the church, & powr from Christ graunted unto them, it resembles a *Democracy.* . . . The power graunted by Christ unto the body of the church & *Brotherhood,* is a prerogative or priviledge which the church doth exercise: I. In *Choosing* their own officers, whether Elders or Deacons. II. In *admission* of their own members. (X,3,5)

Admission to membership was to be restricted to visible saints, and many people were left out.

The *doors* of the Churches of Christ upon earth, doe not by Gods appointment stand so wide open, that all sorts of people good or bad, may freely enter therein at their pleasure; but such as are admitted thereto, as members ought to be *examined and tried* first; whether they be fit & meet to be received into church-society, or not. (XII,1)

Many felt unjustly excluded from worship and communion by this examination for fitness. In England this Massachusetts practice raised eyebrows even among Puritans friendly to New England. Presbyterians, for example, by far the majority of English Puritans, opted instead for general admission to the sacraments except for notorious sinners. But the Cambridge Platform held to trial and examination before admission, which seemed reasonable enough, although Richard Mather's draft and the final document did emphasize charity in the examination:

The things which are requisite to be found in all church members, are, *Repentance* from sin, and *faith* in Jesus Christ.(XII,2)

The weakest *measure* of faith is to be accepted in those that desire to be admitted into the church. . . . Such *charity* and tenderness is to be used, as the weakest Christian if sincere, may not be excluded, nor discouraged. Severity of examination is to be avoyded.(XII,3)

Testimony of confession was to be public, and preferably, personal:

In case any through excessive fear, or other infirmity, *be unable* to make their personal *relation* of their spirituall estate in publick, it is sufficient that the Elders . . . make *relation* thereof in publick before the church. . . . (XII,4)

But whereas (some) persons are of better *abilityes,* there it is most expedient that they make their *relations, & confessions* personally with their own mouth. . . . (XII,4)

A personall & publick *confession,* & declaring of Gods manner of working upon the soul, is both lawfull, expedient, & usefull. . . . Wee must be able and ready upon any occasion to declare & shew our *repentance for sinn, faith unfagned, and effectuall calling.* (XII,5)

Although in Massachusetts a man had to be admitted to church membership before he was eligible to vote or hold office (women were allowed to do neither), the ministers sought, nevertheless, to separate spiritual from civil affairs as far as possible. A man excommunicated from the church did not lose his civil rights:

Excommunication being a spirituall punishment, it doth not prejudice the excommunicate in, nor deprive him of his *civil rights,* and therefore toucheth not princes, or other magistrates, in point of their civil dignity or authority. (XIV,6)

The ministers argued that Congregational churches could be formed without the consent of the government, but conversely an important law of 1636 required approval of both magistrates and neighboring churches.[39]

It is lawfull, profitable, & necessary for christians to gather themselves into Church estate, . . . although the consent of Magistrate could not be had thereunto. . . . (XVII,1)

Puritans believed that the civil authority had no jurisdiction over the inner life of the conscience.

The object of the powr of the Magistrate, are not things meerly inward, . . . as unbeleife hardness of heart, erronious opinions not vented; but only such things as are acted by the outward man. . . . (XVII,7)

They did, however, expect the civil authority to police outward behavior, including speech, and to punish errors acted out in public, as the last section of the Platform explained:

Idolatry, Blasphemy, Heresy, venting corrupt & pernicious opinions, that destroy the foundation, open contempt of the word preached, prophanation of the Lords day, disturbing the peaceable administration & exercise of the worship & holy things of God, and the like, are to be restrayned, & punished by civil authority. (XVII,8)

And also the church was to be established by the government and, if necessary, supported by public taxes. All taxpayers were to meet the cost of the churches, whether they were members or not. In many small Massachusetts towns the salary of the minister was the town's biggest expense.

Necessary & sufficient maintenance is due unto the ministers of the word. . . . People are not at liberty to doe or not to doe, what and when they pleas in this matter. . . . (XI,1,2)

Puritans were so successful in presenting a united front to the world and to history that few realize today how much disagreement there was about the Cambridge Platform. A full third of the Deputies in the General Court voted against adopting it. Some congregations still leaned towards a Presbyterian form of church organization. Others felt that any synodical agreement infringed on their autonomy. Some deputies who voted against it were suspicious that the ministers intended to take control away from the lay brethren.[40] Their suspicion was well founded. All the first-generation ministers had been ordained by bishops in England, and although some publicly renounced their Episcopal ordination, not all were ready to do so. The ministers thus considered themselves a group set apart, endowed with special spiritual authority by virtue of their previous ordinations as well as of their calling. The Puritan laity, on the other hand, had inherited a long tradition of suspicion and resentment of an elite clergy. In England clergymen all too often had been arrogant, snobbish, self-important. An underlying opposition existed throughout the first century in New England between the lay members and their ministers.

Lay members of congregations were directly represented in the government by the deputies in the General Court. The House of Deputies was a small body, usually not more than fifty persons. The magistrates, or Court of Assistants, were an even smaller group, about fifteen. When there was a division of interest between ministers and their congregations, magistrates tended to line up with the ministers and deputies with the laymen. The refusal of one-third of the deputies to vote for the Cambridge Platform was the opening salvo in a long struggle for control of the churches and of the country itself.

The most divisive difference of opinion concerned the issue of infant baptism, already singled out by the General Court as a special reason for calling the synod. Richard Mather in his working draft of the Platform, proposed a liberal policy: infants were to be baptized if one grandparent had been a communicating church member, even though neither parent had experienced regeneration or been accepted into communion. This open policy ran into opposition from one or two ministers at the synod and from many more laymen. The synod was unable to reach agreement. Rather than decide the issue by majority vote, the synod left the entire question of infant baptism out of the Platform altogether.[41]

Work on the Cambridge Platform, from the first call for a synod, in 1646, to publication of its conclusions, in 1651, took six years. It would be a mistake to think that Massachusetts congregationalism, the New England Way, was fixed in these years. Differences in practice always existed. That the Platform has come to be taken as the definitive description of the Puritan church in America is due more to Increase Mather's later, single-minded defense of his father's work than to its comprehensiveness after mid-century. Important changes in the concept and organization of the church were still to come.

HARVARD COLLEGE AND BOSTON

Much happened in Richard Mather's family during the six years between the Cambridge Synod meeting in 1646, and the publication of the Platform. The oldest son, Samuel, earned his M.A. degree at Harvard in 1646 and stayed on to become one of the first college tutors. Nathaniel completed his own M.A. there in 1650. Both young men felt called to the ministry, but openings in Massachusetts were scarce, as civil war in England brought immigration to New England virtually to a standstill. The migration reversed itself a little, with Puritans from Massachusetts much in demand in Oliver Cromwell's England. Samuel and Nathaniel Mather said goodbye to their parents and brothers and joined a stream of young men returning to England in the winter of 1650–51.

Timothy had become a farmer, and, in 1649, at twenty-one, he married Katherine Atherton, the daughter of a wealthy landowner in Dorchester. By the time Samuel and Nathaniel sailed for England, Timothy's wife had given birth to a baby, the first of six children and the beginning of the third generation of Mathers in New England.

Eleazar was twelve in 1649. He and Creasy were constant companions as they roamed through the village of Dorchester, with its soft dirt roads in summer and freezing ice and mud in the eastern Massachusetts winter. Their childhood was filled with uniquely American experiences: Indians and wampum, farmers dressed in homespun, the simple frame meeting house where their father preached on the sabbath. Eleazar was considered the introspective one. Although Increase showed little early interest in books, he was quick to learn, quicker than Eleazar. When Eleazar turned fourteen, Increase had caught up with him in Latin and Greek. Their education would be completed, as Richard's had been, outside the parental home. Custom and social class dictated that the boys should leave home early. In 1651 the two boys left together for Harvard College, two very young men, one fourteen, the other twelve. Neither would return home again to live with their parents. Their departure was a rite of passage into the adult world.

No doubt they walked the nine or ten miles to Cambridge, or possibly, rode in a hay cart drawn down the dirt road by a team of oxen or on a horse behind their father. A few miles from Dorchester, the road to Cambridge passed through the village of Roxbury, where John Eliot, apostle to the Indians, lived. At Roxbury the road forked, to the right to the long narrow peninsula and Boston, to the left north-west through woods to the banks of the Charles River. Across those marshy shores lay the village of Cambridge and Harvard College.

The Massachusetts General Court had created Harvard College in 1636 with an appropriation of £400, but it was three years later before the first building—"Old College"—rose awkwardly above the treetops and the houses of Cambridge, like those of Dorchester built of unpainted, sawn wood with shingled or thatched roofs. Next to Thomas Shepard's meetinghouse was the home of Henry Dunster, president of Harvard College, and across the yard behind Dunster's house rose the big, ugly, angular college building, three stories of wood, topped by great brick chimneys, towering over all other buildings in Cambridge and, for that matter, New England. To the west of this "Old College" was another college building, the Brew House. Students at Harvard usually drank nothing but beer at meals.[42]

Many individuals made private gifts, large and small, to the college endowment, and the largest John Harvard's: all of his personal library and half an estate, valued at seven or eight hundred pounds. The college soon became an important symbol of religious and cultural sufficiency. The mixture of public and private endowment testifies to the New England Puritans' commitment to education and learning. Small gifts to the college over the years reveal how important it was among ordinary people: a belt of wampum, a silver shilling, a half-bushel of wheat. No other European settlement in America, not even the great Roman university of Mexico City, established in 1551, could match New England in this public commitment to education.

If Puritan ministers came out of Harvard, so too did Puritan governors, merchants, lawyers, physicians, soldiers, farmers, and politicians. The charter stated the college's purpose was "the advancement of all good literature artes and Sciences . . . that may conduce to the education of the English & Indian Youth of this country in knowledge: and godliness." No mention was made of a seminary. Roughly half of Harvard graduates in the seventeenth century became ministers of the gospel; half did not.[43] The education that future ministers received, particularly in their undergraduate years, was largely humanistic and based on the literature and politics of Greece and Rome. Freshmen studied logic and Latin literature; juniors continued in Latin and started Greek literature and philosophy; seniors added mathematics, geometry, and astronomy. Theology was reserved for graduate students who were working towards their M.A. degrees.

The mood and tone of undergraduate life were a far cry from the ascetic piety usually associated with Puritanism. Here, for example, is an early verse copied by a Harvard undergraduate into his notebook:

> Take, O take those lips away,
> That so sweetly were fore-sworn;
> And those eyes like break of day,
> Lights that doe mislead the morne.

The verse is Shakespeare, from *Measure for Measure,* and the copyist was Seaborn Cotton, oldest son of Boston's most famous minister.[44]

On the day of their entrance examinations, Eleazar and Increase took their turns standing before President Henry Dunster in his study. Dunster was a specialist in Old Testament languages and must have seemed heaven-sent to the Harvard Overseers, for they had hired him on the spot

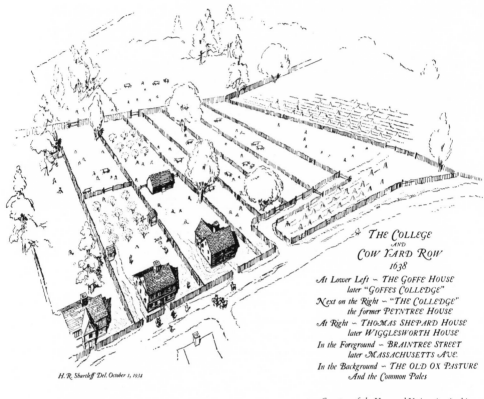

THE COLLEGE
AND
COW YARD ROW
1638

At Lower Left ~ THE GOFFE HOUSE
later "GOFFES COLLEDGE"
Next on the Right ~ "THE COLLEDGE"
the former PEYNTREE HOUSE
At Right ~ THOMAS SHEPARD HOUSE
later WIGGLESWORTH HOUSE
In the Foreground ~ BRAINTREE STREET
later MASSACHUSETTS AVE.
In the Background ~ THE OLD OX PASTURE
And the Common Pales

H. R. Shurtleff Del. October 1, 1934

Courtesy of the Harvard University Archives

Harvard College in 1638, two years after its charter by the General Court. Increase Mather entered Harvard in 1651 and was graduated in 1656. Drawing by
H. R. Shurtleff, 1934

when he came to Boston in 1640 age thirty-one. Fortunately for Dunster, he had married a rich widow, Elizabeth Glover, or he would have
been hard put to survive the coming lean years. He brought a printing
press to Cambridge. It belonged to Elizabeth's former husband and was
set up on Dunster's porch until a better place could be found.

The formal part of Eleazar's and Increase's entrance examination was
conducted in Latin. The boys were asked to translate at sight Virgil,
Tully, and similar Roman authors. Probably they were asked to compose
some Latin verse as well and to respond in Latin to Dunster's conversation. Dunster would certainly have gone on to test them in Greek also,
with passages from the Old Testament and from pagan literature.

Old College, Harvard, built in 1639, replaced by New College in 1676. Drawing by H. R. Shurtleff, 1934

The Library in Old College, Harvard. Drawing by F. W. Hartwell, 1939

But exam or not, considering who their father was, there was little doubt that Eleazar and Increase would be admitted as freshmen. They were given a rank in the entering class, Eleazar at the top of the entire list and Increase next, a testimony both to their skills and to their father's standing in the colony. Sometime later Richard Mather arranged for the first year's tuition and fees: twenty bushels of wheat at £20, a "blacke Cow" valued at five pounds twelve shillings; another, a "fatt Cow" at the same value.[45]

Approximately forty undergraduates enrolled that year. The Mathers were younger than most. The average age of a freshman in those days was almost seventeen years; Increase was a mere babe in such company. As freshmen the two brothers probably shared the same bed in the large dormitory on the second floor of Old College. Rising at dawn, they stumbled downstairs for morning prayers in the great hall below, then ran with the others to the "buttery hatch" to receive their breakfast, handed over a Dutch half-door. Breakfast was a pot of beer and a piece of bread. For a little extra money, a student could get butter or a morsel of cheese. Then came lessons and academic exercises until 11:00 A.M. Dinner, robust fare—beef, bread and beer, and on lucky days a pudding—was served a mid-day in the commons or great hall. The faculty and students ate in the same hall, but sat apart and according to rank and seniority. Afternoon offered a much needed snack from the buttery hatch to break the long fast until supper at 7:30 after evening prayers. In the fall and winter the hall at supper time was unevenly lit by candles and a blaze in the fireplace. For supper, a meat pie perhaps, or oatmeal, eggs, and the ever present beer. On Sundays college students attended the Cambridge meeting across the road and heard the learned and pious Thomas Shepard.

Perhaps it was the heavy meals and beer three times a day, as Increase later said, that caused him to leave Harvard. Perhaps it was the hazing of a twelve-year-old boy away from home for the first time. Whatever the entire explanation, Increase did not stay. "My parents being tender of me, and fearing that the Colledge diet would not well agree with my weake natural constitution of Body, they sent me to Ipswich . . . to live under the roof and be under the constant inspection and instruction of that godly learned divine Mr. John Norton."[46]

The move was portentous. Richard Mather selected a home where the completion of his youngest son's education complemented his own piety and scholarship. Richard Mather and Norton already formed the closest kind of personal bond, for Mather had chosen his younger colleague to act as his own spiritual adviser.[47] Norton had several other boys boarding in his house.

It was probably Richard's intent that young Increase would live with the Norton family at Ipswich for one or two years and then return to the college at Cambridge. But fate intervened to bring him to Boston first. The revered John Cotton had died at sixty-seven in 1651, and the church where he had preached for almost twenty years asked Norton to replace him. The call was a measure of Norton's prestige in the Puritan community. Thus Increase Mather, between the ages of thirteen and sixteen, moved to Boston, under the tutelage of a famous scholar now also pastor of Massachusetts's premier congregation. The combination of influences was enormous. Norton in his role as a second parent became a model, in some ways more clear-cut than Increase's natural father, free from the ordinary psychological struggles between father and son. Norton's influence lay at the heart of Increase's lifelong ambition for recognition as a scholar not only in Massachusetts but in Europe.

LIFE IN BOSTON

In the 1650s Boston was still a frontier seaport just beginning its phenomenal growth in size and wealth, although it hardly yet had the look of either seaport or city. Most Boston homes in 1650 still had gardens and orchards around them and often a stable or cow barn in the back. Virtually all were built of wood, although one or two were brick. Most were one and at most two stories high, with shingle or thatch roofs, and unpainted weathered pine, giving the town a soft and silvery look. In dry weather Boston was a tinderbox, and the thought of fire was a nightmare. The streets and lanes went unnamed, as if they were still country roads. In the whole town only one street was paved with cobblestones, the rest lay naked to sun and rain. Residents threw their garbage and refuse onto the dirt, although after 1666 butchers were required to dump their wastes into Mill Creek, which flowed sluggishly across a narrow part of the peninsula separating the North End from the center of the town.[48] The dirty, rutted lanes, the hurry and push of carts, wheelbarrows, porters, pedestrians, men on horseback, merchants, boys, farmers, sailors, captains, carpenters, and an occasional Indian, this was the Boston of Increase Mather's youth.

Living in John Norton's household gave Increase a privileged place in town. Norton had bought Governor Winthrop's old house on the road leading up the peninsula from the mainland. Only a block or two away and across the dirt road was the large, square meetinghouse of Boston's First Church, the most important pulpit in the colony. Increase, with Norton's other student boarders, attended church service with the colony's largest, wealthiest, and most powerful congregation.

A little further along the road a traveller would come to the Town House, where the General Court met when it was in session, where the magistrates met when they sat as a Court of Assistants, and where Boston town meetings were held. A stone's throw further on was the waterfront, first the Town Dock and a mooring basin for small boats, then the privately owned wharves and warehouses which even this early were beginning to line the shore. Ocean-going ships anchored in the inner harbor. Passengers and freight came ashore in boats. Further out in the great island-dotted bay, past Castle Island, was the outer harbor, where, in later years, big fleets would come to anchor.

Boston was built on the east or seaward side of the hilly peninsula extending north into the inner bay. The original shoreline has long since disappeared under landfills as the modern city has pushed outwards. In those days the bottom or neck of the peninsula, where it joined the mainland, was so narrow that during storms salt spray blew across. The water on the western or landward side of the peninsula, known as the Back Bay, was too shallow for shipping, and low tide exposed odoriferous mud flats. The houses and wharves of Boston clustered together on the ocean side and on the eastern slopes of Beacon Hill. When the wind blew from the east, it brought the acrid smells of the sea, and from the west the softer fragrances of pine woods.

Just north of the Town Dock a canal across the peninsula joined the main harbor with shallow mud flats of the Back Bay. A mill pond was built on this western edge; the canal, Mill Creek, separated the central area around the dock and Town House from the upper end of the peninsula, known then and today as the North End. In the 1650s the North End was mostly open country, but wharves were beginning to be built along the harbor side and a few small homes were going up. This North End would become in Increase Mather's lifetime the most densely built-up part of the city. A second church was gathered there in 1650, ostensibly to accommodate the growing population, but also, one thinks, because of dissensions in First Church. The source of this dissension was a small number of poor, radical Puritans who were increasingly uncomfortable with the growing prosperity around them. The new, second meetinghouse was built in the North End in the winter of 1649–1650.

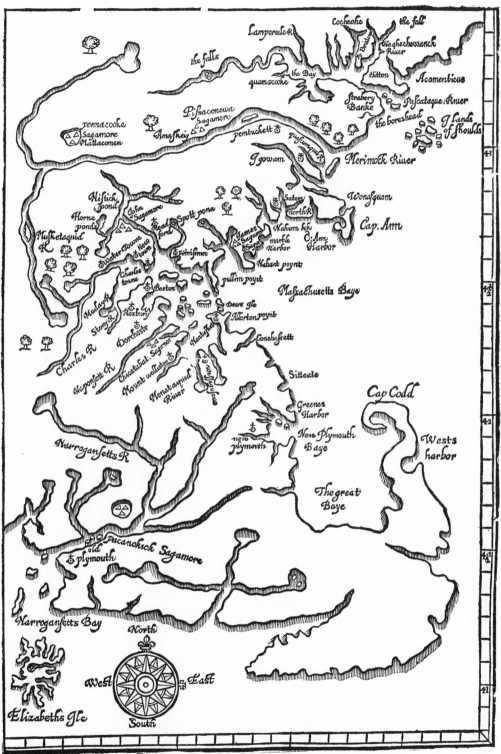

the fall
Cocheoho
Lampereele R.
the falls
the Bay
quamscooke
Weghechessanch River
Hitton
Acomenticus
Strabery Banke
Paseataque River
Piscaconowa Sagamore
Amaskeig
pemtuchett
qusumqusk R.
the boreshead
Ilands of Shoulls
pennacooke Sagamore Mattacomen
Igowam
Merimock River
Nistick pond
Saten North R.
Wonasquom
Horne ponds
John Sagamore
Cap: Ann
Musketaquid
Head ford
Spott pona
James Sagamore
Nahum keke
WaterTowne
New towne
Swimsmer
marble Harbor
O: Ann Harbor
Charles towne
Nehant poynt
pullim poynt
Boston
Massachusetts Baye
Mudavyt
Roxbury
Deare gle
Stony R.
Dorchestr
Allerton poynt
Charles R.
Chicatabot Sagmon
Nantasky
Conchusetts
Naponsett R.
Mount wollaston
Mena tapmd River
Sitteale
Greenes Harbor
Cap Codd
Narrogansetts R.
new plymoveth
New Plymouth Baye
Wests harbor
The great Baye
Pacanokick Sagamore
old plymouth
Narrogansetts Bay
North
West
East
South
Elizabeths Jle

From William Wood, New England's Prospect, *London,* 1635.
Courtesy, Massachusetts Historical Society

Map of Boston and southern New England in 1635

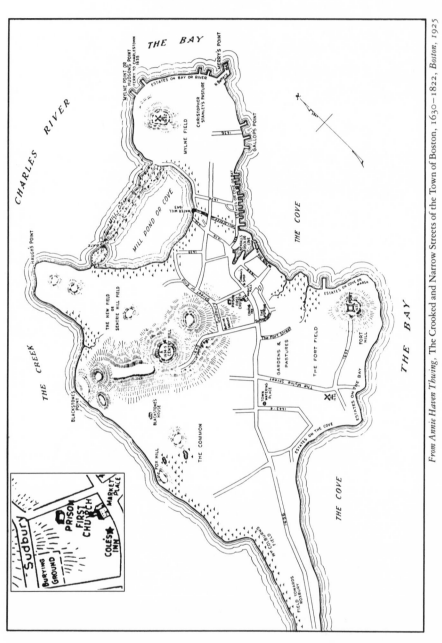

From Annie Haven Thwing, The Crooked and Narrow Streets of the Town of Boston, 1630–1822, Boston, 1925

Map of Boston's streets and buildings around 1645. Increase Mather lived in Boston and attended First Church from ages 12 to 15; the church was across from the marketplace, just northwest of "The Cove." Second Church, where he served, was built in the North End in 1650.

BOSTON'S FIRST TOWN-HOUSE
1657-1711

Boston's first Town House in the center of the marketplace. Stocks were at lower left, a council room and public library above; 1930 sketch drawn from original 1657 specifications

This North Church, or Second Church, would become Mather's home for almost sixty years. When he was living under John Norton's roof, he would have laughed at any such prediction, for the North Church congregation was poor and insignificant, and Increase Mather was making larger plans for himself.

The beginning of the North Church reflected truly the early years of Congregationalism and its interior contradictions. Eight men signed a covenant to worship together, and a church was thereby formed. These founding members and the community of newcomers in which they lived had difficulty in attracting a minister. For several years they held worship services without an ordained minister and therefore without the comfort of the sacraments. One of their number, a humble man of no formal education named Michael Powell, led in prayers and preached the sermons. In 1653 the members proposed ordaining Powell as their minister. Powell, a humble, plain man, had never in his wildest fancies imagined himself a member of the clergy. Nevertheless, he consented, judging it to be God's will. But when the church sought the approval of the magistrates, the magistrates objected. Powell, they said, was "illiterate as to academical education."[49]

The magistrates and their allies, the ministers, would insist that the church in New England be middle-class, bourgeois, educated. However, John Farnum, one of the founders of the North Church, who had no education beyond the Bible, argued that a "gifted" person could speak to things of the spirit just as well as one with a degree from the "niniversity." This belief in the priesthood of all believers, and this hostility to elitist education, were common features of the radical wing of the Puritan movement in England. Other congregations, particularly in Salem, took up Powell's cause and argued that a church might choose a "gyfted" person as pastor, and that the magistrates, as part of the civil government, had no right to interfere. The autonomy of the gathered church was at stake. The government, on the other hand, was determined that, to use William Perkins's language, "the common sort of ignorant people" should not be ordained to the ministry in New England. In the end the case of Michael Powell and the Second Church was taken to the General Court, where the magistrates and deputies agreed that Powell, honest and sincere though he might be, did not have "the abilities, learning and qualifications as are requisite for an able minister of the gospel."[50]

The North Church did in the end find a minister acceptable to the government. He was John Mayo, a somewhat tired and lackluster person who took the job because he was dying of loneliness in a rural Massachusetts village. He was only one of dozens of immigrant Puritan ministers who found that living year-round in a tiny hamlet surrounded by forest with no one to talk to but rude fisherfolk and farmers was more than they had bargained for when they left England behind. Homesickness and loneliness constantly undermined the Puritans' enthusiasm for their exile in America, and over the years no one would feel this more acutely than Increase Mather. But not yet. Now he was young, his father was famous, he himself studied with the great John Norton, whose name was known on both sides of the Atlantic, and he attended the preeminent First Church.

At Norton's, Increase began to experience the first signs of religious conversion. His mother's death, in March 1655 was a catalyst. In her thirty-one years of married life, Katherine Mather had given birth to six sons and raised five of them to maturity, but Increase always felt that he, the youngest, had a special place in her heart. "I was," he wrote of this time in his life, "in extremity of anguish and horror in my soul." Towards the end of May, choosing a day when everyone would be out of the house, he crept into a garret above John Norton's study and poured out his heart to God. "I gave my self up to Jesus Christ, declaring that I was now resolved to be his Servant, and his only, and his forever, and humbly professed to him, that if I did perish, I would perish at his feet. Upon this I had ease and inward peace in my perplexed soul."[51] He was a month short of his sixteenth birthday.

Increase's conversion experience was almost exactly like his father's. The similarity was no accident. Richard Mather, like many of his contemporaries, had kept a diary and written his autobiography to serve as a guide for his children. Increase, too, would tell *his* children how God had entered his life. Such spiritual autobiographies were an important means of passing values and expectations on from one generation to the next. Increase's conversion was like his father's in age, place, and circumstances; at age fifteen this is what Increase had learned to expect conversion to be. Later in life he would cling to this particular kind of spiritual growth as the true form of regeneration. The belief would eventually become old-fashioned, and a new generation would come to think him eccentric.

At home in Dorchester, Richard Mather, alone now with his two youngest sons gone, married a second wife, Sarah Story Cotton, the widow of John Cotton. With Sarah came her youngest daughter, Maria. The marriage united two of Massachusetts's most important families. Later Increase would marry Maria, but now he continued his studies under Norton's supervision, and the year after his experience of regeneration he returned to the Harvard campus and graduated with his class in the summer of 1656. He almost did not pass, but his tutor, Jonathan Mitchell, interceded with the president. Ordinarily he would then have started the regular three-year course of study leading to the M.A. degree, but Increase was more ambitious—he planned to join his brothers Samuel and Nathaniel in England and finish his studies at a real university.

Increase was not alone in his desire to return to England. Many friends and classmates were going back. Nearly a third of the young men graduating from Harvard in the 1650s joined this reverse migration. During that summer of 1657 at least three ships left Boston with men going back; the largest, with fifty passengers, was lost at sea with all on board. In July 1657 a few days after his eighteenth birthday, with tears in his

eyes, Increase bade farewell, as he believed forever, to his father and Eleazar and boarded a ship for England.[52]

ENGLAND: THE REVOLUTION THAT FAILED

And why not? Samuel and Nathaniel had already gone back. All the
circumstances which had driven his father's generation into exile were
changed. Archbishop Laud was dead; the king was dead; England was a
republic under the friendly rule of Oliver Cromwell. There was little to
keep an ambitious young man in America. The belief that New England
had a special errand in the world, as Winthrop had announced in 1630,
had not yet become an article of faith with the generation born in America. On the contrary, the reform of the world seemed to lie with the Congregationalists and Independents in England. New England had been a
necessary refuge, but a temporary one. New England's experiment in
creating the first Congregational churches seemed invaluable to the revolutionaries at home in England. "Tis incredible," Nathaniel wrote from
there, "what an advantage to preferment it is to have been a New Englishman."[53] "To have been. . . ."—Nathaniel's use of the past tense is
telling. The center of action was now in England.

The leaders of English Congregationalism—Thomas Goodwin, John
Owen, Joseph Caryl, John Howe, Philip Nye, and others—were pushing through the Puritan revolution under the protection of Cromwell
and in anticipation of the millennial rule of the saints. In every national
election the Congregationalists were a small minority, but most of them
did not hesitate to accept the help of the army to keep themselves in
power. Most Puritans in England favored a Presbyterian church polity,
one with a national church, centralized authority, and admission to the
sacraments almost as broad as the Anglican communion. The Independents, who were closely allied to New England Congregationalists
in ideas about church government, wanted particular independent
churches, no central authority, and sacraments only for visible saints.
Many of their leaders believed fervently that the Second Coming of
Christ was at hand. They were a minority revolutionary party, kept in
power for the time being by Cromwell and his army.

In America there were several close personal supporters of the Independents. John Davenport, the senior minister at New Haven, was one
of them. Davenport, of John Cotton's generation, was an eminent Puritan, a close personal friend of John Preston and editor of Preston's

works. Davenport's colleague, William Hooke, also supported Independency in England, and Hooke's wife Jane was a cousin of Cromwell's, a sister of one of Cromwell's generals, Edward Whalley, and an aunt of another, William Goffe. Goffe and Whalley were two of the regicides who had voted to execute Charles I. They continued to be close advisors to Cromwell, resisting to the very end any compromise on church polity. As a young man in his twenties, Increase Mather would find himself deeply involved with these older men. They constituted an inner circle of Puritanism with whom he would be in correspondence as long as they lived.[54]

In 1653 the Puritans in England forbade Anglican clergy either to preach in church or to teach in school, just as they themselves had been silenced by Archbishop Laud twenty years before. The parish churches and the livelihood that went with them were turned over to Puritan clergymen. To be sure, many Puritans who were Congregationalists did not want to become priests in these established parish churches and preferred to find their own church fellowship outside the parish system, or to content themselves with lectureships and chaplaincies in the colleges and universities. In all, 130 Congregational ministers displaced Anglican clergy in the parishes. They were less than ten percent of all livings turned over to Puritans. Most of the rest went to Puritans who were Presbyterian in their views.[55]

Samuel and Nathaniel Mather were in the ten percent who displaced Anglican incumbents. Nathaniel stayed in the south of England. He married the daughter of a wealthy Puritan named William Benn and went from one parish to another until he was at last admitted in January 1657 as vicar in the established church at Barnstaple on the southwestern coast of Devon.[56] Samuel became first a chaplain at Magdalen College, Oxford, and then a minister at Leith in Scotland. He later acquired the position of curate in a parish in Lancashire, near his birthplace, but preferred to seek appointments outside the established parishes. He followed Cromwell's army to Ireland, became a Lecturer at Dublin's Christ Church Cathedral, a Senior Fellow of Trinity College, and a colleague of Samuel Winter at St. Nicholas Church.[57] All these were important posts in the top echelon of the invading Puritan culture.

Samuel encouraged his father to send Increase over to Dublin to study for his M.A. degree, and Increase sailed for England in July 1657. He passed through London and Lancashire, visiting friends and relatives of his mother and father, and arrived in Dublin in September. The two brothers had not seen each other since Increase was twelve, and Samuel hardly recognized the tall, eighteen-year-old man who greeted him now. Increase stayed with his brother and sister-in-law and soon enrolled as a student at Trinity College. [58]

Little is known of Increase's year in Dublin, but he seemed almost a foreigner to the other students, with his frontier ways, his narrow New England views of the church, and his obsession with scholarship. His closest friend was Josiah Winter, son of the provost. His father sent money from America for school expenses. [59] He came down with the measles and after that with a mild case of smallpox that gave him a precious immunity afterwards. No record exists of his studies or intellectual growth, but at last, on June 24, 1658, he assembled with his class for commencement ceremonies and to receive his master of arts degree. Increase refused to wear the usual colorful academic robe and hood, and stood out from the others in his plain black gown. He liked to sign his name "Crescentius Matherus."

The provost offered the new master of arts holder a fellowship at the college; the Lord Deputy offered him a church in Ireland; and brother Nathaniel found him a parish church in England. Increase chose the parish church and soon left Ireland behind, thinking it a cold, damp place. He arrived back in London scarcely a year after leaving Boston. There he met John Howe, who was private chaplain to Oliver Cromwell and a great man in the inner circle of Congregationalists. Howe, taking a liking to the younger man, offered him the living at his own church in Great Torrington, while he, Howe, continued in London. Great Torrington was not far from Barnstaple, where Nathaniel was, and Increase jumped at the offer. By winter of 1658–59 he was settled in his new job and only nine miles from his brother.

The Puritan revolution had already started to collapse, the immediate cause of failure the death of Oliver Cromwell, Lord Protector of England and informally the protector of the Independent or Congregationalist party. A more fundamental reason for collapse was the Puritans' failure to create a sound political basis for a republican government. Congregationalists and Presbyterians had missed the chance to reconcile their differences. At a conference in the old Savoy Palace in London, the Congregationalists agreed on a Declaration of Faith and Order which was similar to the Presbyterians' Wesminster Confession (1646) but which left no room for agreement on matters of church organization. This failure to compromise, as much as anything else, cost them the revolution. [60]

Richard Cromwell, who succeeded his father, vacillated first towards Parliament (Presbyterian) and then towards the army (Congregational- ist). In May 1659 he resigned. Events were now moving faster and faster towards the end of the Puritan reforms. Several of the Congregationalists were prepared even now to use the army to stay in power. Among them were John Owen, the regicides Whalley and Goffe, and Joseph Caryl. But these extremists, much admired by Mather, had lost touch with the people. Army officers in London conspired to seize Parliament, but far to the north General George Monck, commander of the army in Scotland, had the good sense to insist that the civil power must rule the military, not the other way around. Monck prepared to march his army south. Faced with the possibility of fighting their comrades in arms, the army outside London deserted the Congregationalist cause. Monck negotiated with John Owen and others, but they would not back down. Finally he marched south and entered London on February 3, 1660.[61] The Pres- byterians in Parliament thought they had won. But Monck called for elections, and the new Parliament, the Convention Parliament of 1660, favored a restoration of the monarchy. A short month later, Charles II stepped ashore at Dover. The Puritan revolution in England was fin- ished. Only in America could it continue. These events utterly destroyed Increase Mather's hopes and plans. With Cromwell dead, John Howe needed to have back his church at Great Torrington. Nathaniel's father- in-law found Increase a new position as chaplain to the English garrison on the Isle of Guernsey, and there he went in April 1659 to live in a grim, stone fortress built on a rocky island in the harbor, not the kind of place Increase wanted. Later that same year he obtained the position of vicar at St. Mary de Load, in Gloucester. But popular acceptance of Puritanism was slipping fast in these last days of the commonwealth, and before long Increase was in trouble over his outspoken, uncompromising views. He returned to the chaplaincy at Guernsey with the feeling that in Gloucester he had been persecuted for his faithful witness of Christ. No sooner was he back on Guernsey than Charles was restored to the throne.

Men and women all over England feared reprisals for the Civil War and the execution of Charles I, but Charles II and his ministers were le- nient. An act of Parliament pardoned all but the fifty-nine regicides and a small handful of others, including one or two New England men like Hugh Peter. Edward Whalley and William Goffe fled to Massachusetts; other regicides were caught and gruesomely executed. The general am- nesty allowed thousands of English Puritans to survive the change of government without penalty, but the revolution was over and a counter-revolutionary current ran strong. The established parish churches were turned back to their original clergy. Nathaniel lost his church at Barnstaple and went to London. Samuel lost all his offices in Dublin, spoke out against the return to episcopacy, and was promptly forbidden to preach in Ireland. He managed to hide himself in his church in Lancashire until 1662, when he was ejected from there as well.

Increase remained safe only so long as Colonel Bingham remained in command of the garrison on Guernsey. When the command changed, Increase was obliged to conform, and when he would not, he had to get out. Again, as when he described his graduation from Trinity College, the reader detects in Mather's autobiography a hint of pride in his own stubbornness. "When the King was proclaimed in Guernsey, I did out of conscience openly refuse to drink his Health . . . I refuse to subscribe to some papers . . . that now wee beeleved the Times were and would be happy . . . ."[62] He went to Dorchester on the mainland, where he could stay with William Benn, and preached frequently to Puritan audiences. His preaching was greatly admired and he could have had a living worth £400 a year, he wrote, if he would conform to the Church of England. He would not.

In January 1661 a handful of Fifth Monarchy fanatics staged an insurrection in London, hoping to bring about the second coming of Christ. They were easily defeated by the army, and their leader, Thomas Jenner, was hanged and disembowelled, his head, arms, and legs cut off and carried across England for all to see. The warning struck home. Congregationalists, including Nathaniel Mather, quickly published a pamphlet to distance themselves from Jenner's wild actions. But their anxieties continued that somewhere, somehow, some hothead would touch a match to the powder. New elections to Parliament in May 1661 replaced the moderate Convention Parliament with the royalist and vengeful Cavalier Parliament. Congregationalists began to flee the country.[63] The Netherlands was the closest refuge. Nathaniel Mather fled there and found a place as minister to an English church in Rotterdam. Increase planned to follow him with a young friend from Boston days, Samuel Bellingham, but Bellingham was frightened by rumors of a massacre and left London before Increase could get there.[64]

Unlike his two brothers, Increase Mather had not married and no family roots held him to England. His older brothers had been born in England, and for them England was home in a way it could never be to him. The emotional pull of his place of birth and childhood drew him back to America. He was the first generation to be American-born, and that made a difference. Perhaps most important, he was still young enough at twenty-two to consider his father's roof his best shelter in an uncertain world.

CHAPTER 2

The Struggle for Identity
[1661 - 1672]

The return voyage was mercifully quick and safe. Increase Mather's ship reached the fishing camps on Newfoundland's southeast coast in August 1661 and after a wait of only ten days—he thought himself lucky—he took passage on a New England vessel headed back to Boston. He landed on September 1 during the last days of New England's summer and went directly to his father's home in Dorchester. Eleazar was there, too, and the three men held an emotional reunion. The next day Richard Mather "shining like the Sun in *Gemini,* and hearing his two sons, in his own pulpit entertain the People of God, . . . [was] an *Happy Father.*" [1]

Increase Mather had offers from a dozen towns across New England but wanted none of them. Seldom did a prospective minister in New England have so many opportunities. "People are apt to run after strangers though they have little in them of real worth," he wrote about himself with unfamiliar modesty. [2] His degree from Trinity College and several years of preaching in England gave him an extra measure of glamour. So did the reputations of his father and brothers, a family dedicated to the service of God. His own exceptional abilities as a scholar and the piety demonstrated by his having been, as he said, persecuted for his faith, all helped explain his high reputation when he was still untried at twenty-two.

The irony was that Increase did not want to stay in Massachusetts at all. Massachusetts was a poor and uncouth frontier compared to England. He considered himself in exile. "Thus was I persecuted out of two places, Glocester and Guernsey, before I was 22 years of age," he wrote later.[3] But in fact Increase was home. With the flavor of the great world still in his mouth, he looked on his rustic surroundings with distaste as a temporary setback, an exile entered into for conscience's sake. But his family and friends saw it differently and offered no sympathy. He confided his anger and frustration to his diary.

The only offer to preach that seemed halfway suitable was to assist John Mayo at Boston's North Church. What made this offer tolerable was its location in Boston, the only New England town with even a semblance of sophistication. So Increase became a "hireling preacher," a man who preached to a congregation for money but stood outside its covenant and in no more meaningful relationship to the members of the congregation than to be paid for his services. He did join a church, but joined his father's in Dorchester, not the North Church, where he preached. "The first winter after my Return," he wrote, "I preached one Lords day with my Father at dorchester, and the other Lords day at Boston to the congregation where I still continue."[4] When Mather crossed Mill Creek on his way to his new church, he was in Boston's North End. The meeting-house there stood about three hundred yards north of the stream, in an area of open fields and scattered houses, not far from the water's edge, where wharves and warehouses were already going up. The meeting-house, now ten years old, had been enlarged with two galleries to hold the growing North End population. When Mather stood in the pulpit to preach, it was as if he stood on the stage of a small, unpainted opera house with orchestra below and balconies rising. The rough-hewn clapboard building, while not at all what he had dreamed of in England, was ideal for his talents, and he quickly made a name for himself as a preacher.

MARRIAGE AND FAMILY

Seven months after coming home, Increase married young Maria Cotton, his step-sister since his father's remarriage in 1656. She was now twenty-one.[5] The historical record tells nothing about their courtship. It does confirm that both were four or five years younger than the customary age of first marriage in New England. Cautious heads might have counselled waiting, and they would have been wrong. The marriage lasted half a century, during which time Maria raised a large family and managed the household by herself. Like most wives of her generation,

her life was in the background of Increase's public concerns and little
about it is known. Like Increase, Maria kept a devotional diary, but it
was unseen by any eyes but hers until her death.

There were powerful personal and psychological pressures for Increase
to marry when he did. Puritan social norms held that men and women
could lead an acceptable life only within a family. The nuclear family of
husband, wife, and children was almost universal in New England. For
Increase to continue in his father's home after having once left it was unacceptable and psychologically unendurable. By marrying he would become the head of his own household and acquire stability and place.
Surely, too, an encouragement to the marriage was Increase's knowledge
that it would join the two most respected ministerial families in New
England. It also solved at once the problem of where Increase would live
while preaching at the North Church. The young couple moved into the
house where Maria had been born, John Cotton's old house in Boston, not
far from the First Church. On Cotton's death it had passed to his three
children: one half to the oldest, Seaborn, and one half divided between
the other two, John Cotton and Maria.[6] Seaborn, a worldly, facetious
man who was six years older than Increase, was a minister in a New
Hampshire village. He and Increase did not get along well, and it galled
Mather terribly that his brother-in-law had part ownership of the house
where he and his bride lived.

Maria Mather, on the other hand, was at home in the house of her
birth and childhood. She took over the management of the household,
which soon came to include domestic servants and a young boarder.
There were a barn and stable, where Increase kept a saddle horse. There
were orchards, a vegetable garden, milk cows. All this Maria managed,
for Increase was completely absorbed in his work, like his father before
him. "I kept close to my study," he wrote years later, "and committed the
management of the affairs of the Family to her."[7] No stories would come
down, as were told years later of Governor Stoughton, of visitors finding
Increase Mather stripped to the waist in his hay fields. Maria gave birth
to their first child there in February 1663, and after that they had children regularly every two years. The first, a boy, they named Cotton after
Maria's father. Then came two girls, Maria in 1665 and Elizabeth, pre-
maturely, in January 1667. These three children lived to marry and have
children of their own. The next child, Nathaniel, born in 1669, lived
only until nineteen. After Nathaniel there would be five more girls and
another son, ten in all.[8]

In this old house, surrounded by his growing family of children and servants, Increase Mather began to shape his life. He was restless and irritable. He wanted more than anything to return to England. He felt hard-pressed for money and blamed his church. He came to hate the old Cotton house and long for one of his own. The room in the house that meant most to him was his study; it was his workshop, a retreat for meditation and prayer, the place where he sought the consolation of his books and manuscripts. He began to assemble his great library. When he took time later, in 1664, to catalogue his books, they already numbered about seven hundred titles, more than a thousand volumes, all sizes and shapes and topics. Mather listed them, not alphabetically, but by size: folio, quarto, octavo, and "small octavo." Here were chiefly volumes of biblical commentary and church fathers, but also the non-Christian Latin and Greek classics, Tacitus, Juvenal, Cicero, Demosthenes, Horace, Plautus, Seneca, Aesop, Lucian, Sophocles, Lucan, and Ovid. Medicine—a practical concern—and history and travel were well represented. Milton, Ramus, and Calvin shared space with the English Puritans Owen, Mede, and Baxter. It was the library of the man who would become the leading scholar of his generation in New England.[9]

When one or another of his children was feverish and cried in the night, Increase came to his library to spend the small hours before dawn alternately praying for his child and losing himself in his studies. Here he composed regular weekly sermons and intermittent Thursday lectures, all memorized to be delivered without notes. Here he sharpened his quill pens and wrote thousands of pages for the printing press, books that would make him famous on two continents. Mather scratched out page after page of the diary he would keep for the next fifty years. On hot summer nights he would strip off his clothes and write almost naked: "Finished & committed [sermon] to memory. Most excessive hot that could not endure clothes on. Heart serious."[10] On the short days of winter, the candles guttered long in their holders, and he drew the black, floor-length cleric's gown close about his legs.

Outside the house Mather was tirelessly social, and hardly a day passed without visitors.[11] He liked important people and wealthy people. Samuel Bache, a rich merchant from England who emigrated to New Haven and then to Boston, became his closest friend. Some years later Sir Thomas Lake, a wealthy Puritan gentleman, built a house in the North End and joined the Second Church. Lake would then come to Increase's aid financially, and many years later, after Maria's death, Increase would marry Lake's daughter. Mather often met with the governor and dined with the artillery officers. He ate out at taverns or at the houses of others, and frequently visitors stayed overnight at his house. Increase Mather had a taste for sophisticated surroundings evident throughout his entire life. Boston alone of the New England settlements could appeal to it.

In 1662 Boston's entire population was probably no more than 2,500 people. No home, church, or place of business was more than an easy walk from his house. In this community everyone saw everyone else, face to face, in the streets or at their places of work or worship. There were no anonymous people; no one was a stranger for long, although strangers, Indians, seamen, and newcomers were always passing through. Boston in Mather's day was different from other New England towns where even a passing stranger was a rarity. Boston's looks—the unnamed dirt roads and the unpainted wooden buildings—belied the fact that the town had become a metropolis. Whatever it looks and size, Boston was the meeting place of legislators, home of the court and the governor, the center of law and authority. The laws of Parliament, so went an old rule of thumb, did not reach across the seas. Massachusetts acknowledged the sovereignty of the king of England, but the charter gave the colony the right to govern itself. Not a single representative of the crown lived in all New England, and no appeal to England was allowed from Massachusetts courts. Boston, rustic as it might be, was, nevertheless, the highest seat of government.

Boston was also becoming a thriving center of trade with routes radiating outward—if not yet around the world, at least all across the North Atlantic. The commerce was managed out of merchants' homes, and silver money was so scarce that much trade was still barter and exchange of goods. Nevertheless, ships crossed and crisscrossed the Atlantic, bringing Boston into contact with the wider world. Boston's ships stopped at the tobacco colonies of Virginia and Maryland, crossed to the West Indies in the Caribbean, traded at Portuguese islands off the coast of Africa, and sailed to England and the European continent. Other ships went northeast to the great international fishing grounds off Newfoundland, where they traded with fishing fleets from England, France, and Spain. From every shore of the North Atlantic Ocean came men, ships, news, opinions, vices, merchandise, and disease.

In 1656 a merchant named Robert Keayne left in his will the money to build a Town House. Following the pattern of English market towns, the ground floor was to be open on all sides to make a gathering place, an "exchange," for merchants, farmers in from the countryside, and traders of all sorts. The second floor was to hold a council room and a public library, for which Keayne's own collection of books provided a start.

Here, around the exchange and in the adjacent streets, grew up the urban setting for Increase Mather's new life. Hezekiah Usher, who owned property across the road where the new Town House would be built, made a large contribution to the building fund. Usher was one of Boston's largest merchants, and he did an important business in books imported from England. His shop was a place Increase Mather loved to haunt. He would spend hours standing on the plank floor of Usher's shop reading in volumes he could not afford to buy. At other times he visited the bookshop of John Ratcliff, who was employed by Usher as a bookbinder.[12] Mather frequently ordered books from England through Usher, who bought regularly from the London publisher and bookseller Richard Chiswell. Chiswell later would publish in London some of Mather's own books. Books from England came packed in wooden barrels, which were unloaded at Town Dock, carried up to the store, and unpacked. News of their arrival was enough to bring Mather around to Usher's shop. When he finished browsing and stood at Usher's front door, he stood at the very heart of provincial Boston, but he carried in his head the ideas being discussed in the bookstalls of London.

SOLDIER OF THE LORD

Although Increase Mather lived in Boston, his mind was focused on the long-fought war of the Lord against Satan being waged in Europe. He believed that the war would end soon in the inevitable victory over the Antichrist. Victory would spell the start of the millennium. The major battlefield was England. He hungered after news of England, and much of his large incoming correspondence was long, hand-written newsletters, which he shared among his associates in America: news of court and palace, political news, news of the church and the restored bishops, news of the Nonconformist ministers and their troubles, military news, social news, news of crops and droughts and miraculous happenings that might offer a key to God's plan.[13] For the Nonconformist minister in Massachusetts these were anxious days. In England their enemies were in the saddle; men feared arrest and persecution. The newsletters were read eagerly but anxiously for news of the Puritans left in England.

This was a century of transition, when receding beliefs in the miraculous and the supernatural mingled easily with advancing beliefs in natural science and rationalism. It did not occur to Mather that there was a separation between the supernatural world of God and the Holy Spirit and the natural world in which he lived. Instead there was in his mind a constant penetration of one by the other. They flowed together without boundary. The invisible world of spirit was the realm inhabited by angels and devils. What happened there could be guessed at sometimes by out-of-the-ordinary events in the visible world of nature. Because Mather, like all Puritan intellectuals, put great emphasis on order and meaning, such events must have some purpose in God's scheme of things. Miraculous events in the natural world were signs and signals. "Last Decem.," he reported to a correspondent, "there were horses seene lighting down from heaven upon the ground in Wales & marching in a warlicke posture, to the Amazement of many beholders. Upon the 3d of March it rained wheate, & Rye, & pease in severall places in Dorsett. A godly Minister that saw it, & tasted some of it writes me word of it. The Tast thereof was very loathsome." [14]

In his own perception of things, Mather was a soldier of Christ waging war against the forces of Antichrist. As a soldier in the great war, he joined the conspiracy to protect William Goffe and Edward Whalley, the two regicides now under sentence of death, who had fled to Massachusetts a year ahead of Mather himself. The governor in Massachusetts had refused to guarantee their safety, so the fugitives went on to New Haven, where the minister, John Davenport, gave them shelter for a time. Even New Haven, however, seemed too public a place, and soon they moved further off, to the frontier village of Hadley on the Connecticut River. The minister at Hadley, John Russell, took them into his house and built on extra rooms for a permanent hideout.

Increase Mather was not back in New England long before he was in touch with all these people. He entered the conspiracy by serving as the conduit through which Goffe sent and received messages from England. Mather hid the clandestine mail within his own packets of correspondence, which he gave to ship captains sailing to London. There the packets were turned over to a friend, who opened them and distributed the contents. Goffe's wife never knew where her husband had taken refuge; in the 1670s she sent her letters to Mather in Boston, and he forwarded them to Hadley. Goffe, in a pathetic attempt to escape detection, addressed his wife as "Mother." The couple never set eyes on each other again. At first the flight of the regicides to New England and their concealment from royal warrant-servers seemed part of the great war. Spies were sent to discover the network of revolutionaries, and their correspondence had the color of holy war. Davenport, who functioned as a center of conspiratorial news, used a simple code to disguise the names of people involved.[15] The conspiracy kept alive Mather's sense of participation in the great fight. "I something feare," he wrote Davenport in the letter quoted above, "whether the times may not be such heere, as that I must fly for it ere long again heere, as in England I have beene faine to doe."[16] He continued to think of himself as a man persecuted for his faith. As the Restoration settlement established itself in England, however, English Puritanism itself changed, the holy war was forgotten, and forgotten too were the fugitives in America. Goffe and Whalley lived out their years buried in the New England countryside.

HALF-WAY COVENANT

The great disagreement that had divided New England Puritans into two camps at mid-century came to a head in 1662. The General Court called a synod of all the churches to answer two deceptively simple questions: who are the subjects of baptism, and ought there be a consociation of churches? The second question would lie dormant until the end of the century, but the first was urgent. The gathered church of visible saints, so revolutionary in the setting of traditional English religious life, ran up against the deeply ingrained tradition of infant baptism. At the extreme radical end of the spectrum of Puritan beliefs, antipaedobaptists abandoned infant baptism altogether, separating themselves at the same time from the Church of England and worshipping in illegal conventicles. None of the early leaders of Massachusetts were separating Baptists. Winthrop, Dudley, Wilson, Cotton, Shepard, Norton, Richard Mather, and others were non-separating Puritans. Even after they had created the particular churches of visible saints, they defended baptism of the infant children of the saints, basing it on the Abrahamic covenant in Genesis 17.7: "And I will establish my covenant between me and thee and thy seed after thee in their generations for an everlasting covenant, to be a God unto thee and to thy seed after thee."

As things soon turned out, a conspicuous number of children of visible saints, baptized in their infancy, grew up without experiencing that rebirth which would identify them as visible saints also. Would their children be eligible as infants for baptism? Richard Mather was faced with this situation in his own family when children were born to his son Timothy in the early 1650s. Neither Timothy nor his wife was a member of a church, and unless the rules were changed, their children would not be baptized. Mather campaigned to enlarge the rules for infant baptism to include grandchildren as well as children of visible

Courtesy, Harvard University Portrait Collection

Portrait, possibly of Charles Chauncy, president of Harvard from 1654 to 1672 and opponent of half-way covenant

saints. But many Massachusetts saints saw such an enlargement of baptism as opening the churches to unregenerate members, and they clung fiercely to the more exclusive baptism.

At a more abstract level, the argument cut into the basic thinking of New England Puritans, for it pitted typology against the ideal of the particular church of visible saints. Typology was a centuries-old method of interpreting scripture. Events described in the Old Testament were understood to foreshadow later events in the New Testament. Carried further, scriptural events could be thought of as prefiguring events in the

John Davenport, senior minister of New Haven and author of *Another Essay for the Investigation of the truth,* a criticism of half-way covenant, with preface by Increase Mather

post-Testament times. Puritans in New England commonly explained their own experience in America as the working out of God's will already prefigured in the Old and New Testaments. Puritans considered baptism analogous to circumcision, and some New England Puritans used typological reasoning to argue that Old Testament circumcision justified the baptism of the infant seed of visible saints. But there were others, notably Charles Chauncy, the president of Harvard College, and John Davenport, the minister at New Haven, who rejected those arguments and gave primary emphasis to the purity of the churches.[17] The community was thus divided in theory as well as in practice.

Seventy ministers and laymen met in synod in March 1662 in the old meetinghouse in Boston. They represented most of the churches in Massachusetts. Richard and Increase Mather were delegates from the Dorchester church. The key to the synod's debate was Proposition Five, since nicknamed the "half-way covenant." Proposition Five said that men and women who had been baptized into one of the churches as infants should be allowed to have their own children baptized also, even if they themselves had not experienced new birth or been admitted into full communion. It would be sufficient for these parents to understand church doctrine and subscribe to the church covenant.

Richard Mather, his old friend John Norton, and Jonathan Mitchell, Increase's tutor in his last year at Harvard, dominated the synod debates. A handful of others opposed them. Charles Chauncy, who was so literal in his interpretation of the Bible that in his early career he would celebrate the Lord's Supper only in the evening at supper time, led the opposition. John Davenport, not from Massachusetts, was therefore not a delegate, but he came to Boston nevertheless and attended the synod. He opposed any loosening of the criteria for baptism. It may have been during these trips of Davenport's to Boston that Increase first came to know the older man. Increase, his brother Eleazar, and John Mayo at the North Church also opposed the half-way covenant, but probably had little influence in the debates. Once, when Increase wanted to read a paper of Davenport's to the synod, John Norton put a stop to it.

Increase Mather publicly opposed his father. When he rebelled in the synod, he was challenging one of the most deeply held tenets of Puritan society. The fifth commandment, "Honor thy father and thy mother," was taken with dreadful seriousness. Thomas Cobbett, for example, advised all children, "Present your Parents so to your minds as bearing the Image of Gods Father-hood, and that also will help on your filiall awe and Reverence to them."[18] When at twenty-three Increase contradicted

the views of his father, of his proxy-father John Norton, and of his college tutor Jonathan Mitchell, he began a struggle for personal independence that reached into his very bowels. Unconsciously he attached
himself to another father figure, John Davenport. Davenport, the same
age as Richard Mather, had been more active in the Puritan movement
in England. After five years at the university, Davenport had begun at
nineteen to preach at St. Stephen's Church in Coleman Street, London.
During the 1620s, increasingly Puritan, he had participated in the organization of the Massachusetts Bay Company and when John Cotton fled
from his parish in 1633, he hid him in London. A few years later, Davenport himself fled to Holland, where he soon engaged in a fierce dispute
over what he thought were lax standards for baptizing infants. In 1637
at Cotton's urging Davenport emigrated to New England and helped
found a colony at New Haven.[19] He had become, after Richard Mather
and John Norton, probably the most admired minister in New England.
Increase now accepted his leadership on the question of baptism in open
opposition to his father.

Richard Mather thought that the most precious gift parents could
give their children was membership in the mystical body of Christ. He
believed that baptism gave the individual a full, personal membership in
a catholic church. Increase, on the other hand, using familiar typology,
argued that baptized men and women who had not gone on to a new
birth in Christ had forfeited their membership and the right to have their
children baptized into any particular church. Davenport went further to
reject typological reasoning altogether and to emphasize also the obligation baptism entailed.[20] Both men wanted to keep the particular
churches free from unregenerate members, which the half-way covenant
seemed to threaten.

When the synod votes were counted, Richard Mather had won. The
synod overwhelmingly favored Proposition Five and the half-way covenant. Increase did not give up; instead he helped organize further opposition, and when the synod report was presented to the General Court
in October, it was young Increase Mather and not Charles Chauncy who
asked permission to present a dissenting statement. That request was
denied, but Increase did come away with the unprecedented permission
of the Court to publish opposition arguments, even though the General
Court had voted to accept the report of the majority.[21] The Massachusetts
press, like that of England, was censored, and publication required a
license. For the first time in its history, the General Court had given permission to publish arguments opposed to a position of the Court. That

permission testified to what soon became all too evident: the colony was divided over the issue of baptism. Lay members of the churches did not agree with the synod majority or with the leadership of their ministers. As a consequence, most churches, including Richard Mather's, refused for years to put the half-way covenant into practice. The representatives of the lay members in the government, the deputies, allowed opponents of the half-way covenant to publish their objections.

Increase turned all his youthful energy to this cause. Charles Chauncy sent an essay against the half-way covenant to London, where it was published with the signatures of Increase, Eleazar, and John Mayo. Increase persuaded Davenport to write against the proposals, and Increase, in turn, wrote a preface, an unsigned "Apologetical Preface to the Reader," in John Davenport, *Another Essay for the Investigation of the truth* (Cambridge, 1663). His unsigned preface was Increase Mather's first published work. Richard Mather and Jonathan Mitchell replied, and in 1664 the press in Cambridge was choked with material relating in one way or another to the synod. Actual publication about the issue ceased in 1664, but Increase continued to act as a center for opposition and collected written arguments against the new baptism from all corners of New England.[22]

This activity brought him into close contact with the most zealous men in Massachusetts, among them John Russell, who was hiding the regicides in his house in Hadley, and Russell's co-conspirator, Peter Tilton, Deputy to the General Court from Hadley and the man who usually brought Goffe's letters to Mather to be smuggled into England. These men feared that the half-way covenant would dilute the pure church of visible saints by offering baptism and hence membership to men and women who never experienced a new birth in Christ. As it turned out, they were correct. Increase fought the change as long as he could. He became widely known as a champion of the original, primitive, revolutionary Congregationalism. At this time, too, Mather began an alliance with the House of the Deputies which would last for thirty years. The deputies, elected by the brethren of each town's church, were generally opposed to the results of the synod. When Increase chose sides in the half-way covenant fight, he had thus taken a political position in addition to a religious one. For the rest of his life, he would put the interests of lay members and their deputies ahead of the interests of the ministers and the magistrates.

NORTH CHURCH

All that summer of 1662 Mather had been preaching at the North Church. Michael Powell, who had been denied ordination ten years before because of his lack of education and was for years the Ruling Elder and popular lay preacher, was suddenly incapacitated by a stroke, and in August Mather struck a bargain to preach every Sunday. He and John Mayo were to divide the weekly offering, £65 a year for Mayo, £50 a year for Mather. Michael Powell's salary was reduced to £25, and that only if enough money remained.[23]

Some older members of the congregation were angry to see their friend Powell replaced by a young man of such a different temperament and social status, but Mather charmed his audience. The more he preached, the more determined the North Church was to have him. Not just full members of the church, but townspeople who had no vote in church affairs, members of the new mercantile class moving into the North End, found in Increase Mather the spiritual leader they wanted. When Mather, still unwilling to settle in Boston, started enquiries about moving to the West Indies, townspeople petitioned him to stay. Yet the present arrangement with the church satisfied no one. Mather was unhappy at preaching for hire; old members of the church were angry at the displacement of Powell; new members wanted a settled minister with strength and abilities to match their own upward thrust. In May 1663, Increase and Maria made a half-step toward accepting the call; they joined the North Church.

Increase's dilemma was that although he knew what he wanted out of life, he was not sure what God wanted for him. He wanted to be at the center of power and to associate with the great scholars of Europe. He wanted the glamour of England, although he knew deep within himself that all the attractions of England were vanities. His true calling was to serve as one of God's ministers. Might that not be here on the edge of civilization? Increase might rebel at the thought of wasting his talents on a rude and unsophisticated people, but he could not escape the fact that Providence had cast him up on these shores, that these people gathered in a true church were calling him to be their spiritual leader. Did not these things reveal God's will? Would he not be wrong to resist? Yet he could not accept that Boston, with its muddy streets and unpainted wooden houses bleaching in the sun, was where he should spend the rest of his life. "This church was very urgent with me to accept of office relation," he summarized later, "but for several years I withstood that motion finding a great averseness in my spirit to comply therewith. I had also a great desire to return to England if liberty for Nonconformity should there be granted. . . . It was some encouragement to me, that the Inhabitants as well as the church did by writing and subscribing their names signify their desires of my Continuance amongst them."[24]

In the end a seemingly trivial issue decided him. He still lived in John Cotton's house in the shadow of that great man, and he longed to move away. The situation created tensions within his marriage. "This morning," he wrote in his diary, "my wife desires me with tears to leave her fathers house, wishing that I would rather leave Boston than live here." Mather told the North Church that he could not accept its call unless it would buy him another house. The church could not do that, but it might rent him one. That was enough, and Increase wrote out his acceptance that very morning.[25] A lifelong commitment was about to be sealed. As it turned out, however, Increase and Maria lived another five years in the old Cotton house before moving to one purchased by the church.

In 1664 it was acceptable for ministers in New England to secure their future in the changing world by entering into written contracts with their churches. The contract that Increase Mather signed with the North Church revealed all his anxieties and uncertainties. He agreed to accept ordination as the Teacher in the North Church provided that he would be free to leave if the Lord called him elsewhere, or if he suffered "persecution" from within the church, or if he had bad health, or if the pay was insufficient. In any of these circumstances "Then (my relation to them notwith-standing) I would be at liberty to return to England, or to remove elsewhere."[26]

The ordination was set for May 27, 1664. In the weeks leading up to ordination Increase was beset by anxieties. On the thirteenth of May he read for the first time his father's response to Davenport's criticism of the half-way covenant, for which he, Increase, had written the preface. Richard Mather confined his arguments to refuting Davenport, and Jonathan Mitchell wrote the reply to Increase's preface.[27] The next day at supper, one of the church deacons told Increase that some of the church said they would contribute nothing to the maintenance of Mayo or young Mather, because they opposed the synod. After reading Mitchell's "Answer to the Preface," Increase noted in his diary only "Heart disturbed with unworthy reflections."[28] In the General Court there was talk that the North End Church should be prevented from ordaining Mather because of the way he opposed the majority of the synod. "At night, my brother S.C. sayd at table that I had acted disorderly in opposing the Synod, & that being disorderly was as bad as drunkenesse or Scandall."[29] The fact is that a large majority of North End Church members wanted Increase not despite of, but because of, his opposition to the half-way covenant.

Increase and his father did not allow their differences over the half-way covenant to disturb their relationship openly. During the months leading up to Increase's ordination, father and son met frequently. Increase described a day at the end of March: "In morning went to Dorchester. There the Lord helped me very graciously in prayer & preaching. Oh blessed be god. I sayd in secret (Lord thou hast called me to this work & I dare & will trust thee for thine assistance). Supped with my father. Came home that night. This was a sweet fast."[30] As the ordination day approached, they continued to meet: "Visited Governor (with Father)"; "My father here this day"; "After lecture walked with father about a mile homewards."[31] Nevertheless, Increase had not slackened his attachment to Davenport. When he received some of Davenport's sermons on May 8, even though it was the Sabbath, Increase spent the midday between morning and afternoon services "in reading mr Davenports sermons sent to me & in secret prayer."[32] Later Eleazer and Increase conferred with the other senior opponent of the synod, Charles Chauncy.[33]

The half-way covenant was not the only thing that weighed heavily on Increase Mather's mind in those weeks. On the night of April 18, Maria's brother, John Cotton, came to the Mather home and spent the night. Namesake of his famous father, one year younger than Increase, and favorite brother of Maria, John Cotton was a cherished friend and a member of Boston's First Church. He was now in desperate trouble. The next morning he confessed to Increase a shocking story of sexual advances made toward two women members of the church. One can only imagine the turmoil in Increase Mather's mind at this revelation. The two lines entered in his diary on this day are illegible, as if their meaning had been too shocking to bear. That afternoon, Increase went to Major General John Leverett, one of the leaders of First Church, "to know what thought of having church meet about J.C." "He sayd," Mather reported in his diary, "thought that best & not before publick congregation;"[34] there would be a meeting of the church membership only. On May 1, 1664, the saints of the First Church voted to excommunicate John Cotton from their fellowship "for lasivious uncleane practices with three women and his horrified lying to hide his sinne."[35] The next month, June 1664,

Cotton made an act of contrition to his church. Increase was deeply torn what to do. "Troubled about J.C.," he wrote, "being very desirous to testify more fully for him. & yet affraid to doe it, because I could not say (*sana conscienta*) that his carriage & demeanore had bin all along suitable to his condition."[36] The next day, Cotton was restored to church fellowship on his "penitential acknowledgement openly confessing his sinnes."[37] Shortly afterwards, he moved to Martha's Vineyard, serving as a missionary to the Indians there. In 1669 he was ordained minister to the church at Plymouth, outside the jurisdiction of Massachusetts, and for the next thirty years he would remain there, an intimate and cherished friend and correspondent of Increase and Maria.

Increase's own ordination day approached, but he could not reach an agreement with the church about his salary. "At night br. Way with me told me that many cryed out against me for covetousness. That mr Mayo especially expressed his dislike at my answers to the church because I mentioned maytenance."[38] Mather's mood vacillated: "Heart in listless frame. . . . Heart in good frame mostly. . . . Heart sometimes lively, sometimes dead."[39] A few days of peace and confidence would be followed by a sudden plunge into despair: "Abhored suggestions ad A. [atheism]," then recovery, "Resolved to walk with God & leave all things to him to order in mercy and faithfulnesse."[40] As the day approached, Increase "spent much time in discourse with br. E[leazar] & T[imothy]. Heart in various frames."[41] Eleazar preached for him on the Sabbath before the ordination, and Increase started to work on his ordination sermon the next day. He "labored to imprint sermon for ordin." in his memory on Wednesday. Thursday was spent in prayer.

On Friday came the special day. Richard Mather and John Mayo "imposed hands" to symbolize Increase Mather's election by the fellowship of church members. He was ordained Teacher, responsible for the instruction and guidance of the church. "In Publick enlarged & broken in Prayer at first," Mather wrote of that day; "Lord helped graciously in speaking his Word."[42]

John Hull, treasurer of the colony, entered in his diary what seems to be an outline of Increase Mather's ordination sermon. It struck themes which would last a lifetime: "Self-interest is too predominant in many. Want of subjection of inferiors to superiors, and too much want of religious care to contain in subjection those under them, is a visible evil among us. Disacknowledgment of the ordinance of councils, and that great breadth of a ministerial judge, is very visible in many churches. Non-acknowledgment of the children of the church to be members thereof, not taking care that their knowledge and life might answer their relation, is also manifest. And many other evils, as grudging at the maintenance of magistracy, and, by too many, of the maintenance of the ministry; likewise pride in long hair, new fashions in apparel, drinking, gaming, idleness, worldliness, &c."[43]

The Monday after his ordination, Increase and Eleazer rode to Dorchester, where they spent the day with their father and step-mother and returned to Boston in the soft summer evening long after dark. Increase went immediately to his study and "composed part of Preface for mr. D. [Davenport's] Sermons."[44] The differences with his father over baptism persisted, and would persist like the evolving plot of a Greek tragedy until their bitter, fated end. Increase was pained when his own actions at the synod were criticized: "Much grieved at the unworthy dealings of them mentioned day before [by Seaborn Cotton]," he wrote later that June and continued with a half-serious wish "to goe for England again & suffer there more under prelacy rather than to stay in N.E. to suffer under them that looked upon as godly."[45] The mutual commitment so recently entered into between Mather and the North Church had brought him neither joy nor peace. He remained troubled in personal life and easily stung by criticism. All summer long he was bothered by "Abhorred temptations ad Atheisme," as on July 29, 1664: "Grieved, grieved, grieved, with temptations to Atheisme."[46] Once after he had lost his temper and said things he wished he had not, Increase admitted to his diary, "heart full of inward bleedings and confusions."[47] His low salary from the church was a constant source of depression and often caused him to think of leaving.[48] In December, he seriously thought about moving to Barbados.[49] All the while he corresponded with the great Protestant scholars at home and abroad: John Owen and Philip Nye in England, Voetius and Hornbeck on the continent, and of course, Davenport in New Haven.[50] The young Increase, who celebrated his twenty-fifth birthday that June felt himself better than his Boston surroundings. "Troubled at the new churches little care of me. Desirous to remove from them if Lord would."[51]

These were, nevertheless, the busiest months of his life, filled with new duties that stemmed from his office within the church. His days were taken up with a constant round of visits and conferences, all noted briefly in his diary, intermixed there with equally brief notes of his omnivorous reading. Frequently Increase was called out of town to other congregations. Late in October, for example, he worked on Saturday until late in the morning, "then rode for Concord. Came to Cambridge about 1h PM. There tarried till 4h for mr [Peter] Bulkleys son. Rode 10 miles in night & dark & very cold, but Lord kept from evil." He preached the Sabbath sermon at Concord and returned on Monday. Coming back through Cambridge he met the Deputy Governor, Richard Bellingham, and they rode on to Charlestown together and crossed over to Boston by ferry just as dark was falling.[52] It was Halloween, though All Saints day was not recognized in Puritan Massachusetts. Guy Fawkes day was recognized a week later; in 1664 it fell on a Saturday. "At night much troubled to see bonfires. Moved with indignation that sabboth should be profaned & wicked superstitions revived."[53] The next month he argued with some of the wealthiest men in his church about celebrating Christmas, "I Con, they Pro."[54] At home the baby was sick. "This day Cotton taken very ill of vomiting & purging. I troubled because loved him so strongly. Strong affections bring strong affliction."[55]

OBSTINATE AND TURBULENT ANABAPTISTS

The congregation Mather so reluctantly joined was divided into two parts. In one were the adult members of the church, who had given proof of their regeneration and signed the church covenant, and their children. In the other were the men, women, and children of the community, who crowded into the meetinghouse every Sabbath, but who had not had the experience of new birth, had not been admitted to the fellowship of the visible saints, had not signed the covenant, and, unless earlier in England, had not even been baptized.

Technically only the first of these groups was the church, but every minister in Massachusetts spoke to both audiences. It has been said that the Puritan ministers preached only to the already saved, but that was untrue of Increase and his generation. To be sure, Mather distinguished the visible saints from the rest and often did speak to them in particular. But he always considered himself an evangelist whose mission was to bring the unconverted to a new birth in faith. The legal relationship between him and the two parts of the congregation was perfectly clear. The inner church of visible saints elected the minister, ordained him, set his salary, admitted new members to the inner circle, and administered the affairs of the congregation. The outer circle attended service but did not receive the sacraments and had no voice in the decisions of the church. In Boston both the First Church and Second or North Church supported their ministers by voluntary offerings every Sunday. In almost all other Massachusetts towns, however, Sunday offerings were insufficient and the ministers' salaries were met by a public tax, which fell on regenerate and unregenerate alike. Men and women who attended church but were not members did not have a direct voice in the colony's government. With a few exceptions, only full church members could vote for governor, deputy governor, magistrates, or deputies. In 1664 visible saints controlled both state and church.

The North End of Boston was very small in 1664. When Increase was ordained Teacher of the North Church, there were forty covenanted members, twenty-three women and seventeen men.[56] These forty were the church, but, as in most other walks of life, it was the men who governed. We can do no more than make a rough guess at the size of the population of the North End itself in 1664. Tax lists indicate that by 1680 about a thousand men and women lived there. In 1664 there might have been as few as fifty families. Even that modest number would have meant that even then church members were a minority of adults at the North End. Perhaps for every adult man who was a member there were two who were not. Nevertheless, all, men, women, and children came to Sabbath service, and all, to a greater or lesser degree, expected the new minister to speak wisely to their needs.

The character of the fellowship in the North Church was changing. As the population grew in numbers and wealth, the church became more middle-class. Entering this religious environment, Mather came as a young, ambitious clergyman who had an exalted idea of his role. Though chosen by the fellowship, in his own eyes Mather stood apart from them in a special relationship to God. Ten years earlier, Samuel Stone had observed that the New England ministers had become "a speaking aristocracy in the face of a silent democracy."[57] The phrase is apt in Increase Mather's case, for despite his staunch defense of the rights of the brethren, he did not think of himself as one among equals. To preach with authority and in the name of God was to preach officially, with all the standing of office, with the power of a special right as an ambassador of God, doing all in the name not of the church but of God. At least one of the founders of the North Church, John Farnum, who believed in the kind of lay preaching Michael Powell had done, opposed the changing emphasis, and Mather had been careful to discuss the differences between him and Farnum with the ruling elders before he accepted their offer.[58]

Farnum was already attending home worship services with a tiny company of Puritans—seven men and two women—organized by Thomas Goold or Gould, who had left the Charlestown church over the issue of infant baptism. The small house church Goold organized may have been the seed of New England's first surviving Baptist congregation. Infant baptism, however, was only one of its objections to the way the Massachusetts churches in general were evolving.[59] John Farnum's complaints reveal how, besides doctrinal issues, the spirit and function of the early gathered church was succumbing to authority and formalism. His disagreements with the new Teacher of the North Church grew worse during the next twelve months. Farnum and Mather were headed towards a collision.

It is apparent from Mather's diary that infant baptism was not the central issue between them. Farnum resented an educated clergy's taking over the church he had helped found, the North Church, his church.

At night John Farnum with me. [Mather wrote] I sayd that hear hee desired to leave church & join with another society, I desired to know what reason had, & and would endeavor to give him satisfaction from the word of God. He answered would not tell me reason but when church came together hee would tell. He not bound to tell everyman, & what I had to doe to enquire. I sayd holy Ghost had made me overseer & what should I answer at day of Judgement if should be sayd such an one going astray & you not used meanes to recover him, therefore I must enquire in fear of God. . . . At last in discourse hee objected against br. Collicott, & that church had no Communion, that mr. Powells maytenance was taken from him, but refused to discourse those particulars. I desired him seriously to consider what it would cost him to rend from church— what would loose by it, & what would get by it. Would loose esteem of many good men, would loose the immediate influence of their prayers & which worst of all, might fear would loose favor of God. He made light of all, & should have esteem of as good as they &c. I told him that erred he held Communion with excommunicate persons which was irregular &c. He sayd that so hee did, was of their meeting, & (sayth he) they are as good men as any of you all, & the church censure [against them in Charlestown] was wicked censure, done by mr Simms & mr Shepard without major part of the Church.[60]

Farnum made impossible demands of the North Church before he would resume fellowship:[61]

1. They must set up the ordinance of [lay] prophecy; 2. They must not baptize infants; 3. They must all be baptized themselves; 4. They must put away their teacher [Mather], and not own him for an officer.

The argument moved into public church meetings. Farnum stubbornly, then angrily sought to justify his behavior and to escape the censure of his fellows.

FARNUM: My heart is broken.

MATHER: But, Brother, we must *see* it broken, by the fruits and effects of it.

FARNUM: You shall not see it.

MATHER: Nay, but we must see it, or how can we receive satisfaction!

FARNUM (bitterly): *You see it!? You shall never see it!* (Later) I did not come here to be snap't and snubbed and snarled at by every one.

As Farnum turned to leave the meetinghouse, Mayo tried to stop him.

MAYO: Brother Farnum, in the name of the church and in the name of Christ, whose church we are you are required to stay and hear what further we have to say unto you.

FARNUM: Don't use the name of Christ to me; I am not one that can stoop and bow to every one.

In private, Farnum's wife came to his defense. "Goodwife Farnum sayd that she believed what her husband reported against mr Mayo & me. I told her that she brake the rule 1.Tim. 5. 19 [against an Elder receive no accusation but under two or three witnesses]. She sayd that was fine thing indeed, then Elders might say what they would when no body was by. She told me that she heard strange things of me, but she would not stand to them, nor tell where she had it. But it must needs be true because reported. She sayd that there were as bad in church as her husband but she perceived the proverb was true that as a man was befriended so his case was ended . . . She sayd that thought it strange that a man must be made an offender for a word." [62] The case dragged on through interminable meetings at Mayo's house and in the meetinghouse.

MATHER: After that the teacher had ended his speech in endeavoring to clear up the rule before the church, this offending party *made a leg* to him in a way of scorn and derision before the church.

And again, in the winter when Farnum took a seat high up in the second gallery, out of sight of all but a few of the congregation, Mayo asked him to come down front. Farnum replied,

You may speak to me here, if you have anything to say to me. I can hear you well enough.

The Farnum affair reached a sad end. Farnum left the meetinghouse one last time, saying, "This place is too hot for me."

"By which words," Mather later reported, "he caused many vaine youths to burst forth into an open laughter in the midst of work so awfull and dreadfull, and went to go out of the congregation. The pastor required him, in the name of

Christ, to stay; but he refused to hear the church, and went away out of the congregation. . . . When he was gone, the pastor did, in the name of the Lord Jesus, the Judge of quick and dead, deliver this impenitent and profane offender unto Satan, for the destruction of the flesh, that the spirit might be saved. Now, out of the hands of Satan, whose at present he is, the Lord, if it be possible, deliver him.

John Farnum was a plain, outspoken man of little education, full of anger, frustrated at not knowing how to deal with the changes taking place all around him, always putting his foot in his mouth. Like many Puritans, he wanted an emotional, informal, egalitarian religious fellowship. It was his misfortune to be in a church that was swept up into a higher social class by the growing prosperity of Boston's North End. This new community had different expectations. Farnum found no peace in his break from the church he had helped found, and, years later, in 1683, when tempers had cooled and new issues occupied men's attention, he was readmitted to the North Church. For the time being, Farnum continued to worship with the small Baptist fellowship. In May 1665 they all signed articles of faith drawn up by Thomas Goold, and seven men and two women rebaptized themselves by immersion. Goold, Farnum, and John George were arrested the next year but released in October. Then in March 1668 they were all arrested.

In a proceeding reminiscent of the synod which preceded Anne Hutchinson's trial in 1637, the General Court arranged a public debate between the Baptists and a panel of orthodox ministers. In the debate, held on April 14 and 15, 1668, questions of church discipline were as important as questions of doctrine. James Allen, minister of the First Church and moderator of the debate, said in his opening remarks: "Your work is to give the reason for your separation from the people of God; and settling up a meeting in the way of Anabaptism: and whether this commonwealth is to allow it."[63] When asked how they could justify leaving their particular congregations, the Baptists gave sometimes contradictory answers. They had separated from the established churches because they objected to the baptism of infants, and because those churches denied them participation in church services, particularly lay prophecy. William Turner: "3 things I separate from you for. 1: Baptizing infants. 2: Denying prophecy to the brethren. 3: A spirit of persecution of those that differ from you." The ministers were assuming too great a role in church worship, for as Turner said the next day, "All the work is not to lie on one parson or teacher as you do."[64]

At the end of two days, the ministers were agreed on their recommendations to the General Court. There could be no question of allowing the Baptist meeting to continue. The question was partly one of schism. Jonathan Mitchell, Increase's Harvard tutor, put it succinctly: "For you to set up a church in the midst of us in opposition to us: this is schism. . . ."[65] The General Court issued a sentence of banishment against three of the prisoners, Goold, Farnum, and William Turner, calling them "obstinate and turbulent Anabaptists."[66]

Then a surprising and prophetic thing happened. Sixty-six persons presented a petition pleading that the sentence was too severe. Several who signed were among Boston's best families, and at least one, Richard Way, was a pillar of Increase's North Church. Several reasons account for the public objections to the court's order. Many people sympathized directly with one or another of the Baptist positions on infant baptism and the governance of the churches. Others reasoned that if the orthodox ministers themselves were divided over infant baptism, as the arguments for and against the half-way covenant revealed, the issues were not fundamental, not enough to justify the severe sentence of banishment. Still others were influenced by repeated urging from English Puritans not to be narrowly intolerant of Baptists. In England Puritans of all varieties were making a united front against the established church. In the face of public protest, therefore, the General Court backed away from the sentence of banishment. The case dragged out over several years, and in the end left the Baptists free to hold their meetings on Noddles Island in the bay.[67] In ten years they would be back in Boston.

A PREACHER'S LIFE

In the North Church, Increase Mather quickly fell into a weekly routine that would last without interruption except for illness for the next twenty-three years. Every Sunday was dedicated to morning and afternoon worship services. Lengthy, extemporaneous prayers played almost as important a part in these services as the sermons, but there was no formal liturgy, as was prescribed in the Church of England Prayer Book. Two or even three ministers might participate at one service, although one was enough. Often Increase exchanged pulpits with colleagues. Special church services were sometimes held during the week, as, for example, Increase's Friday ordination, and sometimes private persons asked ministers to hold services at their homes. Increase frequently preached at Dorchester and his father for him at the North Church. When either Eleazer or Seaborn Cotton were in Boston, they too would preach in Increase's church. He celebrated the Lord's Supper once a month; on these days, Increase's sermons were always "sacramental" sermons on the life of Christ. Mondays without fail Increase began to prepare for his next sermon, and throughout the week he worked to perfect it. Every Thursday afternoon there was a lecture at the First Church, and Mather soon took his place among the regular speakers. After the Thursday lecture, the ministers who had been present met at the home of John Wilson. Sometimes Mather rode out to Dorchester for the Thursday lecture there, and then he would stay for supper with his father and stepmother. They in turn came to Boston several times a year and stayed at Increase and Maria's house, Sarah Mather's home for many years when her first husband had been alive. Every Friday, Increase Mather "committed sermon to memory." Saturday was given to preparing himself for the Sabbath through long hours of "secret prayer."

Such was the skeleton of his week. There always seemed to be more church business than there was available time. One frequent task was to hear relations of spiritual growth upon which admission to the fellowship would be judged. Ordinarily Mather heard these relations at Michael Powell's house. After Powell suffered his stroke this was the only church function he could perform. Most of the persons coming to his house to offer relations were women, who were generally allowed to disclose the evidence of their conversion privately before the ministers.[68] Men were expected to speak publicly before the church. Increase Mather believed most strongly that such an examination of the evidence of a true regeneration was essential. He tried once to prevent his colleague at Salem, John Higginson, from publishing "because he denied necessity of examination de conversion before admission to Lord's Supper."[69] Higginson was not alone, and within fifteen years this question of examination would become a major disagreement among the Puritan ministers in Massachusetts.

Maria Mather adapted her own week to her husband's crowded schedule, always ready to entertain the numerous guests he brought to the house. But her children must have occupied most of her time. Cotton was born in February 1663; Maria came in March 1665, and Increase recorded that she was weaned just a year later.[70] Maria became pregnant again at once, and the next child, a girl, was premature: "About 8h A.M. my wife became ill. About 1h P.M. delivered. Lord helped me much in prayer and sermon. Little sleep in night because troubled that my wife came before her time."[71] When the children were sick, Mather usually noted it in his diary. "Cotton not well which hindered from sleep in latter part of night. . . . This morn Cott. of his own accord sayd to me, Father, Ton would go see God, which words went to my heart lest Lord should take him away by death. Much troubled at his illness being very feverish &c."[72]

John Cotton's embarrassing behavior had not lessened his friendship with Increase. With brother Timothy and his brother-in-law Seaborn Cotton things were different. Increase was on bad terms with both of them. History has left no clue about the cause of his quarrel with Timothy, except that the trouble went back at least to October 1664. Increase rode to Dorchester then "to have T. examined before Father and Elder W. But T. refused to come when Father sent for him."[73] The next February, Increase started out again to Dorchester on the same errand, but was turned back by a snowstorm.[74] In June he forced the issue. Increase had preached in Dorchester that June 25, 1665, and the next day, after reading for a time in his father's library, he "Spent the rest of Time in discourses with my Father. P.M. Tim. sent a note full of revilings. My Father & selfe sent for him twice & he would not come, at last F. sent for him & then he came. Mr. Withington blamed him & not me. I desired they would show me wherein I had done any evill, in words or actions. They could not shew this, he not being able to prove any of his false charges. At last I declared before the elders that I charged Tim. to be guilty of breach of 3, 5, 9 Commandments. Therefore desired that the church & them who stood charged to doe all things without partiality would duely prosecute him. So I left it, & came home. . . ."[75] Whatever the trouble was, that was not the end of it, although Increase referred to his brother less and less frequently in the years ahead.[76]

Bad feeling between Increase and Seaborn is better documented. Seaborn, a royalist in politics, was out of sympathy with the Puritan commonwealth. In the spring of 1665, royal commissioners under the leadership of the Duke of York's agent, Colonel Richard Nicholls, returned from the capture of New Netherlands. They were, besides Nicholls, Colonel George Cartwright, who had a home in Boston, Sir Robert Carr, and Samuel Maverick, a settler in the Bay even before the Winthrop fleet in 1630. Following their instructions from Whitehall, they tried to persuade the Massachusetts General Court to end religious qualification for the franchise, to grant judicial appeals to England, to extend religious liberty to Anglicans, and to adopt an oath of allegiance to the king instead of to the Massachusetts commonwealth.[77] Mather, who knew Cartwright, had tried several times to discuss the issues with him and the other commissioners.[78] When the General Court refused to give in, Mather was elated: "Much revived & exhilerated with account of Court yesterday in declaring for liberties," he wrote in his diary.[79]

But Seaborn Cotton, seemingly encouraged by the presence of the royal commissioners, had gone in the other direction and was now accused of health drinking, a symbolic act of defiance to Puritan politics and a gesture of loyalty to the crown. Increase was angry and ashamed, but could do little. Seaborn wavered and partly excused himself by pleading that he "dranke health only, not with Punctilios of it, such as not kneeling nor compelling to drink up cup."[80] The next year Seaborn's royalist leanings were more pronounced and Increase's embarrassment was all the greater. When Seaborn came to Boston, Increase invited him to preach in the North Church, only to see his deacons walk out: "P.M. My brother S.C. preached for me. This day goodm. Philips was not at Lords supper, & he with goodm. Way & . . . went away after noon because my brother S.C. preached."[81] Later that same year, Seaborn vented his feelings at a meeting of the Boston ministers: "S.C. sayd that the General Court was guilty of rebellion, & that the ministers hereabouts were the Authors of the rebellion and that he (was) confident the country would (go) against the ministers Usurping Authority as they did . . . , and that the ministers hereabouts cryed out against prelacy whereas they themselves were worse than Bishops. That if Christ were here upon earth he would owne the King's Cause against the Parliament. That the Covenant was an abominable thing, and that he abhorred it."[82] With the heir of John Cotton talking this way, it is clear that not everyone of Increase's generation believed in an errand into the wilderness.

In 1664 Governor John Endecott died and was succeeded by Richard Bellingham, who had been lieutenant governor and who was now elected and reelected governor until his death in 1673. The change worked to Increase Mather's advantage, for Bellingham became a close friend. Increase had intended to travel with Bellingham's son Samuel in 1660, when Samuel took fright at events in England and fled the country. Since then there is no record of particular intimacy between the elder Bellingham and Increase until Bellingham's younger son, John, died in September 1665, only a year or two out of college. Mather gave the distressed father spiritual comfort at that time, and the two men were companions after that, often walking together along the streets and byways of Boston.[83] Few other forms of outdoor recreation were available.

Puritans generally turned their backs on play. Twice Mather recorded playing quoits with Colonel Searle, but that was all.[84]

Mather did take a yearly vacation from his church duties. The first recorded holiday was a trip to the Connecticut River Valley to visit Eleazer at Northampton. Increase left Boston on horseback shortly after daybreak one Monday morning in June, and, riding through woods and farmland, he reached Lancaster, a village on the frontier. He spent the night there with Joseph and Mary Rowlandson, the minister and his wife, who hardly suspected the trials they would face ten years later in the Indian war. The next day's ride crossed country where there were no English settlements at all. The party reached an Indian village, where they "lodged between the wigwams." A third day brought them to Hadley on the left bank of the Connecticut River, where Mather spent the night. He easily reached Eleazer's home in Northampton, across the river, the next day.[85]

The Connecticut River Valley in these lower reaches was a land of broad river bottoms, deep soil, and pleasant rolling hills. It had attracted settlers from Massachusetts Bay from the beginning. The two brothers rode down the west bank of the river as far as the falls at Windsor, getting soaked by rain on the way. They stayed at Windsor with John Warham, the minister, a man of their father's generation who had organized the original Dorchester church before leaving England.[86] On the third day of their trip they started home in the afternoon and reached Northampton after midnight, making their way on horseback by the light of the stars and moon. Increase stayed several more days and spent much of his time visiting John Russell at Hadley, returning to Northampton each night. One supposes that it was an act of discretion not to mention in his diary the name of William Goffe, who was still in hiding in Russell's home. Finally the vacation was over. From Northampton Increase and his party rode twenty-eight miles the first day and bivouacked in the woods. The next night was spent again at Lancaster with the Rowlandsons, and on the twenty-third of June he reached Dorchester, Boston, and home by nine o'clock that evening.[87]

After a year Mather was still unhappy with his church salary. Despite his carefully worded contract, the salary was still not fixed. Two months after his ordination, in July 1664, "Br. Way sayd, that they must either part with one of their ministers or else ministers must live poorly."[88] Michael Powell's salary put an extra burden on the church, but older members were unwilling to stop it. They asked Increase to take a smaller share of the weekly offering, £80 a year. He replied, "I answered I would not say anything either that I would be or contra; neither did I judge it convenient for me to say what maytenance was convenient, whether £20, £100, £500 &c and putt them in mind of former promises which they owed."[89] By February he was again praying that an opportunity to leave Boston would present itself: "earnest in prayer that God would remove me from Boston to some other place more comfortable."[90] The most likely alternative seemed to be Barbados, and he started enquiries about "who [was] godly in Barbados." He was, it seems, ready to "lay down my office" for any other opportunity.[91]

When Mather had been ordained, there had been an agreement to divert part of the weekly offering from Michael Powell to Mather. Now some church members wanted to give it back. "To take away that mayntenance which was given to me & bestow it upon mr P. that never labored was unreasonable unconscionable & little lesse than sacreligious," Mather told the church.[92] John Mayo told Mather, "if you take this course youll break the church in pieces."[93] Some accommodation was at last reached, and for an entire year the issue disappeared from his diary. Then in June 1666, it surfaced again: "In morning Lord helped graciously with enlargement in secret prayer, especially in praying that hee would remove me out of Boston to England & there dispose of me where I might have many to do good unto, & where I might have opportunity to follow my studies & increase learning, & where I might have sutable encouradgement in outward respects, & not be distracted in work of the Lord."[94] There is no shred of evidence that Increase Mather in his late twenties felt any more than Seaborn Cotton a sense of a special godly purpose for New England or his involvement in it.

ISRAEL'S SALVATION

In 1665 an extraordinary thing happened in the world of Jewry. From London first, then from Amsterdam, Hamburg, and other continental ports came word that a Jew named Sabbatai Sevi was preaching in Syria that he was the Messiah. Handbills with the news were circulated in European ports, and some Jewish families began to pack their possessions and start back to the homeland.[95] Mather first heard about the Jewish Messiah on February 12, 1666. Excitement gripped him. A Jewish Messiah might presage the conversion of the Jews, predicted in Romans 11 : 26: "And so all Israel shall be saved: and it is written there shall come out of Sion the Deliverer." A conversion of the Jews would mean the near approach of the end of time. Mather immersed himself in books and commentaries about the conversion of the Jews and the millennium, searching every day through writings of Voet, Brightman, Cotton, and Mede, all of them radical millennialists of an earlier generation.[96] He began a series of monthly lectures on Romans 11:26 (and used them to take up a collection for Michael Powell). Three Jews, for whom no identification has been found, visited Boston in August, and Mather "labored to convince that Messiah is come."[97] His colleagues in the ministry were uncomfortable with the public lectures and let him know they wished he would stop. ("At night much troubled to hear that many of the ministers wished I would make an end of preaching de Jews"[98]). The monthly lectures did come to an end; Mather concluded that Sabbatai Sevi was not the true Messiah.

Regardless of what else went on around him, a driving force within Increase Mather compelled him to write. During the summer of 1665 he had started a biography of his father-in-law, John Cotton, a manuscript that was never published and has since been lost.[99] He interrupted that work in the fall of 1665 to write an essay on the "Power of the Magistrates," the principal argument of which was that magistrates had the authority to silence the upstart Baptist community.[100] This too, after many readings by colleagues and many revisions, went unpublished. The following spring and summer of 1666, he concentrated on the conversion of the Jews. Nine months later, in May 1667, he began to transcribe the notes of those sermons into a book-length manuscript. By working furiously all month, he was able to finish in June.[101] John Davenport read the manuscript and wrote a preface. Mather sent it to England, where it was published under the title *The Mystery of Israel's Salvation* (London, 1669) with additional prefaces by William Greenhill and Davenport's one-time colleague William Hooke.

Prodigies, persecutions, wars, sedition, the burning of cities, pseudo-prophets, the downfall of princes, and the conversion of the Jews, Mather wrote, were all signs that the second coming was near. Then the world would dissolve in fire, the renovated world would come into existence, and the saints would live. But, Mather insisted, the current talk among the Jews was mistaken. These events were not a prelude to the second coming of Christ. Mather was cautious. Satan, he wrote, was a spiritual and not a physical adversary. He played down expectations of a physical resurrection. In place of a certain date and a renewal of carnal pleasures, Mather presented the prospect of a spiritual and mystical millennium, when everything would happen in some vague, though not too distant, future time. He criticized the Fifth Monarchy men, who had translated millennial hopes into political action. They were "carnal millennaries," who had erred by anticipating the fifth and seventh vials of the Book of Revelation.[102] Because he did profess to believe in the physical resurrection of the saints of former times, Mather was a chiliast. Yet he was a chiliast who de-emphasized chiliasm. As his son Cotton would put it much later, he was a "sober chiliast."[103]

Writing was a solace. Buffeted by public and private storms during the first years of his ministry in Boston, Mather found withdrawal into his study the perfect solution to his frustrations outside. Writing *The Mystery of Israel's Salvation* gave him hours of pure bliss. Immured and alone, surrounded by silent books, he could escape from human conflicts. "The truth is," he wrote, "that whilst a man is dwelling upon these meditations, he is as it were in heaven upon earth, he hath fellowship with the Angels in heaven. . . . But as for those whose understandings God hath opened to *conceive* and *receive* these truths they see a glory in them above the world, that eye hath not seen, nor tongue can express."[104] After more than half a century, Benjamin Colman would remark of Mather, he "lov'd his Study to a kind of excess, and in a manner liv'd in it from his Youth to a great Old Age."[105]

HIS FATHER'S DEATH

In the winter of 1667–68 Increase Mather buried himself in his books and tried to forget his unhappy dependence on a niggardly church and his sense of a life wasted in provincial Boston. That winter a sequence of events began that was to change everything. First, the aging pastor of Boston's First Church, John Norton, died. In search of a suitable successor, the congregation turned to John Davenport at New Haven, one of the last of the great ministers from the first generation. A majority of the members of First Church, about two-thirds, voted to call him to Boston, but twenty-eight members thought Davenport's opposition to the halfway covenant made him unsuitable, and they protested the choice. The majority quickly overruled them and did so with such lack of tact that the next day the twenty-eight minority members signed a public letter criticizing their own congregation for railroading through the decision.[106]

Davenport was eager to accept the invitation. But his church in New Haven did not want to lose their famous minister, and in a letter to Boston refused to let him go, citing as a reason that the First Church was itself divided on the call. Davenport was determined. My church, he wrote, "decline giving a positive answer, but leave that to me."[107] He came up to Boston in May 1668 to preach for a trial period. Those opposed to him were put under great pressure to change their minds. The First Church asked a council of neighboring churches how it could discipline the reluctant minority, but the strategy backfired when the council recommended that the dissenting minority be allowed to leave and form a congregation of their own. Members of the First Church wanted Davenport, but they also wanted all members of the church to come under his discipline. That insistence on submission to discipline played a large part in the next developments.

The original twenty-eight dissenters requested dismissal for themselves and their wives, so that they could form another congregation. To have broken away without permission would have been schism, which, so read the final paragraph of the Cambridge Platform, was to be prevented by the intervention of the state. Their departure, they said, would leave the old church free to make a unanimous call to Davenport. The majority would not hear of it. The twenty-eight were tricked into leaving the meetinghouse, and when they were gone, the invitation to Davenport was again to put to a vote and passed unanimously. A new letter was sent to New Haven. The church there still raised objections. When their answer reached Boston, Davenport and the ruling elders of the First Church decided to take matters into their own hands. They rewrote the letter and forged the signatures of the New Haven authorities. On the strength of this forgery, on November 1, 1668, Davenport formally accepted his call to Boston's First Church. One week later, he told the twenty-eight men who had requested dismissal for themselves and their families that they would not be dismissed, but must remain under the discipline of the Church. Davenport was determined to impose his will on them. The task, he said, was his "crown" and he wore it proudly.[108]

In January, February, and March 1669, the dissenters refused to take communion from Davenport. On one occasion they left the church in a body when communion began, except for two deacons who felt they had to stay behind to officiate. Davenport harangued these two mercilessly for their "jejeune and poor" judgment, and gave them a week to reconsider their loyalties.[109] On February 12 nearly five hundred people crowded into the meetinghouse to hear the two deacons publicly criticized and voted out of office. Davenport refused repeated requests from the dissenters to call a council of neighboring churches to mediate the disagreements. He argued that to do so would destroy the independence of the particular churches. The twenty-eight wrote to the neighboring churches for help. The churches in Dedham, Lynn, Salem, and the North Church in Boston refused to interfere, but some of the others agreed, and a council was formed. Richard Mather, from Dorchester, because of his age and despite his declining health, was chosen to be its moderator.

The church council met in Boston on April 13, 1669. Richard Mather stayed at his son's house. He went to Davenport's church, but was not allowed inside. Davenport objected on the grounds of congregational autonomy: "I doe not see that you are an orderly council. . . . (This church has) done their duty to the dissenting Brethren."[110] The next day, Mather and three others tried again. They were told they might meet a delegation in a house next door. They were kept waiting there for two hours before anyone came, and nothing was accomplished. Exhausted, Richard Mather returned to his son's home, and that night he collapsed. The next day Increase took his father in a coach back to Dorchester, and within the week he was dead of a stoppage of urine.

At seventy-three Richard Mather had already become weak and blind in one eye; he was growing deaf. His end could not have been far away. Nevertheless, the circumstances of his collapse made it seem that his death was brought on directly by the crisis over Davenport's appointment and indirectly by the argument over the half-way covenant. Richard Mather and John Davenport had taken diametrically opposite positions on the half-way covenant, and Increase had sided notoriously with Davenport. Increase's unconscious rebellion against his father, begun in 1662, had suddenly been brought to its fruition. Now he felt responsible for his father's death.

When Increase Mather wrote his father's biography, a year later, he described this pathetic scene between them a day before Richard died.

"Sir, if there be any speciall thing which you would recommend unto me to do, in case the Lord should spare me upon the Earth, after you are in Heaven, I would intreat you to express it."

At the which, his Father making a little pause, and lifting up his eyes and hands to Heaven, replied,

"A speciall thing which I would commend to you, is, Care concerning the Rising Generation in this Country, that they be brought up under the Government of Christ in his Church; and that when grown up and qualified, they have Baptism for their Children. . . . I have thought that persons might have Right to Baptism, and yet not to the Lord's Supper; and I see no cause to alter my

judgment as to that particular. And I still think that persons qualified according to the Fifth Proposition of the late Synod-Book, have Right to Baptism for
their Children."[111]

There is no independent confirmation that this conversation took
place. The scene and Richard Mather's gestures are hackneyed, the language too formal to ring true. The scene was, nevertheless, how a guilt-
ridden son, after seven years of public opposition to his father, wished it
to be known. Although Increase wrote the scene, he did not have himself
make any response to his dying father's last wish.

The denouement within the First Church parted the veil of harmony
covering the Massachusetts churches. The dissenters from the First
Church, supported by the council of neighboring churches, announced
their decision to form a separate congregation. By law they needed approval from both nearby ministers and magistrates. The former they
had. The latter was more uncertain. Seven out of twelve magistrates approved; five and the governor, Bellingham, did not. The close vote
promised contention and ill will. Nevertheless, on the basis of it, the
dissenters went ahead, and, on May 12, 1669, meeting in Charlestown
to avoid a confrontation in Boston, they organized themselves into
Boston's Third Church. For years these two churches, the First and the
Third, would represent conservative and liberal approaches to the questions of church policy.

Within a matter of weeks after his father's death, Increase received
another personal shock, for the forgery with which Davenport's call had
been facilitated was suddenly exposed. Nicholas Street, Davenport's colleague in New Haven, visited Boston, asked from some quirk of curiosity to see the letter, and recognized at once that his own signature had
been forged to a new document. In July a large group of ministers published their condemnation of Davenport's deception. Increase was among
them, condemning his old ally. He joined his colleagues again in November in a letter to England vouching for the legitimacy of the new
church in Boston.[112]

As if the death of his father and then the exposure of Davenport's intrigue were not enough, at the end of July word came that his brother
Eleazar was dead. As soon as he could, Increase started west, repeating
the trip he had made four years before, but now under frighteningly
different circumstances. As he rode through the forest, his mind was
plunged in darkness. God, he knew, would not let so much as a sparrow
fall without purpose. What should Increase make of these events, a succession of hammer blows, his father's death, Davenport's disgrace, and

now Eleazar's death? All were connected with the synod of 1662, and he himself had been a leader against it. Would he be next? Had he been wrong? Why was God angry? These questions preyed on his nerves, and his health failed. He had not been a week at his sister-in-law's house in Northampton before he collapsed; he ran a high fever, sank into a coma, and for a week lay near death. Very gradually he recovered. By the end of September he was up and about, but the questions still tormented him, and all the month of October, while the river valley blazed in its glory of fall color, Increase struggled in a mood of black despair.[113]

Mather read through Eleazar's diary and the notes from his sermons. He helped the church find someone to take Eleazar's place, Solomon Stoddard—a man four years younger than Increase, born in Boston, a Harvard graduate. Esther Mather, Eleazar's widow at twenty-five, would marry Stoddard later and bear twelve more children. For now she had been left by Eleazar's death with three small children, Eunice five, Warham three, and the baby Eliakim, barely nine months. Eliakim was brought to Boston to live with the Sewall family. Eunice would eventually marry a minister, settle in the frontier community of Deerfield, and die on the winter march to Montreal in 1704. Warham would grow up to try the ministry, then the law, and end up a judge of the Connecticut Supreme Court.

In November, Increase felt strong enough to travel. He must get across the central Massachusetts hills before winter snows blocked the trails. Once back in Boston he kept to his house, mentally and physically exhausted.

THE BIOGRAPHY OF HIS FATHER: AN ACT OF ATONEMENT

Short days and early winter darkness mirrored the inner darkness of Mather's spirit. He seemed frozen in body while his mind raced over the terrifying thought that God had withdrawn his protection. His father, when troubled in spirit, had gone to John Norton for help. Increase sought no outside counsel. He fought his struggle alone, locked day and night in prayer, arguing over and over the basis of his life: "Christ has made requests in Heaven for me; else how am I alive this day? My being brought from the gates of death is because Christ has requested for me."[114] Day after day he recorded his struggles in his diary: "In the close of the day especially, my heart was moved to believe that God would accept of and Answer my poor prayers. 1. Because I drew nigh to him, therefore his blessings will draw nigh to me. 2. Because the things which I asked, and the end why I asked them was for God's glory. Not for my owne sake, but for God's sake. 3. For the honor of his son Jesus Christ. 4. Because nothing but my sins and abominations which this day I confessed before the Lord can hinder the Answer of my prayers; but these can not hinder because they are done away in the blood of Christ; who has loved me and given Himselfe for me, which I know for I feel my Heart loveth Him. 5. because there never was any creature that did humbly seek unto the Lord for such blessings as this day I prayed for, that was denied by him. And surely I shall not be the first whom God will deny. O blessed forever be my dear God in Jesus Christ who heareth prayer." [115]

Gradually Mather regained strength, and, as he did so, his will to act. He set himself four goals: a biography of his father, a book on the problem of infant baptism, another of "practical" value for the children of the church, and a book in Latin. [116] New life began to force its way up through the cold ground of his depression. The book in Latin, a vanity born in earlier years and in imitation of John Norton, was a sequel to Mather's first book about the conversion of the Jews. He finished it in the winter of 1670–1671, but it would be ten years before it was published in Amsterdam as *Diatriba de Signo Filii Hominis, et de Secundo Messiae Adventu* (*Discussion of the Sign of the Son of Man, and the Second Coming of the Messiah*). [117] His other three goals, far more important, laid the foundation of a new life.

Increase wrote the promised biography of his father in the summer of 1670. Writing it was an act of atonement for the guilt he felt over the circumstances of his father's death. He published it, *The Life and Death of that Reverend Man of God Mr. Richard Mather,* anonymously in Cambridge, Massachusetts, that fall. It marked the first great turning point in Increase's life. In it he gave expression for the first time to images and values that influenced his entire generation. Twenty years later, Cotton Mather would use it as a model of biography turned into history. No one in America had ever written biography like it.

Scholars have long treated New England Puritan biographies as if together they comprise a literary genre. Thus, for example, Kenneth Murdock wrote, "Puritan biographies were at bottom didactic. . . ."; Perry Miller and Thomas H. Johnson, "the art of biography as understood by the Puritans was the preparation of case histories"; Cecelia Tichi, "They (biographies) were heavily influenced by a Puritan literary genre developed in England and carried on in the New World"; William Scheick, "In many respects the content of New England Puritan biographies is identical to that of their sermons."[118] These remarks lead the reader to suppose that New England Puritans wrote a number of biographies. Between 1630 and 1690, however, only two biographies were written and published by New England Puritans. John Norton wrote a biography of John Cotton, *Abel Being Dead, Yet Speaketh; or, The Life and Death of that deservedly Famous Man of God, Mr. John Cotton* (London, 1658), and twelve years later Increase Mather wrote the biography of his father.

Life and Death is the first biography written by an American-born writer, the first to be published in America, and the only full-length biography, other than Norton's, to be written in New England before 1691. Although in parts it falls back awkwardly on the precedents of the English genre, *Life and Death* reveals clear signs of Increase's intention to do much more. In 1691 his brilliant son Cotton used biography in the first of a series of lives that would form the basis for his church history of New England, *Magnalia Christi Americana,* and in so doing would influence the writing of American history for a century and a half to come.

Increase's biography of his father was born out of his guilt and confusion over a conflict which, because it had been unconscious, had been unsuspected. The book is suffused with universal problems of fathers and sons.[119] Three generations are represented in it. The story opens with Richard Mather's relations with his father and closes with his relationships with his sons. At every turn the wisdom of the father is presented as paramount: "God intended better for me, then I would have chosen for myself," Increase has his father saying; "and therefore my Father, though in other things indulgent enough, yet in this would never condescend to my request. . . . And good it was for me to be overruled by him, and his discretion, rather than to be left to my own affection and desire."[120] The words are Richard's about his childhood, but Increase could have meant them for his own. The biography ends where it began, with a father giving direction to his sons. Now it is Richard speaking to Increase and his brothers through the father's last will and testament. By this device Increase was able, in the biography, to reassure himself of the paternal blessing he stood in such great need of: "and their *Father* that now speaketh unto them, and with their dear *Mother* now with God, shall exceedingly rejoice in the day of Christ, when we shall receive our Children unto those everlasting Habitations. . . ."[121]

The father-son relationship expressed in this biography became a preoccupation for the rest of Increase's life, finding expression in both politics and religion. It permeated his sermons about Christ: "*God and Christ do confide in one another.* They do, as it were, take one another's word. The Father trusts Christ."[122] The son's obligation to fulfill the father's errand in America would become the cornerstone of Increase Mather's historical mythology and the overriding principle behind his political and ecclesiastical policies. He would return many times to the theme of a father's passing on to his son the cherished covenant with God. He reprinted in the biography in their entirety his father's reasons for emigrating to America. In doing so the son, Increase, was coming to terms with his own situation, beginning for the first time to internalize his father's motives and to make them his own. Increase's flight from England in 1661 took on the same quality as his father's in 1635. Even more important, his presence in Boston became purposeful, as his father's now seemed to him to have been.

Increase summed up all this in a metaphor as influential as anything else he was to say or write. He made Richard a symbol of all fathers of the first generation. Richard's lengthy reasons for emigrating became the motives for founding the colony in New England. The artistically awkward inclusion of all of Richard's "Arguments tending to prove the Removing from Old-England to New . . . not only lawful, but also necessary . . ." word for word, a full third of the entire biography, was appropriate because, in Increase's words, "They are of weight and because Posterity may thereby see what were the swaying Motives which prevailed with the First-Fathers of N.E. to venture upon that unparallel'd Undertaking, even to Transport themselves, their Wives and Little ones, over the rude Waves of the vast Ocean, into a Land which was not sown."[123] Biography here turns to history; the emigration of Richard Mather stands for the emigration of all; his reason for leaving England stands for the reason for Massachusetts's existence; and the reason for writing the biography is that those who follow should know whence they have come and why they are here. "The fathers may have founded the colonies, but the sons invented New England."[124]

At a personal level, Increase's biography of his father established a new direction and meaning in his life. David Leverenz has argued that the collective myths of New England's beginnings were adopted by the second generation "to avoid social and personal conflict," and that they were "rhetorical solutions to the fundamental problem of sons who had followed the pure Father's calling and found . . . the people seemed to be watching for something else."[125] These ideas, derived from psychoanalytical theory, correspond extraordinarily well with Increase Mather's life. Increase wrote his biography to resolve a conflict with his father that

THE
LIFE and DEATH

OF

That Reverend Man of GOD,

Mr. *RICHARD MATHER,*

TEACHER of the CHURCH

IN

Dorchester

IN

NEW-ENGLAND.

By Mr Increase Mather.

Pfal. 112. 6. *The Righteous ſhall be had in everlaſting remembrance.*

Heb. 13. 7. *Remember them who have ſpoken to you the Word of God,*

Rev. 14. 13. *Bleſſed are the dead which die in the Lord : they reſt from their labours, and their works follow them.*

Miniſtri vita cenſura & cynoſura.

CAMBRIDGE:
Printed by *S. G.* and *M. J.* 1 6 7 0.

The Life and Death of that Reverend Man of God, Mr. Richard Mather, Increase Mather's 1670 biography of his father

he could no longer endure. It initiated a perception of the past and an obligation to imitate that past in the future, a "rhetorical solution" which became increasingly inappropriate in the real world.

Increase Mather reached these thoughts at a time when others were coming to similar ideas. In the same month of May in which Increase started on the biography, Thomas Danforth, fifteen years Increase's senior, preached an election sermon called *A Brief Recognition of New England's Errand into the Wilderness*. Two years earlier, William Stoughton had preached in a sermon called *New England's True Interest:* "God sifted a whole nation that he might send choice grain into the wilderness." Printed in 1670, the year of Increase's biography and Danforth's sermon, Stoughton's imagery was joined to that of Danforth and Mather to make up a powerful mythology. A beginning had already been made in Edward Johnson's *Wonder-Working Providence* (1652), where New England was described as "the place where the Lord will create a new Heaven, and a new Earth . . . , new churches, and a new Commonwealth." [126] The young preachers of this second generation completed the myth. Stoughton, Danforth, Mather, and a handful of others created New England in America. They turned back to the first generation to justify and explain national life, and as they did so they revealed a deep sense of their own inadequacy. [127]

The next book Increase started in that year of trial and despondency was a study of what his father's generation had written on the subject of infant baptism. All this was familiar ground after the eight years of argument over the half-way covenant. He completed a book-length manuscript of evidence from the founders of Massachusetts—his father's generation—in support of infant baptism. But he did not publish it. Mather was not yet ready to change his mind on the issues underlying the half-way covenant.

DEVASTATION OF THESE CHURCHES

The laymen and their representatives in the General Court were outraged at the schism in the First Church, and they supported John Davenport. In 1669, prior to the exposé of the forged letter from New Haven, the Deputies chose Davenport to deliver the election sermon in May. He gave a ringing denunciation of the way in which a bare majority of magistrates, aided by the ministers, had agreed to the new Third Church. Election day sermons in Massachusetts were annual events and frankly political. As such, they frequently exposed divisions within the

Puritan community that otherwise found no public expression. That was the case now. The Deputies, representing the lay members of the churches, thanked Davenport profusely for his sermon; but the magistrates, who with the ministers had been the targets of Davenport's criticism, refused to pass a vote of thanks. Political lines had been drawn with Davenport the champion of the ordinary people, the lay brethren. As for his forgery, Davenport never acknowledged any wrongdoing in the forged letter. ("What do you mean, evil?")

The next May, in 1670, Increase's longtime associate from Hadley, Peter Tilton, was returned as Deputy to the General Court. Tilton began an investigation into the circumstances surrounding the creation of the Third Church. The Deputies passed a resolution condemning the ministers for their involvement in it in language more violent than was ever used publicly in Massachusetts before or possibly since: the ministers were guilty of "declension from the primitive foundation worke, innovation in doctrine & worship, opinion & practise, & invasion of the rights, liberties, & priviledges of churches . . . to the utter devastation of these churches, turning the pleasant gardens of Christ into a wildernesse, . . . these are the leven, the corrupting gangreens, the infecting spreading plague . . . which hath provoked divine wrath." [128] The rancor of the Deputies towards both ministers and magistrates over the half-way covenant partly explains why Increase would wait five years to publish his book about infant baptism.

Mather's fourth goal in 1670 was a "practical" book for the children of the church. He finished it on March 1, 1671, as a memorial to his brother Eleazar. He shaped the notes of Eleazar's last sermon into a moving plea for the young children of the churches, the "Rising Generation." In so doing he brought Eleazar, too, symbolically to join him in reconciliation with their father. He gave this book the title *A Serious Exhortation to the Present and Succeeding Generation . . . Being the Substance of the Last Sermons Preached by Eleazar Mather* (Boston, 1671). It is impossible now to tell which words were Increase's and which were Eleazar's. The book is ordinarily listed in bibliographies as the work of Eleazar, which Increase would have wanted. The creative energy which transformed Eleazar's notes into a moving appeal was undoubtedly Increase's. *A Serious Exhortation* makes Richard Mather's death a loss for all. The entire "Present and Succeeding Generation" had metaphorically lost their fathers. They now found themselves adrift in the world. "We are like a company of Children in a Boat that is driven out to Sea, may be it may come to shore, but in greater danger to sink or drown than otherwise. . . . What will become of unskillful Passengers, when Pilot and able Steersman is taken away? *What will become of this generation?*" [129] There could hardly have been a more succinct statement of anxiety and insecurity of Increase's generation.

A Serious Exhortation touched deep chords of feeling in Mather's time and was reprinted twice during his life. The lasting popularity of the book was due less to that first bereavement, when the earliest religious leaders died—John Wilson, Norton, Richard Mather, Davenport all died in the 1660's—than to a mixture of hope and guilt about the next generation. "I know you are apt to complain against the Rising Generation," Increase wrote, "and it cannot be denied there is cause enough. . . . But I beseech you to consider whether you give not too much occasion thereunto: Do they not see *your* Pride, *your* Worldliness, *your* Passion, *your* Vanity? And doth that not harden and stumble them?" [130] "God hath not given his Gospel unto men, that a few *old Christians* may enjoy something of the Presence of the Lord while they live, and then carry away the Gospel and Religion (as worthy Mitchell said) into the cold grave with them when they die." [131]

The four goals Mather had set himself were now accomplished. His own emotional recovery took longer. All during 1670 and 1671 he felt weak and enervated, depressed and despondent. Nightmares tormented his sleep. He lived with the constant fear that his melancholia, his lack of physical energy, and his awful dreams all foretold some approaching catastrophe. "I was sorely molested with the *ephialtes* [nightmares]. I had read in physitians that that disease was a sign that the person subject to it, should be taken with one of these 3 diseases, either 1. Apoplexy; or 2. An Epilepsy; or 3. A Mania. Now Satan set in with my melancholy to perswade me (though there was no ground for it) that this last would be my condition. The thoughts wereof filled me with inexpressible sorrows and fears." [132]

Increase's struggle upwards from depression over the next few years was carried on in the framework and vocabulary of Augustinian spirituality, in the language of which "a primary emphasis on personal experience, human sinfulness, and divine initiative in salvation through grace are the hallmarks." [133] It may have helped his recovery that at last, in 1670, the church purchased a house for him on North Square across from the North Church meetinghouse. Increase and Maria moved there after eight years in the old Cotton home. [134] It was a large frame building, two full stories plus a garret above and a cellar below, where winter provisions, salted beef, corn, dried peas were stored, and with a library and study for Increase on the second floor at the head of the stairs.

The next summer he experienced such deep religious awakening that he began to think of it as a second conversion. It came about this way. In July 1671, Mather took his regular summer vacation at the village of Lynn, a day's ride northeast of Boston, where there were mineral springs. "I there prayed alone under the Trees, and did humbly and believingly (through the Lords grace towards me) betake my selfe to God and to Jesus Christ for healing my bodily distempers." The combination of physical rest and constant prayer seemed to work. As he did often in his devotional life, Mather argued back and forth in prayer. "I believed, because though sin had brought these distempers on me, yet God has accepted the sacrifice which Christ has offered for my sins. . . . And because Christ has Redeemed my body as well as my soul. . . . hee will not deny unto me so small a matter as bodily Health, which is nothing in comparison to eternal glory." As Mather's health improved, he experienced moments of exultation: "After prayer, I went away inwardly rejoycing, because *I have prevayled! I have prevayled! I have prevayled for mercy.*"[135]

The road back to complete physical and emotional health was long and slow, with many setbacks. The nightmares continued intermittently, and Mather lived a seesaw life between depression and exuberance. Much later, in writing his autobiography, he found a date in his diary of which he could write, "Thus were these grievous Temptations overcome. Nor was I after this day, any more molested as formerly." That date was August 2, 1671.[136] Nine months later, he would write, "As I was thus praying my heart was exceedingly melted, and me thought, I saw God before my eyes, in an inexpressible maner, so as that I was afraid I should have fallen into a trance in my study."[137] In November 1672, fifteen months after Lynn, Mather kept a private day of thanksgiving. He reviewed in his diary the many blessings for which he could be thankful, a brilliant contrast to the gloomy entries of the 1660s and an explicit reconciliation to life in Boston. "1. Here God gave me to find my Father alive, and to enjoy communion with him for 7 or 8 years together. 2. Hee has cast my lot in Boston, the most public place in New England where I have had a great opportunity to do service for God and Christ. . . . 6. God has given me many Bookes and manuscripts, which have bin great Helps to me in his service. 7. God has blessed and Increased my Family. . . . 9. God has remembred me when I was brought very low both in body and in spirit, and has restored me to perfect Health again, and this in Answer to many prayers, yea solemn extraordinary supplications before him. . . ." At this place in his diary, without pause in its flow, Increase sang the early verses of the one-hundred-and-third Psalm: "Bless the Lord O my soul, and all that is within me bless his holy Name. Bless the Lord O my soul, and forget not all his benefits, who forgiveth all thine iniquities, who healeth all thi diseases, who Redeems thi life from destruction, who crowneth thee with loving kindness and with tender mercys, who satisfyeth thi mouth with good things, so that thi youth is renewed like the eagles." [138]

In this final, triumphant mood, soaring like an eagle, Mather transcribed six recent sermons in which he summarized as a second rebirth his spiritual trials since his father's death. The six sermons formed yet another book, which he dedicated to his church; it was published in London two years later (1674) under the title *Some Important Truths about Conversion.* These sermons bear on one central theme, expressed most clearly in the title of the first, "A Sound and Thorough Conversion." Mather stressed the absolute necessity of a conversion experience. Only a few of you, he told his readers, are saved. "The larger part of you, amongst whom I have been preaching for years, remain unregenerate." Those of you who have already experienced a new birth, he went on, may expect "a farther and as it were a second conversion." Here he spoke from his own recent experience. We cannot convert ourselves, he emphasized, but can and must pray constantly for converting grace. Even so, the number saved will be small compared to the number headed for destruction. [139]

In his preface to the six sermons, Mather was frankly autobiographical. He credited the church's prayers as well as his own for his recovery. For the first time in his life, he expressed a commitment to his ministry in New England. His tone was solemn, even morbid, as he warned his church that he would soon be dead. "These truths were spoken to you by one whom God brought out of his grave on purpose that so he might declare these things to you." [140] This prediction of an imminent demise would continue to characterize Mather's writing for the next fifty years. More important were the convictions burned into his mind about the experience of conversion. With the completion of *Some Important Truths,* Mather had written more than most of his colleagues were to do in their lifetimes. He was still only thirty-one. He had at last found his place and purpose in God's plan for New England.

CHAPTER 3

God's Agent on Earth

[1672-1676]

The world was a new place to Increase Mather after 1672. He had been, he believed, on the threshold of death, but was brought back to life in a physical renewal and a symbolic, or spiritual, rebirth. "These truths," he wrote to his church in 1672, "were spoken to you by one whom God brought out of his grave on purpose that so he might declare these things to us. . . . I have long expected that Christ would come and call for me, but I knew that until my work be done, I am immortal."[1]

Until my work be done, I am immortal! Mather strove to create a presence befitting, as he saw it, God's agent on earth. He sought to convey through his very appearance the awfulness of his ministry. He must always be serious, never lighthearted. He disciplined himself not to laugh in public. Cotton wrote years later that his father could be "pleasant" in the company of his close friends, but in general, "He maintained a Serious Temper of mind, and such a *Gravity* as made all sorts of Persons, wherever he came, to be struck with a Sensible awe of his Presence, as much as any ever were of a Roman *Cato's*; Yea, *If he laughed on them, they believed it not. . . . His very Countenance carried the Force of a Sermon with it.*[2]

After his brush with death in the winter of 1669–1670, Mather often reflected on his own mortality. New England Puritanism was a religion that kept death constantly in mind, and in these years Mather exaggerated the characteristic.[3] In 1672 Increase learned of his brother Samuel's death in Dublin. Now from a family of five ministers only he and Nathaniel were left to be messengers of God. "And is it so indeed?" he mused on the first day of the year 1675. "Doe I live to write any thing in the year 1675? Who could have thought that it could have bin so, when I was so near unto death above five years agoe?"[4]

The nature of his diary changed. Mather began to record regular, devotional practices. Before 1669 his religious introspection had been matter-of-fact. Now the meagre "Heart Serious" of the 1660s gave way to effusive prayers, copied down verbatim after having been delivered extemporaneously on his knees in his study. He began a regular monthly assessment of his spiritual state, first itemizing "Causes of Humility" one by one, and following those with a parallel list, "Matters of Supplication."[5] These accounts are charged with feeling. From his struggle with depression, Mather emerged into a period of intense religious emotionalism.

A GROWING FAMILY

Outward circumstances had not changed materially. Mather still found himself short of money, in debt and miserable because of what he believed to be shabby treatment by his church. He recorded his sense of humiliation over and over in his diary, and prayed repeatedly to be rescued. "O that the Lord Jesus . . . , would either give an Heart to my people to looke after my comfortable subsistence amongst them, or . . . remove me to another people who will take care of me."[6] Relief came when Sir Thomas Temple and Captain Thomas Lake joined the church in 1670 and soon made large contributions to it and to Mather.[7] At this time the North Church purchased a house for Mather on Clarke's Square across from the meetinghouse.[8] Increase and Maria had four children when they moved there. A fifth child, a daughter, was born in the new house in November 1671. They named her Sarah after Maria's mother. Three years later, a third son came, named Samuel after Increase's oldest brother. Maria's nephew John Cotton, Seaborn's son, came to live there too.

In the spring of 1675 little Nathaniel, almost six years old, fell sick and almost died. He lay vomiting and feverish, his small body contracted in abdominal spasms. Night after night, Increase prayed beside the boy's bed. He could do nothing else. "Little doe children think," he wrote, "what affection is in the heart of a Father. Let the Lord doe with me & mine what seemeth him good. I desire to Trust in his power & mercy."[9] Increase's response to his child's sickness was the same as his response to his own: prayer and supplications to the Lord. He always seemed to find space in his diary when his children were sick.

Nathaniel got no better, and a few days later Sam, a baby of less than a year, was sick too. "There hath bin much Health in my Family for a long time," Increase reasoned. "God has spared the lives of all my children. . . . I have nothing to say but to lie down abased before him."[10] The next day he spent in prayer. "His Mother, & his Brother Cotton were with me in my study after a day of secret Humiliation before the Lord, when I thus prayed for the child, all of us weeping for him." Increase could not help seeing himself through young Cotton's eyes. "Now I thought it might be some discouredgment to Cotton in case Hee should see that his poor sinfull Fathers prayers were not heard; therefore I humbly pleaded that with God."[11]

In two days, the baby recovered. Mather was exhausted with sleepless nights. He stayed up until two o'clock in the morning working on the next day's sermon and carried his heightened emotions into the pulpit. One listener confessed afterwards he had been so moved that he had almost cried out in the meetinghouse. Nathaniel passed more than twenty intestinal worms, and his fever subsided.[12] That crisis was over, but the summer of 1675 brought an epidemic of bronchial infection. By August 12, Mather reported that all of his six children were down with colds and coughs. Samuel, a year old that month, suffered from fever in the hottest part of the summer. This crisis also passed, but Samuel and Nathaniel were sick again in the spring of 1676. This time, Samuel nearly died. The exhausted parents could offer only prayers and afterwards tears of gratitude.[13]

Of all the children, Cotton, born in 1663, was clearly the leader. He learned early to read and write English, Greek, and Latin, and became exaggeratedly pious. For years he plagued his brothers and sisters, and his classmates when he could get away with it, with his overweening piety. He was forever composing prayers, devising routines of meditation, and catechizing his younger brothers and sisters.[14] What Increase felt about his extraordinary son is hard to say, but Cotton demonstrated a hero worship of his father that would develop into a neurotic dependency. In the summer of 1674 when Cotton was eleven years old, his father enrolled him at Harvard College. He withdrew the boy that same summer, for reasons that are unclear. Cotton had developed a stammer in his speech, possibly a result of the nervous tension of separation from his home. Or perhaps the older boys in the college dormitory had hazed him because the eleven-year-old already had a stammer in his speech and was peculiarly vulnerable.[15] The intense piety with which the parents confronted this setback to their firstborn is revealed in Mather's diary: "October 7. 1674. I fasted and prayed before the Lord because of my son

Cottons Impediment in his speech. At the close of the day, I called him and his mother into my study. Wee prayed together and with many Tears beweyled our sinfullness, and begged of God mercy in this particular, and solemnly gave the child to God upon our knees, begging the Lord to accept of him. I can not but Hope that the Lord has heard me, and will in some comfortable measure remove this evill in his owne Time. However, whether God will hear me or no, I am resolved to Trust in him, and to wayt upon him for a gracious Answer, and so let him do with me and mine what seemeth him good." [16]

Harvard College was now on the edge of disaster. When President Chauncy died in 1671, the Overseers persuaded Leonard Hoar to come from England to take the post. Hoar, a man of Increase's generation, had been graduated from Harvard a year ahead of Increase and like Increase had gone to England in the euphoric 1650s. There he took a church and made an advantageous marriage. Ejected from his church at the Restoration, Hoar had lived on his wife's estate and continued his studies in medicine, science, and biblical criticism. The attraction of becoming president of the Puritan college drew him back to New England. In December 1672, Hoar was installed as president of Harvard. There were few students and less money. The college building—dormitory, library, classrooms, and dining hall all in one—was dilapidated. Hoar, a man of rigid and unrealistic expectations, soon made himself hotly disliked by both the students and the two teaching fellows, Urian Oakes and Thomas Shepard. Students began to leave; others wrote satirical verse about the new president. Both teaching fellows resigned. The essence of the complaints, with a discretion characteristic of New England society, was kept out of public record, even when Hoar's conduct of college affairs was discussed in the General Court. Some people said that Hoar was responsible for the deterioration; others, like John Hull, believed that if "those that accused him had but countenanced and encouraged him in his work he would have proved the best president that ever yet the college had." [18] Increase Mather, by then a member of the Board of Overseers, was of Hull's opinion. By October 1674, with only three students left, Hoar's ability to maintain discipline was seriously in doubt. In the last analysis, Harvard was controlled by the General Court. The Deputies voted to dismiss, but the Magistrates wanted to give Hoar one last chance. All the paid staff except the president were dismissed, and Hoar's salary was reduced by a third. Hoar and his young wife suffered through a long, silent winter, and in the spring of 1675 he resigned. [19] The Overseers began promptly to remake the college. They reappointed Urian

Oakes and Thomas Shepard as teaching fellows and restored their salaries. Urian Oakes hesitantly allowed himself to be appointed acting president while continuing as minister at Cambridge. Increase Mather, who
had defended Hoar all the previous year, was appointed a non-teaching
Fellow and a member of the Corporation.

Mather was expected, apparently, to promote those principles of rigor
and discipline that Hoar had represented but had failed to implement
successfully. Mather himself was a logical candidate for the presidency,
but he would not consider leaving Boston for rustic Cambridge. According to scuttlebutt among the undergraduates, Mather wanted to move
the college to Boston and be president there. Always thin-skinned,
Mather was stung by this gossip and complained bitterly to Oakes.
Oakes found him difficult, but tried his best. "I must bear with their
Jealousy," Mather reported of one such conversation. Oakes "professed
his desires that I might be at Cambridge."[20] The college treasurer,
Thomas Danforth, coming to Oakes's support, told Mather that "those
Reports about reflections on me in Cambridge were slanders and false-
hoods, & desiring that I would not believe them. And that if I would
accept of the Presidentship, it would be selfe denial, &c."[21] That same
month, Increase took Cotton for the second time to live at the college.[22]

Leonard Hoar did not live long after his humiliation. He and his wife
moved to Boston, and in November Increase was called to their house in
the middle of the night to find Hoar dying. Hoar asked Mather to take
care of his young nephew. The next day he was dead.[23]

Increase Mather was now not only on the Board of Overseers *ex officio*
as the minister of one of Boston's three churches, but also on the Corporation as a Fellow, and hence involved in the day-to-day operation of the
college. By the time Cotton Mather received his bachelor's degree from
the hands of acting president Urian Oakes, Oakes and Mather had made
up their differences. In the preface to Mather's *Mystery of Christ,* Oakes
referred to the author as "my intimate friend" and urged that these "excellent sermons" be "read over and over." His own unexpected death
only two days before the commencement exercises in 1681 would again
leave the overseers facing their old problem of finding a president.

JEREMIAD

One wintry day in February 1674, Increase Mather preached the first
of the great sermons that were to make him famous. It was a jeremiad,

The Day of Trouble is near. [24] He asked Urian Oakes to write a preface, and published the sermon that same year.

Of all the many styles of sermons in Puritan New England, the jeremiad has taken the firmest grip on the American imagination. It takes its name from the austere foreboding of the Old Testament prophet Jeremiah. Mather took this text, however, from Jeremiah's contemporary, the prophet Ezekiel, Chapter 7, verse 7, "The morning is come unto thee, O thou that dwellest in the land: the time is come, the day of trouble *is* near, and not the sounding again of the mountains." According to the Geneva Bible, "morning is come" meant the beginning of punishment is started; "sounding again of the mountains" was a voice of joy and mirth, which was not to be. For this text he chose the line between, "the day of trouble is near." [25]

Mather slowly and meticulously proceeded through all the mandatory steps of the sermon form. First the text was examined word by word for meanings of language. Then the doctrine was drawn from the text: God sometimes brings great trouble on his own people. By "his own people" Mather meant, and everyone in his meetinghouse knew he meant, the church members sitting before him.

Very carefully he divided and subdivided his doctrine, building a case like a lawyer, taking nothing for granted: your name is John Doe? You live at such and such a place? You are the brother of the deceased? The case was made in abstractions, the evidence drawn from scripture and ancient history. Some in the audience concentrated to keep the succession of logical points in mind; others wondered when he would get to the point. Afternoon came before Mather mentioned New England for the first time. There had been a lunch break, of course, as there was every Sunday, although on most Sundays the afternoon sermon was separate from the morning's. This time, Mather picked up exactly where he had left off, elaborating part four of his doctrine. At last he finished his development of the doctrine and came to the "Uses." The audience became more alert. Now he would apply the lesson to their own situation.

In his first application of the text, Mather referred to something already mentioned in abstract: visible saints in the audience before him would be punished for their sins. The coming troubles, Mather said, were meant to awaken the faithful to the fact that the "Last Times," that is, the millennium and then the end of time itself, were near. A sure sign of the approach of the "Last Times" would be great sorrows in the world. Mather quoted Matthew 24:6, 7, 8: "Ye shall hear of wars and rumours of wars. . . . For nation shall rise against nation, and realm against realm, and there shall be pestilence, and famine, and earthquakes in divers places. All these are but the beginning of sorrows." For the first time that day, Mather leaned towards his audience and spoke directly to them: "What do we hear of at this day," he asked, "but wars and rumours of war?" He referred to Europe, but. . . . Are we safe? Shall not the storm fall on America? on New England? He had his audience's attention. He brought the subject nearer home. Think of the deaths of our own ministers and magistrates. "When Kings call home their ambassadors, it is a sign they will declare war." It was a simple argument by analogy, but it was effective.

Up to this point, Mather had concentrated on building anxiety among those visible saints, who had reason to feel secure. "Sinful Security," Urian Oakes was to say later, "is the great Disease of the last times."[26] Two-thirds of the sermon had been devoted to convincing the righteous that they were not safe from punishment. He began a catalogue of weaknesses in which every member of the church could find some recognition of self. "We can now see little difference between Church-members and other men. . . . Professors of Religion *fashion themselves according to the world.* And what *Pride* is there? Spiritual Pride . . . , yea, carnal, shameful, foolish Pride, in Apparel, Fashions, and the like. . . . Disobedience . . . in Families, in Churches, and in the Commonwealth. And is there not Oppression amongst us? Are there no biting Usurers in New England . . . that grind the faces of the poor?"[27]

Men have given up on family prayer. Why? They have not time, they say. Why not? How is your time taken up instead? Mather supplied the answers to his rhetorical questions: your time is consumed with worldly interests, with making money. "*Oh this World, the World* undoeth many a man, that thinks he shall go to Heaven when he dieth. And in this respect our Land is full of Idolatry. . . . We have changed our Interest. The Interest of *New England* was Religion, which did distinguish us from other *English Plantations.* . . . now we begin to espouse a Worldly Interest and so to choose a new God."[28] Who would deny it? Boston's North End was filling up with merchants, artisans, ship chandlers. The waterfront was crowded with docks and warehouses. More and more ships built in local shipyards and outfitted by Boston merchants were plying the seas in search of goods and profits.

The effect of the sermon was to add shame and guilt to insecurity. Next came a feeling of expectancy. "Signs have appeared. By signs I mean Prodigies." He spoke of fabulous and dreadful legends out of England's past, lurid and fantastic accounts of armies seen marching in the sky, the noise of battle, clanging armor. He drew from the rich imagery of the prophets, reminding his audience that it had rained blood at York on the day the Danes landed to pillage England. He quoted Isaiah 29:6: "*Thou shalt be visited by the Lord of hosts with Thunder and with Earthquake, and great noise, with storm, and tempest, and the flame of a devouring fire.* Hath it not been so with us? We have been visited . . . with terrible Thunders and Lightnings."[29]

The sermon drew to a climax of horror. The image Mather had chosen was a cloud of blood. His language moved easily from images of dark thunderclouds to the symbolic cloud threatening the land, a dark, billowing "cloud of blood." Several times he repeated the phrase "a cloud of blood." "There is a black Cloud over our heads, which begins to drop upon us." Silence filled the meetinghouse, the eerie quiet before the storm. Will it rain blood on our heads?[30] Then, quickly, he gave release from the horror. "This is *Immanuel's land.*" Here was the key to the jeremiad. "This is *Immanuel's land.* Christ by a wonderful Providence hath dispossessed Satan, who reigned securely in these Ends of the Earth, for Ages the Lord Knoweth how many, and here the Lord hath caused as it were *New Jerusalem* to come down from Heaven; He dwels in this place."[31]

Mather now shaped for his audience the self-image that was becoming the central, mythic idea of his generation. New England was "as it were a little Nation." Because we are the Lord's children and in covenant with him, Mather told his people, the Lord will punish us, but he will not destroy us. "God hath culled out a people, even out of all parts of a Nation, which he hath also had a great favour towards, and hath brought them by a mighty hand, and an out-stretched arm, over a greater than a Red Sea, and here hath he planted them, and hath caused them to grow up as it were into a little Nation; And shall we think that all this is to destroy them within forty or fifty years? Destruction shall not as yet be." And again, later, "God cannot finde in his heart to destroy us."[32]

This sermon placed Increase Mather among the first rank of his generation of Puritan preachers. In it he wove together many of the themes of his contemporaries: William Stoughton's *New England's True Interest* (1668), Samuel Danforth's *Errand Into the Wilderness* (1670), and his own image from his father's biography of the first fathers crossing "over the rude Waves of the vast Ocean." The next year, when a cruel Indian war devastated Massachusetts, Mather pointed triumphantly to the spread of war to New England as a fulfillment of the prophecy contained in *The*

Wo to Drunkards.

TWO

SERMONS

Teſtifying againſt the Sin of

Drunkenneſs :

Wherein the *Wofulneſs* of that Evil, and the Miſery of all
that are addicted to it, is diſcovered from the
WORD of GOD.

Preached by *INCREASE MATHER*, Teacher of
a Church in *Boſton* in *New-England.*

Iſa. 5. 11, 22. *Wo unto them that riſe up early in the morning, that
they may follow ſtrong drink, that continue untill night, till Wine
inflame them. Wo unto them that are mighty to drink Wine, and
men of ſtrength to mingle ſtrong drink.*
Prov. 23. 29, 30. *Who hath Wo? Who hath ſorrow? —— Who hath
Wounds without cauſe? —— They that tarry long at the Wine.*
Hab. 2. 15. *Wo unto him that giveth his Neighbour drink: that
putteſt thy bottle to him, and makeſt him drunken alſo.*
1 Cor. 6. 10. —— *Nor Drunkards, ſhall inherit the Kingdome of
God.*

CAMBRIDGE:
Printed by *Marmaduke Johnſon.* 1673.
And Sold by *Edmund Ranger* Bookbinder in *Boſton.*

Wo to Drunkards, two sermons by Mather, 1673, condemning drunkenness as a
moral laxity that brings divine punishment

The Day of Trouble is near.

TWO
SERMONS

Wherein is shewed,

What are the Signs of a Day of Trouble being near.

And particularly,

What reason there is for *NEW-ENGLAND* to expect

A Day of Trouble.

Also what is to be done, that we may escape these things which shall come to pass.

Preached (the 11th day of the 12th Moneth, 1673. being a day of

HUMILIATION

in one of the Churches in *Boston.*

By *INCREASE MATHER*, Teacher of that Church.

Ezek. 33.7. *O Son of man, I have set thee a Watchman to the house of Israel, therefore thou shalt hear the word at my mouth, and warn them from me.*
Matth. 24.6,7,8. *Ye shall hear of wars, and rumours of wars — For Nation shall rise against Nation, and Kingdome against Kingdome: All these are the beginnings of sorrows.*
Luke 21.28. *And when these things shall begin to come to pass, then look up, and lift up your heads, for your Redemption draweth nigh.*

Cambridge: Printed by *Marmaduke Johnson.* 1674.

The Day of Trouble is near, a jeremiad by Increase Mather, lamenting spiritual decline in New England; printed in Cambridge in 1674

Day of Trouble is near. He believed that the mantle of the Old Testament prophets had fallen on his own shoulders.

The Puritanism of Increase Mather's generation, however, was far more complex than a jeremiad alone suggests. English Puritans, deprived of the spiritual comfort of the confessional and the absolution from sin, had always sought assurance of Christ's mercy. Mather regularly gave them this assurance in sermons couched in a language of joyful certainty in Christ's redeeming love. Mather expressed this side of Puritanism best in sermons preached once a month when he celebrated the Lord's Supper. The theme running throughout them is Christ's love and his redemption of man from the consequences of sin. The language was the language of love, fellowship, and mutual devotion, of encouragement and assurance. His sermons are reminiscent of John Cotton, whose rhetoric was effusive with a vocabulary of love and sexual imagery.[33] Cotton's sermons on the first book of John seem to have served as a model for at least one of Increase's.

Increase's sermon images have the same simple, visual quality that they have in his jeremiads, although now the message is hope instead of fear. "Jesus the *Son of GOD* does as it were take the believing soul by the hand, and leadeth him into the *Presence*-Chamber. He opens the door for him, and presents him before the *Father of Glory,* and sayes Behold O Father, Here is a soul that I dyed for, this soul is washed in my blood, and therefore do thou look upon him with a favorable eye for my sake."[34] In the strict logic of Calvinist theology, there could be no certainty about election; God's choice of saints was in the last analysis secret. But Increase did not preach strict logic or offer a rational argument. Born and educated like his colleagues in the broad stream of Augustinian piety, he sought to touch the feelings of his audience, to convert their hearts, by appealing not to the mind but to the affections, particulary to their need for assurance. "Thy salvation is *certain.* . . . By (being) reconciled to God by the *death* of his Son, we are *saved* by his *life.* . . ."[35] So did Mather try to assuage the Puritans' universal longing for certainty, for assurance.

To those in his audience who had not yet had an experience of regeneration, he held out the same sweet promise of a certain salvation, if only they would come to Christ. "O Christless Sinner, look about thee and see where thou art! Thy soul is hanging over the mouth of hell by the rotten thread of a frail life: if *that* break, the devouring Gulf will swallow thee up for ever. . . . Awake thou that sleepest and rise from the Dead, and *Christ shall give thee Light.* . . . *Here is a matter of glorious Consolation,*

and Encouragement unto those that come to Jesus Christ. There is admirable
Sweetness and Consolation in these two or three words. JESUS *THE*
MEDIATOR."[36]

To the converted and unconverted alike, Mather's sacramental ser-
mons balanced the terror of the jeremiad by guaranteeing that the Old
Testament had been replaced by the New, that the wrath of Jehovah had
been mediated by the love of Christ. "JESUS is better than *Moses.* The
New Testament than the *Old. . . .*"[37] He used a new metaphor: "Christ as
Mediator is the Father of the *new world.*"[38] The jeremiad and the sacra-
mental sermon ended on the same note, proclaiming the special place of
New England in the scheme of things: this is Immanuel's Land; Christ is
Father of the New World.

In 1675 Mather began to collect some of these sacramental sermons
for a book. War and other writing projects interrupted the work, but by
the end of the decade he had seven sermons ready, and he asked his friend
Urian Oakes to write a short foreword. The volume was not published
until 1686, with the seven sermons dating from the 1670s, one as early
as 1672, and an eighth, added later, all published under the title *The
Mystery of Christ.*[39] Scholars have misread the character of New England
Puritanism during the 1670s either by focusing on the language and
content of the Jeremiad to the exclusion of other kinds of sermons, or by
believing mistakenly that Mather's sacramental sermons in *The Mystery of
Christ* represent a change of outlook after 1680.[40]

CHARIOTS OF WAR

In the summer of 1675, Increase Mather was preoccupied with the
health of his children and with what was happening at the college. Few
people in Boston were even aware of the trial in Plymouth of three
Wampanoag Indians charged with murder. The murdered man, John
Sassamon, one of the few Indians to have studied at Harvard college, had
been for a time the English-speaking secretary to the chief sachem of the
Wampanoags, Metacomet, whom the English called King Philip after
Philip of Macedon. Later he left Philip and joined a Christian Indian
village. In midwinter, 1674−75, he told the authorities in Plymouth
that there was talk among several tribes of resisting the English hegem-
ony, and, soon afterwards, he was murdered. His body, shoved under the
ice on a pond, went undiscovered until the spring thaw. A witness then
came forward to identify three Indians as the killers, but information
about a conspiracy was not made public until their trial at Plymouth.[41]

Even then, the possibility of an armed contest over occupancy and control of New England did not enter the Puritans' minds. But war was coming, and it proved to be a powerful catalyst for change.

By 1675, the English probably outnumbered the Indians in New England two to one. Although the Indians remained attached to their traditional social and political forms, they had quickly adopted English technology, particularly metals and textiles. Indian soldiers in 1675 invariably fought with musket and steel tomahawk, though they might rely on bow and arrow after the first discharge of firearms, because it was quicker to fit arrow to bowstring than it was to reload the cumbersome flintlock muskets. One on one in the field, the Indian could easily hold his own as a warrior. Indian society could not, however, bend its entire culture to the rational prosecution of a sustained war. For that, the centuries of European experience proved far superior.

In June 1675, a few days after the executions at Plymouth, a frontiersman named Benjamin Church was clearing farmland on the disputed border between Plymouth and Rhode Island. Rumors had already flickered through the forests that Philip of the Wampanoags was ready for war. A party of Indians from the nearby Sogkonate tribe approached through the woods to bring a message from their chief. Their sachem Awashonks, a woman, was having a dance and asked Church to attend. On horseback Church followed the messengers and soon reached the scene of Awashonks's dance. She broke off dancing when Church appeared and came to talk.[42] Philip, she said, was getting ready for war against the English and wanted her to join with his people. Six Wampanoags who were at the dance were already dressed for war, painted, hair trimmed down to the scalp-lock, armed with powder and shot and a musket. Church advised Awashonks to seek safety with the Plymouth government and set out for Plymouth with the warning. He reached Governor Winslow's house on June 16, and on the 20th Wampanoags attacked the frontier town of Swansea. By the twenty-eighth an English force from Massachusetts and Plymouth had assembled and engaged scattered Indian war parties along the Plymouth-Rhode Island border. But, to Church's disgust, the English commanders dillydallied through July and so lost the chance to encircle Philip and his warriors. Philip led his entire tribe, men, women, and children, by canoe and by foot through the forest out of their homeland. His way was now clear either southwest to join the large tribe of Narragansett Indians in eastern Connecticut, or northwest to the Nipmucks in central Massachusetts.[43]

On August 2 the Puritans learned what direction Philip had taken when the isolated village of Brookfield in central Massachusetts was overrun and destroyed by Nipmucks, who had been persuaded by Philip's presence in their lands to join in a general war against the English. From Brookfield the fighting spread north to the Merrimac and west to the Connecticut River. Many of the numerous, small Massachusetts tribes, which the settlers had long believed to be loyal and trustworthy, now turned against the English. In September the Commissioners of the United Colonies (Connecticut, Massachusetts, and Plymouth) met and recommended a full-scale war effort. The Court of Assistants created a committee for war finances, and on September 17 it published a call for a day of repentance.[44] The proclamation explained the Indian attacks in terms of Massachusetts's provocation of the Lord and stated that victory in war could only come with the Lord's help, earned through sincere reformation, humility, and faith. Meanwhile, Indians in the Connecticut River Valley ambushed and destroyed a large English force at Bloody Brook. A few days later, the largest town in the valley, Springfield, was attacked and a third of its buildings were burned to the ground.[45]

The Massachusetts General Court assembled on October 13 to put the colony on a war footing. It gave emergency powers to a handful of military commissioners, who thereafter conducted the war under powers passed by the General Court under the title *Laws and Ordinances of Warr*.[46] Defense was taken out of the hands of local militia and turned over to the military commissioners, who promptly developed an overall strategy. The commissioners designated in every threatened town specific houses as garrison houses. Troops ordered to the town would be quartered there. In case of an attack, townspeople were to seek refuge in the nearest garrison house; their own homes and farm buildings would not be defended. Some of the smaller frontier towns were judged by the military commissioners not worth defending, and the government in Boston advised the residents to evacuate their women and children.

Across Massachusetts the government raised troops of volunteers, and, when they were not enough, drafted men from the eastern towns considered not to be in danger. The towns where these troops were sent were required to provide food and lodging for the troops and pasturage and stabling for their horses. The scale and effectiveness of the Indian attacks came as a surprise. Indian war parties numbered hundreds of warriors; they moved quickly, and the English seldom knew their whereabouts or what target was next. The Indians, on the other hand, always seemed to know where the relief columns were. The General Court quickly recognized the need to modernize its own tactics. Mounted troops were ordered to arm themselves with carbines instead of the sword, and foot soldiers abandoned pikes in favor of muskets. The government in Boston ordered the purchase of a thousand firearms through Boston merchants, a resource closed to the Indians.

The defensive strategy of Massachusetts perhaps did more than the devastation of Indian attacks to dissolve the homogeneous, tradition-bound, self-governing Puritan communities. The sudden appearance of large bodies of armed troops in the small, closely knit towns quickly undermined their coherence as communities of family and church fellowship. Rural villages, where no one ever before had lived outside a family structure, were now suddenly swollen with outsiders who had no family ties to the residents. Single men drafted from their own families in distant parts of the colony were moved about from town to town as the commanders in Boston saw fit. The newly written Articles of War superseded the ordinary law of the colony. The military commissioners in Boston, not town fathers, now made decisions about lives and property. And when towns were overrun, burned, and evacuated, hundreds of families streamed towards Boston and other coastal towns, uprooted entirely from their rural isolation. Thus did the Indian war undermine the City on a Hill.

GOD'S PUNISHMENT

Increase Mather held a very different understanding of the war from the military commissioners. The rational pursuit of victory in terms of troops and armaments concerned only secondary causes. In Mather's mind, nothing happened unless it was God's will that it should happen. If Puritans wanted victory, they must understand God's purpose in unleashing the dogs of war, and discover how meekly to acknowledge his righteousness. The Thursday after the General Court first met in October was Increase Mather's turn to deliver the weekly afternoon lecture in Boston. He could expect the entire General Court to be present, the Governor, Deputy Governor, and all the Assistants and Deputies. In the growing crisis of war, the prospect was daunting. "I prayed with Tears in my study, before I went to preach," he wrote, "that the Lord would be with me, & owne & bless my labors for the glory to his name, & so as to cause Reformation of those things which are displeasing to him in the Countrey."[47]

When the meetinghouse filled up that October afternoon, Mather told his audience that the war had come as a punishment. New England had sinned. Had he not foretold this very thing in his sermon *The Day of Trouble is near* the year before? Had he not then quoted from Matthew, "And ye shall hear of wars and rumors of wars"? Were not these attacks on Massachusetts towns a call to awaken men to repent their sins? Were not the terrors of Indian attacks the fulfillment of prophecy and the just consequence of a covenanted people backsliding? Mather rehearsed the catalogue of sins he had itemized in his jeremiad in 1674: a lessening of godliness, a growth of worldliness, even among the elect; pride, expressed in new fashions of dress and hair; disobedience to parents, teachers, ministers; oppression in the marketplace by merchants and laborers alike.[48]

That Thursday lecture catapulted Mather into leadership in Massachusetts. To be sure, his ideas were widely held among the ministry and accepted by the colony's leaders. An accident of the calendar, however, had given Mather the opportunity to speak first, and in the ensuing twelve months he held on to and reinforced his role as principal spokesman for the ministers. When a committee of the General Court asked the ministers in Boston for their advice, they followed Mather's lead, even to paraphrasing the catalogue of sins in his jeremiad *The Day of Trouble is near*. As a consequence, the General Court drafted and passed into law on November 3, 1675 an omnibus statute under the general title "Provoking Evils," which identified the backsliding for which God was presumably punishing this people and provided correctives, which, when carried out, would end the war. "Provoking Evils" was the most complete enactment in the seventeenth century of New England's notorious "blue laws."[49]

Some of the minister's recommendations could remain recommendations only. Even the war emergency would not permit the government to dictate to the churches. For the rest of it, the laws followed the minister's suggestions to the letter. "Long hair like women's hair is worn by some men," and "some women wear borders of hair, and their cutting, curling, and immodest laying out their hair, especially among younger people. This Court doth declare against this ill custom as offensive to them." The Court authorized grand juries to make presentations and county courts to proceed against both men and women for violations of the code about hair length and style. It was the same for dress. The law spoke of "the evil of pride in Apparell," of "strange new fashions both in poor and rich, with naked breasts and arms," and "superfluous ribbons, both on hair and apparrell."

As for Sabbath attendance, the town officers were ordered to close the doors of the meetinghouse so that no one could leave before service was over. These same officers were required to designate special seating places for children, where they could be kept under stricter watch. If children were not brought to Sabbath service, their parents were to be fined or the children whipped. Laws already on the books against swearing and profanity were strengthened by punishing anyone who overheard a neighbor swear and failed to report it.

The law "Provoking Evils" came down heavily against the sale and abuse of alcohol. Drunkenness had been one of Increase Mather's earliest preoccupations. There were problems with alcoholism among members of his church, and his first publication in Massachusetts under his own name had been a sermon against drunkenness in 1673.[50] Residents of towns were now strictly enjoined from going to taverns, which were in theory only for travellers away from home. As well try to hold back the tides, as to stop Englishmen from tippling. An illicit underworld of drinking places sprang up. Men and women sold alcohol from their homes without licenses. To stop the practice, the law sought to create a network of citizen-spies appointed by the county courts. The clientele of these early speakeasies were servants and apprentices, and the law cracked down on "inferiors absenting themselves out of families whereunto they belong, in the night, and meeting with corrupt company without leave."

Other scofflaws came from a better, wealthier class of person, as the legislation explained: "Whereas there is a loose and sinful custom of going a riding from town to town, and that oftentimes men and women together upon pretense of going to lectures, but it appears to be merely to drink and revel in ordinaries and taverns, which is in itself scandalous and is to be feared a notable means to debauch our youth, and hazard the chastity of such as are drawn forth thereunto." Finally, in the face of steady inflation of prices and wages, the General Court ordered both merchants and laborers to abstain from charging exorbitant prices. County courts and grand juries were authorized to enforce the rule of a fair price.

There was little that was actually new in the social restrictions of the 1670s, but it was in these ten years that the attempt to legislate morality reached its high water mark. The strict mores of the earliest years of settlement were by now competing with older and more traditional patterns of English life. This change in social behavior did not necessarily mean that the men and women of the generations born in Massachusetts were less virtuous than their fathers. Rather, the development of the colony's internal economy from its very Spartan beginnings now offered greater opportunity for traditional English diversions.

The legislation gave prominence to the asceticism that characterized Puritan morality throughout its long development in England and in America. Yet the asceticism of Massachusetts was strikingly different from the worldly asceticism Max Weber described in his influential essay *The Protestant Ethic and The Spirit of Captialism.* Weber used Richard Baxter's *Saints' Everlasting Rest* and *Christian Directory* to demonstrate a connection between asceticism and capitalism. Specifically, Weber found that Puritan asceticism "turned much more sharply against the acquisition of earthly goods than it did in Calvin," and that "the real moral objection is to relaxation in the security of possession. . . . It is only because possession involves this danger of relaxation that it is objectionable at all. . . . Not leisure and enjoyment, but only activity serves to increase the glory of God. . . . Waste of time is thus the first and in principle the deadliest of sins. . . . Loss of time through sociability, idle talk, luxury, even more sleep than is necessary for health . . . is worthy of absolute moral condemnation."[51]

Puritan asceticism in Massachusetts, and in particular the asceticism that found expression in the law "Provoking Evils," was of a different kind. The sin in sociability, idle talk, and luxury was not wasted time but debauchery, loss of chastity, disobedience, and above all pride. Pride in person, pride in a fine bosom or handsome head of hair, prideful ostentation of latest fashions—these were Mather's *constant* targets. His condemnation of all manifestations of human pride was the exact counterpart to Puritan preaching of the inescapable corruption and vileness of natural man. All that was flirtatious, merry, jocose, or high-spirited Mather condemned because it disguised human corruption and diverted attention from God's righteousness. Apprentices who stole away at night were guilty of disobedience and corrupt company. Men and women who rode from town to town were guilty of scandal and debauchery. Neither squandered time nor lack of productivity were his concerns. Nowhere in his long career did Increase Mather publish a sermon on the necessity of hard work in one's calling, however much he demonstrated it in his own life.

The General Court of Massachusetts treated the law "Provoking Evils" as if it were as central to the war effort as was the "Ordinances of Warre." As long as both strategies went hand in hand, Massachusetts had a single

Several

L A V V S   A N D   O R D E R S

Made at the S E S S I O N S *of the*

GENERAL   COURT

Held at Boston *the* 13th *of* October 1675.

As also at the S E S S I O N S *of* C O U R T *held at* Boston, *the* 3d. *of* Novemb.

1 6 7 5.

And Printed by their Order,

Edward Rawson   Secr.

C A M B R I D G E,

Printed by Samuel Green.   1 6 7 5.

Several Laws and Orders, issued by General Court in 1675, including "Provoking Evils," listing moral correctives for ending King Philip's War; printed by Samuel Green in Cambridge

John Leverett, governor of Massachusetts during King Philip's War, who disagreed with Mather and "Provoking Evils"

vision of the world and heaven. For the time being, Mather was content:
"In the morning as I was sitting alone in my study, I was suddenly moved
by the spirit of God, & wonderfully melted into Tears, with a firm perswasion that God would make me his mouth, & owne the words I should
speak, in his name."[52] That conviction finally put an end to any linger-
ing doubts or fears of "horrid temptations to atheisme."

MATHER VERSUS WILLIAM HUBBARD

The military strategy adopted in November 1675 seems in hind-
sight to have been dictated as much by the English desire to acquire Indian lands west of Narragansett Bay as to defeat those Indians who were
on the warpath. Most of the warring Indians were now in central and
western Massachusetts. The United Colonies, however, chose as their
first military effort a preemptive strike against the Narragansett Indians
in eastern Connecticut. On December 18 an English army of about a
thousand soldiers worked its painful way towards a Narragansett town
located on four or five acres of rising land surrounded by swamp. Here a
thousand or fifteen hundred men, women, and children were living for
the winter in a village crudely fortified by a wooden palisade. Inside,
wigwams and wood and bark huts were crowded closely together.[53]
Stumbling over the frozen hillocks, pulling free from tangles of briars,
breaking repeatedly through thin ice into ankle-deep water, the English
forces reached the palisaded town. The winter days were short. That
afternoon they attacked, and, after a sharp fight, gained entrance and set
fire to the wooden huts. As the occupants came stumbling out, no
quarter was given to age or sex. The English casualties were heavy, about
eighty men killed and many more wounded. No accurate figure of Indian losses seems possible. After the Great Swamp Fight, the forces of
the United Colonies stayed in a miserable winter camp near Wickford,
on the edge of the Narragansett country, hoping to pursue and finish off
the Indians in Connecticut. The rest of the New England frontier was
relatively quiet. Philip had gone west to Albany to try to enlist the help
of the Mohawks. Fortunately for the English, he was unsuccessful.

Increase Mather was not concerned with strategies and alliances. The
real battle lines, he thought, were at home in man's fight against his sinful nature. The reformation in public life that the new laws were supposed to bring about was slow to take place, and Mather himself began
to be criticized for belaboring the sinfulness of the people. As always, he
was acutely sensitive to criticism. "The season cold & my Heart like it,"

he wrote that December; "I find that outward things will discompose the spirit."[54] By January 1676, he was blaming the magistrates for not enforcing the laws, and when it came his turn to preach the Thursday lecture again, he denounced them. Afterwards the ministers dined with the governor, lieutenant governor, and magistrates.

Governor John Leverett had little in common with this young clergyman who kept harping on the sins of the people. Leverett had been admitted a freeman of the colony in 1635, four years before Mather was born. He had served as deputy from Boston to the General Court in 1649 and had been one of that minority that had voted against the Cambridge Platform, a fact which, if known to Mather, must have prejudiced him against the older man.[55] Leverett, too, had gone back to England during the revolution and had served under Cromwell. He was a soldier and a gentleman, not a priest. Humility was not his strong suit. After seven years as a magistrate, he was elected to succeed Bellingham as governor in 1673. Now he was a wartime governor, and the lives of men and women rested on his leadership. He had no patience with Mather's talk that the real enemy was not the Indians and the real battlefield was not in the garrison houses and the frozen countryside.

Neither Leverett nor the magistrates had liked Mather's Thursday lecture that bleak January afternoon. At their dinner together, Mather talked about the growing drunkenness in the colony. Leverett, who should have known, growled out that there had been more drunkenness in the early years than there was now. Mather took the remark personally. William Stoughton, one of the magistrates, made matters worse with a weak joke: Mr. Mather would have to preach a recantation sermon. "No," Mather blurted out, "but if men would not accept my labors God will." Still hot under the collar when he reached home, Mather vented his anger in his diary, where he blamed Leverett for issuing licenses to the growing number of taverns in Boston. "No wonder that N.E. is visited, when the Head is so spirited."[56]

Two weeks later, the Narragansetts slipped away from the army facing them and attacked Pawtuxet, Rhode Island. Soon they were up along the western frontier in Massachusetts with Philip's forces. The settlements there were in greater danger than ever. Men and women turned against all Indians. At Chelmsford there was an ugly incident. Captain Samuel Mosely, schooled in the brutality of the West Indies and now a militia officer in Massachusetts, led a party of self-appointed vigilantes to bully, threaten, and in the end kill two Christian Indians. Captain Mosely liked a fight and always found volunteers.[57] To Mather the news from

Chelmsford meant only another wrongdoing for which the colonists would be punished. The Indians, he said, were God's agents, a scourge with which he punished the unrepentant English. Rage against the Indians was inexcusable; the enemy was within. It was not a popular point of view.

Mather was losing his audience. One Friday early in February, he spoke to a special meeting of his own church, just the members this time, about a hundred men and women. He hammered away at the real cause of the war and the need for reformation. Then he read parts of "Provoking Evils" from the pulpit. To his dismay, Mather got a sullen response. After the meeting, two pillars of his congregation, Captain Lake and John Richards, stayed behind to tell him so. "When ministers did lay a solemn charge upon the people," they told him, "it might take with the ignorant, but no rational men would regard what was sayd the more for that." Mather replied that "Truth had more Authority with it when it came in such a way . . . because it came from a Father." He reminded them of Hebrews 13.17: "Obey them that have oversight over you."[58]

On Feburary 10, 1676, Indians attacked Lancaster, some fifty miles northwest of Boston. The attack was half expected, and all but the most foolhardy had already retreated to the garrison houses. Joseph Rowlandson was the minister at Lancaster, and his home was one of the garrison houses. That day Rowlandson himself was in Boston to seek more troops for the defense of his town. Even without him, there were thirty-seven people in his house on the night of February ninth. At sunrise Mary Rowlandson looked out a window and saw smoke rising above the trees. Gunfire was clearly audible. No one dared venture out, and before long, Indians appeared and quickly surrounded the house, shooting at it from all sides. The rooms on the ground floor became pungent with the smell of burnt powder as the defenders fired back. As always, the Indians sought some way to set fire to the wooden building, by shooting flaming arrows onto the roof or by pushing or rolling a burning cart against the walls. Behind the Rowlandson house rose a short, steep hill. After several hours, when three of the defenders had already been wounded by gunshot, the Indians succeeded in rolling a burning cart downhill against the house. The men, women, and children inside were caught between the flames and smoke inside and the howling enemy outside. Mary Rowlandson took one child in her arms and another by the hand and stepped out of the door. She stood in the dooryard frozen in horror. "I had often before this said," she wrote later, "that if the Indians should come, I should chose rather to be killed by them than be taken alive but when it came to the trial my mind changed." Shaking in extremity of terror at what she had witnessed and at what lay before her, Mary Rowlandson was taken captive with her children.[59] Long before he reached home, Joseph Rowlandson could see the columns of smoke rising in the winter air. Of the thirty-seven people in his house, twelve were already dead, including his brother, sister-in-law, nieces, and a nephew. His wife and children were gone. Rowlandson returned to Boston and sought out Increase Mather. Together they went to the Council. Some means must be found to effect an exchange of prisoners.[60]

The war continued to go badly for the English. On the twenty-first, Medfield was attacked and burned to the ground, despite the presence of a large force of militia in the garrisons. Medfield was twenty miles from Boston. The General Court was in session, busy night and day with war measures. More troops were drafted. Discipline in garrison houses needed to be sharpened. The treasury was empty, and loans from bankers and merchants were needed. They would be repaid with lands taken from the Indians. Christian Indians were interned on Deer Island in the bay. They were given little food, and lacked shelter, but at least they were safe from mobs. Captured Indians, when they were not executed by hanging or being "knocked on the head," were sold into slavery on Barbados. A bounty was offered for any Indian found "skulking" about in the woods, dead or alive.

February was a cruel month. Mather's North Church held a day of humiliation; there were services morning and afternoon. Then an epidemic sickness struck Boston, and there was no word yet of the Rowlandson family. Indians were reported within ten miles of the city. "The Lord have mercy on his Jerusalem every where," Mather prayed. "Pitty N.E. Sanctify these Judgments. Have Compassion on them that deep sufferers in this day of Calamity. Restore Peace to this land. Preserve Boston from desolating judgments. Amen! O Lord Amen!"[61]

In fact, although it was not apparent yet, the English were winning the struggle. Large bands of Wampanoags, Narragansetts, Nipmucks, and others, men, women, and children, were moving about the forests in involuntary migration. Stores of food had been lost, and the annual fishing camps on tidal rivers and at the seashore were impossible. Furthermore, spring planting for the coming year was virtually out of the question. It was only a matter of time. Entire family bands were reduced to living off the land, surviving on berries, grubs, insects, lily roots, acorns, and nuts. If a horse or cow fell into their hands, it was consumed, even its ears and hooves. They caught and ate bear, deer, beaver, turtles, frogs, squirrels, dogs, skunks, snakes, and porcupines. But the lack of the usual diet of beans, corn, squash, and seafoods drew on their energies. Many sickened during the winter months, and the privation gradually took its toll. Mary Rowlandson, a prisoner, saw it all. "I laid down my load, and went into the wigwam, and there sat an Indian boiling of horse's feet (they being wont to eat the flesh first, and when the feet were old and dried, and they had nothing else, they would cut off the feet and use them). I asked him to give me a little of his broth, or water they were boiling in; he took a dish, and gave me one spoonfull of samp, and bid me take as much of the broth as I would. Then I put some of the hot water to the samp, and drank it up, and my spirit came again. He gave me also a piece of the ruff or ridding of the small guts, and I broiled it on the coals."[62]

Plunged in its own fears and miseries, Boston was as yet unaware how close the English were to winning. John Hull's diary for these months tells the story in laconic Yankee style:

Feb. 10. Lancaster spoiled by the enemy
21st. Medefeild in part burned by ditto.
March 13. Groton burned
26th. Marlborough burned in part.
1676, 28th. Rehoboth assaulted.[63]

Mather strove with little success to mount a general movement to renew church covenants. Even as he did so, he heard of the attack on Groton, where Samuel Willard was minister. Willard's home was one of the garrison houses and heavily defended. Unable to break in, the attackers burned the meetinghouse nearby and taunted the defenders: "What will you do for a home to pray in now?" Willard's house survived the attack, but Groton was heavily damaged, and the town was abandoned. Willard came to Boston along with the other refugees. For him, at least, the war had opened up a new future. By mid-April, every English town on the edge of settlement was abandoned and refugee families found shelter where they could. Dunstable, Groton, Lancaster, Marlborough, Menden were all gone. Indian attacks now concentrated on the next ring of towns: Andover, Chelmsford, Billerica, Woburn. Sudbury came under attack for the second time on April 21, and a major battle ensued as both sides brought up reinforcements. Losses were heavy, and many English dead were left in the field.

It was the Indians, however, who could least afford the losses. Mary Rowlandson watched the warriors return from Sudbury and remarked to herself that although they claimed a great victory and many of the enemy killed, they were more subdued than ever. Her own master brought back a pillowcase with Holland lace and told her to make a dress for his youngest child. In another wigwam she was fed by an Indian who had killed two Englishmen that day and brought back their clothes. The Indians, who did not have a spinning or weaving technology, prized European clothing highly and often made it their principal loot. "I looked behind me, and there I saw bloody clothes with bullet holes in them; yet the Lord suffered not this wretch to do me any hurt; yea, instead of that, he many times refreshed me: five or six times did he and his squaw refresh my feeble carcass."[64]

On May 1, 1676, negotiations for Mary Rowlandson's release were begun. The Massachusetts Council sent letters by two Christian Indians to the council of sachems at Watchusett in central Massachusetts. Mary Rowlandson recorded, "Then came Tom and Peter, with the second letter from the Council, about the captives. Though they were Indians, I got them by the hands, and burst out into tears; my heart was so full I could not speak to them; but recovering myself I asked them how my husband did, and all my friends and acquaintance: They said, They are all very well, but melancholy. They brought me two biscuits, and a pound of tobacco."[65] Joseph Rowlandson did not know that during her captivity his wife had stopped smoking. She distributed the tobacco given to her among the Indians who had been kind to her, commenting later that the Indians were desperate and would smoke bark, if need be. Tom and Peter returned to Boston, but were back within a week with an Englishman to continue ransom negotiations. After much bravado and haggling, while Mary waited anxiously, scarcely able to hope, an agreement was reached. There followed an extraordinary scene in the camp as men and women crowded around the departing captive. "Some asked me to send them some bread," she wrote, "others some tobacco, others shaking me by the hand, offering me a hood and scarf to ride in; not one moving hand or tongue against it. Thus hath the Lord answered my poor desire, and the many earnest requests of others put up unto God for me. . . . O the wonderful power of God that I have seen, and the experience that I have had: I have been in the midst of those roaring lions, and savage bears, that feared neither God, nor man, nor the devil, by night and day, alone and in company: sleeping all sorts together, and yet not one of them ever offered me the least abuse of unchastity to me, in word or action. . . . I speak it in the presence of God, and to His glory. God's power is as great now, and as sufficient to save, as when he preserved

Daniel in the lion's den; or the three children in the fiery furnace. I may as well say as his Psalm 136, 1, *Oh give thanks unto the Lord for He is good, for His mercy endureth forever.*"[66]

The battle at Sudbury and the ransom of Mary Rowlandson mark the war's turning point. That year elections came earlier than usual. The General Court and townspeople of Boston assembled on May 3 for the election day sermon. As always, it would be a political statement. For that very reason, the choice of ministers to deliver these sermons alternated between the deputies and the magistrates. In 1676 it was the magistrates' turn to choose a speaker, and they asked William Hubbard of Ipswich. They chose him partly to counteract Increase Mather, who was more and more irritating in his insistence that the war was the fault of the English and that the magistrates were negligent in their duty to enforce the moral law. William Hubbard was Leverett's age, almost twenty years older than Mather, and one of the earliest graduates of Harvard. In 1656 he had become the junior minister at the church in Ipswich. His style of speaking, his rhetoric, his whole approach to the issues of the day differed from Mather's. Not that Hubbard was unorthodox in his Puritan doctrine, for he was not. Nor was it that he had abandoned a providential world view, for he had not. What set Hubbard apart from Mather in 1676 was reasonableness. "Sweet Reason" Benjamin Colman would call it in the next century. Reason and moderation were his keynotes. Even the title of his sermon conveys the change of tone and attitude: "The Happiness of a People in the Wisdome of their Rulers Directing, and in the Obedience of their Brethren Attending unto what Israel Ought to Do." Not only did it proclaim the government had been wise in its conduct of the war, but it suggested that happiness would follow a quiet obedience to the government, rather than breast-beating abasement before God.

Hubbard was a precise man, who loved to spin out the logical implications of his argument. Always he strove toward a cautious middle ground. On the question of toleration of other religions, for example, he wrote, "It is scarce possible to give any general rule about Toleration, that will suit with all times and places." That remark alone was enough to put Hubbard and Mather on opposite sides. The conduct of the war, however, was the main issue and the reason the magistrates had chosen Hubbard for this occasion. Hubbard agreed with Mather that God had a controversy with New England; but his analysis of the provoking evils was put in such a way as to have a meaning far different from Mather's.

"I shall instance but in two things . . . most likely to render us obnoxious," he wrote. They were: "1. Spiritual Pride. 2. A Spirit of Worldly-mindedness." To be sure, Hubbard rehearsed at length the evils of worldliness, the self-conscious and proud hair styles, the immodest dress: "Let all due testimony be borne against this kind of pride." Hubbard went on, however, ". . . but it is another sort, spiritual pride, that is so offensive in the sight of God, and is indeed the root whence the other springs." Spiritual pride, "some secret heart evill" too deep-hidden for church censures or published laws to mend, this was the real root of God's anger with New England. Not pride in dress, but secret pride in spirit. That finger pointed, if it pointed at anyone, straight to Increase Mather.[67] The General Court paid to have Hubbard's sermon printed, and he dedicated it to Mather's *bête noire,* Governor John Leverett.

MATHER'S HISTORY OF THE WAR

Increase Mather had just begun to write a history of the war when Hubbard delivered his election day sermon. Mather stopped work on his history to answer Hubbard, working steadily night and day for a week.[68] He wanted to place the war in the context of a providential world view in which the war served some purpose of God's and in which the Indians were the agents of that purpose. No other explanation seemed possible to him. He detected in Hubbard's sermon a fundamental difference. Hubbard explained the war primarily in secular terms of troop movements and war material. Mather saw a separation between religious and worldly ways of understanding. He laid out in the simplest language the nature of New England's errand, the role of the ministers in Puritan society, and the reason why the Scriptures were used as they were to understand events. Discarding the sermon form, he wrote an essay instead; then freed from the formal requirements of the sermon and intent on explaining an unpopular view of the enemy, Mather presented one of his most readable explanations of the Puritan world view. When it was published, he called it *An Earnest Exhortation to the Inhabitants of New England.*

Early in this essay, Mather explained and justified his constant use of scripture. To him biblical events had as much relevance as events in 1676. Whatever happened in history, that is in time, was related vertically to God outside of time.[69] He did not think of events as a sequence of cause and effect in the world. "The wayes of God," he wrote, "are ever-

AN EARNEST
EXHORTATION
To the Inhabitants of
New-England,
*To hearken to the voice of God
in his late and present*
DISPENSATIONS
As ever they defire to efcape another Judgement, feven times
greater then any thing which as yet hath been.

By *INCREASE MATHER*; Teacher of a Church
in *Bofton* in *New-England.*

Lev. 26.23,24. *And if you will not be Reformed by thefe things, but
will walk contrary unto me, then will I walk contrary unto you, I
will punifh you, yet feven times for your fins.*
Jer. 13.17. *But if you will not hear it, my foul fhall weep in fecret
places.*
1 Cor. 10 11. *Now all thefe things hapned unto them for enfamples,
and they are written for our Admonition, upon whom the ends of
the World are come.*

B O S T O N
Printed by *John Fofter*: And are to be Sold over againft
the *Dove*. 1 6 7 6.

An Earnest Exhortation, 1676, by Mather, placing King Philip's War in context of
providential world view; printed by John Foster

A BRIEF

HISTORY

OF THE

VVAR

WITH THE

INDIANS

IN

NEW-ENGLAND.

From *June* 24. 1675. (when the firſt *Engliſhman* was Murdered by the *Indians*) to *Auguſt* 12. 1676. when *Philip*,
alias *Metacomet*, the principal Author and
Beginner of the War, was ſlain.

Wherein the Grounds, Beginning, and Progreſs of the War, is ſummarily
expreſſed. Together with a ſerious EXHORTATION to the
Inhabitants of that Land.

By *INCREASE MATHER*, Teacher of a Church of
Chriſt, in *Boſton* in *New-England*.

Lev. 26. 25. *I will bring a Sword upon you, that ſhall avenge the quarrel of the Covenant.*
Pſal. 107.43. *Whoſo is wiſe and will obſerve theſe things, even they ſhall underſtand the*
loving Kindneſs of the Lord.
Jer. 22. 15. *Did not thy Father do Judgment and Juſtice, and it was well with him?*

Segnius irritant animos demiſſa per aures,
Quam quæ ſunt occulis commiſſa fidelibas.   *Horat.*
Lege Hiſtoriam ne fias Hiſtoria.   *Cic.*

London, Printed for *Richard Chiſwell,* at the Roſe and Crown in St. *Pauls*
Church-Yard, according to the Original Copy Printed
in *New-England.* 1676.

Courtesy of the John Carter Brown Library at Brown University

A Brief History of the War with the Indians, 1676, reflecting Mather's confidence
that he related events "truly and impartially"; reprinted in London at the Rose
and Crown, St. Paul's Church-Yard for Richard Chiswell

lasting; wherefore he brings the same Judgements upon his People now as in the dayes of old, in case there be the same transgressions." It followed that, "if then we would know why Droughts, Blastings, &c. have been upon our Land, let us search the Scriptures, and see for what sins those Judgements have befallen God's Israel of old."[70] If the people wanted to understand the war, "let us look into the Scripture and there see what sins have in former ages brought the punishment of the *Sword* upon a professing People: and if those very sins are prevailing amongst us, write upon it, that it is for them, that this Judgment is come upon us."[71]

Hubbard's sermon had criticized the secret pride of some ministers, but the ministers, Mather wrote, play an all-important part in understanding the war, for it is they who are chosen by God to be his messengers. Never mind that from time to time ministers may be wrong. The important thing is that they are the Lord's Watchmen and Seers, "and therefore you may expect that God will communicate Light to you by them."[72]

It was necessary to know what sins had caused God's anger in the past and what same sins offended God in contemporary Massachusetts in order to effect a reformation, "*a due execution of wholsome laws which are founded on the Word of God.*" Mather pointed to the magistrates. They were responsible for enforcing the law. His tone was carefully calm and impersonal, but the meaning was clear enough. "I have read, that it is a rule in *Politicks, that a bad Executioner of Laws is worse than a violator of them.* Our defect is not so much in respect of the want of good Laws, as in the non-execution of those Laws that are good. It were better never to make Laws for the suppressing of Evils that are provoking in the sight of God, than not to see them faithfully executed when they are made."[73]

A case in point was the proliferation of drinking places, licensed and unlicensed. Mather continued to believe, despite his quarrel with Governor Leverett, in a golden age of the first fathers. "When as our Fathers were *Patterns of Sobriety,* they would not drink a cup of wine nor strong drink, more than should suffice nature, and conduce to their health, men of latter time could transact no business, nor hardly ingage in any discourses, but it must be over a pint of wine or a pot of beer, yea so as that Drunkenness in the sight of man is become a common Sin, but how much more that which is Drunkenness in the sight of God."[74] Mather refused to dine with the Artillery Company on the occasion of their annual election of officers that June, "because it was in an ordinary, contrary to the Law established, as considering, it would not be possible to

Reforme the common sort of people in things of that count, if Leaders did not set before them a good example."[75]

The most scandalous behavior during the war, Mather thought, was how the English treated the Indians, with no distinctions between friend and foe: "What madness and rage hath there been against all Indians whatsoever."[76] "I doe believe," he wrote, "that many Englishmen that look with disdainfull eye upon these poor Praying Indians, shall see a number of them sitting down with Abraham, Isaac and Jacob in the Kingdome of God, when I pray God they may not see themselves shut out." Mather was shocked that even church members were guilty of indiscriminate racism.[77] He stubbornly chose this time of danger, of all times, to take up the Indians' cause.

The lumping together of all Indians caused people to forget the missionary aspect of New England's errand in the wilderness; other colonies were started for material purposes but New England for religious purposes, Mather said in his essay. "Our Fathers came hither to this end, that they might *Propagate the Gospel,* and be instrumental to set up the Kingdome of the Lord Jesus amongst the *Heathen.*"[78] It was a great sin that so little had been done to that end. The men of the first generation would be saddened, if they knew the spirit of the present generation, "who will neither believe that there is any good work begun amongst the Indians, nor yet desire and pray that it might be so."[79] Mather quoted the charter of the company, which gave it as an official purpose of the colony to win the Indians to Christianity. When he published *An Earnest Exhortation,* he included with it John Foster's woodcut of the Massachusetts seal, which in a masterpiece of irony showed a nearly naked Indian speaking the words "Come over and help us."[80]

Both Mather and Hubbard agreed that land hunger was a cause of the war and a threat to the Puritan communities. Families were beginning to move out of organized towns into the wilderness. "Let there be no more Plantations erected in New-England," Mather wrote, "where people professing Christianity shall live like Indians, without any solemn invocation on the name of God, and altogether without instituted worship."[81] "*Land! Land!* hath been the Idol of many in *New-England:* whereas the first Planters here that they might keep themselves together were satisfied with one Acre for each person, as his propriety, and after that with twenty Acres for a Family, how have Men since coveted after the earth, that many hundreds nay thousands of Acres, have been engrossed by one man, and they that profess themselves Christians have forsaken Churches and Ordinances, and all for land and elbow-room enough in the World. Lot would forsake the Land of Canaan and the Church . . . that he might have better worldly accomodations in Sodome. . . ."⁸²

Assuming the war against the Indians would be won, what should be done with the Indians' land? Mather proposed it should be used to support public education. "Should *Academical Learning* fall in this land, it would be one of the saddest Omens that could be. Ignorance and Barbarisme would overspread the face of succeeding generations. . . . If ever God shall give us the lands of our enemies, I cannot think how they can be disposed of better, or more to Gods glory, and publick advantage, than for the support of schools. And what a wonderfull providence will it be, if Barbarians should occasion the promotion of *good Literature?*"⁸³

Mather saved *An Earnest Exhortation* until he finished his *Brief History of the War with the Indians in New-England.* He was so pleased with the *Exhortation* that, when he wrote the preface to the history, he said, "the thing which I mainly designed in the history, was the subsequent *Exhortation* which is annexed herewith, wherein I have desired to approve myself as in the sight of God, speaking what I believe God would have me to speak, without respect to any person in this world."⁸⁴ The one thing he said he would have changed in the *Exhortation* was to provide more emphasis on the importance of carrying out the mission to the Indians as the first fathers' errand. "It is a great pity then, that we in *New-England,* who do not come behind others in Profession, and Pretences to Religion, should fall short in real endeavors, for the promotion, and propagation of Religion, & Christianity amongst those that have been for ages that are past, *without God, and without Christ and strangers to the Commonwealth of Israel.*"⁸⁵ Thus did this obstinate preacher address the thousands of New England men and women who had lost members of their families in the Indian war.

Over the summer of 1676, the tide of war turned strongly in favor of the English. By mid-June the government felt secure enough to offer amnesty to Indians who surrendered. Every week bands of Indians came in to the settlements. Often their men volunteered to change sides and help the English hunt down the enemy still in the woods. When the English went on the offensive, they found the help of these new Indian allies invaluable. The government declared June 29 to be a day of public thanksgiving. In August, tough, woods-wise Benjamin Church, that same man who had been warned by Awashonks of Philip's impending attack, led a party mostly of Indians, many of them veterans of the fight against the English six months earlier, in a search for Philip and his shrinking band. After a hair-raising chase, they caught up with him. Metacomet, known to the English as King Philip, was shot in the field by an Indian in Benjamin Church's party. They carried his head in triumph to Plymouth; the severed hands went to Boston for display.[86] It was Church, the prototype of the later American frontiersman, who brought the war to its close. Mather would have said he was the secondary cause.

When peace came at last, Increase Mather clung to his dire warnings. Even if God's punishments were over for the time being, that was no reason to relax in security. Moral reformation still had not come about. "God forbid," he wrote, "that we should act as if we were delivered to do abominations, for then it is certain that the continuance of this affliction would have been a far greater mercy, than deliverance out of it."[87]

Mather explained in the introduction to his history of the war that he had begun it when he read several inaccurate and even malicious accounts suspected of being written by Quakers.[88] In fact, however, his beginning seems more closely associated with William Hubbard's delivery of his election day sermon, "The Happiness of a People." Mather wrote morning and afternoon for the next two days on "Hist of warr with Indians,"[89] but within a week he put it aside to write *An Earnest Exhortation*. He resumed work on the history in June, finished the "Exhortation" by July 26, and finished the history on August 21, having written of the summer's climactic events as they were happening.[90]

Mather expressed in his preface the same concerns about writing history that he expressed in his biography of his father: a combination of diffidence and justification. "I hope that in one thing," he wrote, "(Though it may be in little else) I have performed the part of an *Historian,* viz. in endeavouring to relate things truly and impartially, and doing the best I could that I might not lead the *Reader* into a Mistake. *History* is indeed in itself a profitable Study. . . . Yea and it is proper for the Ministers of God to ingage themselves in Services of this nature."[91] *An Earnest Exhortation* and *A Brief History* were printed both separately and together in the fall of 1676, and by winter Richard Chiswell published an edition of the history in London. It sold five hundred copies before it was upstaged by another history of the war, this one by Hubbard. Chiswell sent the remainder of the London edition to Mather to distribute as he pleased.[92]

Hubbard had worked during the winter of 1676–1677 on his own history of the war. It was a much longer work than Mather's and one which was far more secular than Mather's in its treatment of historical causation. He finished and published the book in the spring of 1677.[93] Mather at once went over it looking for mistakes.[94] Hubbard's history covered the whole span of Puritan-Indian relations. To compete with it, Mather followed his own history with a short book on the relations between the Indians and the English from the time of settlement to the start of King Philip's War. This new book, *A Relation Of the Troubles which have hapned in New-England, By reason of the Indians there* (Boston, 1677), concentrates on the Pequot war of 1637. Mather's interest was less in a narrative record than in filling out his interpretation of the role the Indians played in providential history. He repeated the awkward combination of narrative history and theoretical essay by adding *An Historical Discourse Concerning the Prevelancy of Prayer* to the new book. Mather's efforts at writing history were obsolete even in his own day. His histories of Indian wars were not reprinted in the colonial period, while Hubbard's went through seven editions.

CHAPTER 4

Spiritual Leadership

[1676-1680]

It was November 1676. The war was only just over. Increase Mather tossed fitfully in bed. It would not be daylight for several hours. The dark city huddled under a cold rain, and outside his bedroom a wind swept off the bay. Suddenly Mather started up awake. Did he smell smoke? Before he reached the window he heard the first shouting in the streets. Boston was on fire.

The Mathers' house was downwind. Increase and Maria bundled up the children and got them out and through the wet streets to safety. By the time Increase had returned, he could hear the roar of flames. He ran upstairs with the two older boys—Cotton was thirteen, John, Seaborn's son, nineteen—and tried to save his library. He piled the most important manuscripts in Cotton's arms, then sent him off. He and John grabbed books from the shelves and threw them down the stairs. Maria, below, directed friends who had come in to help. They emptied the linen chests, pulled the bedding off, and saved almost everything, even the chairs, although heavier pieces had to be left. Outside in the street, Increase's books lay piled up in the rain. Someone in the crowd filched a little money from the heap of household furnishings.[1] When daylight came, the roaring of the fire was audible inside the study, and a hundred books and manuscripts still lay scattered about in Mather's rooms. He had to leave them behind. From the street, he and Maria watched as their home burst into flames. Not far away, the North Meetinghouse caught fire and was consumed in a brilliant inferno, collapsing into a mountain of charred timbers that steamed and hissed in the drizzle. From downwind they heard a succession of explosions as houses were blown up in a desperate effort to stop the fire's steady march. All told, seventy or eighty other houses were destroyed by the flames despite the cold rain. Scores of families who were members of his congregation lost everything. "This was the Fatal and dismall day," Mather wrote.[2]

Waking up in a strange bed the next morning, Increase reflected on what had happened. The habit of mind that sought to learn God's will in every event found no exception now. He and his wife had had a narrow escape but managed to save most of their possessions. "Surely, I see that God is a Loving and tender hearted Father, inasmuch as Hee is pleased to Correct me with so much gentlenes."[3] Two weeks later in a letter to John Cotton in Plymouth he expressed similar feelings.

"I see," Increase wrote, "that He is a tender hearted and loving Father in that he doth correct me with so much gentlenes, notwithstanding all my unworthy walkings before Him. He hath showed peculiar loving kindness to me (however vile and sinful) in this dispensation. It is true that my home is burnt . . ."; he went on to describe his losses before returning to God's purpose.[4]

"God (and I believe his angells) did so influence me that I could not sleep. . . ." He was amazed that he had urged Maria only weeks before to move, "because I feared desolation and fire was coming where I lived." How could he explain such a premonition? Once more Increase felt he had a prophetic power. Was it possible that God would really make some special use of him? The thought was overpowering, only to be whispered to his closest friend. "I would not have you speak of it," he wrote his brother-in-law, "so long as I am alive."[5] Meanwhile, Mather wrote, his congregation was impoverished and he feared his own weakness in faith may have been the cause of this fire. "I see plainly that I am so far from being able to keep judgement off from others, that I cannot keep it off from my own House.[6]

North Church was soon rebuilt, bigger than ever, a three-story wood frame building, heavy in design, with a gambrel roof and a square clock or bell tower.[7] The building was erected on the same triangular piece of land, Clarke's Square, within a shouting distance of the wharves and ware-houses at the water's edge. The Mather family lived for most of 1677 in a rented house. There Maria gave birth to another baby girl, Abigail. Sarah Cotton, Maria's mother, had died the year before, and in the summer of 1677 the old Cotton house was sold by the children. With Maria's share of £100, she and Increase purchased land of their own near the rebuilt church.[8] The house lot, one hundred feet by sixty feet, was on a street later to be named Hanover or Middle Street. In 1677 the North End was still rustic enough for it to be designated in the deed as "the street that leads from the Water Mill towards Winimeset ferry-place." The property on one side was owned by a widow and on the other by "Jethro the Negro." There Increase and his wife built a house, the first one of their own and the house in which they were to live out the rest of their lives.[9]

Even the losses to Mather's library in the November fire were restored. Leonard Hoar's widow, Bridget, who had married Hezekiah Usher, Jr., the Boston bookseller, offered Increase his choice from her first husband's books. Mather picked out ninety-seven titles, plus "pamphlets of diverse sorts." The books covered a broad spectrum of interests: theology, history, medicine, natural science, and philosophy. His library now rivaled Harvard College itself.[10]

THE DANGER OF APOSTASY: A CHALLENGE
TO THE MAGISTRATES

In the long run, Mather came to see the fire as another warning, like the Indian war. He was thinking of that warning and the sins of the country when the deputies asked him to preach the election day sermon in May 1677. It would be the occasion for another round in the political tug-of-war between deputies and magistrates. A year before, William Hubbard had pacified the General Court with his "Happiness of a People in the Wisdome of their Rulers." Now it was the deputies' turn, and they expected a different message from Increase Mather. They were not disappointed. In the most important election sermon of his life, *The Danger of Apostasy,* Mather cried out that the ruling magistrates and ministers were allowing New England to fall into sin. Surely they would suffer.

Mather reminded his audience of the mythic role of the first fathers in New England. "Let me speak freely (without offence to any) there never was a Generation that did so perfectly shake off the dust of Babylon, both as to Ecclesiastical and civil Constitution, as the first Generation of Christians that came unto this land for the Gospel's sake, where was there ever a place so like unto New Jerusalem as New-England hath been? It was once Dr. Twiss his opinion that when *new-Jerusalem* should come down from Heaven *America* would be the Seat of it. Truly that such a Type and emblem of new-Jerusalem, should be erected in so dark a corner of the world, is matter of deep meditation and admiration."[11]

You, the children of this New Jerusalem, Mather told his audience, should have obeyed our fathers. He quoted part of a passage from the book of Judges familiar to everyone, Judges 2 : 17: "And yet they would not harken unto their Judges, but they went a whoring after other gods. They turned quickly out of the way which their fathers walked in obeying the commandments of the Lord, but they did not so." Twice more in repeated phrases, Mather made the words an accusation of the apostasy of his own generation: "the Children did not so. . . . the Children did not so." The ominous rhetorical phrase, repeated and repeated again, sent a thrill through his audience. [12]

Increase singled out twelve men sitting in front of him in places of honor: the governor and eleven magistrates. The first responsibility, Mather said, rests with you. You are the rulers and the examples to all of us. He touched on their failure to support a learned ministry in every town, their failure to guarantee good grammar schools or to support the college. Magistrates, he said, had allowed towns to be built without even a church for public worship. They had permitted unorthodox worship to continue unrestrained. Mather was alluding both to the Baptists and to the Quakers. Each group had been meeting in private houses in Boston since 1674.

John Hull noted in his diary that year, "This summer, the Anabaptists that were wont to meet at Noddle's Island met at Boston on the Lord's Day. . . . Some Quakers are also come and seated in Boston. Some of the magistrates will not permit any punishment to be inflicted on heretics as such." Samuel Sewall noted this extraordinary event on July 8, 1677: "In Sermon time there came in a female Quaker, in a Canvas Frock, her hair disshevelled and loose like a Periwigg, her face as black as ink, led by two other Quakers, and two other followed. It occasioned the greatest and most amazing uproar that I ever saw. Isaiah I.12.14." [13] "Sinfull Toleration," Mather called it: "indeed the *Toleration* of all Religions and Perswasions, is the way to have no true Religion at all left." [14]

Pride, Mather said, was everywhere. To be sure, magistrates could not rub out pride from men's hearts. But they could prevent outward pride in dress; they could prevent drunkenness and the debauching of the Indians by drunkenness. "Certainly (much honoured in the Lord)," he addressed the magistrates directly, in front of everyone, "if your blessed Fathers and Predecessors were alive, and in place, it would not be so; If *Winthrop, Dudley, Endicot* were upon the Bench, such profaneness as this would soon be suppressed." [15]

Then came the threat: If you have "become cold and indifferent in things of God . . . you may believe it, that God will *change* either *you* or your government *ere long.*"[16] Never had the magistrates had such a tongue-lashing in public.

Magistrates alone were not responsible. Ministers, too, Mather said, must bear part of the blame, because some ministers admitted unregenerate persons to the sacraments. He put his finger on the most sensitive of all issues in New England Puritan worship: "I wish there be not Teachers found in our Israel, that have espoused loose, large Principles here, designing to bring all persons to the Lords Supper, who have an Historical Faith, and are not scandalous in life, although they never had Experience of a work of Regeneration on their Souls. . . ." The neglect of the experience of regeneration, he said, was the foundation of the great apostasy.[17] New England had never been agreed on this point. Thomas Hooker and Thomas Shepard had both argued that the hopes of a new birth might be sufficient and that faithful candidates should be encouraged to the Lord's Supper as a preparation for the experience.[18] Now some members of the next generation were developing these preparationist theories, and Increase Mather sensed, accurately, that they would destroy the church as he knew it.

After magistrates and ministers, Mather turned to the people and the people's elected representatives, the deputies. He did not rebuke. His tone changed from judgment to encouragement. He pleaded with the deputies and the people of this New Jerusalem to live up to their fathers' principles, and urged them to promote a general renewal of church covenants. With a few quiet words, Mather brought his sermon to a close.

Increase had presented himself more frankly than ever before as the spiritual leader of New England. He threw down the gauntlet to the ruling magistrates and the ministers, declared himself the champion of the brethren of the churches, and called the people of Massachusetts back to a vision of their holy purpose in America. The sermon outraged Governor Leverett and the magistrates and they refused to print it. Mather had anticipated their anger. What honor has a prophet in his own land?

THE BOSTON PRESS AND THE POWER OF
THE PRINTED WORD

The power of this New World Jeremiah would be in part the power of the press. Thirty years earlier, the handpress President Dunster had acquired with his wife's estate had served all the colony's needs. When Dunster retired, he sold it to the college. At first the presswork was done by Stephen Day, and later by his son Matthew. Soon, however, Samuel

WUNAUNCHEMOOKAONK NASHPE

MATTHEVV.

CHAP. I.

a Luke
3.23.
b Gen.
21.3.
c Gen.
25. 26.
d Gen.
29. 35.
e Gen.
38. 27.
f 1 Chr.
2.5.
Ruth
4.18.

g 1 Sam.
16.1.
& 17.
12.
h 2Sam.
12. 24.
i 1 Chr.
3.10.

k 2 Kin.
20. 21.
1 Chro.
3.10.

l 1Chr.
3. 16,
17.

Ppometuongane *a* book Jeſus Chriſt, wunnaumonuh David, wunnaumonuh Abraham.

2 *b* Abraham wunnaumonieu Iſaakoh, kah *c* Iſaak wunnaumonieu Jakobuh, kah *d* Jakob wunnaumonieu Judaſoh, kah weematoh.

3 Kah *e* Judas wunnaumonieu Phareſoh kah Zarahoh wutch Tamarhut, kah *f* Phares wunnaumonieu Ezromoh, kah Ezrom wunnaumonieu Aramoh.

4 Kah Aram wunnaumonieu Aminadaboh, kah Aminadab wunnaumonieu Naaſſonoh, kah Naaſſon wunnaumonieu Salmonoh.

5 Kah Salmon wunnaumonieu Boazoh wutch Rachab, kah Boaz wunnaumonieu Obeduh wutch Ruth, kah Obed wunnaumonieu Jeſſeoh.

6 Kah *g* Jeſſe wunnaumonieu David ketaſſootoh, kah *h* David ketaſſoot wunnaumonieu Solomonoh wutch ummittamwuſſuh Uriah.

7 Kah *i* Solomon wunnaumonieu Rehoboamoh, kah Rehoboam wunnaumonieu Abiahoh, kah Abia wunnaumonieu Aſahoh.

8 Kah Aſa wunnaumonieu Joſaphatoh, kah Joſaphat wunnaumonieu Joramob, kah Joram wnnnaumonieu Oziaſoh.

9 Kah Ozias wunnaumonieu Jothamoh, kah Jotham wunnaumonieu Achazoh, kah Achaz wunnaumonieu Ezekiaſoh.

10 Kah *k* Ezekias wunnaumonieu Manaſſes, kah Manaſſes wunnaumonieu Ammonoh, kah Ammon wunnaumonieu Joſiaſoh.

11 Kah Joſias wunnaumonieu Jechoniaſoh, kah wematoh, ut papaume na uttooche máſinneóhteámuk ut Babylon.

12 Kah mahche miſſinneohteáhettit ut Babylon, *l* Jechonias wunnaumonieu Sa'athieloh, kah Salathiel wunnaumonieu Zorobabeloh.

13 Kah Zorobabel wunnaumonieu Abiudoh, kah Abiud wunnaumonieu Eliakimoh, kah Eliakim wunnaumonieu Azoroh.

14 Kah Azor wunnaumonieu Sadokoh, kah Sadok wunnaumonieu Achimoh, kah Achim wunnaumonieu Eliudoh.

15 Kah Eliud wunnaumonieu Eleazaroh,

kah Eleazar wunnaumonieu Matthanoh, kah Matthan wunnaumonieu Jakoboh.

16 Kah Jakob wunnaumonieu Joſephoh, weſſukeh Mary noh mo wachegit Jeſus uttiyeuoh áhennit Chriſt.

17 Nemehkuh wame pometeongaſh wutch Abrahamut onk yean Davidut, nabo yauwude pometeongaſh ; neit wutch Davidut onk yean ummiſſinohkonauh ut Babylon, nabo yauwudt pometeongaſh : neit wutch ummiſſinohkonaoh ut Babylon nó pajeh uppeyonat Jeſus Chriſt, nabo yauwudt pometeongaſh.

18 Kah Jeſus Chriſt *m* wunneetuonk yeu mo, nagum okaſoh Maryboh kah Joſeph quoſhodhettit (aſquam naneeſinhettekup) miſkauau wutché keteauónat naſhpe Naſhauanittooh.   *m* Luke 1.27.

19 Neit weſſukeh Joſephuh wunnomwaénuœoh, matta mo wuttenantamœun wutáyímáuoh muſſiſſewautut, unnantam kemeu nuppogken yeuoh.

20 Webe natwontog yeuſhog kuſſeh wutangelſumoh Lord wunnaeihtunkquoh ut unnukquomuonganit, noowau, Joſeph ken wunnaumonuh David, ahque wabeſiſh nemunon Mary kummittamwos, newutche uttiyeuwoh wachegit, ne naſhpe wunneetupanatamwe Naſhauanittœur.

21 Kah woh neechau wuſiaumon woh kuttiſſowen *n* Jeſus, newutche woh wadchanau ummiſſinninnumoh wutch ummatcheſeongaſhnooóut.   *n* Luke 1.31.

22 Wame yeuſh n nihyeupaſh ne woh n niſh toh anoowop Lord naſhpeu manittoowompuh noowau.

23 *o* Kuſſeh peenomp piſh wompequau, kah piſh neechau wannaumonuh, kah piſh wuttiſſowenouh Emanuel, yeu nauwuttamun, God kuwetomukqun.   *o* Iſaiah 7.14.

24 Neit Joſeph omohket wutch kouénat, wutuſſen uttoh áaukqut wutangelſumoh Lord, kah neemunau ummittamwuſſoh.

25 Kah matta oowaheuh nó pajeh wunneechanat mohtommeeinitcheh wunnaumonuh, kah wuttiſſowenuh Jeſus.

CHAP. II.

JESUS *a* neekit at Bethlem ut Judea ukkeſukkodtumut Herod Sontim, kuſſeh waantamwáenuog wamohettit wutchepwoeiyeu Jeruſalemwaut.   *a* Luke 2.6.

A 2   2 Noo-

Courtesy, American Antiquarian Society

Seal of Massachusetts Bay Colony, designed in 1629 and printed in 1676 in *An Earnest Exhortation* from woodblock by John Foster, first printer in Boston and also astronomer and friend of Mather

Green became the printer in charge and sire of a great line of American printers.

Meanwhile, in England a Puritan missionary society to the American Indians, the New England Company, had raised money to send another press to America for the use of John Eliot, who proposed to print the Bible in Algonquian. The society sent over a young, rambunctious printer named Marmaduke Johnson to do the work. The Indian press was put with the other in a little-used brick building on the college campus. By 1663, Marmaduke Johnson had printed Eliot's Indian Bible. Johnson went to England for a visit and brought back his own press, the colony's third, and new type. He wanted to set up in Boston, but the General Court refused.

History has left no direct record why the General Court refused at first

Printing press used by Isaiah Thomas, the type of press used by all colonial printers

to license a printing press in Boston. Most likely the court believed, like governments elsewhere in the English-speaking world, that printing presses were dangerous. The seventeenth century was everywhere one of revolutions and civil war. All governments felt insecure. One recalls the remark of Sir William Berkeley, Governor of Virginia, in 1671: "I thank God, there are no free schools nor printing, and I hope we shall not have these hundred years; for learning has brought disobedience, and heresy, and sects into the world, and printing has divulged them, and libels against the best government. God keep us from both!" [19] As long as there was a printing press in Masssachusetts, the General Court reasoned, it was much better that it be isolated in the village of Cambridge and not in Boston, which had been since the days of Ann Hutchinson a more turbulent, volatile place, a busy seaport and the seat of government. When the prohibition was eventually lifted, book publishing in Massachusetts began an explosive growth. Increase Mather would be at the center of it.

For the time being, all three printing presses operated in Cambridge. More volumes came off the Indian press for Eliot's "Indian Library." Commercial printing and printing on government order was done by Samuel Green, Marmaduke Johnson, or both of them together, though their relationship was strained when Marmaduke courted one of Green's daughters without permission. The younger man persisted in trying to move to Boston, and in 1674 he finally received permission. Perhaps Mather played a role in this decision; on the same day that the General Court issued Marmaduke Johnson a license to print in Boston, it placed Mather and Thomas Thacher, minister of the Third Church, on the board of licensers. [20] Johnson moved his printing equipment to the city, but he died on Christmas day, 1674, before he could open for business. It was a critical moment in the history of American publishing.

Increase Mather thought he knew just the person to take over the press in Boston. It was John Foster, a friend from Dorchester, ten years younger than himself. Foster had been baptized by Richard Mather, had been graduated from Harvard College, and had then taught school off and on in Dorchester. He was interested in things mechanical and scientific. He had an artist's and a craftsman's turn of mind. He copied a portrait of Richard Mather, cut a woodblock from it, and produced the first print made in English America. [21] He drew a map of New England and cut a woodblock of that, too, another first. The map was soon pirated and reprinted in London. [22] His woodblock of the Massachusetts seal printed in *An Earnest Exhortation* (1676) would become one of the most commonly used emblems in the history of New England printing. Pre-

sumably Foster cut the woodblocks from which he illustrated his annual
Boston almanac and possibly the majestic cut of King David playing a
harp used in Russell's *Cambridge Almanac* of 1684.[23] Later Foster would
become an amateur astronomer and contribute to Isaac Newton's great
work on the movement of the planets. Encouraged by Increase Mather,
and perhaps with a loan from Mather and John Eliot, Foster purchased
the Johnson press and opened for business at the Sign of the Dove, in
Boston in 1675.[24]

The first two books off Foster's press were sermons by Mather,[25] both
examples of Puritan sensationalism well chosen to appeal to a hungry
reading public. One had been preached at the hanging of two men convicted for murder—the crowd had been so large, five thousand some
said, that beams holding up the galleries in the North End meetinghouse began to crack, and the whole performance had to be moved to the
larger South meetinghouse. The other sermon was a memorial Increase
preached for men killed and maimed in an explosion aboard a ship in the
harbor. Among the dead were two of the wealthiest men in the North
End, John Freake, a merchant whose portrait in sumptuous dress was
painted shortly before the explosion,[26] and the son-in-law of Major
Thomas Clark, who had given the land for the new North End meetinghouse; and Captain Scarlett, another merchant prince of Puritan Boston,
whose wharves and warehouses bordered the water's edge on the North
End. These first two popular books began Foster's bid to shift the center
of publishing from Cambridge to Boston. Samuel Green fought the
competition. He started legal proceedings to repossess the type Foster
had acquired with Marmaduke Johnson's estate. The legal battle dragged
on, and although Green finally won, Foster by then had acquired new
and better type from England.[27] Increase and his son Cotton and John
Eliot of Roxbury all helped Foster in this struggle. Within five years,
Foster's press had eclipsed the older ones in Cambridge, and Boston
was on its way to becoming the center of book publishing in English
America.

In 1675 New England ministers ordinarily did not write books or
publish sermons at their own initiative. Certain kinds of sermons were
published as a matter of course—for example, funeral sermons, or the
last sermon of a retiring minister. After 1670, election day sermons were
often but not always printed. In the 1670s most sermons published in
Massachusetts were of these kinds. Much of the other output was reprints of popular devotional books. Thomas Shepard's sermons printed

after his death as *The Sincere Convert* (Cambridge, 1641), appeared in nineteen editions by 1692.[28] Shepard and John Cotton were the popular spokesmen for Puritan spirituality from Richard Mather's generation. In the decade of the 1670s, only three men published sermons on their own account: Samuel Danforth, Samuel Willard, and Increase Mather, and Mather published three times as much as the other two put together. Yet so new was it for a minister in New England to publish, that before 1675 Increase Mather had published only twice in New England under his own name, and then often with a prefatory apology.[29]

Samuel Danforth published a sermon on a sensational criminal trial for sodomy; that was as far as his publishing genius went. Samuel Willard, on the other hand, shared Mather's creative drive. Willard was a year younger and two years behind Mather at Harvard. When Increase went to England in the 1650s, Willard went to minister to the small town of Groton on the extreme northwestern frontier. In 1673 he published a collection of sermons delivered there, *Useful Instructions for a Professing People in Times of Great Security and Degeneracy.* To have published a collection of sermons from so small and isolated a village, and at a time when no one else in Massachusetts was doing it, is evidence of Willard's great personal confidence and inner drive. Groton was overrun during the Indian war, and Willard came to Boston. In 1678 he accepted the pulpit of the Third Church, and, true to its origins, became Boston's most liberal minister. Mather and Willard soon dominated the religious life of the city. Willard earned a reputation as a gentle, warm-hearted man, quite unlike the image Increase chose for himself. But these differences of personality were trivial in comparison to their agreement on fundamentals. Willard and Mather held a similar view of Christian history and New England's place in it. They would work closely together on almost every important church issue for the next twenty-three years.

Increase Mather was the first to exploit fully the potential of the printing press. In the decade of the 1670s, when Danforth published one sermon and Willard his one collection, Mather published eight volumes of sermons, two of which were collections. Besides these, he had published the biography of his father, his two histories of the Indian wars, and his two books on baptism. Most of his sermons were not outrageously long, as is sometimes imagined, but usually from fifteen to twenty pages in printed version, no longer than an ordinary university lecture today. A single sermon delivered in two parts, morning and afternoon, would be longer, of course, but a preaching performance of two hours was exceptional enough for Mather himself to remark on it. Sermons were ordinarily not written out beforehand, but Mather, like others, kept a permanent record in outline form of the sermons he preached.[30] Sometimes when he prepared sermons for the press, he took the occasion to lengthen them with further examples and illustrations, and since he did not preach from a written text, preparing a sermon for the press was a creative act that involved restating the ideas in fresh language. Later in his career, Mather would work from shorthand notes taken down as he preached, and later, too, he would have the help of his son Cotton as a stenographer and amanuensis. For the present, however, Increase hunched for hours on end over his writing table and scratched out his own manuscripts with a quill pen. No wonder the daily entries in his diary are scribbles. More than once he apologized for his bad handwriting. Time for his books always had to be squeezed into the never-ending schedule of sermons. Time became more and more precious as the years passed.

Mather preached and wrote in a plain style. No one had explained more carefully than his father-in-law how and why a plain style in preaching brought men and women nearer to God. Ultimately, John Cotton had said, those who were to experience God would need no language at all, but would apprehend the essence of Christian love directly. Meanwhile, a plain style helped men and women approach in their earthly lives the perfect community of love and fellowship. Mather studied Cotton's books and manuscripts carefully, and when he preached on Christ, he tried to echo his illustrious ancestor. He used his own father as a model, too. Richard Mather, "studiously avoided obscure phrases, Exotick Words, or an unnecessary citation of Latine Sentences. . . . The Lord gave him an excellent faculty in making abstract things plain."[31] And Increase wrote of himself, *"Those few in the world that know anything of me will testify that my continued practice is Plainness in delivering the Truths of God,"* and, "Plain food is best *in a spiritual as well as a natural sense."*[32]

Plain, however, did not mean unlearned or narrow-minded. In his preface to *Some Important Truths* (1674), Increase stated emphatically his belief in the importance of a liberal arts education. When he was gone, he told his church, they must replace him with a man of "humane learning." "Believe not those that would perswade you that Schools of Learning, Colleges, &c. are Antichristianism, or late Popish Inventions." And do not forget books. "Books are Talents in God's service. They are a weariness to the flesh, but a testimony to be produced."[33] Nor did plain style mean a simple rhetoric. Literary style in the Boston of Increase Mather's day was heavily influenced by the demands and opportunities of public oratory. The Puritan sermon—text, doctrine, uses—dictated rhetorical form as precisely as the Prayer Book did the Anglican liturgy. English Puritan preaching since the sixteenth century had emphasized a plain meaning to a plain audience. In the seventeenth century, it also emphasized oratorical skills that heightened the audience's emotional response. Furthermore, Mather's written style was different from his spoken style. Consider, for example, the following excerpt from an introduction Mather wrote to a sermon published by a colleague: "The Lord intended some great thing when He planted these Heavens, and laid the foundations of this Earth, and said unto New England (as sometimes to Sion) *Thou Art My People:* And what should that be, if not so a Scripture-Pattern of Reformation, as to Civil, but especially in Ecclesiastical respects, might be here erected, as a First Fruits of that which shall in due time be accomplished the whole world throughout, in that day when there shall be one Lord and his Name one over all the earth."[34] The structure of the passage is complex, even though the cadences cry out to be spoken aloud.

Sermons accounted for fewer than half of the books Mather published, at least in the first thirty years of his writing career, but they were a significant part of his work, usually published in groups of four to six. They fell into many categories, some evangelical, pleading and urgent in tone, as Mather sought to open his audience to conversion or to reassure those already converted; others were topical sermons about recent events, political sermons delivered to the General Court, moralistic sermons about contemporary life, prophetical sermons warning of the dreadful consequences of sin. The prominence given these last, the jeremiads, in the history of American literature should not obscure the full range of preaching or distort the place of the jeremiad in seventeenth-century American culture. All Mather's sermons were cast in a conventional form that progressed inflexibly from an analysis of the text to its uses in everyday life. A measure of Mather's creative power was his ability to explore other literary forms. He was one of the very few men of his generation to do so. He published history, biography, theology, and science, and in doing so he used a wider range of literary forms than any other person in New England in his century, only to be outdone in the end by his son.

Writing and publishing became for Mather a principal means of exerting influence and gaining fame, if not fortune. He assiduously sent copies of his works to colleagues in America and England. Recipients, particularly from isolated towns and villages in New England, were warmly grateful for this connection with the great world of ideas and literature. A measure of Mather's growing prestige in the Boston book world was the number of times he was asked to write introductions "To The Reader" in other ministers' books. He became easily the most important spokesman in print of his generation. The impact of all this on the literary culture of Massachusetts is incalculable. Mather's example encouraged others. His patronage of John Foster and the first press in Boston started an expansion of printing that accelerated to the end of the century, long after Foster himself was gone. It is easy to see Mather's reflection in his son Cotton's enormous production, or in the writing and publishing of Samuel Sewall, Increase's lifelong friend and admirer.

BOOKS AS INSTRUMENTS

For four years Mather waited to declare himself publicly in support of the half-way covenant. During his recovery from the trauma surrounding his father's death, he had gathered together statements favoring infant baptism from the leading men of that first generation—his father, his father-in-law, his foster father John Norton, and several English spokesmen. As early as April 1671, Increase organized this material into a book. He circulated it to some colleagues and thought of publishing it then. For some reason he did not; perhaps the widespread popular hostility to the half-way covenant and the Third Church kept him from announcing his own change of mind.

Now, however, he made his position clear by publishing the manuscript, *First Principles of New-England* (Cambridge, 1675), and by writing and publishing a new book, *Discourse Concerning Baptism* (Cambridge, 1675), in which he argued the correctness of his stance. But he went further, and cracked open a door through which crowded, in the next quarter century, ideas which would revolutionize Massachusetts ecclesiology.

The question of infant baptism, he wrote, had not to do with grandparents, but with the fitness of the parents themselves.[35] If the parents were "visible believers," whether or not they were members of a particular church (for which an experience of regeneration was necessary), then their children were eligible for baptism: "*Visible believers have right to Baptisme for themselves and theirs.*"[36] Such baptism made children members of a visible, catholic (i.e., universal) church, distinct from and prior to membership in a particular, covenanted church. When Increase Mather wrote of a single, catholic church of visible members, he went beyond the Synod of 1662 and helped lay the groundwork for changes in the sacrament of baptism, the role of the ministry, and the nature of church membership.[37]

Strongest objection came from Dublin, where older brother Nathaniel wrote of Increase's new ideas, "I confess I beleeve not one of them."[38] Nathaniel had gone to Dublin on Samuel's death in 1672 and now served as minister to Samuel's congregation. Times were bitterly hard for him. His church was harassed by the Restoration government; it was impoverished and forced to meet illegally in private homes.[39] Perhaps this experience of persecution kept Nathaniel from accepting the more expansive ecclesiology of Increase, whose experience in America was one of steadily rising prosperity and support from the wider society. Nathaniel returned to the issue again in 1681–1682, after Increase had published another book on infant baptism:[40] "Surely your arguments for Infant Baptism are not, meethinks, cogent," Nathaniel wrote. "Your making children members of the Catholik visible Church . . . I confess I doe much wonder at. But I see Congregational principles are lost in New England, & all to open a dore for a larger administration of Baptisme."[41] And two weeks later: "As to the notion of a Church catholik, visible, integrall," none of the old writers support it. "The company or body, as you call them, of professing beleevers throughout the world are in truth no company, no body, having no compaction amongst themselves any more than the loose stones in the highways in Ireland . . . are an house."[42]

If these remarks from his older brother troubled Increase, he gave no sign of it. His two books on baptism published in 1675, which would have roused a storm of protest five years earlier, appeared without a ripple. He turned his attention to the growing body of church members, the baptized children, who were members of the church in name but all too often not regenerate. One afternoon in 1675, he sat down with the church records before him to figure out as best he could who were the "children" of his own North Church, that is, who were baptized in it, but not full, communicating, regenerate members. To his dismay, he found he could not tell for sure who had been baptized in his church and who had not. Mayo's records were almost useless and his own for the past ten years not much better.[43] As near as he could make out, there were in 1675 eighty-one baptized children of his church. They came from sixteen families. Some were already adults, twenty-two, twenty-four, and even in one case twenty-seven years old.[44] During the five years before the war, thirty-seven adults had joined Mather's church, and in the five-year period following the war, new memberships would rise to sixty-two. But baptisms grew faster; the proportion of "children" to adult

members was rising. By the end of the decade, the North End church
would have 144 adult members and 135 baptized "children."[45] These
were the Rising Generation, and their progress towards a new birth and
church membership became Mather's major preoccupation.

As Mather directed his evangelism at these young men and women,
his religious emphasis became more and more tribal. He seemed to argue
a preemptive right to church membership based on family. "Now God
hath seen good," he preached in 1678, "to cast the line of election so, as
that it doth (though not wholly, and only, yet) for the most part, run
through the loins of godly Parents. There are, it is true, Elect Children,
who are not born of Elect Parents, but there are few (if any) Elect Parents
without Elect Children."[46] He worried endlessly over his own children,
and frequently recorded in his diary his prayers for one or another of
them: "After I had prayed, as I was in my garden, and had this *soliloqui,*
'God has heard my prayer for this child, God will answer me, and the
child Shall live to do service for the lord his God, and the God of his
Father.' My heart was melted before the Lord, which meltings I think
were the worke of his Holy spirit. And therefore I am not altogether
without hope, that this child shall be blessed and made a blessing in his
generation. Amen! O God, in Christ Jesus, Amen!"[47] Or again, in his
diary: "Sept. 9. 1677. Quickened at the Lords Table, especially in praying that God would remember his Covenant with children, saying before
the Lord, Lord! our Fathers and mothers (as for many of us wee may say it)
are now in glory, and you wilt bring us to be with them, and also our
children after us, so as that they, and wee, and our children shall together
sound forth thi prayses to eternity."[48]

Thoughts like these brought Increase to heights of emotion: "In
speaking thus, Tears gushed from me before the Lord. I trust prayer and
Faith shall not be in vain. Oh! I have prevailed and obtained mercy for
my poor children. Amen! Lord Jesus!"[49]

These were feelings Mather could not say aloud. The conventions of
his Puritan culture prevented any father from expressing such tender
thoughts about children in public. Instead, in sermons and books Puritan
ministers confronted children and their parents with a fierce, judgmental
picture of childhood designed to terrify youth into an awareness of sin and
repentance. The most popular books for children were James Janeway's *A
Token for Children* and New England's own Michael Wigglesworth's long
poem, *The Day of Doom,* both relentlessly foreboding. Mather followed
the pattern. One day he addressed the six- and seven-year-old children
before him in the meetinghouse with these terrifying thoughts, not

original with him but formulae in the rhetoric of Puritan child-rearing. "If you dy and be not first new Creatures, better you had never been born: you will be left without excuse before the Lord, terrible witnesses shall rise up against you at the last day. Your Godly parents will testifie against you before the Son of God at that day."[50]

Mather often threatened even the youngest children that their parents might desert them at the day of judgment. His own father had said as much to him.[51] He preached and wrote, "I will most certainly profess unto Jesus Christ at the day of judgement, Lord, these are the Children, whom I spake often unto thy Name, publickly and privately, and I told them, that if they did not make themselves a new heart, and make sure of an interest in Christ, they should become damned creatures for ever-more; and yet they would not repent and believe the Gospel."[52] These warnings and threats were often accompanied with graphic images. In one of his most popular sermons, *The Wicked Man's Portion* (the same exe-cution sermon with which John Foster had opened his printing business in Boston), Mather warned the children in his audience thus: "*Disobe-dience to Parents* is a sin that is often punished with untimely death. . . . All you *disobedient children* that are here before the Lord this day, hearken to the Word of the Lord. There is a Scripture which methinks should strike Terror and Trembling into your Souls, It is that Prov. 30.17. *The eye that mocketh his Father and despiseth to obey his Mother, let the ravens of the valley pick it out, and the young eagles eat it.*"[53]

Many children, he said, are afraid to challenge their fathers and there-fore show their rebelliousness to their mothers. "It is to be feared," Mather warned them, "that such children will come to the Gallows, and be hanged in Gibbets for the ravens and eagles to feed upon them if they will."[54] Modern readers should beware of reading such sermons as ex-pressions of Puritan parents' true feelings. Such statements were conven-tions required by an absolute and literal belief in heaven and hell. In this same sermon, Mather found a subtle and indirect way of expressing those parental feelings convention forbade him to say outright. To illustrate the fate of disobedient children, he chose the story of Absalom from 2 Samuel, in which Absalom is caught by an overhanging tree branch, and while he is helpless, his enemy Joab thrusts darts into his body and has him cut down and killed. So much Mather recounted to his audience as an example of what happens to children who disobey their parents.

What Mather did not repeat, but what was familiar to everyone, was the rest of the story: the news of Absalom's death is brought to his father, King David, who was broken in grief. "And the King was moved, and

THE
FIRST PRINCIPLES
OF
NEW-ENGLAND,

Concerning
The Subject of Baptisme
&
Communion of Churches.

Collected partly out of the Printed Books, but chiefly out of the *Original Manuscripts* of the *First* and chiefe *Fathers* in the *New-English Churches*; With the Judgment of Sundry Learned Divines of the *Congregational Way* in *England*, Concerning the said Questions.

Published for the Benefit of those who are of the Rising Generation in New-England.

By *INCREASE MATHER*, Teacher of a Church in Boston in *New-England*

Deut. 32.7. *Remember the dayes of old,----Aske thy Father and he will shew thee, thy Elders & they will tell thee.*

Plal.102.18. *This shall be written for the Generation to come.*

Nihil mihi Authoritatis assumo, sed quæ ab alijs disperfa velut in ordinem Epitomata, Confcribo. *Veget. L. 1. C. 8.*

CAMBRIDGE
Printed by *Samuel Green*, 1 6 7 5.

The First Principles of New-England (1675), in which Mather defends infant baptism and the half-way covenant

THE NECESSITY
OF
REFORMATION
With the Expedients fubfervient
thereunto, afferted;
in Anfwer to two
Q U E S T I O N S

I. *What are the Evils that have provoked the Lord to bring his Judgments on New-England?*

II. *What is to be done that fo thofe Evils may be Reformed?*

Agreed upon by the
ELDERS and MESSENGERS
Of the Charches affembled in the

SYNOD

At Bofton *in* New-England,
Sept. 10. 1 6 7 9.

*Mal.*3.7. Even from the dayes of your Fathers yee are gone away from mine Ordinances, and have not kept them, Return unto me and I will return unto you,
faith the Lord of Hoft : but ye faid, Wherein fhall we return ?

Rev. 2. 4,5. Neverthelefs I have fomewhat againft thee, becaufe thou haft left thy
firft love. Remember therefore from whence thou art fallen, and Repent,
and doe the firft works; or elfe I will come unto thee quickly, and will remove
thy Candleftick out of his place, except thou Repent.

B O S T O N;
Printed by *John Fofter.* In the Year, 1 6 7 9.

The Synod of 1679, third in Massachusetts's history, which sought to foster religious revival by urging congregations to renew their covenants

went up to the chamber over the gate, and wept: & as he went, thus he said, O my sonne Absalom, my sonne, my sonne Absalom! Wolde God I had dyed for thee, O Absalom, my sonne, my sonne!"[55]

The Geneva Bible has a gloss here which explains that David accepted God's judgment as just, but retreated into his room, because "he colde not otherwise hide his fatherly affection toward his sonne."[56] The logic of Puritanism required parents to accept God's judgment as just and perfect, even if it were the death, or worse, the damnation of their own child. Grief had no place in that scheme of things. God's will is perfect. Therefore Mather, like David, had to hide his feelings. His choice of the Absalom story, with David's heartbroken cry at its end, even if that ending was secret like the cry itself, was Increase's way of making known his feelings as a parent. When he prepared this sermon for the press, Mather revealed indirectly his feelings about the Rising Generation: "for whose sakes," he wrote, "I am most willing not onely to Preach, and to write, but to dye, if I may but thereby Promote their *Conversion* and *Salvation*. . . ."[57] This unique public statement is an echo of David's "Would God I had died for Thee, O Absalom, my son, my son!" As the Geneva Bible said of David, so must Mather "hide his fatherly affection."

The Rising Generation became Mather's most popular theme, and John Foster soon found himself printing many of Mather's sermons on it singly and in collections. *Pray for the Rising Generation,* preached in 1678, was published that year and reprinted in 1679 and 1685. *A Call to the Rising Generation* and *Remember Now Thy Creator in the Days of thy Youth* were preached and published in 1679. *The Wicked Man's Portion* appeared in 1675 and was reprinted in 1685. Foster also printed a second edition of *A Serious Exhortation to the Present and Succeeding Generation* (1677). Increase distributed many copies of all these books far and wide, sending them to friends in New England and old England, too.

SMALLPOX: A WARNING FROM A STERN GOD

In the summer of 1678, disaster struck Boston. A smallpox epidemic, dreaded Old World killer, brought havoc to the seacoasts of the New World, wherever ports were open to ships from Europe. The small towns in the interior, or those fishing villages with little or no contact with Europe, were relatively safe. Mather's own light infection of smallpox in Ireland in 1659 had given him immunity, but now in the summer of 1678 all his family was exposed. The Mathers were lucky. The two older boys, Nathaniel and Cotton, had light cases and soon recovered. The babies of the family, Samuel (age three) and Abigail (one year), escaped altogether. But seven-year-old Sarah fell sick, and Maria, the oldest girl, was stricken so seriously they feared for her life. Increase prayed in anguish day and night. Fifteen-year-old Cotton, already showing his flair for language, wrote to his uncle in Plymouth: "To have coffins crossing each other as they have been carried in the streets;—To have, I know not how many corpses following each other close at their heels,—To have 38 dye in one week,—6, 7, 8 or 9 in a day. Yet thus it has lately been, and thus it is at this day."[58]

One hundred eighty died by October 3, 340 by early November, which was perhaps ten percent of Boston's population, a terrible mortality.[59] To Mather, the epidemic, like the war and like the fire, was a dreadful warning from a merciful but stern God. "We have seen the red Horse amongst us," he wrote, falling back on the language of the Book of Revelation, "even bloody judgements and desolation, but are not bettered thereby. Now there is a pale Horse come, and his Name that sits thereon is Death."[60] His mind fed on the strange prophecies of that last book of the New Testament and he entered into its dream-like world. He came to feel himself to be a latter-day prophet who, like the prophets of old, had a mission to call mankind to repentance.

On March 16, 1679, Governor John Leverett died. Simon Bradstreet was chosen to serve for two months until the general elections in May. Bradstreet, in his seventies now, was one of the earliest settlers and held in great reverence. He was also far more sympathetic than Leverett had been. This was the opportune moment for Mather to renew the campaign he had started during the war for a general recognition of New England's backsliding and a renewal of piety. He arranged with Foster to publish *Danger of Apostacy,* and after the May elections had returned Bradstreet again, Mather and eighteen other ministers petitioned the General Court to call a synod of all the churches for the purpose of enquiring into the causes of "God's controversy with us."[61]

REFORMING SYNOD

The inspiration to hold a synod, only the third in Massachusetts's history, may have come from a correspondent in England, Thomas Jollie. In April 1677, Jollie, minister to a small Puritan congregation in Lancashire, opened a correspondence with Increase Mather on the strength of what friends had told him of this powerful New England preacher. Jollie's mental world was rich in biblical imagery and rhetoric, and his effulgent letters could only have flattered Mather's own sense of being a chosen instrument of God. "The Lord hath sett watchmen upon Jerusalem's walls," Jollie wrote, "who will not give him nor his people rest untill her righteousness goe forth as brightness and her salvation as a lamp that burneth; until hee establish and make Jerusalem a prais in the earth. The Lord, I perceiv, hath given you a spirit to give warning; cry aloud, and spare not: the hous of Jacob needs crying to, as well as the God of Jacob."[62]

Mather quickly responded, sent books, cried out about New England's apostasy, and told of the fearful epidemics and fires that were surely God's punishment of a sinful land. Jollie made a suggestion: "The advice I humbly offer for your awakning to duty in the reforming of your manifest evills and for preventing of threatning ruin is, that a Synod bee gathered to that purpose. . . . (I) suppose your Magistrates are Church-members, . . . and soe may bee present at such a Synod as Magistrates or as Messengers of the churches. There will the Teaching Elders be present to stir up one another, and to stir up the Magistrates to their duty."[63]

Mather liked the idea. A synod would give him an opportunity to confront the sinfulness of the people and the slackness of the magistrates. It would also be an occasion to repair the damage being done by some ministers who were straying from the old ways. In his mind, he linked a synod with another strategy for reviving religious interest, the encouragement of entire congregations to renew their church covenants in a special ceremony.

Covenant renewal was not itself new. The practice had gone on sporadically since the earliest church in Massachusetts, and there had been a flurry of renewals during the war. On March 21, 1677, the last Sabbath of the outgoing year, the appropriate time for rebirth and renewal, Mather preached to his father's church in Dorchester *Renewal of Covenant the Great Duty* (Boston, 1677). The sermon became for him the start of a campaign to persuade all the churches in Massachusetts to renew their covenants. It would be an engine of reformation, an exercise of piety. By a general renewal of church covenants across Massachusetts, God's chosen people would reappropriate the spirituality of the first fathers.[64]

Not everyone agreed. Although church covenants had been a characteristic of the unique pattern of New England churches, even in Richard Mather's day it had been necessary to defend the practice against some who thought it unscriptural.[65] Now in the next generation there were new objections. Solomon Stoddard not only denied in 1677 the legitimacy of church covenants, but began to question whether a person's rela-

tion of spiritual growth could be used to determine his or her regeneracy.[66]
If regeneration could not be demonstrated, the attempt to exclude all
but proven visible saints from the Lord's Supper fell through; and that
would lead, perhaps, to inviting persons full of faith and hope to join in
the Lord's Supper as a way of moving towards regeneration. That spring,
Increase Mather inveighed against weakening admission requirements
in both his major published sermons, *Renewal of Covenant the Great Duty*
(March) and *Danger of Apostasy,* the election sermon in May. Perhaps he
had Stoddard in mind. Two years later the General Court called for a
synod.

By September 10, 1679, the long days of summer were shortening
into fall. The morning sun rose noticeably later and more to the south
with each passing day. A hint of frost was in the air. In the towns and
villages of Massachusetts, men stacked firewood against the winter. In
Boston, Increase Mather observed his colleagues assemble for the synod,
his synod. He knew he had strong allies among the other ministers. John
Russell from Hadley was a staunch supporter. Also from the Connecticut
River Valley came a new minister, Edward Taylor, then America's greatest living poet but secretly so, a protégé of Mather's and an outspoken
champion of both the church covenant and experiential rebirth.[67] Urian
Oakes, the witty president of Harvard College, "my intimate, dear
friend," was there. Thomas Cobbett from Ipswich would support him
and would be listened to because of his great age. "I know no other exter-
nall means left to further our reformation," Cobbett had written a year
earlier, "but a solemne renuing of Covenant with God by all & every of
our respective churches."[68] And Samuel Willard, the brilliant colleague
at Boston's Third Church, uncomfortably soft on the question of a public
relation of personal experience, was Mather's staunch supporter on covenant renewal.[69]

On the first day of the synod, Mather made an issue of the fact that
churches had sent their ministers but not representatives of the lay
brethren. In recent years, the ministers had begun acting more and more
apart from the brethren who had ordained them. Increase Mather stayed
with the original ideal and insisted now that the synod must have lay
representatives as well as ministers. He won this point on that first day,
and no votes would be taken until lay representatives of all the churches
were present.[70] A week was lost while messengers went back to the
towns. Meanwhile, the synod chose a committee to draft a working
paper, a committee which Mather and his allies easily dominated.
On the seventeenth, a week late, the synod met again. This time the

brethren were represented. They voted unanimously to adopt the Cambridge Platform of 1648 "in its substance," which meant some changes might be made. On the nineteenth, the drafting committee gave its report. It was now Friday, and the delegates were anxious to get home. They took up the committee report item by item, but only got to the third before they encountered a disagreement.[71]

The third proposition had to do with admission to the Lord's Supper. The report recommended that no one be admitted to full membership and the Lord's Supper without the church having a chance to examine his or her religious state. The draft read thus:

That both Churches and Elders be most watchfully and strictly circumspect in admission unto full communion in the Lord's Supper, . . . that none be admitted but upon satisfactory account given unto the Church of their knowledge, faith, and experience as a sufficient ground (in the judgment of charity) to hope that they are sincere converts and are able to examine themselves and to discern the Lord's body according to Direction.

The committee backed up its recommendation with this passage from 1 Corinthians 11:28, 29:

That persons may not come in their unregeneracy and so be hardened, judicially sealed, and shutt up in their Hypocrisy and Apostasy, eating and drinking judgment unto themselves. And that the Table of the Lord be kept pure, and not be polluted and profaned by unworthy communicants.[72]

Many of the ministers at the synod thought that the role of the church in examining candidates for admission was overstated. Solomon Stoddard, in particular, favored a more positive outreach. After a general discussion, Stoddard proposed alternative wording to the third item and offered to debate it then and there. Mather took him on. Urian Oakes agreed to act as moderator. Stoddard proposed to substitute for the committee's language a statement that adults who "make a solemn profession of faith and repentance" ought to be admitted immediately to full membership and the Lord's Supper. There was no reference to a relation of experience here, and no role for the brethren, either. Mather argued that the church must have an opportunity to examine the candidate's opinions and judge the sincerity of his or her faith. In this difference of opinion, Mather followed his father's generation. The Cambridge Platform was clear and unambiguous: "such as are admitted thereto as members ought to be examined and tried first, whether they be fit and meet to be received into church society, or not." All the early ministers, Cotton,

Norton, Richard Mather, had expected it. The Platform recommended that "severity of examination is to be avoyded," but examination there should be.[73] That, however, had been in 1647. By 1679 the Congregational churches were no longer what they had been thirty years before. Stoddard spoke for all those who perceived, however uncertainly, that the church was becoming, and had to become, the church of the whole people, not a select few. The experiences of a very few could not forever serve as the only measure of true religion. In these changed circumstances, the examination for admission, no matter how much it avoided severity, seemed inappropriate.

Stoddard and Mather each spoke once, and then debate was cut off. The synod participants were impatient, and time was short. They voted to substitute Stoddard's language for Mather's. The committee's wording was lined out and Stoddard's inserted. Stoddard and Mather were to elaborate their positions in writing during the winter ahead, but for the time being the issue was settled. Henceforth, any church in Massachusetts which so wished had the synod's approval to dispense with the examination of a candidate and rely merely on his or her profession of faith and repentance. No great wave of church admissions followed, but the New England Way was changing bit by bit.[74] The rest of the committee's draft was adopted with little change. Working late that day, the synod wound up its business. Mather took credit for the overall success of the synod, and if the changes put forward by Stoddard bothered him, he made no mention of it. "Now God in his providence," he wrote some years later, "did both put respect upon me, and (which was a farr greater mercy) gave me an opportunity for some peculiar Service in his Name. . . . There were like to be great heats about the synodical Questions which had bin agitated Anno 1662. But The Lord favoured me so farr as to make me instrumental for the prevention of all differences, so that things were carried on with great unanimity. The conclusions of that synod together with the epistle dedicatory to the General Court were my composure."[75] After the representatives of the churches went home, Mather sat down to draft its formal report. Cotton helped as amanuensis, and the final manuscript report that went to the General Court was in his handwriting. The whole was then published at the government's order as *The Necessity of Reformation* (Boston, 1679).

In his "epistle dedicatory," Mather again used the images he had used in the biography of his father: "Our Fathers . . . ventured themselves and their little ones upon the rude waves of the vast Ocean, that so they might follow the Lord into this Land." He likened that journey to the flight of "our Father Abraham from Ur of the Chaldees, or that of his Seed from the land of Egypt." The myth of a chosen people on an errand for the Lord was woven deeper into the consciousness of New England. [76]

One cannot today read through the report of the synod without sensing the members' dismay at the changes taking place around them. Most of all they perceived a lessening of commitment to God. "Men cease to know and fear, and love and trust in him, but take up their contentment and satisfaction in something else." [77] Point by point the report drove home this conclusion. It spoke of "an insatiable desire after Land, and worldly Accomodations, yea so as to forsake Churches and Ordinances, and to live like Heathen, only so that they might have Elbow-room enough in the World. Farms and merchandising have been preferred before the things of God." [78] Many of the changes now catalogued had been identified during King Philip's War: changes in dress, family life, public drinking, and failure to attend church on the Sabbath. All this was taken almost verbatim from the 1676 law "Provoking Evils." [79] As a consequence of this weakened piety, God was angry. "That God hath a Controversy with his New-England People is undeniable." [80] They pointed to the war, the fire in Boston, the smallpox epidemic. "Would the Lord have whetted his glittering Sword. . . ? Would he have said, Sword! goe through the Land, and cut off man and Beast? Or would he have kindled such devouring Fires . . . if he had not been angry?" [81]

What was to be done then? Men in authority must be examples for others. The Platform of 1648 must be acknowledged, and the churches must be kept pure. Churches should support two ministers instead of only one. The magistrates must see to it that towns taxed themselves to pay better wages to their ministers. Over and over again, the synod singled out the magistrates and charged them to enforce the laws against profanity, heresy, schism, disorder, drunkenness, and breaking the Sabbath. Most of this came straight from Mather's 1677 election day sermon, *The Danger of Apostasy*. Churches should renew their covenants: "Solemn and explicit Renewal of the Covenant is a Scripture Expedient for Reformation." Three of the recommendations of the synod repeated almost word for word what he had urged in his sermon at Dorchester in March 1677. [82] This part of the synod's report would in the years ahead become the basis for a widespread use of renewals throughout Massachusetts.

Last, but not least in view of the literary culture beginning to develop in Boston, were the recommendations about education. "The interest of Religion and good Literature," the final report read, "have been wont to rise and fall together." When the separation between England and New

England became more and more evident after 1660, men like Urian Oakes and Increase Mather came to realize their absolute dependence on Harvard College. "These Churches had been in a state most deplorable, if the Lord had not blessed the Colledge, so as from thence to supply most the Churches, as at this day." If the reform was to succeed, the college and the schools must succeed too.[83] Books were "talents in God's service." "The interest of Religion and good Literature" went hand in hand.

In all of it Increase Mather's hand is evident, and often the language itself was borrowed from earlier sermons and books. He treated the synod as a personal triumph. It put a public stamp of approval on the argument he had clung to throughout King Philip's War—these calamities are the consequences of our backsliding. In some subtle way, the success of this synod perhaps also served in his mind to establish his own achievements as equal to his father's in 1662.

When the General Court met in Boston in October, it approved the synod's report and recommended it to the churches of Massachusetts, "enjoyning and requiring all persons . . . to a carefull and diligent reformation of all those provoking evills mentioned therein . . . that so the anger and displeasure of God, which hath binn many ways manifested, maybe averted from this poore people, and his favour and blessing obteyned, as in former times."[84] *As in former times. Provoking evills. Anger and displeasure of God.* These phrases were touchstones of the mythic history, the Christian world view. If anyone suspected then that these words had lost their meaning, it was not recorded.

Mather planned a covenant renewal for North Church. He wanted again, as at Dorchester three years earlier, to hold the ceremony at the end of the old year, the beginning of the new, a time for renewal. On March 17, 1680, the service took place. Samuel Willard came to preach in the morning, and Mather preached his own sermon, *Returning unto God the Great Concernment of a Covenant People* (Boston, 1680), in the afternoon. The covenant, not the old, original one of 1650, but a new and larger one, was read. "We do . . . each one of us, for ourselves, and jointly as a church of the living God, explicitly renew our Covenant with God, and with one another. . . ."[85] The men of the church raised their right hands to signal assent; the women stood. When John Foster printed Mather's renewal sermon and the text of the covenant, he used a decorative headpiece emblematic of death and rebirth—a skeleton rises from its coffin, cherubs trumpet on either side.[86]

In May the synod was to reconvene and adopt a confession of faith.

The drafting committee, with Mather and Willard both members, decided to recommend the Savoy Declaration of Faith written by the Independents in England in 1658 just before the curtain fell there. But early in May, Mather became exhausted, weak, feverish. Determined to see the synod, his synod, through to its end, he forced himself to its meeting. "Whilest I was in the Synod," he wrote later, "the intenseness of my mind about the work before me, made me forgett my illness. But at night I could not sleep, nor eat in the day Time."[87] He was elected moderator for the meeting, and on May 11 and 12 the synod adopted the Savoy Declaration of Faith. Mather collapsed, exhausted but filled with pride and satisfaction.

CHAPTER 5

New Worlds of Science and Hope
[1680-1686]

CHALLENGES FROM RIGHT AND LEFT

"My illness proved a dangerous feavor," Increase Mather wrote. He was ill for months. "After I was recoverd of it, an Ague, and a sore cough (thought to be a consumption cough for I did often spit blood) brought me very low." [1] By July he was able to rouse himself to say family prayers, but not until September could he dress himself and cross the square to the meetinghouse. On September 12, 1680, he administered the Lord's Supper for the first time since the preceding April. [2]

Mather, restored to health after this long and frightening illness experienced a new sense of well-being. Leading the synod of 1679 and the renewal in his church had sapped his vitality, but in their success he seemed at last to have escaped from his father's shadow and gathered new spirit. The vestiges of anger at his church and at provincial Boston melted away, as it became evident that Massachusetts had accepted him as its religious leader.

Week after week that fall and winter of 1680–1681 Mather noted in his diary signs of the acceptance of his leadership. "Dined with Magistrates. . . . After Lecture with Lord Culpepper [the new Governor of Virginia]. . . . Visited Sir Edmond Andros [Governor of New York]. . . . Dined with Commissioners [of the New England Confederation]. . . . With Mr. Willard, Governor, etc. . . . Dined with Magistrates. . . . Discourse with Deputies. . . . Dined with Soldiers [of the prestigious Artillery Company]. . . . After Lecture with Magistrates. . . . " [3] The ministers of Boston met, usually at Willard's house, each week after the Thursday afternoon lecture, and while Simon Bradstreet was governor, they were repeatedly asked to advise him and the magistrates on public policy.

Nevertheless, such was the personality of this intense man that he hardly knew how to accept the good things life had to offer. It was the nature of his Puritanism that he must turn every benefit inside out. "How should these Mercyes humble & make me vile in my own eyes?" he asked himself, and then went on to reflect that if the summer's illness had not taken his life, it was because God had more for him to do: "I believe and pray, that Hee will help me to doe something more for the honor of Jesus Christ, & the good of his church, in my generation." Yet even that confidence Mather must turn to pain rather than joy: "And who knows but at last, Hee may give me to suffer for his Name & glory?"[4] New challenges to the old ways were not long in coming.

Mather had established himself as the conservative champion of the New England church as it had been put in place by his father's generation. He would defend it against change from those who wanted more leniency in admission to membership and from the antipaedobaptists, who wanted more strictness. The Baptist congregation, once forced to retreat to Noddles Island, was now back in Boston. They built a meeting house on the edge of Mill Pond in the North End. In March, 1679, the town authorities nailed its door shut. "So perverse were they," Mather wrote, "that they would not meet in a private house, but met this Sabbath out of doors [illegible] their meeting place."[5] Their leader, John Russell of Worcester, even had the temerity to answer Increase Mather's *Divine Right of Infant Baptism* with his own book. He could not publish his small book in Massachusetts, where Mather and Willard were licensors of the press, but did publish it in London, and copies were available in Boston by December 1680. In it he made two particularly troublesome points. One was that for years now the Baptists and Congregationalists in England had been in communion with each other, "Brethren of the Congregational Way." The other was that the English Baptists, and those in Massachusetts, too, accepted almost without change the Savoy Declaration of Faith. Under these circumstances, Russell asked, why could not the churches in Massachusetts extend the right hand of fellowship, as their brothers in England had done?[6]

Mather and Samuel Willard were outraged by Russell's book, and both set to work at once to write rebuttals. Russell's death that winter did nothing to assuage them. Mather turned the responsibility of a reply over to Willard, contributing his own notes of his old struggle with John

Courtesy, American Antiquarian Society

"The blessed and gracious God, seems now to have given me a new Life," page from Mather's diary, September, 1680, after his recovery from illness

Farnum. In early 1681 Willard published the rebuttal to Russell under the title *Ne Sutor Ultra Crepidam*, "Cobbler, stick to your last." (Russell was said to have been a shoemaker.) Mather wrote the introduction.[7] The book is in many ways a peevish attack on the social inferiority of the Baptists and their lack of formal education, in addition to a refutation of their arguments. Willard and Mather were angry, not because the *doc-*

trine of adult baptism roused their emotions, but because many Baptists, like John Farnum, had persisted in rejecting ministerial authority. Discipline, not baptismal doctrine, Mather wrote, was at stake. In a small community, he argued, there was no room for two churches, as there was in England. "That which is needful to ballast a great ship, will sink a small boat."[8] There was widespread sympathy among Boston laymen for toleration of Baptists, but Willard and Mather opposed it, and for the time being they carried the day among the ministers.[9]

Meanwhile, word came from the Connecticut River Valley that Solomon Stoddard was proposing to undermine the churches in a very different way. The warning came in a long letter to Increase from John Russell at Hadley, not far from Stoddard's Northampton church. Stoddard, Russell wrote, would now dispense with not only the narrative of conversion experience prior to admission, which had been his point at the synod two years earlier, but conversion itself as a precondition to the Lord's Supper. "Our good Brother Stoddard hath bin strenuously promoting his position concerning that right which persons sound in doctrine of faith, & of (as he calls it) a holy Conversation, have to full communion."[10] Russell, an old foe of the half-way covenant, blamed Stoddard's proposals on the actions of the Half-Way Synod and assumed Mather would be the principal defender of the old way. In the event, Stoddard's own church did not support his radical change at this time, and Mather is not known to have acted on Russell's letter.

The same letter from Russell told about an awe-inspiring phenomenon common to the entire northern hemisphere. A comet flared across the night skies in the winter of 1680–81, drawing crowds out into the streets of Moscow, Paris, and London, as well as the villages of New England. "The Lord hath been aloud alarming all of us by the awfull stretching out of His sword over us in the late Comett," Russell wrote; "the most tremendous appearance that ever my eyes saw. . . ."[11]

JOHN FOSTER: ASTRONOMER AND PRINTER

One winter's night in November 1680, Mather slipped out of the warmth of his bed and, bundled against the chill, went out of doors into Clarke's Square. Across the eastern sky over the dark roofline of the houses opposite was the streak of light. The printer John Foster had spotted the comet first in Boston, and now it was Mather's turn to be the student, as his printer tutored him about the stars. Foster was a philomath, as interested in astronomy as in woodcuts. Through the rest of

November, all of December, and on into January, whenever the skies
were clear enough, Foster made careful records of the comet's apparent
course by plotting it against the background of fixed stars. On December 10 he joined forces with Thomas Brattle, who had just finished
his M.A. at the college, to use the college telescope to calculate the
comet's position. Both men were familiar with the contemporary astronomical literature of Europe and with the new Cartesian philosophy.

In the Boston almanac for 1681 Foster printed his and Brattle's detailed observations, together with an essay about the motion of comets.[12]
Later in 1681 Brattle sent the observations to John Flamsteed, the astronomer at the Royal Observatory in Greenwich, and from there they
found their way into Isaac Newton's hands and were included in his great
Principia Mathematica (1689). Newton gave credit to "the observer in
New England."[13]

The drama of the comet and Foster's enthusiasm wakened Increase
Mather to a new world. The scientific revolution of the seventeenth century, which he had earlier barely recognized, absorbed more and more of
his attention. He began to read what he could find about astronomy and
particularly about comets. He spent hours poring over histories and en-
cyclopedias. That January 1681, in his Thursday afternoon lecture,
Mather summarized this research in a sermon, *Heaven's Alarm to the
World*. Foster promptly printed it, accompanied by a long introduction
in which Mather discussed his new learning. With a brief nod to those
who had written about the physical and mathematical aspects of comets
("some to good purpose and edification"), Mather confined himself to
making "a theological Improvement thereof." The nub of his thoughts
was that the comet was certainly a warning of some great calamity, and
calamities were a portent of the end of time.

Heaven's Alarm to the World was the last book printed by John Foster
before his death. In the six years since Mather had helped him start in
Boston, Foster had worked important changes in the character of New
England printing. He had become the quintessential Yankee jack-of-all-
trades. A man of diverse interests, printer and publisher, artist and illus-
trator, mathematician and astronomer, John Foster both guided the elite
and also pushed Boston's printing presses in the direction of popular culture. From his press came such essentially popular works as Mather's sensational sermons *The Times of Men* and *The Wicked Man's Portion,* and new
forms of literature: Mather's and Hubbard's histories of King Philip's War,
Thomas Thacher's *Brief Rule* (a single broadside of instructions for care of
smallpox), and the first American edition of Anne Bradstreet's poems.

The poems had been published in London in 1650 and were reprinted by Foster in a new and enlarged edition, with new poems found among Bradstreet's papers after her death. Who initiated this second edition, what reading public it was expected to serve, and how it was received are questions that cannot yet be answered. Neither can the more general questions of who decided what books to publish, how were they paid for, how many were printed, at what price did they sell, and who read them.

During Foster's brief time as a printer in Boston, the press turned towards a wider reading public. Execution sermons and similar works of a sensational character appeared henceforth with increasing frequency. In 1674 Foster had compiled the almanac, printed in Cambridge by Samuel Green, for the year 1675; when he moved to Boston, he began a second almanac and Massachusetts supported two almanacs for the rest of the century: "The almanac,—most despised, most prolific, most indispensable of books, which every man uses, and no man praises, the very quack, clown, pack-horse, and pariah of modern literature, yet the one universal book." [14]

In Europe, the largest readership for almanacs was workers and peasants at a level of culture where literacy merged imperceptibly with illiteracy. These European almanacs often had a rough, topsy-turvy humor that poked fun at wealthier and more powerful members of society, at gentlemen, clergy, shop owners, and the like. Such wry humor was expressed frequently through an ironic reversal of character, for example, the immoral clergyman, the dishonest judge, the cowardly knight. In New England, far from springing up from a semi-literate culture, almanacs were produced by the quasi-official Massachusetts press and were compiled by members of the elite culture, often students or tutors at Harvard College. Written by the "Cambridge dynasty," they were aimed at a higher and more sophisticated audience than in Europe. In one rare example of New England wit it was ignorant countrymen, not the upper classes, who were ridiculed. [15]

Astrology inevitably crept into the almanacs. The proclivity of Puritans for the natural sciences made it inevitable, for the almanacs themselves were exercises in natural science, and almanac writers in Massachusetts in the 1670s and 1680s were hard-pressed to distinguish between successful advances in astronomy and the organized fancy of astrology. [16] In this they were no different from the great scientists of Europe. Even Johannes Kepler made a living casting horoscopes. One has only to leaf through one or two annual issues of the Royal Philosophical

Society's *Transactions* to realize how confused with each other were fact and fancy, method and madness. Puritan ministers, the intellectual authorities of New England, were similarly confused.

John Sherman, minister at Watertown, kept a foot in both camps. In the 1674 almanac, he published a brief essay on Kepler's theory of planetary motion, as well as a jumbled horoscope, which "portends no small evil" for the coming summer. In 1676 he seemed explicitly to reject astrology. After giving details of a conjunction of Saturn and Mars near the Pleiades, he wrote "what these signify I shall not say, but leave their Effects to Gods Providence and mans observation. And leaving Starlight, I shall make use of that far more resplendent and glorious of the Sun of Righteousness shining out to us in holy Scriptures." In the almanac for 1677, Sherman expressed perplexity: "Though I never was so Astrologically opinionated, as to think that the Stars were intended for windows, through which poor mortals might peep and steal a look into the sacred Decrees and secret Counsels of the most High: yet sure I am, they are a considerable part of The Heavenly Host; Deut. 4.19 by which as Instruments the Sovereign Lord and Ruler of the World bringeth about and Effecteth great things, Judg. 5.20." [17] Cotton Mather in 1690 disparaged the almanac as "that *little* but *spreading* thing . . . [subject to] that common abuse, of being an engine to convey only silly impertinencies, or sinful superstitions, into almost every cottage in the wilderness." [18] But that was after John Tulley and Sir Edmund Andros and reflects very changed circumstances. In 1683 Cotton had prepared one himself.

The New England almanacs, written by the "Cambridge dynasty" and for an educated public, must nevertheless have reached the least literate reading public in America as in Europe. When Foster introduced illustrations into the Cambridge and Boston almanacs, he could only have moved them further in a more popular direction. Foster, like his predecessors, mixed science and astrology. His first woodcut, in the Cambridge 1675 Almanac, is of the sun casting the shadow of the earth on the moon, an illustration of the Copernican heliocentric system. Later in 1678 in his Boston Almanac he printed a woodcut of the Man of Signs. Had he lived longer, his role in New England's culture might have been more vividly recognized, but he only lived six years after opening his shop in Boston. He was a sick man when he published Mather's *Heaven's Alarm* in March 1681. When he moved back to Dorchester, he made a will that left twenty shillings each from the proceeds of the sale of his

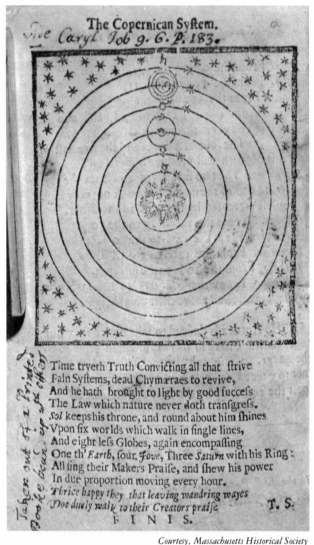

"The Copernican System," first such illustration published in New England, from John Foster's almanac, 1681; New England almanacs were directed at a more sophisticated audience than their English counterparts

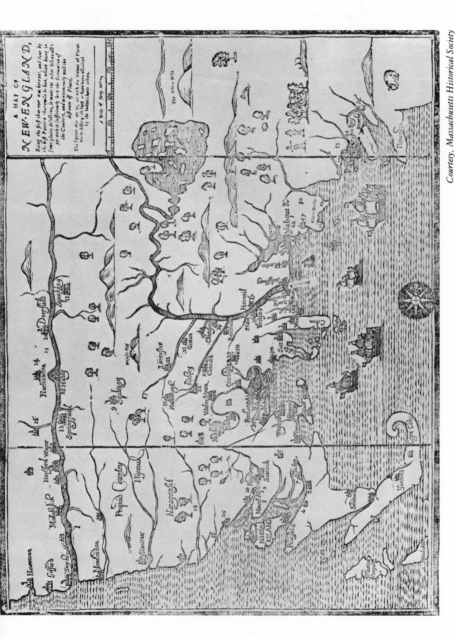

Courtesy, *Massachusetts Historical Society*

Map of Boston and New England in 1677; woodcut by John Foster, printed in
William Hubbard's history of King Philip's War

Courtesy, Museum of Fine Arts, Boston

Headstone for the grave of John Foster, "the ingenious mathematician and printer," who died in 1681 at 33. Increase
Mather's words carved on the stone: "Living you studied the
stars; dying, I pray you, Foster, ascend above the aether; learn
to measure the highest heaven."

printing shop to his three patrons: Increase Mather, Cotton Mather, and
John Eliot. In September he was dead of consumption at the age of
thirty-three.[19]

The inscription on Foster's gravestone is an emblem of the relationship
between Foster and Increase Mather. In the form of a dialogue between

Foster and Mather, it is also emblematic of the relationship between Puritan religion and natural science:

IM ASTRA COLIS VIVENS; MORIENS, SUPER AETHERA FOSTER
SCANDE, PRECOR; COELUM, METIRI DISCE SUPREMUM.
JF METIOR, ATQUE MEUM EST: EMIT MIHI DIVES IESUS:
NEC TENEOR QUICQUAM, NISI GRATES, SOLVERE[20]

IM:Living you study the stars; dying I pray you, Foster, ascend above the aether; learn to measure the highest heaven.
JF:I measure it, and it is mine; the Lord Jesus has bought it for me, nor do I owe anything, but to pay thanks.

For the smaller footstone, a line from Ovid was chosen, which in its translation announced in unmistakable terms the arrival of a Yankee culture: "ARS ILLI SUA CENSUS ERAT—OVID. SKILL WAS HIS CASH."[21]

PURITAN AS SCIENTIST

August 1682. Midsummer and hot in Boston. Increase Mather had taken a ten-day vacation with his son Cotton the month before. *Practical Truths*, his latest collection of sermons, was at the printer's, and he was already transcribing the next. John Rogers, president-elect of the college, had not yet moved to Cambridge, and the Overseers asked Mather to manage the commencement again. There was not one B.A. graduate that year. Mather managed the ceremonies in August. Ten days later, he saw another comet.[22]

Two weeks after that, on August 31, 1682, it was again Mather's turn to give the Thursday Lecture. As he had eighteen months earlier, he would make the comet the subject of his talk. He turned for his text to the story of Exodus, where Moses said the people would not believe and God gave him a sign, saying, "And it shall come to pass, if they will not believe thee, neither hearken to the voice of the first sign, that they will believe the voice of the latter sign." Eighteen months before, a comet had blazed its way across the winter sky. Plainly people had not listened to the warning. This second comet, then, was the latter sign. Mather's Thursday Lecture, *The Latter Sign Discoursed*, soon published, was peculiarly quiet and unemotional. It carried none of the vibrancy of *Heaven's Alarm,* nor any of the rhetorical drama of Mather's great jeremiad sermons, but simply warned that "men ought to hear the voice of God in signal providences, especially when repeated."[23] The emotional quiet of this sermon, however, concealed Mather's own excitement at the second comet in as many years. This time, Foster was no longer there to help, but Mather was ready to study on his own. He threw himself into the search for God's meaning behind the events.

A week after his Thursday lecture, he found a copy of Johan Hevel's *Cometographia: totam naturam cometarum, . . . exhibens*, published in Danzig in 1668 in Latin. It contained a physical description of comets, lavishly and beautifully illustrated, together with the best information from the great observatory in Danzig. It outlined the history of all recorded comets and their supposed relation to the history of mankind. For the next fourteen months, Mather plunged into this subject. He pored over every book he could find on astronomy and on the occurrences of comets in human history. He read astronomical works by Giovanni Batista Riccioli, Gotefridus Wendelinus, Stanislaus Lubienietsky, Jacques Bernouilli, Johannes Kepler, Robert Hooke, Christian Longomontanus, and Willebord Snell.[24] He discovered the *Transactions* of the Royal Philosophical Society. He walked to Cambridge to study until midnight, searching through the college library and looking at the comet through the college telescope.[25]

The telescope was a disappointment; he could make out only a faint blur. But the library drew him back again and again. He discovered the *Miscellanea Curiosa . . . sive Ephemeridium Medico-Physicarum Germanorum*, published in Latin and known in English as the "German Ephemerides," modelled on the Royal Society's *Transactions*.[26] The Royal Philosophical Society, established in London some twenty years before and now an important engine of the scientific revolution, excited Mather enormously. In April 1683, he met with a few others at Samuel Willard's house to plan a "philosophical society" in Boston. It held its first meeting on April 30, 1683, and met thereafter on the last Monday of every month at the Mather house on Clark Square. Papers were read in imitation of the London model. Mather sent at least one of his and Cotton's papers to Europe, where it was published (in Latin) by Wolfgang Sengurdius in *Philosophia Naturalis* (Leyden, 1685). Some of the meetings were moved to Willard's home; later in the year they were occasionally skipped, and, in the end, the project fizzled out. The last meeting of the Boston Philosophical Society recorded in Mather's diary took place on December 10, 1683, but the interested members continued their activities for at least two more years.[27] In time, Cotton Mather would succeed to his father's place, become a fellow of the Royal Society, and contribute dozens of papers to its annual meetings.

One thing seems certain. The dwindling away of a philosophical society devoted to natural science was not the result of opposition from religion. The Boston Philosophical Society may have failed to catch on simply because there were too few men of sufficient education and leisure in the city. Outside Boston and the cadre of young teaching fellows at the college, there were few who could give much time to serious study. Most Puritan ministers led lonely lives, and their intellectual interest was stifled in the countryside. The Boston Philosophical Society may not in itself provide evidence to support Robert Merton's hyphothesis that Puritan values encouraged the development of modern science, but Increase Mather certainly believed that the Roman Catholic church impeded it. "But notwithstanding these Arguments are so convictive and demonstrative," he wrote in his book on astronomy, "its marvellous to see how some Popish Authors (*Jesuites* especially) strain their wits to defend their *Pagan* Master *Aristotle* his Principles. *Bullialdus* speaks of a *Florentine* Physitian, that all the Friends he had could never perswade him once to view the Heavens through a *Telescope*, and he gave that reason for his refusal, because he was afraid that then his Eyes would make him stagger concerning the truth of *Aristotles Principles*, which he was resolved he would not call into question. It were well, if these Men had as great veneration for the Scripture as they have, for *Aristotles* (if indeed they be his) absurd Books *de cœlo Sed de his satis*." [28] Modern science, in Mather's eyes, was a Protestant undertaking.

THE NATURAL ORDER AND GOD

Increase Mather was a man with a passion for knowledge. His experience with astronomy inspired three books in rapid succession: *Kometographia, Or a Discourse Concerning Comets* (Boston, 1683), *An Essay for the Recording of Illustrious Providences* (Boston, 1684), and *The Doctrine of Divine Providence* (Boston, 1684). All were about two basic questions, how does God intervene in the natural order of things? and, what meaning do those interventions have for mankind?

The Puritan mind was divided. On the one hand, it conceived of the world, the universe, as rational. The strong connection between Puritanism and science during the seventeenth century had its foundation in this belief. On the other hand, all Puritan leaders held the conviction that in his immensity God could never be entirely comprehended by the mind of man. Creation was "divisible into the 'natural government' and

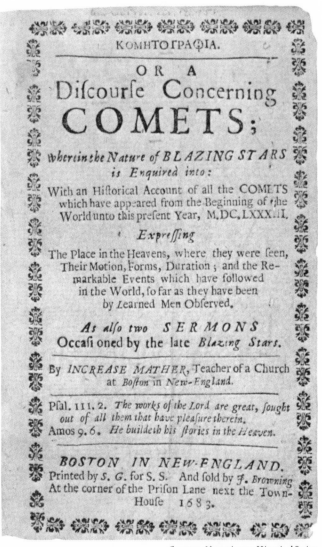

ΚΟΜΗΤΟΓΡΑΦΙΑ.

OR A
Diſcourſe Concerning
COMETS;

Wherein the Nature of *BLAZING STARS*
is *Enquired into*:

With an Hiſtorical Account of all the COMETS
which have appeared from the Beginning of the
World unto this preſent Year, M.DC.LXXXII.

Expreſſing

The Place in the Heavens, where they were ſeen,
Their Motion, Forms, Duration ; and the Remarkable Events which have followed
in the World, ſo far as they have been
by *Learned* Men Obſerved.

As alſo two SERMONS
Occaſioned by the late *Blazing Stars*.

By *INCREASE MATHER*, Teacher of a Church
at *Boſton* in *New-England*.

Pſal. 111. 2. *The works of the Lord are great, ſought
out of all them that have pleaſure therein.*
Amos 9. 6. *He buildeth his ſtories in the Heaven.*

BOSTON IN NEW-ENGLAND.
Printed by *S. G.* for *S. S.* And ſold by *J. Browning*
At the corner of the Priſon Lane next the Town-
Houſe 1683.

Courtesy, Massachusetts Historical Society

Mather's *Kometographia. Or a Discourse Concerning Comets,* exemplifying Puritan
fascination with natural science; printed by Samuel Green, Jr., in 1683 in Boston
and sold by Joseph Browning at his shop at the corner of Prison Lane, near the
Town House

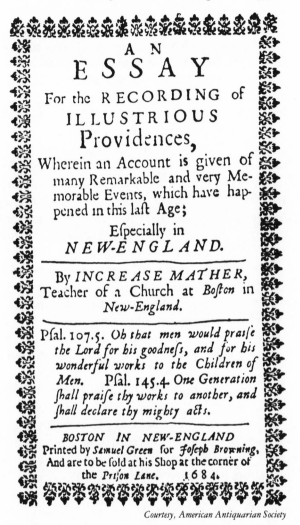

AN
ESSAY
For the RECORDING of
ILLUSTRIOUS
Providences,

Wherein an Account is given of many Remarkable and very Memorable Events, which have happened in this laſt Age;

Eſpecially in
NEW-ENGLAND.

By *INCREASE MATHER*, Teacher of a Church at *Boſton* in *New-England.*

Pſal. 107.5. *Oh that men would praiſe the Lord for his goodneſs, and for his wonderful works to the Children of Men.* Pſal. 145.4 *One Generation ſhall praiſe thy works to another, and ſhall declare thy mighty acts.*

BOSTON IN NEW-ENGLAND Printed by *Samuel Green* for *Joſeph Browning,* And are to be ſold at his Shop at the corner of the *Priſon Lane.* 1684.

Courtesy, American Antiquarian Society

An Essay for the Recording of Illustrious Providences, by Increase Mather, dramatizing the hand of God in the world; printed by Samuel Green, Jr., in 1684

the 'supernatural government.' The former provided knowledge about the creation through second causes or discoverable natural laws; the latter indicated that ultimately the ways of God and His operation were beyond comprehension."[29] This was the dual vision that allowed Mather to become an enthusiast of the scientific revolution, while at the same time maintaining his religious beliefs in an immanent God directing human affairs in ways inscrutable to man. While the dual vision allowed Mather the freedom to speculate in two quite different idea systems, it also made his writing about the natural world and about history blurred and contradictory. In the end, he chose to believe in an inscrutable God over against a world knowable through science.

Kometographia illustrates the contradictions inherent in his thought. It shows a Puritan deeply interested in contemporary science without altering religious beliefs formed on the basis of the Old and New Testaments. The book starts out with an accurate review of what the new science had to say about comets, but ends up, somewhat like Mather's most lurid jeremiads, with ominous predictions of impending doom. For all his Puritan objection to astrology, Mather was never able to disentangle astronomy, astrology, and his understanding of a providential world.

In *Kometographia*, Mather felt himself at the forefront of a new world of discovery. "I may hope that my labour herein, will not be altogether unacceptable to the *English Reader*," he wrote, "since there never was yet (so far as I understand) an attempt of this kind by an *English* hand. My chief design, is to inform and edifie the ordinary sort of *Readers*." [30] The physical nature of comets occupies only two chapters, and the remainder of *Kometographia* is given over to history. The point was to discover and demonstrate what significance comets had for human history. Unlike planets, comets were thought to occur only once, uniquely. Mather took it for granted that they were set in motion by God. History, he believed, showed that comets almost always preceded some great calamity. For example, the first recorded comet preceded the death of Methuselah and the Flood. Modelling his account on Johan Hevel's *Cometographia: totam naturam cametarum*, Mather recounted the devastations, wars, floods, famines, hurricanes, plagues, or volcanoes that had followed comets in the past. It is a history packed with legend and the miraculous, a history more like Fox's *Book of Martyrs* than the secular history of his own day, a history predisposed to the lurid, the sensational, and the catastrophic. Above all, it was a history governed by the assumption of God's Providence.

The issue was, were comets only signals, or were they causes of earthly events as well? In *Heaven's Alarm* (1680) and *The Latter Sign Discoursed* (January 1682) Mather had stuck to a single, clear position: comets are signs and warnings, but not causes. That was the traditional New England position. John Cotton had held it: "Comets are Signal, though not causal: They are Signal as to changes of Divine providence which befall men, though they have no causal influence upon the minds of men." [31]

Mather, rummaging around in all the literature, came to a different opinion. Whereas "judicial astrology," which predicted specific events in the lives of certain individuals, was unacceptable to him, "natural astrology" was not. Comets did have consequences in the natural world. "Such a *Saturnine* Comet as this was (in 1682), hath a natural influence into, and therefore does portend a cold and tedious Winter, much Snow, and consequently great Floods; Malignant and Epidemical Diseases; in special the Plague." He went on to cite a score of floods, storms, and fires which "have already happened in Europe" because of the recent comet.[32]

His conclusions then were: 1) "Ever since the World begun, that Comets have never appeared, but soon after miserable Wars, mortal Diseases, etc. have followed." 2) "I see no sufficient reason why we should not suppose them to be not only signal but causal. . . . It is undubitable that the true Planets and fixed Stars have a natural influence into such things . . . And therefore it is not impossible but that Comets may have the like natural influence . . . causing Droughts in one place, inundations in another, Earth quakes in another, etc. according to the occult qualities which are in the subjects of their influence." But 3) "Whereas, *Wars, Commotions, Persecutions, Heresies, the Death of Princes, Changes,* and *overturnings in the World* do usually happen after the appearance of such Stars, they seem *only signal* and not causal of such events."[33] "The merciful and righteous God useth to discharge his Warning pieces before his Murdering pieces go off. Thrice happy they who take the Warning."[34]

Mather wrote that the comet of 1682 was all the more ominous in that "some rare *Conjunctions of the Superiour Planets* happen this year also."[35] He went on to suggest that this year's conjunction would forecast the conversion of the Jews and the "utter ruin of Rome" by the year 1694.[36] The more Mather speculated about the future, the more sensational his thoughts became: "Desolations by burning are at hand. . . . great Revolutions and Changes. . . . new and unheard of Diseases."[37] As in his fiercest sermons, the Puritan preacher was swept up by his apocalyptic rhetoric. The final chapter of *Kometographia* follows his own jeremiad pattern in a steady buildup of anxiety. Prediction of the exact punishments was not to be tolerated. ("God delights to battle *Judicial Astrologers,* when they presume to know the times and the seasons, which he hath kept in his own power.")[38] But know at least that the evils must be expected. Calamity is at hand. The End of Time.

These thoughts led naturally to his next project. On November 29, 1682, after three months of intense work, Mather finished *Kometographia,* and, two months later, on January 30, 1683, he wrote out the chapter headings for his next book, *An Essay for the Recording of Illustrious Providences*.[39] *An Essay* also reflects the mixed and often contradictory intellectual currents of its age. Years before, Mather had found in his friend Davenport's papers a 1658 proposal to publish stories which would dramatize the hand of God in the world. Those had been the climactic days of the Puritan revolution. Mather saved the paper, and in 1681 he proposed to his colleagues that they all collect and forward to him authentic accounts of mysterious events that would illustrate God's providence for New England. Much of the material for *An Essay* came to his hands this way.

A secondary theme was acts of creation, as distinguished from acts of Providence. It was while he was working on *An Essay* that Mather and Willard organized the Boston Philosophical Society and some of the papers read there found their way into *An Essay*. Chapter Four, titled "Philosophic Meditations," discusses topics similar to those that fill the pages of the Royal Society's *Transactions*: lightning, magnetism, meteors, chemicals, and gases. Increase Mather insisted that even here materialistic explanations were not always sufficient. Some acts of creation were outside of human understanding: "There are Wonders in the Works of Creation as well as Providence, the reason whereof the most knowing among Mortals, are not able to comprehend.[40]

A third theme dealt with the invisible world of spirits. A tide of skepticism was rising in Europe; the tales of the miraculous used by Puritans to demonstrate God's providential intervention were losing credibility. Joseph Glanville, Fellow of the Royal Society, had already raised the alarm in a widely read book, *Sadducismus Triumphatus* (London, 1666). To combat skepticism, Glanville used witchcraft as the most tangible evidence of supernatural forces at work. It was a frank attempt to hold on to the world of spirit in the face of a growing materialism. Glanville, a noted rationalist, reflected the crosscurrents of thought in his age; he argued at another point that "Reason and Reason alone" was capable of proving all the fundamentals of religion.[41] In *An Essay* Mather took the position that the existence of witches proved against skeptics the existence of a spirit world; he devoted three chapters to "Things Praeturnatural which have happened in New England," "Daemons and Possessed persons," and "Apparitions."

An Essay was in fact an immense collection of stories and reports gathered from near and far to illustrate several distinct concerns of Mather's generation. He himself was editor (yet another form of literary expression!). He worked furiously during the year and was able to finish in December 1683.[42] Joseph Browning, a new arrival on the publishing scene in Boston, arranged for the huge manuscript to be printed by Samuel Green, Jr., who had taken over management of John Foster's press. Browning shipped part of the press run, unbound, to England. There it was bought by the publisher George Calvert, who tipped in a new title page and issued a Boston-manufactured English edition at the same time the Boston edition appeared.[43]

The third book inspired by the comets was *The Doctrine of Divine Providence*. It dealt with the question of first and secondary causes, the natural world, and the world of Providences. Mather preached the four sermons that constitute this volume in a series of Thursday lectures during the spring and early summer of 1683, while he was working on *An Essay*.[44] A year later, *An Essay* was finished, and he started to transcribe his sermon notes for the press. Nearly finished in May 1684, the work was interrupted by an illness, but was taken up again in August. In the end he added two other sermons, one sent over from Ireland by Nathaniel, and he sent the manuscript to the press in October 1684.

In *Doctrine of Divine Providence* Mather dealt more explicitly than elsewhere with questions of the natural order and apparent anomalies within it. The greatest and most awe-inspiring Providence was creation itself: "That Law and Course of Nature which He hath Established in the world is a great and marvellous work."[45] Events outside the ordinary course of nature occur, and these are "Signs and Prodigies."[46] Whatever happens is according to God's will and foreknowledge, "tho' as to second causes they might have been otherwise, yet as to first cause things are infallibly accomplished, as he that is in Heaven has determined."[47] When events seem contrary to their natures, it "*is a clear demonstration that they are over ruled by a divine hand.*"[48] "There are eminent preservations and deliverances, which everyone may see the Name of God written upon them in plain legible characters."[49] But also "*Many works of Providence are deep and incomprehensible.* . . . They are out of the reach of men. . . . His ways of Providence are unsearchable."[50] Taken together, the three books written in 1683–1684 constitute Mather's fullest exposition of natural science and providential world history. They are in some ways an extension of the epistemology in *An Earnest Exhortation* (1676). Rationalism, experimental science, astronomy, and astrology all whirled around in Mather's head, mingled with deep-seated convictions about God's providence. Like most of his contemporaries in England, Increase Mather was seldom able to separate or wholly reconcile them.

With his *Doctrine of Divine Providence* Mather opened a new chapter in his relations with printers and publishers. Since Foster's death, the Boston press had been operated by Samuel Green, Jr., who had been working with his father at Cambridge. Samuel Sewall for a few years oversaw the publishing end of Foster's business. Sewall did not like it and soon bowed out. Meanwhile, Joseph Browning (Brunning originally; he was of Dutch birth.) arrived to enter the publishing business. Then in 1684 a newcomer, Richard Pierce, obtained a license to open a second printing shop in Boston. Four years earlier, Pierce had married Sarah Cotton, Seaborn's daughter, and hence had become part of the family, husband to Maria's niece. Increase Mather at once gave his own business to the young printer, usually in conjunction with Joseph Browning as bookseller. *Doctrine of Divine Providence* was the first of several important new books printed under this arrangement. The combination of Pierce and Browning also brought out new editons of several of Mather's earliest popular books, such as *Wicked Man's Portion*. In 1686 Pierce received from Edward Randolph the printing business of the royal government. After Sarah's death in 1690, Pierce got no more of Mather's business.[51]

COTTON MATHER

Urian Oakes died in the summer of 1681, shortly before the Harvard commencement, which he as president was expected to conduct. The next day, at Oakes's funeral, several Overseers asked Mather to take charge of the commencement ceremonies for the candidates for the master's degree, among whom was his son Cotton. Mather responded point blank: "I did absolutely & preremptorily decline it, also to Mr Gookin in privacy I manifested my resolution not to meddle in that matter." Days later, the Overseers asked Mather to oversee the whole commencement. Again he refused, but in the end he was persuaded, and on August 9, 1681, Cotton Mather received his M.A. degree at his father's hands.[52]

After commencement, the search for a president started again. This time the Corporation and the Overseers unanimously chose Increase Mather. He was in a dilemma. To a man of his personality and ambition, the prestige of the college presidency was enormously appealing. At the same time, to leave Boston for the village of Cambridge was unthinkable. Complicating his choice were his Puritan convictions about calling or vocation: if God wanted him to serve in this new capacity, serve he must. How should he know? Reluctantly he said he could not accept unless his church voted to release him. Mather's relief when his church refused to let him go was clear. Even so, he continued to wrestle with the perplexities of the problem until October, when he finally made up his mind, and at a dinner with the Magistrates told them he could not accept.[53]

The entire affair had brought him much closer to the college than before. During the winter of 1681–1682 the Corporation often met at his house. He began to visit the college library frequently, to preach occasionally at Cambridge, and, it appears, to brush up on his Greek. These were the months also when Mather was first drawn to the study of astronomy, and he searched far and wide for books on the subject, in the library in the Town House, in John Foster's library, and most of all in the college library.[54] In September and October of 1682 he stayed to midnight at the college identifying books held in duplicate as the result of two large gifts from England. In the end, Increase seems to have used his position as College Fellow to purchase about one hundred duplicates that he then passed on to Cotton.[55]

Mather became involved in November 1681 in the choice of another non-resident fellow (should it be Samuel Willard or James Allen from First Church?) as well as the search for a new president.[56] The choice for president fell first to Roger Torrey, and when he declined, to John Rogers, a classmate of Urian Oakes. Increase Mather did not like Rogers, and when he was elected nonetheless, Mather resigned from the Corporation.[57] This was the second resignation, for Mather had done the same thing in 1676, when Oakes and he had disagreed over the Hoar business. Unwilling to share authority, unable perhaps to compromise, he chose resignation instead. Both times he was talked out of it.

Although Increase's threats to resign irritated his colleagues, no blemish of character was apparent to Cotton. To his son he was a giant figure. Cotton had been thirteen and fourteen years old when his father rose to prominence during King Philip's War. When the great fire swept the North End in 1676, Mather's certainty that God had given him prophetic powers, a "particular faith," as he called it, affected the son deeply. At that impressionable age, Cotton too formed a bedrock conviction that his father was specially chosen of God.[58] During the next five or six years, when Cotton Mather passed through his adolescence, this belief, explicit and often articulated, became the conscious basis for his obsessive veneration of his father. In an elegy commemorating the death of Urian Oakes, Cotton referred to himself as "I the *dumb* son of *Croesus*."[59]

In 1680 North Church voted to employ Cotton as an assistant preacher. Within the year, he was preaching once a week at an annual salary of £70. Mather's feelings about his son were ambivalent, and never more than when considering Cotton as his assistant in the church. Several times he proposed other men as possible assistants. The more his congregation admired Cotton, the more he dragged his feet. When New Haven invited Cotton to come there, Increase seemed to encourage the move. It took four years, 1680–1684, and repeated votes on the part of the church members before Cotton was at last ordained as pastor in association with his father. Even then, Increase accepted grudgingly, since they "could not agree to calling any other."[60]

Was this reluctance based on jealousy? Even as a young man, Cotton was brilliant, more brilliant than his father. Or did Increase distrust Cotton's exaggerated piety? In his private devotions, Cotton was unrestrained: "This Day, with Anguish of Soul, in The Sense of my own Sinfulness, and Filthiness, I cast myself prostrate, on my Study-floor with my mouth in the Dust"[61] Or did Cotton's richly ornate language, so different from Increase's plain style, make Increase hesitate? Two years after Cotton was finally ordained, Samuel Sewall, an old-fashioned Puritan, found Cotton's language in questionable taste: "disgusted for some expressions; as, sweet-sented hands of Christ, Lord High Treasurer of AEthiopia, Ribband of Humility—which was sorry for, because of the excellency and seasonableness of the subject."[62] Increase's whole lifestyle, like his prose, was stubbornly, ideologically plain, severe, ascetic. Cotton's was flamboyant and exhibitionistic. Cotton was an extrovert. He exuded an energy and outwardness that the father would never match. In Cotton, Increase had a tiger by the tail.

Or was it that Increase delayed his son's ordination in order to make doubly sure that this extraordinary mercy was God's will and not some self-serving fancy? Increase Mather was excruciatingly humble before divine Providence. If God in his wisdom so decreed that father and son should serve together in the same church, that would surely come to pass even if Increase proposed alternatives. Increase's later gratitude at his good fortune in having his son as colleague seems sincere. Still, the ambivalence remained. In July 1682, Increase profusely thanked his church for choosing Cotton: "You . . . have so many ways obliged me, that I cannot think my Son, or anything that is mine, too good or too deare for you. . . . And I am really sensible to your affection manifested toward myself in the great love and respect you have showed to one . . . so nearly related to me."[63] Increase then postponed Cotton's ordination another three whole years. At last, despite it all, and after years of procrastination, Cotton was ordained pastor of the North Church. As if making one last, despairing, subtly indirect reference to his anxieties about the partnership now formed, Mather preached a sermon that contained the story of Aaron and his son Eleazar (Numbers 20:26), in which the mantle of priesthood is passed from the father to the son—and the father dies.[64] The story is typically ambivalent, as well suggesting that Increase was now content to pass on his authority to his son as that he felt threatened with death. Or did not the one entail the other?

Aside from these doubts and ambiguities, Increase Mather took great pleasure in his family. One June day in 1681, he worked in his study from five o'clock in the morning until nine, and then went by boat with his wife and seven children to Winisemet, beyond Charlestown.[65] The next year he noted in his diary for August 14, 1682, "Walked around the Town with all my family." He had eight children by then. Cotton, twenty-one and preaching regularly, lorded it over the others. The two oldest girls were quite grown now. Maria, eighteen, and Elizabeth, sixteen, were sure to have carried themselves with great modesty. Little is known of their lives. Perhaps they helped their mother or perhaps they lived away from home, as sons often did, to learn about child rearing and household economy. Maria's first marriage was still six years away and Betty's fourteen. Like many women in those days, both girls would marry late, be widowed, and marry again. Nathaniel, next in age, was a student at Harvard in 1682. The most introspective of the children and the least robust of the Mather men, Nathaniel would increasingly immerse himself in books, only to succumb to an incurable disease before he was able to make a place for himself in the world. Then there were the little ones—Sarah, Samuel, Abigail, and Hannah, the youngest. As they walked about Boston's busy streets that summer day, Maria Mather was already big again with child. These years when Increase took his vacation out of Boston, he took Cotton with him, a vacation for both, and Cotton was a great help as secretary. One year they spent ten days in Dedham and "Went a Fishing in Dedham River." The next they went to Lynn, where the mineral springs were. On these joint holidays, father and son both preached in the local church and worked on Increase's next books.[66]

CONFIDENT YEARS

At no time had Increase been so happy. Everything seemed to be turning out well. Even the book he had written in Latin twelve years before, when he still longed for a European reputation, was, surprisingly, printed in Holland: *Diatriba De Signo Filii Hominis Et De Secundo Messiae Adventu*

(Amsterdam 1682). Abraham Kick in Amsterdam sent Increase a copy, and Increase wrote back to ask for fifty more to distribute here and there.[67] At least one went to the West Indies, to his old friend Samuel Bache, who had moved to Port Royal, Jamaica. Bache wrote to Boston, "I have lost since I came to this place more than three thousand pounds—yet, blessed be God, nothing but my owne." Bache's fortune was still large enough for him to make Increase a present of forty pieces of eight, as well as engage in a discussion of the intricacies of Mather's Latin book.[68]

Increase had also been diligent in maintaining ties with his brother Nathaniel, in Dublin since 1671. He and Increase kept up a steady correspondence, and Nathaniel never hesitated to act the older brother, correcting Increase's scholarship, reproving him for caving in on the question of baptism, criticizing his reliance on certain Puritan authorities, and ridiculing his belief in the effects of comets on human affairs. It was increasingly clear that the brothers' fortunes were very different. In contrast to Increase's large family, prosperous church, and important position in Boston, Nathaniel grew steadily poorer. His only daughter was nearly blind from a congenital defect. His small Dublin congregation met in private homes. Increase insisted on keeping the family connection alive. Twice he sent portraits of himself to Dublin and badgered Nathaniel to send his own portrait to Boston, a luxury Nathaniel could ill afford. The importuned portrait was at last sent, at a cost to Nathaniel of £3 9s.[69]

Increase also urged his brother to send over a sermon of his own, so that it could be printed in Boston. Finally Nathaniel acquiesced, and Increase added Nathaniel's sermon at the end of his own collection in *Doctrine of Divine Providence*. Nathaniel, however, was intent on another and more important work of scholarship. He labored to see into print brother Samuel's writings. In 1680 Nathaniel had published in London several of Samuel's sermons under the title *Irenicum*. Increase read them in Boston two years later. Much more important, Nathaniel strained all his resources to edit and publish Samuel's large book on typology: *Figures and Types of the Old Testament* (London, 1683), which became one of the two most important treatments of the subject in English at the end of the century. It had two printings, in 1683 and 1685, was reprinted in London in 1695, and was reset for a second edition in 1705.[70] In the beginning Nathaniel had to struggle to get it published at all. The London printer demanded an advance. Nathaniel raised a subscription at seven shillings per unbound copy. Bound copies were priced at ten shillings. Nathaniel apologized to Increase for sending him an unbound copy in fascicles. The publisher had given him only ten. He sent other copies to three of his American nephews: Cotton, Nathaniel, his namesake, and Warham, Eleazar's son.[71]

Figures and Types was a conservative treatment of typology, in which the method was confined to an exegesis of scripture. Samuel examined the ceremonies of worship in the Old Testament and explained how these "types" were "fulfilled" in the New Testament worship ceremonies, called "anti-types." He did not at all go on to suggest that events of his own lifetime fulfilled prototypes of biblical times.[72] It seems probable that Samuel's conservative typology helps explain Increase's conservatism, for the younger brother held Samuel in great respect. Increase was much less free with his typology than Cotton was to be.

In July 1682, Increase finished writing the preface to yet another collection of sermons, *Practical Truths Tending to Promote the Power of Godliness* (Boston, 1682). Publication costs were paid for by a subscription within his church, and in the preface addressed to his congregation, dated July 5, 1682, Increase expressed his appreciation with unprecedented warmth. Ten years earlier, he had felt it important to remind this same congregation that although he had preached to them for years, most of them remained unconverted. Now he wrote of love and gratitude: "If I (who, you will all say, have not been wont to flatter you) take notice of some vertues, wherein the Lord hath caused you to excel, . . . Not a Minister in *New England* [is] more happy than myself, in respect of a loving, and obedient People." "If I knew how to requite your love, I would do it!" "I have no other way to manifest my longings after you all, but by Prayers night and day for you, and *by Writing* as well as by Publick Ministrations, and personal instructions." "The Lord grant that both Speaker and Hearers, Writer and Readers, may rejoyce together in the day of Christ, in that they have not labored in vain!" This was as close to a public display of emotion that the man who schooled himself not to smile would ever come.[73] That preface was so personal, so emotional, so effusive that it offended a few old-timers accustomed to the greater restraint of an earlier age. John Higginson of Salem, son of Massachusetts's first minister, thanked Mather for the book of sermons, which he found satisfactory, "onely some both of Boston & here think the sermons would have been more usefull, if the Preface had been left out, but that may not be the apprehension of all."[74] So much for sentiment in New England.

In his private diaries, Mather expressed himself equally pleased with his lot, and here too the tone contrasts with the heartache of ten years before. Four months after he wrote the preface to *Practical Truths*, he made this unusual entry in his diary: "I have designed to set more Time apart this day than usually, To bless the Lord for such mercyes as these, viz God hath given me to be improved in his grand work. Hee hath given me to write as well as to preach for his Name, And improved me in some special Services, and given me acceptance amongst his people, all my sins and unworthiness notwithstanding. Hee hath remembered me in my Low estate, and spared my life diverse Times when near to death; And these 2 last years blessed me with Health. Hee hath preserved the Lives of all my children. Raised up my eldest son to improvement in the Lords work, my ears hearing and eyes beholding of it. Hee hath given me Comfort in other of my children. Hee hath given me a comfortable habitation. Hee hath so ordered by his providence as that I have a more Liberal Mayntenance, than any minister in N.E. And hath moreover, sometimes cast in unexpected supplies whereby I & mine have been refreshed. Hee hath given me many Bookes, as helps in his Service.

"Bless the Lord the God & Giver of these mercyes, O my soul, bless the Lord, bless the Lord!" [75]

Mather's good feelings about himself, his family, and his church were reflected in his preaching and writing throughout the 1680s. The awful threats of punishment for sins that seemed to dominate so much of the 1670s tended to disappear before a new mood of confidence and hope. Mather loved to demystify religion, a goal which lay at the heart of the earliest Puritan movement, and which partly accounts for the importance given to the plain style in preaching and writing. In *Practical Truths Tending to Promote the Power of Godliness* he gave clear, organized, easy-to-understand directions for worship. Pray, he urged his audience: in the "constant and conscionable practice whereof, so much of Religion doth consist." These are no threatening jeremiads, but simple directives for leading a moral and religious life. In the process, Mather strove to express complicated ideas simply. *"Baptism is a sign and seal of that Covenant which God hath through Jesus Christ, graciously established with the children of men."* [76] "Who are the true subjects of [the Lord's Supper]? Except men have experienced a work of regeneration in their souls, they are not meet subjects of this holy Ordinance." It is a "great evil" when unregenerate persons participate. [77] "It is necessary that we should know and believe, that the words ['this is my Body, etc '] are figurative and not to be taken in a proper sense." [78] The uniform tone of these 1682 sermons is hopeful and moderate. "Beware of excessive toiling and moiling in the World, because that doth incline to sleepiness. And remember to be temperate in all things." [79]

In 1686 Mather published two more collections of sermons in the same evangelistic vein. They would prove to be his last such published collections before he and all Massachusetts were caught up in English imperial politics. One of the new collections was the group of sacramental sermons preached in the 1670s and only now published, *The Mystery of Christ Opened and Applyed*, the evangelical character of which has already been described.[80] In the 1686 preface to these sermons, Mather took aim at the tide of rationalism and atheism rising in Europe. He quoted John Owen, "We have now a great number who oppose the Person and Glory of Christ under a pretence of *Sobriety of Reason*," and added his own sarcastic dart against educated people: "*You may know much in the Tongues of Arts (as the Devils do), yea and have a doctrinal historical knowledge of Christ, too, and yet not savingly know the truth as it is in Jesus.*"[81] Knowledge in and of itself was not sufficient. "There is moreover saving knowledge which is a special grace of the holy Spirit, peculiar to the Elect of God, h.e. when a man knoweth the truths of the Gospel, so as to feel the transforming sanctifying power of them in his own Soul. Job 17.3. This we fitly call the *grace of knowledge*."[82]

The most pietistic of all Mather's books was made up of sermons preached in 1684–1685 and published early in 1686: *The Greatest Sinners Exhorted and Encouraged to Come to Christ*. "*The Law must be preached,*" he wrote, "*inasmuch as thereby is the* Knowledge of Sin, *without which men will never be duly sensible of their need of* Christ. *But it is the* Gospel (*and not the Law*) *which is the* word of Faith. *Sinners will never come to Christ except they be perswaded of His* Ability and Willingness to save. *This the Gospel doth make known, as also that the gracious God is ready for His Son's sake to pardon all those that truly repent.*"[83] The lead sermon in this collection was preached on the text John 6:37: "And him that cometh to me I will in no wise cast out." Thus in the 1680s did Mather preach the Gospel of forgiveness. His greatest ambition was to bring people to Christ, to save souls.

The new outreach had already proved successful. Mather noted dramatic increases in new members and in baptisms in 1681 and 1682. Emblematic of the evangelism of these years was the return of John Farnum after almost twenty years of excommunication and association with the Baptists. Farnum now asked for reinstatement, and after a full confession before the congregation, he was welcomed back to the North Church.[84]

It occurred to Mather now, in the forty-sixth year of his life, that he should write his autobiography. During the closing months of 1685 he sat down with the many volumes of his diary to write his life's story. The idea and the form it took were not original with Mather. Others, notably his father and his father's colleague Thomas Shepard, had written autobiographies at about the same time in their lives.[85] Like Shepard, and probably like his father, Increase wrote for his children, and like them he had no intention to publish. Such autobiographies were family documents. It is clear in the opening address and in later references to them that Mather meant by his children both his sons and daughters. "Dear children," he started, "[you] are all of you so many parts of myselfe; and dearer to me than things which I enjoy in the world."[86] We will not live long together here on earth, he went on, but if we "meet in Heaven and be forever with the Lord, that's happiness enough. I am not altogether without hope concerning my own Interest in Christ. I have thought that the relation of what the Lord has done for your Father, and the wonderfull experience which hee has had of Gods Faithfullness towards him, might be a meanes to cause you to give yourselves entirely to the Lord Jesus, and to endeavor to walk with God."[87]

The confidence in his own "Interest in Christ" does not hide another feature of Mather's Puritanism, his premise that God will faithfully hold up his end of the covenant. This belief played an important part in Mather's recovery from the dark days of 1671, when he had written "There never was any one (I think so) that came to God . . . that yet was denied his Request." Mather went so far as to argue with himself then, and repeated it in his autobiography now, that he must be saved, because if it were not so, "others after my decease, that should see the papers which I had written and kept as remembrances of my walking before God, would be discouraged. For they would see and say, "Here was one that prayed . . . and believed . . . and yet hee perished . . . Hee would tell others, and then they would conclude that there is not so much in prayer, and that Faith is not such a mighty thing as the word of God sayth it is . . . "[88]

The autobiography, however, was meant to be more than a lesson in Puritan spirituality. Mather wanted his children to know their father's life history. In this Increase was no different from his own father or Thomas Shepard. All three men organized their autobiographies as narratives of their external as well as their spiritual lives. Like all historians, they were selective. Increase devoted as much space to his four years in England, 1657–1661, as he had to the preceding eighteen years, even though those earlier years included his conversion, his mother's death, his education at John Norton's, and Harvard. He then spent only half as much space on the troubled years when he came back to Boston, married, and was ordained as teacher in the North Church. He was frank about matters another person might have glossed over: his dislike of Boston in the 1660s, his temptations to atheism, and his reluctance to join the church.[89] He was equally open about not at first wanting Cotton to be his associate in the church. ("I was very backward in consenting to their desires, because of my Relation to him. But considering the church could not agree in calling any other, I gave way to their Importunity."[90]) But there was one subject, crucial in Mather's life, that he could not bear to examine. It was the synod of 1662. Increase made no mention of his earlier disagreement with his father over the half-way covenant. Increase's physical and emotional collapse after the deaths of his father and Eleazar, and his recovery and renewed spiritual assurance, constitute the central portion of the story.[91]

The autobiography has an awkward structure. The narrative is often interrupted with long quotations from the diaries. Chronology is several times ignored, as it was in Increase's biography of his father. Substantial passages seem to have been added as afterthoughts. For example, after the narrative of events reached 1685, he wrote, "Thus have I related the story of my owne life for more than 46 years, so farr as I am able to recollect, and think convenient to express."[92] But then he went on to note in great detail the prayers he had offered over the years for each of his children. He afterwards turned to moments of spiritual exaltation. Many of these he copied down, for the "edification of the children."[93] The autobiography thus served several purposes, some devotional, some not. For the time being he put the manuscript away among his other papers.

CHAPTER 6

Dominion of New England

[1684-1688]

The English government was slow to take up the challenge of overseas colonies. Parliament acted first by passing legislation to keep trade with the colonies in the hands of English merchants and ship owners. Disposition of American lands was considered to be in the king's prerogative—part of the king's domain—and royal government, as distinct from Parliament, was slow to turn its attention to America. Charles II created a Council for Foreign Plantations under the presidency of Sir Anthony Ashley Cooper, Earl of Shaftesbury, a brilliant man sympathetic to English Dissenters and parliamentary law. It was Shaftesbury who employed John Locke to draft a constitution for Carolina that included religious toleration for all. He soon was in opposition to the prerogative party in England. In 1675 Charles II reorganized the oversight of colonial affairs with far-reaching consequences for English America. The old Council for Foreign Plantations was replaced by a Committee of the Privy Council for Trade and Plantations. Members of this committee came to be known as the Lords of Trade. They were supported by a rapidly expanding office staff under the direction of William Blathwayt, and they were to supervise the American colonies for the next twenty years. The Lords of Trade, usually dominated by the Tory Lord Treasurer, Thomas Osborne, Earl of Danby, were immediately responsible for the decisions in England that revoked Massachusetts's charter by 1684 and replaced the independent Puritan colony with a royal dominion.

FISSURES IN PURITAN SOCIETY

Underlying conditions in New England that brought on these decisions to overthrow the Massachusetts government are centered in economic competition.[1] In the long run, economic competition was far more corrosive to the harmony of Puritan Massachusetts than religious differences like those between Mather and Solomon Stoddard or the Baptists. A desire for land underlay the corruption of Puritan social organization, Puritan government, and Puritan values. The biggest single battle was over title to the so-called Narragansett Lands, bounded on the east by Narragansett Bay and the west by the ill-defined border of Connecticut. The largest single consortium of speculators—the region was too large and the prize too much sought after for a single person to have a chance—was the Atherton Associates, headed by Major Humphrey Atherton, whose daughter married Timothy Mather. Even after the boundary between Connecticut and Rhode Island was drawn in the 1660s, competing groups presented a welter of conflicting titles and claims to these potentially rich farmlands, and their lobbying in London brought royal intervention in New England from the Restoration to the end of the century.[2]

The same is true of land claims north of Boston between the Merrimack and Piscataqua Rivers. Massachusetts extended its jurisdiction over four towns in this region during the 1640s, although its charter ran only to the southern bank of the Merrimack. Between the Merrimack and the Piscataqua, the region known later as New Hampshire, the land had been granted in the 1620s to Captain John Mason, and now his heir Robert Mason, resident in England, laid claim to it. Here again land speculation and contested land titles brought the royal government to interfere in the affairs of the Puritan commonwealth.[3] After King Philip's War, the Nipmuck Country of central Massachusetts was opened for settlement and became a third enticement for land-hungry settlers and for speculators.[4] The poison appeared not only among big speculators. In every Massachusetts community men and women more interested in private property than in Christian fellowship quickly appeared. In Dedham, for example, after only twenty years, the town proprietors closed the door to newcomers and kept for themselves and their heirs the public lands within the town boundaries.[5] In Andover, which was settled in 1646, the first comers made their control of public lands permanent in 1662, after sixteen years.[6] The population, spurred on by extraordinary fertility and low infant mortality, put increasing pressure on the settlement patterns of the earliest decades, and by the 1670s families were moving away from village centers. But big speculators were those who carried their cases to London and set in train the actions that would soon destroy the Puritan state. William Bradford gave the land hunger its earliest and most poignant expression when he sorrowfully described Plymouth as "like an ancient mother grown old and forsaken by her children."[7]

Next to land hunger, overseas commerce worked to change the early Puritan way of life. After 1660, commerce between American colonies and between the colonies and England became the dynamic force in Massachusetts's economy. A complex web of trade routes reached from the cod fisheries off Newfoundland and the forests of white pine in New Hampshire all the way south to the sugar islands in the Caribbean, east to the Portuguese-owned Wine Islands in the eastern Atlantic, and north to England itself. The regulation of this complicated ocean traffic was laid down in three acts of Parliament, the Navigation Acts of 1660, 1662, and 1673. When New England merchants entered into ocean commerce, inevitably they entered into a system of rules and regulations set forth by the government in London. It was therefore to London and not Boston that they turned for privilege, license, or arbitration. Commerce, then, as well as land, caused the English government to intervene in the affairs of Massachusetts. Questions of religion mattered very little. Whitehall was largely indifferent to religion in America, demanding of Massachusetts only liberty for an Anglican church in Boston. New England merchants frequently visited London, where they negotiated business and established social and family ties with London merchants. During their London sojourns they made a small but vocal lobby in the Exchange and were a ready source of firsthand advice for the policy makers at Whitehall. These colonial entrepreneurs, merchants, and land speculators alike saw that the center of power lay in London.

There grew up, consequently, an uncertain but nonetheless important division in New England between those who had affairs in London, and so tended to be mindful of the larger world of Europe, and the large majority of people who seemed in their own minds to live quite independently of the old country. This was the critical division in the crisis looming up. The division was partly geographic: Boston, Salem, Ipswich, and a few other coastal towns developed as seaports with frequent connections overseas. The interior towns, like Sudbury, Lancaster, Billerica, and scores more, were a world apart, isolated from Europe. The division was partly one of economic class: by and large, land speculators and merchants were wealthy people; those who lived simple farming lives, and whose commerce was limited to carrying firewood to Boston or provisions to weekly markets, were likely to be poor and less well educated. The division was also partly one of temperament, sentiment, and personality. Not everyone living in Massachusetts after the Restoration was an ascetic Puritan, and even people who thought of themselves as Puritans felt a tug from English fashion and English loyalties. All these things tended to separate people who were favorable to England from those who were indifferent or hostile. The lines converged at Boston, the bustling seaport, the center of wealth, the center of cosmopolitan fashion, and of course, also the locus of the Puritan government and the leadership of the Puritan church.

Hence there was a "moderate" party, so called because its members favored compromise and moderation in disputes that arose between Massachusetts and England. And there was the "popular faction," so called because it was more numerous, poorer, and less well educated. When it came to a vote on a specific issue, the assistants or magistrates were almost evenly divided between the two positions, sometimes voting this way, sometimes that. The deputies always voted overwhelmingly with the popular faction. This political division reflected the fact that the assistants or magistrates were always men of wealth and education, while the deputies, except in the cases of one or two seaports, were the representatives of interior townspeople. It is impossible to know what percentage of adult males were eligible to vote in general elections. In Boston it may have been as little as one in eight by 1685, although in the smaller towns the proportion would have been much higher.[8] The deputies therefore were heavily biased towards a religious conservatism no longer clearly representative of the majority of the population. The position of the ministers in this division between moderate and popular attitudes towards England was awkward. For the most part, ministers allied themselves with the magistrates. There was a clear-cut class interest here. Wealth, education, and self-perception all tended to ally the ministers with the moderate party and the magistrates. But ministers were pulled the other way by the members of their churches and by the opposition of royal and Episcopal England.

END OF INDEPENDENCE

For fifteen years after the Restoration Massachusetts managed to maintain virtually complete *de facto* independence of England. In 1676 the course of events took a new direction.[9] In London the new Committee for Trade and Plantations had charge of colonial affairs for the crown. One of the first men to petition it for redress of grievances was Robert Mason, grandson of the first patentee of New Hampshire. He wanted to collect rent on his lands there. They had been settled in four small villages from Massachusetts and were presently governed from Boston. The Lords of Trade sent a courier to Massachusetts to instruct it to respond to Mason's claims, and they also told the courier to look about him and make an evaluation of the Puritan colonies. The person chosen for this job was Edward Randolph, a cousin of Mason's.[10] If there was ever an evil genius behind the downfall of the Puritan commonwealth in Massachusetts, it was Edward Randolph.

Randolph arrived in Boston in 1676 toward the close of King Philip's War. Crusty Governor John Leverett gave him short answers, among them the observation that the laws of Parliament did not reach beyond the four seas. Despite this rebuff Randolph probed into the politics of Massachusetts and the other New England colonies. It did not take him long to discover the split between the moderate party and the popular faction. On his return to London, he reported that the best men of the colonies were out of sympathy with the Puritan government in Massachusetts and would support royal intervention. Meanwhile, Randolph said, Massachusetts harbored the regicides Goffe and Whalley, denied Anglicans and Quakers religious opportunity, ignored Parliament's laws of trade, coined their own money, employed their own oath of fidelity instead of the oath of allegiance to the king, and allowed only members of the churches to vote. In short, he reported, Massachusetts had formed itself into a commonwealth and governed itself by laws repugnant to the laws of England. The Massachusetts General Court decided to send two agents to negotiate about New Hampshire, and when they arrived in London at the end of 1676, they were confronted with a barrage of questions stemming from Randolph's report.

The agents, William Stoughton and Peter Bulkeley, had been given little leeway by the General Court and were able to make only weak denials of the accusations. The Lords of Trade asked the attorney general to present legal opinions about rescinding the Massachusetts charter or having the charter submitted voluntarily by Massachusetts for appropriate modifications. Before anything could be resolved, in the fall of 1678, a political crisis developed in London around the person of Titus Oates and his stories of a Popish plot to assassinate the king. In the ensuing uproar the Earl of Danby was impeached, and the work of the Lords of Trade came to a sudden halt, but not before Mason was ruled to be entitled to rents from New Hampshire farmers and the king was advised to send his own governor there. Agents Stoughton and Bulkeley were allowed to return home, after three years, with instructions to Massachusetts to send back agents more fully authorized to negotiate changes in the charter.

The Massachusetts General Court now had to face again the prospect of complying with the Lords of Trade or not. Until January 1681, it delayed a decision whether or not to send agents as requested. It asked the ministers in Boston to give their opinion, and at that time Increase Mather voted with the majority to send the agents, thus taking a typically moderate position.[11] The elected leaders of the popular faction, Thomas Danforth, the Deputy Governor, and Samuel Nowell, a magistrate, railed against the ministers. "The governor and several of the Magistrates, declared their thankful acceptance of what was done, but Mr. Danforth, the dep. Governor, reflected upon it, as if it tended to cut off some of the Countrye's Libertyes. Several of the elders expressed their resentment of those reflections amongst which I was one," Mather wrote.[12] Edward Randolph at the back of the room witnessed the same scene and reported it to London: Danforth "makes satyrical reflections upon them [the ministers], calls them the betrayers of their liberty, etc., Mr. Dudley, one of the Magistrates, replys; but Mr. Stoughton could hardly contain himself, that both Governor and others were ashamed of Mr. Danforth's discourse."[13]

After another long procrastination, two agents were dispatched to London. Both of them were close associates of Mather. One was Joseph Dudley, son of one of the founders, and a wealthy farmer in Roxbury. When graduating from Harvard College, Dudley had toyed with the idea of entering the ministry, and Mather had talked to him about serving as his assistant at North Church.[14] Dudley had chosen a life of politics instead. The other agent was John Richards, a merchant, a member of Mather's church for twenty years and an intimate friend. It was he who kept Mather fully informed of the negotiations between the agents and the Committee for Trade and Plantations.[15] Every letter from London made it seem that Massachusetts would soon lose its cherished independence, but it took the arrival of a royal governor for New Hampshire to make Mather join sides with Thomas Danforth and the popular faction.

The Lords of Trade selected as governor of New Hampshire a man named Lionel Cranfield. They could hardly have made a worse choice. Cranfield's political incompetence, personal greed, and overweening arrogance made New Hampshire a sobering example of what Massachusetts might expect if the king were to revise the Bay Company charter and send a governor there as well. Cranfield arrived late in 1682, and after a formal dinner at the Town House in Boston, which Mather attended with the other ministers, made his way to his post in New Hampshire. He frankly intended to use the position to make his fortune. To his disgust, Cranfield found that unlike the West Indies, New Hampshire offered slim pickings. He dissolved the elected assembly and announced his intention to govern only with the aid of a council appointed from London. There followed a pathetic little *opéra bouffe* rebellion led by Edward Gove, who was soon arrested and sent to jail in Boston. Mather visited him there twice and got an earful of Cranfield's misdoings. Ultimately Gove was taken to England and released. Even Edward Randolph, a stickler for authority, thought Gove a harmless person. [16] In his reckless attempts to make a fortune, Cranfield managed to alienate every economic and political interest in New England. In London, meanwhile, Joseph Dudley and John Richards tried to fend off the Committee for Trade and Plantations. Their instructions explicitly forbade agreeing to any fundamental changes in the charter, and they stuck to their guns. Eventually the committee sought to force the issue by a court action in the form of a writ of *Quo Warranto*. If it were successful, this writ would result in the nullification of the Massachusetts charter. The writ was issued in June 1683. At Edward Randolph's suggestion, Charles II promised the Puritans that if the colony resigned its charter without a court trial, the crown would make only minimum changes in it. If, however, the colony contested the writ in court, then the men responsible for that decision would be held personally responsible in England. [17]

MATHER AND THE POLITICS OF INDEPENDENCE

How should Massachusetts, that City on a Hill, respond? The General Court met on November 7, 1683. The entire transatlantic Puritan community entered into the debate and advice came from all quarters. Submit the charter for amendments, or appear in court and contest the writ and warrants. With the example of New Hampshire so close to the north, Mather threw his weight to the popular faction: resist to the end. "Several papers were brought to me," he wrote, "some that came out of England or Holland others written in New England which argued for the Negative. I put those arguments into Form, and added some more of my owne, and then communicated them to some of the Magistrates, who so well approved of them as to disperse copyes thereof, that they came into many hands, and were a meanes to keep the Countrey from complying with that proposal." [18] On December 5 the die was cast when a vote was taken in the General Court. The popular faction won. Massachusetts would defend its charter in the courts. They wrote to London to employ an attorney, one Robert Humphreys, Esq., Inner Temple. Peter Bulkeley expressed the exasperation of the moderate party: "By such (ape-like) overfondness, wee are hugging our privileges and franchises to death and preferre the dissolution of our Body politique, rather then to suffer Amputation in any of its limbs." [19]

That same December in New Hampshire Edward Cranfield ordered that the ministers there must celebrate the Lord's Supper according to the Anglican Prayer Book. [20] In Boston, a town meeting was called to select men for jury duty, and Samuel Nowell turned it into a referendum on the General Court's decision to protect the charter. All adult men in Boston ordinarily participated in town meetings, but on this occasion only freemen, that is church members, were asked to vote. They were certainly no more than a third of the adult men, probably fewer. After the non-free withdrew, Increase Mather was asked to speak. In a short but passionate speech Mather urged the townsmen not to submit to regulation of their charter by Whitehall. The body of the speech made large use of Old Testament precedents and of what had just happened in New Hampshire under Cranfield. "I hope there is not one Freeman in Boston," he closed, "that will dare to be guilty of so great a sin." "Many of the Freemen wept," he later wrote, "and they said generally, we thank you Sir for this instruction and encouragement." When the vote was taken, no one in the room voted for submission of the charter. [21] The speech had been a great success. It was Mather's first experience with political speech making. He was overwhelmed and exhilarated with the response.

Leaders of the moderate point of view were openly critical of his meddling in the political life of the colony. His diary entries shortly afterwards reveal his agitation over the criticism. "Mr. W. sayd that paper of Arguments & c. had done more mischief to N. E. than King & Courts." And again, "With Magistrates & Ministers at the Townhouse. Mr. W. sayd that the paper of Arguments was a Libell. Some others sayd it was worse than the Libell." [22] Events in New Hampshire strengthened the popular faction. Cranfield arrested Joshua Moody for refusing to use the Anglican liturgy, and although he was released soon, both Seaborn

Cotton and Joshua Moody fled to Boston in the face of the Governor's threats.[23] New Hampshire had become an all-too-obvious object lesson of what royal government could mean for Massachusetts.

The annual elections that spring were extraordinary. Anonymous pamphlets criticized Governor Bradstreet and other moderates, a public criticism of standing authority unheard of in the earlier days of the colony. To many it was a sure sign of political decay.[24] In the outcome, Simon Bradstreet was reelected, and again Thomas Danforth came in second as Deputy Governor. But Joseph Dudley and other moderate magistrates lost their places. William Stoughton and Peter Bulkeley were so disgusted at the success of the popular faction that they refused to take their seats. Into the magistracy came leaders of the popular, anti-English faction. Most fateful among these was the election of Elisha Cooke, a man two years older than Mather, his contemporary at Harvard, and a Boston physician. In 1668 Cooke married the daughter of then governor John Leverett, to which alliance, perhaps, may be traced the eventual rancor between Cooke and Increase Mather. Cooke had been elected a deputy for Boston in 1681 on a platform of resistance to England. By 1683 he had been chosen Speaker of the House of Deputies, and now in 1684 he replaced Dudley among the Magistrates. The hostility between Cooke and Dudley became a constant of Massachusetts politics. Meanwhile, Mather had become clearly associated with the anti-English faction. Edward Randolph wrote after the election, "I find all are mad in your country, and that *Mr. Mather the Bellowes of Sedition and Treason, has at last attained his end in setting his fools a horseback. If they do not mend their manners, some of them may ride to the divill.*"[25]

TREASON OR A FORGERY?

Not long after that, Mather had a bad scare. It seemed he would be accused of treason for letters written to Amsterdam. A political struggle in England had forced the Earl of Shaftesbury to flee, and he had taken refuge in Abraham Kick's house in Amsterdam, where he died in 1683. Kick was one of Mather's correspondents. It is not surprising to learn that a packet of letters addressed to Kick was intercepted and turned over to one of the English Secretaries of State. One of the letters was critical enough of the English government to warrant in those days an arrest for treason. Edward Randolph identified it as coming from Increase Mather's pen.[26]

The first Mather knew of it was when he heard that some letters of his to Amsterdam had been stolen and turned over to the government in London. Mather was frightened. "I being in some distress of spirit," he wrote, "because I hear, that some letters which I sent to Holland, are fallen into the hands of them at Whitehall, doe humbly vow unto The Lord, if God will save me out of this distress; and if he will be so gracious as to send tidings from London, that he has delivered me from the malice of those that designed evill against me. Then the Lord shall be my God, and I will (Christ helping of me) endeavor to doe more for his glory than every yet I have done." [27] Later Mather learned that his letter was printed in the Tory *Observator* and a copy taken to Barbados and talked about throughout the Caribbean. [28] He became more and more worried. "I am told that a letter of mine sent to Amsterdam is carried to Whitehall, and the Toreys say it is Treason, and that I shall be sent to London, so that my estate and life is struck at. . . . I likewise hear that the great ones in England are offended at what I spoke to the Freemen in Boston." [29]

Mather was enormously relieved when he finally saw the letter in question. He got a copy at long last in November from Joseph Dudley, who in turn had it from Edward Randolph. The letter was a forgery, he said, based on an original, but clearly concocted to get him in trouble. [30] Mather blamed Randolph for the deception. As for the denouement of this little drama, Randolph, writing to Simon Bradstreet, reported only that the Secretary of State, on being told that Increase Mather was the author of the letter, scoffingly replied, "What, is it that Star-Gazer, that half-distracted man?" and let the matter drop. [31]

Once Mather saw the letter and denounced it as a forgery, his anxiety disappeared. He described in detail to Dudley how unthinkable were the statements he was supposed to have made, and he hugged himself with pleasure over his role as martyr. [32] "I could now read the Booke of psalmes with particular application and more feelingly than ever in my life before," he wrote. "I could now say, princes have sat and spoken against me. I am filled with the contempt of them that are at ease. The proud have had me greatly in derision. They have forged a ly against me. They have digged pits for me. The wicked have wayted for me to destroy me. Deliver me not to the will of mine enemies; False witnesses are risen up against me, and such as breath out cruelty. And innumerable other passages in the Psalmes could I then read and pray over so as never before nor since." [33] At another time, he wrote in the same vein: God "has so farr gratified my desires of suffering for him, as that my Name has bin cast forth as vile, and wicked men in England, Scotland, Ireland, Holland, Barbados, Nevis, etc.—have bin speaking all maner of evill of me falsely. And I would faign hope that the ground of these my sufferings has bin, because I have desired to approve my selfe faithfull to the Lord Jesus and to his Kingdome and Interest." [34]

The fate of the Puritan commonwealth, meanwhile, was being decided in London, at Whitehall. The writ of *Quo Warranto* issued in 1683 proved defective on a technicality, but a writ of *Scire Facias* served the same purpose. At the instigation of the Committee for Trade and Plantations, Massachusetts's charter was extinguished. The Lords of Trade could now proceed to establish a more appropriate form of government. They recommended merging New Hampshire, Maine, and Plymouth settlements with Massachusetts. They were inclined to include Rhode Island and Connecticut, too, but because those two colonies still had valid charters, further legal action was necessary. The form of the new government was at yet undecided. Charles II wanted to appoint Colonel Piercy Kirke governor. Kirke had recently returned from the English garrison at Tangiers, where he had earned an evil reputation for brutality. His appointment to govern Massachusetts with regular troops would have been a disaster. The new governor would have a council appointed by the king. The Lords of Trade recommended an elected legislative assembly, too, but word came down from the king's chambers to omit it. [35] Months passed before these decisions could reach Boston. Meanwhile, successive rumors filtered across the Atlantic, each one more ominous than those that preceded it.

POPULAR CULTURE IN PURITAN BOSTON

In the fall of 1685, when Massachusetts was seemingly open to invasion by whatever ungodly people the king might choose to send, a young man arrived in Boston who advertised himself as a dancing master. A cheeky person by all accounts, Francis Stepney was reported as saying he could teach more divinity in one lesson on the dance floor than Mr. Willard or the Old Testament. True or not, Stepney certainly did advertise dancing lessons, and even scheduled them on Thursday, in competition with the traditional Thursday lectures. A deputation of the town's ministers complained to the magistrates. Samuel Sewall had just been elected to the magistracy, and he reported of the ministers' petition: "Mr. Moodey said, 'twas not a time fore N. E. to dance. Mr. Mather struck at the Root, speaking against mixt Dances."[36] Not surprisingly, the magistrates ordered Stepney to discontinue his lessons.

It was symptomatic of the vast changes taking place in Boston that Stepney had allies among the wealthy men and women of the city. Fifty-five years after John Winthrop's arrival, there were gentry in Boston who showed little of his asceticism. Samuel Shrimpton, reputed to be the richest man in Boston, put up bond for Stepney's appearance at court, and a trial was insisted on. Increase Mather wrote ruefully that "many in Boston, yea, some church members did encourage him."[37] With people of wealth and position behind the dancing master, the affair dragged on for another six months, until at last, by June 1686, Stepney fled the city with a warrant for his arrest and several unpaid creditors at his heels.[38]

Long before then, Increase had written a small volume called *An Arrow against Profane and Promiscuous Dancing*, a short but ponderous analysis of dancing, written at the request of the other ministers and filled with absurd word inventions quite unlike Mather's usual style. For example, Mather wrote that the issue had nothing to do with "*Pyrrhical* or *Polemical Saltation*: i.e. when men vault in their Armour," or sober dancing of men with men, women with women. The issue had to do only with "*Gynecandrical Dancing*, or that which is commonly called *Mixt* or *Promiscuous Dancing*, viz. of Men and Women . . . together." Nevertheless, the book does convey Mather's personal disgust at public intimacies. "If the Holy Prophet *Isaiah* were alive in these dayes, he would not call a *stretched neck, and wanton eye, a Mincing as they go*, by the name of good carriage. . . . In this debauched Age: frequent *Osculations* amongst those that are not in any conjugal Relation, is called good Breeding, Gentile behaviour, and the like."[39]

Such stilted and artificial language was unusual. Shortly after *An Arrow*, Mather preached a sermon at the opposite end of the stylistic spectrum and far more representative of New England Puritan culture: *A Sermon Occasioned by the Execution of a Man found Guilty of Murder*. Mather's sermon is more important for its place in the overall occasion than for its development of his thought or style. James Morgan, a convicted murderer, was brought to Second Church on the Sunday morning of March 7, 1686. Cotton Mather preached. That afternoon the prisoner was taken to First Church, and Joshua Moody preached. Four days later the convicted man was taken to First Church again, and Increase Mather preached the Thursday lecture. This time, after the sermon Morgan was led to the gallows, passing on foot through streets and lanes crowded

A Sermon Occasioned by the Execution of a Man found Guilty of Murder, 1686

with gaping spectators. The whole proceeding over several days was an elaborate public spectacle designed both to instruct and entertain.

All three sermons were printed. Increase Mather's was a characteristic harangue. He was at the height of his powers as an orator, and his audience surely numbered several thousand in the multi-tiered meetinghouse. Starting calmly, Mather moved relentlessly towards an emotional climax in which he turned to the condemned man, rehearsed his confession, pleaded with him to believe in Christ, and assured him that if his repentance were sincere, on the very moment of death his soul would be transported to the right side of God, his sins forgiven, and his eternal life in heaven assured. I cannot forgive you, Mather told the prisoner before him; only Christ can judge your sincerity.

The publication of all three "execution sermons" in one volume gave a new twist in the history of Boston's book trade. One of the principals was Joseph Browning, who had already published *Kometographia* and *Doctrine of Divine Providence*. In 1686 another book publisher, an Englishman named John Dunton, arrived in Boston just in time to witness Morgan's execution. Dunton was a mountebank, and his role in the history of book publishing in Massachusetts is, like the history of the almanacs, an illustration of an elite press invaded by entrepreneurs of popular culture.[40] He and Browning arranged to publish all three execution sermons, and a large printing was run with separate title pages for the two publishers. Browning advertised his at his shop in Boston, Dunton opened a shop in Salem. Dunton soon afterwards returned to London. Each publisher brought out a second edition, one in Boston in 1687, the other in London in 1691. Increase Mather was uneasy over such commercial use of the sermons. In the preface he wrote, *"The Sermons . . . are Published to gratifie some who have been perhaps too importunately, desirous to have it so. . . . "* He hinted that in their hurry the publishers had pushed him to transcribe only part of his sermon.[41] But Mather's reservations were not strong enough for him to forego the publishers' offer. The appearance, even briefly, of European book publishers like Dunton, and the evident commerical success of Browning mark the start of a new period in Boston's literary history. Publishing was becoming increasingly varied and increasingly oriented toward popular tastes.

PRESIDENT PRO TEMPORE OF HARVARD COLLEGE

Harvard College had had a string of bad luck. After Urian Oakes died in 1681 and after Increase Mather declined to leave Boston, the Overseers finally reached an agreement with John Rogers. Rogers had preached in his father's church at Ipswich, but had chosen to follow the career of a physician. Rogers had been offered the presidency earlier, in 1677, but had turned it down then after months of procrastination. He was a sweet-tempered but self-indulgent man and did not assume his duties right away. Increase Mather was prevailed upon to conduct the commencement ceremonies in the summer of 1682, and for the next year the campus was left without the discipline or leadership of a president. Rogers did finally come, but he died suddenly, one might almost say perversely, in less than a year.[42]

Again the Overseers and the Corporation started their search. Both Joshua Moody and Michael Wigglesworth were canvassed and refused the job. The undergraduates meanwhile became increasingly rowdy. High jinks were the order of the day. On one occasion several undergraduates stole some turkeys and cooked them upstairs in the dormitory. The incident and attendant outrage were widely publicized.[43] Doubtless Mather was kept fully informed, for his son Nathaniel was in his senior year, and his nephew, Seaborn's son John Cotton, a resident tutor. Another nephew, Warham Mather, Eleazar's oldest son, was also a senior and due to graduate with Nathaniel.

In March 1685, the Overseers came back to Increase and asked him to be president *pro tempore* while they continued their search. Under the proposed arrangement he would not have to leave his church in Boston. The Corporation offered to keep a horse for him at Charlestown. Mather could take the ferry that crossed the bay between the North End and Charlestown. From there it was but a short horseback ride to the village of Cambridge and the college. Mather accepted the offer.[44]

Old College building, to which Increase and Eleazar had journeyed thirty years before, had long since been razed to the ground, and in its place now was a massive brick building called locally New College, but later designated Old Harvard Hall. Increase plunged into his new responsibilities there with enthusiasm. His college salary of £100 he gave away, £50 to clear up old debts of the college, £50 to be shared between the two tutors. He was determined to pull the college out of the doldrums caused by the long periods without leadership. He made weekly trips and often stayed in Cambridge overnight. He imposed a new and stricter discipline, and the next year drew up a new set of College Laws.[45] All students were again required to live and eat in the college buildings and to attend all scheduled exercises and study periods. No student was allowed to buy or sell or trade anything without his parents' permission. Upperclassmen were strictly forbidden to force freshmen "by blows, threats or language of any kind" to go on errands for them.

Equally important was Mather's influence on the curriculum. He began by warning the students that he would expect orations at commencement time in Greek and Hebrew as well as in the traditional Latin. He ordered the tutors to require undergraduates to translate every day "at least 20 verses in the N.T. out of English into Greek."[46] It seems probable, too, that Mather changed the curriculum to discontinue ethics as a separate area of study. If such was indeed the case, it was an attempt to make scripture the sole guide in moral questions and ignore pagan ethical writing.[47] "It is much to be lamented," he wrote in 1689, "that many Preachers in these days have hardly any other Discourses in their Pulpits than what we may find in *Seneca, Epictetus, Plutarch*, or some such Heathen *Moralist*. Christ, the Holy Spirit, and (in a word) *the Gospel* is not in their Sermons."[48] Mather introduced the study of contemporary physics through the use of the notes of Charles Morton's *Compendium Physicae*. Numerous propositions from it were presented at the commencement exercises by 1687. Morton's book, however, was unpublished and circulated only in manuscript.[49]

Mather's announcement about Greek and Hebrew brought cries of anguish from the students. Why learn a dead language? No one in Massachusetts could speak Greek or Hebrew. Nine students signed a witty, sophomoric letter "to demonstrate how ridiculous it seems . . . to pronounce a Greek, but much more an Hebrew oration in such an auditory."[50] But Mather, who had been practicing his own Greek since 1682, knew what he was about. That summer at commencement, one of the letter writers gave a Latin oration, two others gave Greek orations, and Mather's own son Nathaniel gave one in Hebrew. President *pro tempore* Mather also gave an oration in Hebrew in praise of academical learning.[51] Afterwards, Mather stayed on campus for the better part of a week to put a stop to the end-of-the-year drunkenness that had become an annual scandal.

In September 1685, under Increase Mather's leadership, the corporation chose two new resident fellows, John Leverett (the grandson of Governor John Leverett) and William Brattle, young men in their early twenties, classmates who had graduated together from Harvard in 1680. With them as resident tutors Mather reinstituted regular student disputations. Undergraduates were required to debate assigned topics in

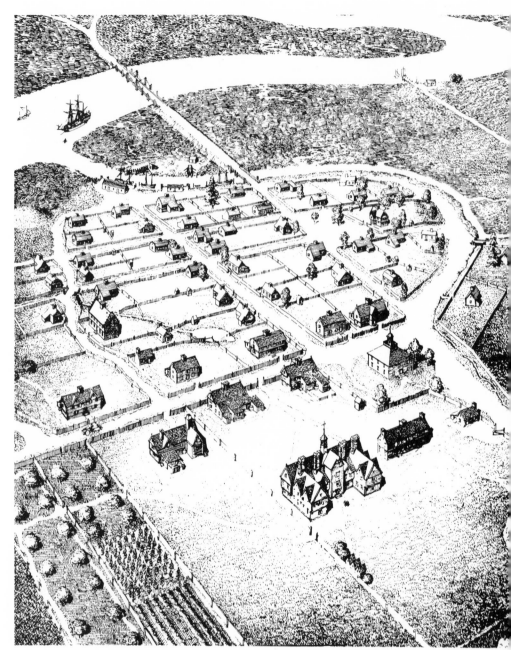

"Bird's-eye View of Harvard and Cambridge in 1668," Old College in foreground, Indian College to the right (west), Cambridge meetinghouse (square building southwest). Increase Mather was elected fellow of Harvard in 1675 and president in 1685. Drawing by H. R. Shurtleff, 1934

New College, often called Old Harvard Hall, built in 1676, destroyed by fire in 1764. Drawing by F. W. Hartwell, 1939

the great hall. Mather himself continued his visits, and sometimes moderated these debates. He heard graduate students dispute once a fortnight until winter storms kept him from crossing over the bay.[52]

The search for a permanent president who would reside at Cambridge continued. Charles Morton was a possible candidate. Increase Mather wrote him in 1685 to see if he would leave his Puritan academy at Newington Green outside London. Morton did decide to come to Massachusetts, but before he reached Boston the colony had lost its charter and with it control over the college. In the end it was only the text of Morton's lecture notes that came to rest at the college. Charles Morton himself became minister at Charlestown.[53]

DOMINION OF NEW ENGLAND

All this time, Massachusetts Bay Commonwealth was in limbo. In Boston people knew the charter had been withdrawn, but no official confirmation had arrived and nothing definite was known of what was to replace the General Court. Without official word, New England fed on rumor, which every ship brought. Boston, at any rate, and some of the larger towns, were fast becoming polarized between those who looked forward to a new government and those more staunchly Puritan who cherished the existing order. Puritans themselves were divided, for some wanted to resist to the very end, even if it incurred the wrath of the king, while others were more pragmatic and wanted to plan how the charter government could surrender with the least loss of power.

Governor Bradstreet asked the ministers in Boston to advise the General Court, and more than thirty ministers met at Monks Tavern, where they had their midday meal and debated the issues. Some said that to refuse a royal message when it came until the General Court could sit and discuss it would be the act of "Rebels and Traitors." Samuel Willard called such a course of delay a "madness." Increase Mather, on the other side, commented that if Willard's grandfather had heard him, he would have "boxed his ears." [54] By three or four o'clock that afternoon the ministers voted, and a majority advised that, when a royal message came, Governor Bradstreet should wait until the General Court assembled before acknowledging the demise of the government. The elected officials were divided too, some saying, let us submit now, others arguing, let us wait at least until we have orders from Whitehall. In the towns some officials refused to act for fear of subsequent punishment, while other townsmen refused to pay taxes, saying the Massachusetts government had already been abolished. [55]

Late in August 1685 came reports out of England of Monmouth's Rebellion. James Scott, a bastard son of Charles II, had been made Duke of Monmouth. When Charles II died in 1685 and James, Duke of York, assumed the throne, Monmouth landed on the coast of England and tried to raise the country. As many as six thousand men came to his flag, but Monmouth's Rebellion was crushed at the battle of Sedgemoor, July 6, 1685. Colonel Piercy Kirke of Tangier did grim service for the king by hunting down rebels, and Sir George Jeffreys, Chief Justice of the King's Bench, began the judicial proceedings that gave to his circuit the nickname "Bloody Assizes." Hundreds of prisoners were hanged and their corpses placed in iron cages at crossroads and market towns, a gruesome warning to others who might dispute royal authority. Hundreds more were transported into near slavery in the sugar plantations in the West Indies. People in Massachusetts, contemplating their own relationship with royal authority, were not slow to get the message.

On Friday, November 13 came news that Lady Lisle, the mother of Leonard Hoar's widow, Bridget, who had remarried in Boston, had been beheaded in England. Her crime was that she had sheltered two men who were later convicted of joining Monmouth's Rebellion. She was sentenced to be burned at the stake, but as an act of clemency was beheaded instead. All of the roughly three thousand people who lived in Boston knew Bridget Usher and what had happened to her mother and why. Should the colony continue to ignore the crown's judgment against the charter? Wednesday next Thomas Danforth and Joseph Dudley had stinging words for each other in a meeting of the magistrates. On November 20, a dark day, starting to snow, the magistrates and deputies met in General Court and agreed to adjourn until February, but to reassemble at once if ships came with a royal message. Later Samuel Shrimpton, possibly the richest merchant in Boston or all New England, for that matter, announced that in his opinion no act of the General Court since the charter had been vacated had any validity. Samuel Sewall noted that "this Monday we begin palpably to dye." [56]

Christmas day, New Year's, Twelfth Night all came and went uncelebrated in Puritan New England. Winter settled in in earnest. A hard freeze started on January 22. Even the best houses in Boston grew chill when one moved away from the great fireplaces. In the Third Church, Sewall observed, the frozen bread "rattles sadly" in the communion plate. The inner harbor began to freeze over. By January 28 the bay was a sheet of ice as far out as Castle Island. [57] A ship tied up there, and its passengers could be seen walking across the ice, a small knot of dark figures bundled against the cold. There was no royal messenger, but the arrivals brought news: Edward Randolph was coming on a ship of war and bringing a royal commission to form a temporary government, which would consist of a council not elected like the Court of Assistants, but named by the king. Joseph Dudley, one of Massachusetts's own, was named to be the president of this council. [58]

Still Randolph himself did not come, and week after week the divisions within Boston became sharper. Some magistrates would no longer attend meetings, saying it would be treason. But the adherents of Thomas Danforth seemed to be growing in numbers. On April 15, 1686, nominations for the election of magistrates and deputies were made, as if these were ordinary times. Bradstreet and Danforth were renominated to be governor and deputy governor. Dudley, Bulkeley, and Stoughton, the Tories, had few votes, but enough for nomination. Danforth charged Samuel Shrimpton with treason for saying there was no government and persuaded a grand jury to indict him. A warrant was issued for Shrimp-ton's arrest and he was released on his own recognizance with trial sched-uled for May 1686. Election day for another year of government under the old charter was set for May 12.[59]

On election day the sentiments of the voters, almost all of whom were church members, were made clear. Assistants who advocated resistance as long as possible received the most votes: Samuel Nowell, 1269; Elisha Cooke, 1143; James Pynchon, 1295. Those who had argued for giving in to the crown at once received generally only half as many votes: Dudley, 500; Bulkeley, 436; Stoughton, 664. The division, roughly, was two to one. How the unenfranchised majority would have voted is not known.[60]

Two days later the Frigate *Rose* sailed into Boston harbor, Edward Randolph disembarked, hired a horse, and rode straight away to Dud-ley's home in Roxbury. The fateful time had come, the policy of delay was a policy no longer. On the seventeenth Dudley met members of the Gen-eral Court in the Town House. The old government sat and stood crowded close together on one side of the room, and on the other side sat or stood those members of the new council who were in the city: Dudley, Major Pynchon, Captain Gedney, Robert Mason of New Hampshire, Ran-dolph, Wait Winthrop. Some were outsiders, like Mason and Randolph; others, like Wait Winthrop, and his brother Fitz, not yet present, and Dudley himself, were men whose fathers had founded Massachusetts; three of the new council, Dudley, Pynchon, and Gedney, had been elec-ted just days before by the freemen.[61]

Dudley exhibited the documents Randolph had brought from En-gland: the judgment against the charter, his own commission with the broad seal of England on it, a commission for admiralty. Danforth tried to speak for the outgoing government, but Dudley cut him off. There was, he said, no other government but the king's government now. On May 21 the old General Court met for the last time. If there was any thought of resisting, few counselled it. The end had come. Samuel Nowell offered a prayer of thanks that they had been able to govern in God's name for fifty-six years. Samuel Sewall proposed they sing a psalm, and that was done, verses 17 and 18 from Habbakuk:[62] "Although the fig tree shall not blossom, neither shall fruit be in the vines; the labour of the olives shall fail, and the fields shall yield no meat: the flock shall be cut off from the fold, and there shall be no herd in the stalls. Yet I will re-joice in the Lord, I will Joy in the God of my salvation." That afternoon Dudley boarded the *Rose*. About five o'clock a twenty-five gun salute boomed out from the cannon on Castle Island. The frigate answered, then the cannon on Noddles Island, then the battery at Charlestown, then the frigate again. Wave after wave, the salutes rolled over Boston harbor and echoed from Beacon Hill, while ships and forts alike hoisted their flags. What would happen to New Jerusalem now? [63]

That the old charter government should have fallen to royal authority was an inexplicable reversal of providential history. The course of events shattered any belief sustained over the last twenty-five years that the king and bishops, the servants of Antichrist, were about to be bound in chains or that New England had been chosen as the place of Christ's second coming and the start of the thousand-year rule of the saints. The course of events in the real world worked fundamental changes in Increase Mather's way of thinking, changes that Mather himself was perhaps unaware of but that nevertheless were representative of New England's shift from a providential world view to a modern, secular outlook.

On the face of it, manners and practices in Boston did not change very much, surely in the smaller towns hardly at all at first. Nevertheless, some changes did come, and in terms of the cultural revolution begun by the first settlers, these changes were fundamental. Slowly the old English calendar came back with Christmas, Shrove Tuesday, Easter, saints' days and the celebration of the royal birthdays and coronations. Mather, Willard, et al., lost control of the press to Edward Randolph. The Boston almanac, which was prepared for 1685 and 1686 by Nathaniel Mather, was put out by John Tulley, a recent arrival from England. Astrology was prominent in it, and in 1688 Tulley even published some bawdy verse. [64] Health drinking, card games, cockfights, bonfires, swearing and oaths also returned to Boston. A maypole was set up in Charlestown, cut down, and set up again. Sailors from the frigate fought with townsmen outside taverns, and wealthy merchants made their way home in carriages, roaring drunk from Roxbury, where Dudley lived. When theatrical sword playing was begun one Thursday afternoon, Mather observed, "the Devil has begun a Lecture in Boston on a Lecture-day which was set up for Christ." [65]

The counterrevolution, however, was not complete. Mather wrote a book, *A Testimony Against Several Prophane and Superstitious Customs* (London, 1687), in which he explained the long-standing Puritan objections to these practices. Although the first edition was printed in London, Richard Pierce reprinted it in Boston the following year, censorship notwithstanding. After all was said and done the maypole did not survive, the dancing master fled, stage plays were outlawed before they began. Most shopkeepers stayed open on Christmas, and conscientious Puritans like Samuel Sewall resigned offices that asked too much of them. As for drunkenness and promiscuity, that was an old story and the change was one of degree. New England after fifty years of Puritan rule would never be like old England again.

Furthermore, Dudley was sincerely interested in preserving some important institutions of New England, among them the college. With the dissolution of the charter government, Mather and the two resident tutors resigned. Dudley and his council, however, met at Cambridge in July 1686 and requested Mather to assume the title of Rector "and make his Usuall Visitations." Leverett and Brattle too were asked to take up their jobs again, so that as a practical matter the college continued without interruption.[66]

Anglican church services were introduced into Boston, and the sky did not fall. Robert Ratcliff now offered the service according to the Prayer Book to all who wanted it. At first he conducted services in the Town House, where the deputies had formerly met. A pulpit was carried upstairs for the purpose. Joseph Dudley attended, and kept a foot in both camps by maintaining his membership in the Puritan church at Roxbury, as well as attending Anglican service. From its beginning, the Anglican service was as much a way of declaring a political and social position as it was a road to eternal salvation. There was little the Puritan ministers could do. An essay by Mather reviewed the Puritan arguments against the liturgy of the Prayer Book. Cotton Mather had it printed anonymously in Cambridge in November 1686, under the title *A Brief Discourse Concerning the Unlawfulness of the Common Prayer Worship*.[67] It was the third tract written by Increase Mather to counter the invasion of New England by old England's non-Puritan culture.

In December 1686, Sir Edmund Andros arrived with two companies of soldiers to take over the reigns of government. Andros, an army officer and an experienced colonial administrator who had been lieutenant governor in New York, 1674–1681, held a royal commission to be Governor-General of the Dominion of New England. This new political entity was designed to include ultimately all the colonies from Maine to Delaware. It would be administered by an army officer who would be responsible directly to London, assisted by a council named from London. There would be no legislature of any kind.[68]

Sir Edmund quickly exercised his power. He asked to let Ratcliff use Willard's meetinghouse, and when the church refused, Andros commandeered the keys. Thereafter as long as Andros was governor Samuel Willard's regular congregation waited in the street until the Anglican services were over. The new governor moved in more important ways to reorganize Massachusetts life, although he did nothing else to interfere with the Puritans' free conduct of worship. Because in English law a corporation cannot itself create another corporation, and because Massachusetts was by its charter a corporation and not a sovereign power, the validity of the towns and their powers to distribute land, delegated by the General Court, was in doubt. Andros started proceedings against all existing land titles issued by the towns. The new policy threatened everyone. Owners were expected to petition for confirmation of old titles, and to pay fees and an annual quit rent.[69] Andros also levied taxes with the advice of his council but without the consent of any elected representatives of the people. This too became a grievance. When the townspeople of Ipswich, led on by their minister John Wise, balked, Andros arrested thirty persons there. The ringleaders were brought to Boston, tried, convicted and sentenced in a special court of oyer and terminer. It was at this trial that the remark was said to have been made and since attributed to several of the examining judges, "Mr. Wise, you have no more privileges left you than not to be Sould for Slaves." All the ringleaders were fined, and Wise was stopped from preaching until he apologized in November 1687.[70]

Long before then, Increase Mather saw a different strategy of resistance. James II, unable to get Parliament to repeal laws against his Roman Catholic allies, had issued a royal decree, a Declaration of Indulgence, which suspended the test act and penal laws against dissenters. News of the declaration first reached Boston on May 18, 1687. To Increase Mather the Declaration was an answer to his prayers. He wrote in his diary: "I am now wayting and praying for an earthquake, which shall issue in the downfall of the Lords enemies and the exaltation of Christ's Kingdome and Interest."[71] That summer the earthquake came. On May 27, 1687, James ordered that this Declaration of Indulgence be published in all the colonies, where his officers were to see that the terms were followed.[72] Surely, Mather thought, this would protect New England against the rough hand of Sir Edmund Andros.

In September Mather suggested to the other ministers that they write James II an expression of their gratitude, and when the ministers agreed with the plan, they appointed Mather to carry it out. He sent the letter to "some Gentlemen in London," one of whom was probably Stephen Lobb.[73] Lobb was a Dissenting minister at the Fetter Lane Church and a relation to Mather by marriage. (Stephen Lobb's father, Richard Lobb, and Nathaniel Mather had married sisters.) The Dissenting community

Sir Edmund Andros, governor of Dominion of New England from 1686 to 1689, when he was deposed

BY HIS EXCELLENCY
A
PROCLAMATION.

WHEREAS His MAJESTY hath been graciously pleased, by His Royal Letter, bearing Date the sixteenth day of October last past, to signifie That He hath received undoubted Advice that a great and sudden Invasion from *Holland*, with an armed Force of Forreigners and Strangers, will speedily be made in an hostile manner upon His Majesty's Kingdom of *ENGLAND*; and that altho' some *false* pretences relating to *Liberty, Property,* and *Religion,* (contrived or worded with Art and Subtilty) may be given out, (as shall be thought useful upon such an Attempt;) It is manifest however, (considering the great Preparations that are making) That no less matter by this *Invasion* is proposed and purposed, than an absolute Conquest of His Majesty's Kingdoms, and the utter Subduing and Subjecting His Majesty and all His People to a Forreign Power, which is promoted (as His Majesty understands) altho' it may seem almost incredible) by some of His Majesty's *Subjects,* being persons of wicked and restless Spirits, implacable Malice, and desperate Designs, who having no sence of former intestine Distractions, (the Memory and Misery whereof should endear and put a Value upon that Peace and Happiness which hath long been enjoyed) nor being moved by His Majesty's reiterated Acts of Grace and Mercy, (wherein His Majesty hath studied and delighted to abound towards all His Subjects, and even towards *those* who were once His Majesty's avowed and open *Enemies*) do again endeavour to embroil His Majesty's Kingdom in Blood and Ruin, to gratifie their own Ambition and Malice, proposing to themselves a Prey and Booty in such a publick Confusion:

And that although His Majesty had Notice that a forreign Force was preparing against Him, yet His Majesty hath alwaies declined any forreign Succour, but rather hath chosen (next under GOD) to rely upon the true and ancient Courage, Faith and Allegiance of His own People, with whom His Majesty hath often ventured His Life for the Honour of His Nation, and in whose Defence against all Enemies His Majesty is firmly resolved to live and dye; and therefore does solemnly *Conjure* His Subjects to lay aside all manner of Animosities, Jealousies, & Prejudices, and heartily & chearfully to *Unite together* in the Defence of His *MAJESTY* and their native Countrey, which thing alone, will (under GOD) defeat and frustrate the principal Hope and Design of His Majesty's Enemies, who expect to find His People divided; and by publishing (perhaps) some plausible Reasons of their Coming, as the specious (tho' *false*) Pretences of Maintaining the Protestant Religion, or Asserting the Liberties and Properties of His Majesty's People, do hope thereby to conquer that great and renowned Kingdom.

That albeit the Design hath been carried on with all imaginable Secresie & Endeavours to surprise and deceive His *MAJESTY,* HE hath not been wanting on His part to make such provision as did become Him, and, by GOD's great Blessing, His Majesty makes no doubt of being found in so good a Posture that His Enemies may have cause to repent such their rash and *unjust* Attempt. ALL WHICH, it is His Majesty's pleasure, should be made known in the most publick manner to His loving Subjects within this His Territory and Dominion of *NEW-ENGLAND,* that they may be the better prepared to resist any Attempts that may be made by His Majesties Enemies in these parts, and secured in their trade and Commerce with His Majesty's Kingdom of *England.*

I Do therefore, in pursuance of His *MAJESTY*'s Commands, by these Presents *make known* and *Publish* the same accordingly : And hereby Charge and Command all Officers Civil & Military, and all other His Majesty's loving Subjects within this His Territory and Dominion aforesaid, to be *Vigilant* and *Careful* in their respective places and stations, and that, upon the Approach of any Fleet or Forreign Force, they be in Readiness, and use their utmost Endeavour to hinder any Landing or Invasion that may be intended to be made within the same.

Given at *Fort-Charles* at *Pemaquid,* the Tenth Day of *January,* in the Fourth year of the Reign of our Sovereign Lord *JAMES* the Second, of *England, Scotland, France* and *Ireland* KING, Defender of the Faith &c. Annoq; DOMINI 1688.

By *His* EXCELLENCY's *Command.*
    JOHN WEST. d'. Secr'.

E. ANDROS.

GOD *SAVE THE* KING.

Printed at *Boston* in *New-England* by R. P,

Governor Andros's 1688 broadside warning of Dutch invasion of England during reign of James II

in England was sharply divided over how to react to James's Declaration of Indulgence, some being quick to seize what advantage they could, while others thought its toleration of Roman Catholics too high a price to pay. Stephen Lobb was an active spokesman for the former group and as such had access to the court. James, eager to recruit friends in any quarter, expressed himself pleased with the letter from the Boston ministers, and when a copy was printed in the *Gazette* and found its way back to Boston in January 1688, men there were suddenly buoyed with hope.[74]

Mather had already pushed his strategy further. In October 1687, the same month John Wise was tried in Boston, Mather urged churches (as well as their ministers) to thank James for his Declaration of Indulgence. Ten churches agreed to do it. Some suggested that this time the letter should be taken over by someone who could lobby in person for their interest. Mather himself seemed the logical messenger.[75] To Increase the thought was breathtaking. For eighteen years he had not thought of returning to England. And now. . . .

As usual, he fasted and prayed alone in his study. Then he put the question to the members of his church, telling them "I knew not how to discern the mind of God, but by them. And that if they sayd to me Stay, I would stay, but if they sayd to me Go, I would cast my selfe on the providence of God and go in his Name."[76] To Mather's surprised delight the church, which had refused to lose him to the presidency of Harvard College ten miles away, now sent him across the ocean to England.

It was now December 1687. Mather quickly made plans, and just as quickly Edward Randolph tried to foil them. On the day before Christmas he had Mather arrested on a charge of defamation. Randolph said Mather had lied in 1684, when he had accused Randolph of forging the letter to Abraham Kick. He sued for £500 damages. The charge was a transparent effort to keep Mather from sailing to England. Trial was scheduled for January 31. Instead of a hand-picked jury of "common-prayer men," which Mather had feared, all the jury but two were members of congregations. Even Samuel Shrimpton, in a rare show of solidarity, put his carriage at Mather's disposal. The verdict was, innocent. Randolph was ordered to pay the court costs. Governor Andros himself, to whom Mather had told his plans face to face, made no effort to stop his going. Only Thomas Danforth seemed skeptical, for Danforth could not believe that the Puritans would win anything solid from King James.[77]

Again plans were laid. At the end of March, Mather was to sail in the ship *President*. He made no secret of his purpose to seek an interview with

James II. He told Governor Andros so in a private interview and preached a farewell sermon.[78] Randolph tried again to stop his going by swearing out another warrant. This time Mather avoided arrest. Willard and Moodey came to pray with him, and two days later Mather stole out at night in disguise to avoid being served a warrant by the constable set to watch his home. He reached the ferry at the North End, was rowed across the black waters of the bay to Charlestown, where he stayed at Cotton's father-in-law's house. A few nights later he moved again, with Cotton this time and his third son, Samuel, now almost thirteen.

At dawn father and Sam were taken by a fishing boat south to near Plymouth harbor. They stayed on board, out of sight, seasick, for several more days. At last on April 7 a watcher from Boston came to say that the *President* would sail that day. Mather and Sam were taken in a small ketch to intercept the ship. Cotton, left behind, climbed Beacon Hill to watch the square-rigger spread canvas and pull out of Boston harbor. He saw following her a smaller boat sent by Randolph to make sure that Mather was not sneaked aboard. Randolph's men were too late and the *President* quickly outdistanced the police boat. Hours later in the far distance, Cotton wrote that he could see the ship heave to as a tiny dot approached over the sparkling sea. Mather's ketch pulled alongside; he and Sam climbed aboard. The *President* fell off again, her sails filled, and "that crazed star-gazer," the "bellows of sedition," set forth for London, the king, and the future of New England.[79]

CHAPTER 7

Representing Massachusetts in London

[1688-1691]

The first days on the *President* were stormy, and Mather was seasick, but he soon recovered and enjoyed the rest of his six-week voyage, except for a toothache that sometimes made it impossible for him either to study or to pray. On most days he managed to pray with the crew, and on the Sabbath he conducted services morning and afternoon. They sailed through icebergs for three days in April and watched one of them over-turn, sending up a cloud of gulls. Closer to England, in foggy weather the ship narrowly missed a rocky headland before finding clear weather in the Channel. Mather and his son Sam left the *President* to go ashore at Weymouth on the south coast on May 16, 1688.[1]

After twenty-three years he had almost forgotten how different this precious, long-settled, cultivated land was from the dark forests and scattered villages of New England. In Weymouth old friends greeted them, one inviting them to dinner, another to spend the night. The afternoon after coming ashore, Mather preached the Thursday lecture at Melcomb, then rode by horseback to Dorchester, the town for which his American birthplace had been named, to preach the Sunday sermon. It was to be this way as long as he was in England, passing from one Dissenting congregation to another, lodging with old acquaintances and new, always asked to preach. When he left England four years later, he remarked with pride that he had been able to preach on every Sabbath during his stay.

Father and son made their way on foot, horseback, and public coach across southern England towards the great city of London. Spring that year was late and cold, but by early summer the hedgerows were alive with nesting birds, the fields bright green with their first crops.[2] As they moved towards London, Mather planned how he would seek out the network of Puritan and family connections which would help him. On the outskirts of the city they circled north to the home of Major Robert Thompson in the village of Newington Green. Major Thompson, a wealthy Puritan merchant and member of the East India Company, was also a member of the New England Company, incorporated in 1649 as the Society for the Propagation of the Gospel in New England. In 1692 he would become governor of the company, a key person in Massachusetts's English connection. Major Thompson's principal trading partner in New England was John Richards, pillar of Mather's North Church and treasurer of Harvard College. Also at Newington Green was a famous academy for Dissenters started by Theophilus Gale, whose books were well-known to Mather and whose connections with the New England clergy and with Harvard were numerous. Another academy for children of Dissenters had been started by Charles Morton, who was now in Massachusetts. In his place was Stephen Lobb, who would play an important part in Mather's first encounters with the government.[3] More important, Nathaniel himself was now established in London as minister to the Lime Street Church, a Nonconformist congregation with strong ties to Massachusetts. John Collins, a Harvard graduate two years ahead of Nathaniel, had preached there since the Commonwealth years. When Collins died in 1687, the congregation wrote to Nathaniel in Dublin to come to them;[4] he quickly won a position of influence among Nonconformists in London. Nathaniel was on hand to smooth the way for his younger brother.

Almost daily that first glorious summer, Increase Mather walked or took a coach into the city from Newington Green. The village has long since then been enveloped by industrial London, but in those days the road ran through open farmland for a mile and a half to Islington, and on the other side of that village again between fields until it reached Clerkenwell, at the edge of urban building. From Clerkenwell Mather took St. John's Street, still twisting and turning like a country lane, but now built up solidly on both sides. At Smithfield Market he could turn left via Holburn and Cheapside, pass the building site for St. Paul's, and go to the Exchange in the heart of the old city. This was the most likely place to find Massachusetts men and news from home. Or at Smithfield he could turn right and work his way past the Inns of Court and the densely built Holburn and Strand to Charing Cross. At Charing Cross began Scotland

Yard, Whitehall, and the great rabbit warren of government offices. Beyond Whitehall lay Westminster Palace and the Abbey. Nearby across the Park was St. James's Palace. Some days on his way to Whitehall Mather went straight to the Thames below Smithfield and took a boat to Whitehall Stairs, more expensive but certainly more comfortable and less dangerous than pushing through the narrow, crowded roads and alleys.

THE PURITAN AND THE STUART KING

Ordinarily Whitehall would have been the last place one would have expected to find a Puritan minister in late-Stuart England. But James II was desperate for support, and Mather was opportunistic enough to seize the moment. So on May 30, 1688, the black-robed Puritan and the Catholic Stuart king of England met in the Long Gallery at Whitehall. Stephen Lobb had arranged the friendly audience. Mather spoke of the address his church had sent and James asked him to read it then and there. When Mather had finished, the king assured him of his good wishes. That afternoon Mather dined with Stephen Lobb and in the evening they met with other Dissenting ministers at the house of William Penn, the great Quaker leader. Mather stayed in London that night and did not get back to Newington Green until late in the long summer evening of the following day, filled with excitement at this beginning.[5] Penn was an old personal friend of the king's. He had no cause to like Mather, who had consistently opposed granting Quakers a place in Massachusetts. Nevertheless Penn was broad-minded enough to cooperate with Mather in pursuit of the larger goal of *rapprochement* between James II and the Dissenters. Mather was somewhat grudging in recognition of Penn's help: "To give mr. Pen [Penn] his due, Hee did in my hearing in the King's closet . . . advise King James to be kind to his subjects in New England."[6] Two days later, on June 1, James gave Mather a long interview, this time in his private quarters instead of the more public Long Gallery. Their conversation focused on Sir Edmund Andros's administration. The king asked Mather to put his criticism into writing, and promised relief.[7]

For the rest of the month Mather busied himself around London. He made the acquaintance of more friends of the Whig and Dissenting causes. He rode, walked or took coach back and forth to Newington Green, or if the hour had grown too late, as it frequently did, he lodged overnight at a Mr. Ball's house in Hoxton Square, near Shoreditch. On Sabbath days he preached, usually at Newington Green, but sometimes in the city of London and in Westminster. The tooth that had given him so much trouble on the passage over was drawn by a London surgeon at a cost of nine shillings. On June 15 he went in the afternoon to Westminster Hall to watch and hear the trial of seven bishops.[8] The Archbishop of Canterbury and six of his bishops had refused to order the king's Declaration of Liberty of Conscience read in their diocese. In a rash move to force the issue, James arrested them all. London's populace supported the Protestant bishops against the Roman Catholic king. When the bishops were brought to trial, the great hall was jammed with spectators. The seven bishops in the dock, the Lord Justices of the King's Bench, the learned counsel before them, resplendent in their robes, were a brilliant, awe-inspiring sight. Mather elbowed his way into the edges of the crowd to watch, his emotions ambivalent. Bishops had been a focal point of Puritan opposition in his father's generation and during his own youth in England. But now the bishops themselves were representing resistance to the crown. That same Declaration of Liberty of Conscience that they refused to acknowledge gave him an excuse to appear before the king. The world was suddenly more complicated than it had seemed.

Mather watched one of the great state trials of the century. In the afternoon the charges against the seven bishops were dismissed. The crowd went wild with delight. Outside John Evelyn observed "a lane of people from the King's Bench to the water-side, upon their knees as the Bishops passed & repassed." That night London and the surrounding villages glowed with the light of bonfires and reverberated with the ringing of bells.[9] The setback for James proved to be at least a temporary advantage for Mather. More than ever the king needed allies. When Mather took his case before the Privy Council's Committee for Trade and Plantations, the council members knew well enough the king's dilemma. The Lord President of the Privy Council, the Earl of Sunderland, inquired just what it was that Mather wanted of the king. "I Replyed," Mather wrote, "that His Majestys declaration might there take place, that liberty & property might be secured to us." "Hee [Sunderland] told me, Hee would wayt on the King for his directions, and I might rest assured it would be done; and that if I designed to return to N.E. it should be done before that, & I should carry it with me."[10]

On July 2 Mather went for his third audience with the king, accompanied by Stephen Lobb and John Owen. A month earlier James had asked that Mather bring in his charges against Andros in writing, and since then Mather had worked with Samuel Nowell and Elisha Hutchinson to prepare them. These allies, both outspoken leaders of the popular faction, happened by good fortune to be in London that summer. Hutchinson was a prosperous merchant, a neighbor of Mather's in the North End, and a lifelong friend. Nowell, a Magistrate in Boston, had been among the earliest opponents of any compromise with England. In 1686 he had received more votes for magistrate than any other candidate. He, more than most, emphasized the duty of government to protect property. Together, Mather, Nowell, and Hutchinson, acting as private citizens only, drew up a "memorial" of charges against Andros and a "petition" of actions they hoped the king would take. The three principal points of the petition were confirmation of land titles, creation of an elected assembly, and awarding of a royal charter incorporating Harvard College. The language was that of Whiggery, not Puritanism, a response to Nowell's influence. Mather himself abandoned religious and biblical rhetoric for the duration of his stay in London. Henceforth in England he was to speak the language of liberty and property.[11]

Everything seemed to go remarkably well, almost too well to be true. James referred the petitioners to the Committee for Trade and Plantations, and when they presented their requests there on August 10, Mather reported to his diary that committee "readily granted all that was desired excepting one particular." The one particular which the Commitee would not recommend to the king was an elected assembly. Sunderland balked at that.[12] Nevertheless, the three Puritans in London had every reason to be jubilant. The next day Mather dispatched the good news to New England.[13]

Mather now embarked on a campaign to see through the bureaucracy the promises that had been made. He spent virtually every day pursuing the "N.E. Affair," in the City or at one of the offices in Whitehall or Scotland Yard. The out-of-pocket expenses were great. Mather had already borrowed small sums from Lobb and Hutchinson, and on August 29 he went with Nowell and Hutchinson to visit Stephen Mason, a New England merchant in the City. Together they borrowed £200 to see the work through. Mather, who kept daily accounts during his London stay, at once began to lay out this capital where it would do the most good: ten guineas, a great sum then, to the attorney general on August 30, again on September 11 and 12. Each time there must be a guinea or a half to the clerk, too. And there were the daily costs of coach hire, fees to scriveners to write out papers, payments for suppers or wine for influential people. All through September and the early weeks of October Mather lobbied hard.[14]

It was too late to gain anything from James's government. The coming revolution made it impossible to bring the king's promises to fruition. On September 26 Mather managed another audience with James, urging him to expedite his promises. "Trouble yourselfe no further," the king reassured him, "I will take care that the thing be done with Expedition." But the things were not done, and on the sixteenth of October, Mather was back again. "Property, liberty, and the Colledge," he wrote, "would be confirmed unto us." It was the last time Mather saw the king. [15]

THE DEATH OF A CHILD

The summer had been enormously stimulating. Mather had begun friendships with many of England's spiritual leaders: Richard Baxter, a grand old man of English Nonconformity, recently released from prison, whose *Christian Directory* would remain a classic statement of Nonconformist piety for two centuries; Dr. William Bates, the so-called "silver tongued divine," a close friend of Baxter; John Flavel, a prolific Nonconformist preacher and writer, who asked Mather to provide an introduction to a new book. Many others in every quarter of greater London welcomed Mather to their homes and to their pulpits. [16]

Both Increase Mather and his son Samuel outfitted themselves with new clothes, from boots to gloves, and early in the summer he sat for a life-size oil portrait by the Dutch painter van der Spriett, and commissioned Robert White to make an engraving from it. Mather took the coach out to Windsor to visit sympathizers to the cause of New England; he took time out for tours of the "Kings and Queens lodgings, with the other rarities and glories in Windsor Castle." Not long after he and Sam went to the Tower of London, where they "saw all the rarities." [17]

Introduced everywhere as the Rector of the college in Boston, Increase Mather warmed and expanded in this environment as never before. Before leaving Boston he had been in correspondence with a continental scholar, John Leusden, and had written him a long letter in Latin detailing the missionary efforts of New England Puritans among the Indians. Still in touch with Leusden during the summer, Mather published the letter in London. The exact reasons for publishing it at this time are obscure, but the fourteen-page book, *Successu Evangelij Apud Indos in Nova-Anglia*, was to have as extraordinary a publishing history as anything Mather wrote. There were two small editions in London that summer, and Leusden wrote Mather that he was bringing out an edition in French. Within a decade *Successu Evangelij*, which had no discernible influence on race relations in America itself, appeared in thirteen editions and five languages. If it did nothing else, it helped Mather establish his name in the world of international scholarship.[18]

The summer months had seemed little short of triumphant. Even though Mather had ventured to England as a private person, he had had repeated audiences with the king and many members of the government. He thanked God, on August 1, 1688, for "My finding acceptance with the King and other great ones," and prayed for "Wisdome from above to manage the great affair which I am come to England about."[19] That great affair, the "N.E. Affair," came to take on a reality and substance far greater than he had been able to imagine in Boston. By the end of the summer it seemed possible that he would be able, with the help of only a few like Samuel Nowell, to restore Massachusetts's ancient privileges. With unbounded energy he lobbied members of the government to this end. But the early hopes began to sink in September and October as the real immobility of the English bureaucracy began to be apparent, and as the domestic problems of James diverted attention from other matters. On October 16, the day of Mather's last audience with the king, his friend and ally Samuel Nowell died. The threat of a revolution preoccupied men's minds. Mather's mood turned pessimistic, and by November 3 he admitted to himself "the delayes and unsuccessfulness of my undertakings for N.E." He prayed now that his God would "Hide me under the Shadow of his wings in this evill & dangerous time & place. . . . Return me to N.E. & to my Family again, in much mercy."[20]

In Boston there was a growing puzzlement over the delays. Joshua Moody wrote to Mather, "Your acceptance with his Majesty . . . make us like men that dream. . . . Only when I doe consider & chew upon what I have heard of the modes of Court, & what unaccountable intreagues there are on foot in the world, I am willing to believe with discretion."[21] Moody was cautious. He wondered why, despite Mather's glowing reports of his success with James, John Palmer had been appointed chief justice for Massachusetts under Governor Andros, when everyone knew Palmer was an old crony of the governor's and hostile to Puritans. "We know [not] how to reconcile these things," Moody wrote, "that there should be so much favor at Court for us, and that yet such a man should be sent over in such a place of trust, who is so much disaffected to us." How could it be, he asked, that Mather did not even know of Palmer's appointment? Moody did not understand that events on each side of the Atlantic followed their own paths. In addition several people in Boston were upset at Mather and Nowell for having named them in the list of charges against Andros. "Some of which have been concerned to think whether it was so prudent & kind to expose them till the pinch came."[22] Mather's son Nathaniel wrote from Salem to his brother Cotton, "Will not those who bear an Ill will to [our father] and his designs, make such an Improvement of it as may be hurtful and Prejudicial to him?"[23]

John Cotton, Maria's brother, on the other hand, was overwhelmed with the drama of Mather's success. "I could hardly perswade myselfe," he wrote, "that you would adventure into the Royal prescence, with resolution, soe to speake and declare as you have done. . . . I doe not know, nor did I ever heare that ever any one man run soe great a hazard attended with such circumstances for this people as you have."[24] Maria Mather, at home in Boston, often climbed the steps to her husband's study to pray and meditate, and to write her own devotional diary. "I kept a Fast alone in the Study," she wrote on December 17, "to request of God that he would afford Assistance to my Dearest now in England, that he may do Service for God, and for His New-England Israel."[25]

By the end of the year, the summer's promises from James proved to be no more than summer promises. "Or else," Moody wrote, "after so many good words & large promises, something would have been sent to give us a little present Relief . . . "[26] Though Moody did not know of it, events in England were bringing James II's rule to an end. In London John Evelyn was astounded when at the end of October he found that his fellow countrymen were actually hoping for a foreign invasion. On November 5 William of Orange landed on the south coast with an army. By December 2 the key garrisons of Plymouth, York, Hull, and Bristol had declared for the invader. Evelyn saw "the Greate favorits at Court, priest[s] and Jesuites, flie or abscond: Every thing (til now conceiled) flies abroad in publique print, and is Cryed about the streetes. . . . The Popists in offices lay down their Commissions & flie. Universal Consternation amongst them. It lookes like a Revolution."[27]

The Whig revolution of 1688–1689 did not at first appear to Mather the blessing it later became. He had pinned his strategy, after all, on James's Declaration of Liberty of Conscience. Now James had fled, and as far as Mather knew the Anglicans would be back in power. Whitehall was in chaos. Mather went to the coffee shops of the City to hear the news and to read the political pamphlets. But there was personal news as well. At the Exchange Mather heard the terrible news that his son Nathaniel had died.

The young man had been dangerously weak all his life. After he finished his last year for the master's degree at Harvard, following Mather's departure for London, he had gone to Salem for a cure. He was under the care of a physician there, but to no avail. Increase wrote in his diary, "As for me, I can not express how great my loss is in being deprived of such a praying son! I have done so little for Gods children, since I have bin in the world, that Hee may justly take mine from me. Yet Hee is so gracious as to leave me 2 sons & 6 daughters still. The Lord continue their lives, & pour his spirit on them all." [28] At Newington Green, Mather grieved for his son, depressed and frightened also at the confusion created by the revolution. Characteristically he blamed himself: "My sins the cause of this and all other sorrowes." As he looked at his son Samuel, who had just turned fourteen, he hoped that Nathaniel's death would be the means of Samuel's conversion. [29] Mather put his grief aside to write out a summary of Governor Andros's misdeeds. Some of his London allies urged him to have it printed in anticipation of Parliament's reassembling late in January. He did so, the title, *A Narrative of the Miseries of New England* (London, 1689), perhaps expressive of his personal despondency over his son's death. [30] He paid £1,5s to have it printed.

REVOLUTION AND A TRANSFER OF POWER

The revolution forced Mather to change his strategy. Friends who had helped him with James were now out of power. He must form new alliances and seek out new allies for his colony. He turned first to Philip Lord Wharton, the fourth Baron Wharton, a grand old man of Nonconformity, who as a youth during the Civil War had sided with Parliament against the king. Wharton had become an intimate of Oliver Cromwell. After the Restoration he continued to stand squarely for the rights of Dissenters and with principles of parliamentary government, but when James II came to the throne he thought it prudent to travel in Europe. One of those who invited William of Orange to invade England, he was made a member of William's privy council afterwards. Lord Wharton would become Mather's chief ally at court.

The other principal person with whom Mather allied himself at this turning point was Sir Henry Ashurst, eldest son of a rich London merchant famous for his charitable gifts to Dissenting ministers. The father had been treasurer of the Society for the Propagation of the Gospel in New England and a major financial backer of John Eliot's Indian Bible. When Increase's brother Nathaniel first arrived in London in 1650, he had used Alderman Ashurst's London home as an address for mail from

New England.[31] After the senior Ashurst's death in 1680, his two sons, Sir Henry and William, had continued to support their father's causes. The Whig-Protestant revolution of 1688 gave both of them the opportunity to enter public life. William was knighted in 1689, and became Lord Mayor of London in 1693; later he was treasurer of the Society for the Propagation of the Gospel in New England and after Major Thompson's retirement in 1696, Governor of the Company. Sir Henry Ashurst entered Parliament, where he became Mather's most valuable ally amongst the parliamentarians as Lord Wharton was at Whitehall. Sir Henry also joined other wealthy men to exploit the natural resources of New England; he helped form a consortium that bought the Mason family's title to New Hampshire and thereafter competed fiercely with other merchant-speculators for special trading privileges.[32] Such possible conflicts of interest notwithstanding, Increase Mather found Ashurst indispensable.

Early in January 1689, Mather moved from Newington Green into rooms in London so that he could be closer to Whitehall and to the Exchange, one or the other of which he tried to visit every day.[33] In the short winter days Mather could ill afford the long walk out to Major Thompson's. It seems probable that Mather rented a room from "Cousin" John Whiting, Copthall Court, Throgmorton Street. He was certainly living there in April 1689. The outcome of the revolution was still uncertain. James had fled to France and was in alliance with its Roman Catholic king Louis XIV. William of Orange and his English wife Mary Stuart occupied Westminster Palace. A parliament had been called for January 22; in the meantime the peers conducted a provisional government. Every day brought new rumors and new hopes.

The first week of January was bitterly cold. London was blanketed with snow. Thin columns of smoke rose from thousands of chimneys. The Thames froze from bank to bank. On January 8 Mather dressed himself in his best clothes and made his way to Lord Wharton's home, and the two went in his lordship's carriage to St. James's Palace, where Lord Wharton introduced Mather to William of Orange. Mather presented a petition he had drawn up and signed on his own authority for the restoration of Massachusetts's old charter. Wharton spoke strongly in favor. William responded that he would do what he could; that they should go to see his English secretary, William Jephson, who, as it happened, was a cousin of Lord Wharton's. A thaw began that day, a good omen. Shortly afterward the Privy Council's Committee for Trade and Plantations prepared a circular letter to the royal governors in America instructing them to keep their present offices, but Mather, learning of the letter, arranged with Jephson to have the one to Sir Edmund Andros held back. Of all the royal governors, only Andros failed to receive early confirmation of his position under the new regime. In later years, Mather thought that this alone was worth his voyage to England.[34]

The transfer of power from James II to William and Mary had been effected. By the end of January a working agreement was reached in Parliament. The throne was declared vacant, and William and Mary were invited to accept it jointly. A lengthy Declaration of Rights, accompanying the invitation, guaranteed a constitutional government. Mather walked that day to Newington Green and Major Thompson's, where a worship service was held in "solemn thanksgiving because of the Nation's deliverance."[35]

PARLIAMENT OR WHITEHALL?

James II, in an effort to control Parliament, had abolished many corporate and borough charters. Restoration of these charters was one of the first concerns of Parliament, and Mather lobbied hard to include colonial charters in the legislation. "I had an ally in Mr. Hampden, Chairman of the Grand Committee For Grievances in The House of Commons," Mather wrote later, and also Alderman Love and several other London merchants in the House.[36] On February 2 the House of Commons agreed to debate a bill that would restore borough and corporate charters in the plantations as well as in England.[37] In the next frantic six weeks, among the busiest of his life, Mather lobbied on two fronts at once, seeking to ensure that the lumbering bureaucracy of Whitehall would implement William's promises, and at the same time building a party in Parliament that would accomplish the same thing through legislation.

Many staff members at Whitehall opposed concessions to Massachusetts. Among them were men who worked for the Secretaries of State, the Privy Council, its Committee for Trade and Plantations, in the offices of the Attorney General, Treasury, Commissioners of the Customs, and Admiralty. They respected authority, legitimacy, and control centralized in London. They had little or no sympathy for the Puritan cause and for the most part fully supported Andros's record as a governor first in New York, then in Massachusetts.[38]

"If New England be restored to the usurped Privileges they had in 1660 . . . ," one of them pointed out, "It will so Confound the Present settlement in those Parts, and their Dependence of England, that 'tis

hard to say where the Mischeif will stopp, or how farr the Acts of Navigation will be over throwne thereby."[39]

Mather adroitly appealed over their heads. Lord Wharton arranged
another interview with the king, and this time Mather persuaded William to recall Sir Edmund Andros.[40] The pressure was on at Whitehall:
"With such Power and Ardour is this Designe carried on and by those
who perhaps suspect not the Intention of the Republicans who solicite
them, that no Man dares open his Mouth to the Contrary for feare of
being Crusht."[41] Nevertheless, Mather and his allies were unable to
achieve their ultimate goal of restoring the old Massachusetts charter. Sir
Robert Sawyer, the former Attorney General who had prosecuted the
writs against it, reviewed for the committee all the earlier arguments,
and Mather had to give up any hope that these judgments would be over-
turned. The committee concluded that there should be a new Massachusetts charter to "Preserve The Rights and Properties of the People of New
England," but "Reserve a Dependence on the Crown of England." From
late February through May 1689, Mather and his friends lobbied in vain
at Whitehall for a more satisfactory resolution.[42]

All that spring, Mather hoped he could bypass the reluctant Committee for Trade and Plantations and all the other opposition at Whitehall
and arrange for Massachusetts to be included within the Corporation
Bill, slowly working its way through the House of Commons. "I also
became acquainted," Mather wrote later, "with the leading men in the
convention parliament, particularly, Edward Harley, John Thompson,
Mr Sacheveril, Alderman Love, Mr John Hampden, John Somers, the
three mr Foleyes, and others."[43] With the help of Ashurst and Wharton
he tried to win votes. He cultivated dozens of men of Whig inclinations
who were sympathetic to the old Puritan cause. He often and successfully sought to influence their wives, for many of whom the religious
element was paramount. It cost him enormous amounts of time and not
a little money.[44]

A war of pamphlets began, and Mather contributed two publications,
New England Vindicated and *A Further Vindication of New England*, both
published in London anonymously. These were short, specific arguments
aimed at including New England in the provisions of the Corporation
Bill.[45] Opposition pamphlets took the position that strong imperial control was desirable if England's colonial sovereignty and commerce were
not to suffer. A remarkable feature of these political tracts is how thoroughly Mather adopted a political rhetoric. The language of his Puritan's
providential world view virtually disappeared to be replaced by the lan-

guage of Whig politics. Later in the summer he wrote another piece under the title *A Brief Relation of the State of New England* (London, 1689), in which he endeavored to give sympathetic English readers a quick sketch of Massachusetts's history. It too is a skillful, secular piece of writing without a hint of the Puritan in it.[46]

The writing closest to Increase Mather's heart, however, had nothing to do with politics. It was the biography of his son Nathaniel written by his oldest son Cotton, received in manuscript in London on January 23, 1689. It was titled *Early Piety Exemplified*. In the confusion of the move into London and the daily trips hither and yon, Mather misplaced the manuscript. He was miserable. In February the manuscript turned up again and his spirits rose. In a day of deep emotion he and Nathaniel, namesake of the dead youth, read the biography aloud together. The brothers agreed to have it published in London, and Increase saw it into print in March. It brought a renewed surge of strength. "My Nathaniel has left a good, and by the printing of his life, a lasting name behind him."[47] His son was memorialized; the king in council had ordered Andros's recall; Parliament had voted to include New England in the bill to restore charters. In the early warm spring that followed the bitter cold of January, the fields around London were green and beautiful. "Bless the Lord, O my Soul."

REVOLT IN THE COLONIES

The arrival in London of Mather's good friend Samuel Sewall, in the middle of January 1689 helped compensate for the loss of Nowell's companionship. Sewall was a determined tourist, and in his company Increase and his son set off on several long excursions outside the city. At the end of March they all went by coach to Maidenhead, Abbingdon, and Oxford.[48] Three weeks later they were off again, this time down river to Greenwich Observatory, where they talked to the Astronomer Royal, John Flamsteed, to whom Foster's and Brattle's observations of the comet in 1682 had gone. Mather had already interested himself in getting scientific instruments to take to Massachusetts: February 7: "A.M. At Gresham Colledge &c. P.M. About Telescopes &c." February 8: "My brother N. & my Sam walked to a lapidary, & to one that made baroscopes &c."[49] At the end of June the visitors from Boston hired a coach to take them to Cambridge, where they visited Emmanuel College, nursery of many Puritans of their fathers' generation.[50]

Perhaps the most consequential extracurricular activity Mather engaged in in 1688–1689, however, was his promotion of Harvard College. He had persistently asked James and then William to establish Harvard by independent charter, all of which in the end came to nothing. More important was the search for private endowment. As early as September 1688, he was in touch with Sir Robert Thorner, a wealthy Puritan whose acquaintance with the Mathers went back to the time Increase and Nathaniel had fled England in 1660. In 1688 Thorner added a bequest to Harvard to his will. Even more important he appointed a nephew, Thomas Hollis, as a trustee of his estate. Through this connection Hollis became interested in the college and ultimately, often encouraged by Mather, became one of its greatest benefactors. Mather's pursuit of private endowment would continue for the remainder of his life.[51]

June brought alarming news from home. The people of Boston, following the logic of events in New England, not knowing that Andros was to be recalled, staged their own rebellion. On April 18 rebels seized and imprisoned the governor and the small company of English soldiers under his command. By the twentieth the Frigate Rose and the fort on Castle Island were in their control. The revolt srpead sporadically to other colonies on the eastern seaboard. In May and June a militia company in New York under the command of Jacob Leisler seized power when Francis Nicholson, Andros's Lieutenant Governor, sailed for England, and in August in Maryland a party of armed planters calling themselves the Protestant Associators took over the government. In all three revolts the rebels proclaimed their loyalty to the new monarchs in England.

Mather and Samuel Sewall were on a tour of Cambridge when news of the rebellion reached them. "We were surpris'd with joy," Sewall wrote in his diary.[52] But Mather quickly saw difficulties. He had been expecting Andros's recall. Armed revolt would have to be explained carefully. Accompanied by Lord Wharton, he went to the king, gambling on a bold approach: "I presume your majesty has bin informed of the great service which your subjects in New England have done . . . in securing that Territory." He played on the fact that although William was secure in England, James was raising troops in Ireland, while parts of Scotland were disaffected; France was at war with England, and who knew what was happening in the colonies. Mather described the rebellion in Boston as a defense against invasion from New France rather than a revolt against Andros.[53]

The strategy worked, at least for the time being. William accepted Mather's interpretation of the overthrow of Andros and promised he

AT THE TOWN-HOUSE in

BOSTON:

April 18th. 1689.

Sir,

OUr Selves as well as many others the Inhabitants of this Town and Place adjacent, being surprized with the Peoples sudden taking to Arms, in the first motion whereof we were wholly ignorant, are driven by the present Exigence and Necessity to acquaint your *Excellency*, that for the Quieting and Securing of the People Inhabiting this Countrey from the imminent Dangers they many wayes lie open, and are exposed unto, and for Your own safety; We judge it necessary that You forthwith Surrender, and Deliver up the Government and Fortifications to be preserved, to be Disposed according to Order and Direction from the Crown of *England*, which is suddenly expected may Arrive, promising all Security from Violence to Your Self, or any other of Your Gentlemen and Souldiers in Person or Estate, or else we are assured they will endeavour the taking of the Fortifications by Storm, if any opposition be made.

To *Sr.* Edmond Andross Knight,

Wait Winthrop	*Elisha Cook.*
Simon Bradstreet.	*Isaac Addington.*
William Stoughton	*John Nelson.*
Samuel Shrimton	*Adam Winthrop.*
Barthol. Gidney	*Peter Sergeant.*
William Brown	*John Foster.*
Thomas Danforth	*David Waterhouse.*
John Richards.	

Boston Printed by *S. Green.* 1689.

Proclamation, signed by fifteen leading colonists urging Andros to "Surrender and Deliver up the Government"; read from Boston's Town House, April 18, 1689

Joseph Dudley, imprisoned with Andros in 1689 and later acquitted; served as
governor of Massachusetts from 1702 to 1715

would have a letter written for Mather to carry back to Boston acknowledging the rebellion in his name. Mather's relief was immense. You can become Emperor of America if you want, he told William.[54] The Committee for Trade and Plantations was less readily satisfied. Nevertheless, after a hot debate, it agreed to a letter to Boston, authorizing the rebel government to continue in power until a permanent settlement could be reached.[55] The Boston rebellion broke up the Dominion of New England and placed the burden of initiative back on the men in London. It thus was a milestone in New England's history. Mather had up to then been fighting at best an even battle with Blathwayt and others who wanted to keep the status quo. Now that the Dominion was fragmented, Mather's influence was powerful enough to preclude any likelihood that it could ever be reassembled.[56] The Corporation Bill, which Mather hoped would restore the old charter, was still in Parliament and the subject of heated debate. By August it seemed to some to have no chance of passing that session.[57] Nevertheless, Mather professed in his autobiography some years later that he had been confident of the outcome: "There being no apparent danger, but that the Bill would be carried to perfection," he wrote, "I thought I might with Joy and good Tidings in my mouth return home to New England."[58]

Perhaps Samuel Sewall's plans had something to do with Increase's decision to go home. Sewall had come over on the ship *America*, commanded by William Clark, and planned to return on the same vessel when it sailed in August. Mather booked passage for himself and Sam, and in a hustle and bustle they packed up everything, the big oil portrait, their new clothes, books, and instruments for the college, and on August 20 left London by coach for Gravesend and then on to Deal, where the *America* lay at anchor in the harbor with other vessels to sail in convoy once the winds changed. For more than a week they fretted there. Once all the passengers were summoned aboard, but two days later were sent ashore again.[59]

Three days later young Samuel Mather was ill with a fever. A local doctor induced vomiting and the next day opened a vein to draw off seven ounces of blood. Samuel grew worse, and in another day the diagnosis was apparent. Smallpox.[60] In the next few days while the fleet still waited a change of wind Mather wrote Governor Simon Bradstreet and his son Cotton to tell them of the success of the Corporation Bill and of the king's letter authorizing Massachusetts to continue its present government. The wind turned, the other passengers for New England boarded, and the convoy sailed. In Deal, through the month of September, Mather nursed his son back to health. In October they took the coach to London.[61] That winter parts of Mather's letters were published in Boston in a broadside, *The Present State of New-English Affairs*.[62]

Mather returned to find a Parliament in which the political tide had turned against him. The Tory or Court party, which had grown in influence, opposed the Corporation Bill when it was re-introduced. The bill was vigorously debated. Government officers with experience in colonial administration lobbied to exclude the colonies from a general restoration of charters. The 1689 uprisings in Boston, New York, and Maryland had helped the Tory cause, because moderate Whigs now looked askance at such contempt for authority. Tories held it against Massachusetts that Sir Edmund Andros was kept in prison, and Edward Randolph sent back scathing reports of the Massachusetts government. Mather lobbied night and day to keep New England in the bill. When at last it did pass the House and was sent to the Lords, almost every colony except New England and Virginia had been excluded by special provisions.[63] Debate in the House of Lords began on January 11, 1690. The next morning on his way to Westminster Mather wrapped himself in his heaviest cloak against the cold, passing fallen chimney pots and uprooted trees in St. James's Park. For two weeks he lobbied in Lords to keep New England in the bill. His spirits alternately plunged and soared. But before the issue could finally be resolved by a vote, William prorogued Parliament and then early in February dissolved it. There would have to be new elections before anything more could be done. Mather wrote of his frustration: "That Parliament being unexpectedly Prorogu'd and Dissolv'd, a whole Year's *Sisyphean Labour* came to nothing."[64]

William, displeased with the Whigs, placed the Tory President of the Committee for Trade and Plantations, Sir Thomas Osborne, Earl of Danby, now made Marquis of Carmarthen, in several places of the highest trust. This was a bad turn for Mather, since Carmarthen had all along favored a strong military governor for New England and had been president of the committee when the charter was withdrawn and Andros sent as governor. Election campaigns dominated the political world in February and March. The Tories won a majority. The Corporation Bill, a Whig issue, was dead and with it any chance Mather had had of restoring Massachusetts's charter through Parliament.[65]

MASSACHUSETTS'S CHARGES AGAINST ANDROS
AND DUDLEY

The rebellion in Boston the previous spring had brought together the factions which had divided the Puritan community. Samuel Shrimpton, as well as Thomas Danforth, William Stoughton, and Governor Bradstreet, no less than John Richards and Elisha Cooke, all signed the revolutionary manifesto, "Declaration of the Gentlemen, Merchants, and Inhabitants of Boston" which was read from the Town House on the morning of April 18, 1689. The overthrow of Andros's government was popular across the entire spectrum of Boston and New England society. Within a month a convention of representatives from Massachusetts towns, the largest representative assembly ever held in the colony, gathered in Boston. After much wrangling between moderate and radical factions, the convention voted to restore the government as it had existed under the old charter until London decided on a permanent settlement, but with one revolutionary change. The convention voted for a franchise based on a small property qualification rather than on church membership.[66] Even with this concession to a secular state, however, many moderates who had been willing to throw out Andros were unwilling to return to the old charter, and they began individually to disassociate themselves from the government. As they did so, political authority in Massachusetts was steadily undermined.

Contradictory information streamed across the Atlantic to England. Some supported the rebellion, others condemned it; some asked for the old charter back, others requested a new charter, and still others favored the appointment of a royal governor and direct administration from England. The general population of Massachusetts, country people who had no correspondents in England, the ordinary people, were in a rage against Sir Edmund, against Randolph, against Joseph Dudley, and all those who had participated in the Dominion government. They insisted that Andros and the others be kept in prison. Dudley was at first allowed house arrest at his home in Roxbury, but a clamoring mob alarmed the Council of Safety, and he was returned to the jail. Andros was kept in a dungeon on Castle Island. Randolph wrote his many letters to England "From the Common Gaol in New Algeires."[67]

While the principals were under arrest, evidence was sought against them. Every Massachusetts town was asked to collect affidavits against the jailed men. Randolph's trunks yielded up a treasure of correspondence to England, which was held against him and used to incriminate others. By December 1689, a mountain of documentation had been assembled and a seven-man committee appointed to sift through it and bring order to the accusations of misrule. Anger and self-righteousness run through the affidavits sworn out by hundreds of persons in the towns of Massachusetts and New Hampshire. They held it against Sir Edmund Andros for "intollerable fineing him and excessive charges. . . . unhumaine destroying of souldiers that were here Imprest. . . . to the common prison and that without any crime done by him, a most hellish way to undoe men. . . . Rayseing mony contrary to the liberty of Free born English Subjects." Dozens of complaints were made against Dudley: "Coppie of twelve of his owne Letters, which declare his Malitious Spirrit, and manifest his Treacherous minde against the Massachusetts Colloney, Chiefly to Augment his fortune and Avenge himself for being left out of the Majestry—did he not break his freeman's oath? . . . Notorious things done. . . . his encroachment on all and every side. . . . makeing a pack-horse of the law as if it must attend him and George Farewall his child (the Attourney) as they pleased. . . . would not suffer them to speak. . . . called them from County to County, and would not suffer them to have a Jury."[68]

Even in the abbreviation of these many affidavits and testimonies one reads the voice of ordinary people grown used to governing themselves in their own interest, used to electing their own governors and clergymen, used to self-respect and the respect of their government, now suddenly subjected to the overbearing hauteur of the upper classes of old England, the voice of a people already accustomed to an unspoken social revolution, a social revolution that the Dominion of New England had seemed about to reverse but which had now marvellously been justified by the Glorious Revolution in England itself.

The men who governed in Boston would, of course, receive an order from London to send Andros, Randolph, and the others to England. The Committee for Trade and Plantations wrote that letter in June 1689, but Boston did not admit to receiving it until November, a not impossible delay in the notoriously slow and unsure communication between England and New England, but one which also possibly reflected the Puritans' determination to delay, delay, delay as long as humanly possible. The prisoners were not released until February 1690, by which time the Committee of Safety had sifted through the evidence against them and compiled a dossier on each of fourteen men held prisoner.

Massachusetts read the good news Increase sent from Deal in September 1689, still unaware of the collapse of the Corporation Bill in Par-

liament in the meantime. When orders for the return of Andros and
Randolph came, the interim government appointed two men, Elisha
Cooke and Thomas Oakes, to join Mather and Sir Henry Ashurst in England as official agents of the colony. It instructed them to negotiate
a return of the old charter with whatever additional privileges they
deemed desirable. Perhaps foremost in their responsibilities was to press
the charges against Andros, et al. and thus justify armed revolt.[69] Elisha
Cooke and Thomas Oakes represented the extreme, popular wing of the
political spectrum in Boston. They were Harvard classmates. Both had
practiced medicine in Boston, and in 1684 Cooke had been elected to the
Court of Assistants in place of Dudley. Oakes had been elected speaker of
the House of Representatives in the interim government. In England
Increase Mather and Sir Henry Ashurst became now for the first time
official spokesman for Massachusetts.

Two ships sailed from Boston at almost the same time, the one carrying Sir Edmund Andros, Dudley, Randolph, and about eleven more; the
other carried Cooke and Oakes. The two agents landed in the west at
Bristol at the end of March and hurried by public coach across southern
England to London. They went at once to Mather's lodgings in the city.
Sir Henry Ashurst arranged an interview with the king for the next
week, and the week after that with Queen Mary. Meanwhile, Andros's
party reached London and went promptly to Whitehall. The Committee
for Trade and Plantations left word at the Exchange for the agents to
come to the Council rooms in Whitehall. Once there they were told they
must put in writing the objections against Andros. The four agents retired to Mather's room and drafted a hasty response. None wanted to sign
their names to the draft, and their attorney, Robert Humphreys, advised
them not to, pointing out that the charges were brought by the people in
Massachusetts as a whole, not by the agents as individuals. All four
understood that, if the prisoners were found innocent, they would surely
sue whoever had signed the "objections." Mather said of himself and Sir
Henry Ashurst, "Wee had bin children had we (signed) it upon their
saying they could prove what was asserted," and "We had not seen what
proofs they had brought with them."[70]

Perhaps what happened in Whitehall in the next few weeks could have
been avoided, perhaps not. It was, in any event, a disaster for Massachusetts. On April 17, 1690, the Committee for Trade and Plantations convened around the big table in the council chamber. Against the wall on
one side stood the four men acting for Massachusetts, together with their
legal counsel and their attorney. Across the room crowded sixteen men

released from jail in Boston, their legal counsel, and a small crowd of supporters from within the city. The Lords of the Committee took their seats. William Blathwayt, secretary to the committee and chief of staff in the Plantation Office, hovered at the Marquis of Carmarthen's elbow.

Carmarthen asked that charges against the prisoners be read. Sure enough, no sooner had the first been read, than Joseph Dudley broke in with the request that the authors sign "the Charge delivered in against them, that they might know who they had to answere, and to have satisfaction if they cleared themselves." Carmarthen adopted this suggestion and asked the agents to sign the charges. "We appear here in behalfe of the Country that imploy us," they said. It did not satisfy Carmarthen, who wanted to know, "Who imprisoned Sir Edmund Andros and the rest?"

"The Country, my Lord," answered Sir John Somers, Counsel for the agents, "the people of the place."

Sir Robert Sawyer, late attorney general and now counsel for Sir Edmund Andros, broke in brusquely here, "You say it was done by the people, but it was by the Rabble spirited by the faction to overthrow the Government."

Carmarthen had the last word: "You say it was done by the country and the people, but that is nobody. Let us see A. B.C.D. the persons that will make it their case and make this charge, that we may know who we have to do with, for that paper is not signed by anybody."

The argument dragged on until other members of the committee grew restless, some taking sides with the agents, some clearly favoring the prisoners. At last Carmarthen turned to the agents, "Gentlemen, here has been a pretty deale of time spent. My Lords will give his Majestie a true and impartial account of what has been sayd on both sides, and waite on his Majesty's further pleasure in the matter, and you may withdraw for the present."[71] The next day the Privy Council dismissed all charges against Andros and the others, and the day afterward they were received in audience by William.

The whole affair was talked about and laughed about around London as a triumph for the Tories. Mather was humiliated: "Those oppressors did not only come off with flying colors," he wrote, "but insulted over their Adversaries. . . . The Agents of N. E. are on this account Exposed in the News Letters and Ridiculed in the City and Countrey."[72] Worse than humiliation was a possibility that William would re-appoint Andros governor of New England! For one thing, it was becoming all too evident that the provisional government in Boston was unable to defend

---

This is Publifhed to prevent Falfe Reports

An Extract of a Letter from Mr. Mather, To the Governour, Dated Sept. 3. 1689 from Deal in Kent.

THe Houfe of Commons Ordered a Bill to be drawn up for the Reftoration of Charters to all Corporations. Some Enemies of *New-England* did beftir themfelves on that Occafion. But it has pleafed God to fuccced Endeavours and Sollicitations here fo far, as that N. E. is particularly mentioned in the Bill.

It has been read twice, and after that referred unto a Committee for Emendations. What concerns N. England paffed without any great oppofition. The Bill has been in part read the third Time, and the Charters of N. Eng. then alfo paffed without Objection. Only fome Additional Claufes refpecting Corporations here, caufed Debates fo that the Bill is not as yet Enacted.

In the latter end of *June*, a Veffel from *Mount Hope* arrived here, which brought your Declaration of *April* 18. with an account of the Revolution in *New-England*. The week after I went to *Hampton Court*, and had the favour to wait on His Majefty, who told me, That He did accept of, and was well pleafed with what was done in New-England, and that he would order the Secretary of State to fignifie fo much, and that His Subjects there fhould have their Ancient Rights and Priviledges reftored to them.

The King has fent a Gracious Letter (which was delivered to me, and if I return not my felf, I fhall take care that it be fent to you) bearing Date *Auguft* 12. Wherein He fignifies His Royal Approbation of what has been done at *Bofton*, and affures you that the Government there fhall be fetled, fo as fhall be for the Security and Satisfaction of His Subjects in that Colony, and in the mean time bids you go on to Adminifter the Laws, and manage the Government, according as in your Addrefs you have Petitioned.

My Lord *Mordent* (now Earl of *Monmouth*) bade me affure you that He would be your Friend, and he bade me tell you from him, That your *Charters fhould be reftored to you by Act of Parliament*.

I have been with moft of the Kings moft Honourable Privy Council, who have promifed to befriend *New-England* as there fhall be occafion for it. The like I may fay, of all the Leading men in the Parliament.

I have been in the *Downs* a fortnight, and Aboard Mr. *Clark*, feveral Nights, but the Wind has been againft us. And we now hear that the *New-found-Land* Convoyes (on whofe Affiftance we had a Dependance) are gone.

Superfcribed To the Honourable
Simon Bradftreet, *Efq.*

Governour of the Maffachufets Colony in N-England.

A Paffage extracted from the publick News-Letter, Dated July 6. 1689.

The people of *New-England* having made a thorow Revolution, and fecured the publick Criminals. On *Thurfday* laft, the Reverend and Learned Mr. *Mather*, Prefident of the *Colledge*, and Minifter of *Bofton*, waited on the King; and in a moft Excellent Speech laid before His Majefty, the State of that People; faying, *That they were fober, and Induftrious, and fit for Martial Service ; and all with their Lives and Interefts were at His Majefties Command, to tender the fame unto His Majefty : That they defired nothing but His Majefties Acceptance of what they had done, and His Protection ; and that if His Majefty pleafed to encourage and Commiffion them, He might eafily be Emperour of* America. His Majefty affured him, that He was pleafed with what was done for Him, and for themfelves in the Revolution, and that their Priviledges and Religion fhould be fecured unto them.

Extracted from a Letter of Mr Mather, to his Son, Dated Sept. 2. 1689.

On *July* 4. The King faid unto me, *That He did kindly Accept of what was done in Bofton. And that His Subjects in New-England fhould have their Ancient Rights and Priviledges Reftored and Confirmed unto them.* Yea, He told me, *That if it were in his power to caufe it to be done it fhould be done,* and bade me reft affured of it.

The *Charter-Bill* is not finifhed, becaufe fome Additional Claufes refpecting Corporations here in *England* caufed a Debate; and the Parliament is for fome weeks Adjourned.

Befides the Letter from the Kings Majefty, whereof we have notice as above ; there is now arrived, an Order from His Majefty to the Government, bearing Date, *July* 30. 1689. Requiring, That Sir Edmund Androfs, Edward Randolph, *and others, that have been Seized by the people of Bofton, and fhall be at the Receipt of thefe Commands, Detained there, under Confinement, be fent on Board the firft Ship, bound to England, to anfwer what may be objected againft them.*

Bofton, Printed and Sold by Samuel Green, 1689.

1689 newsletter, printed in Boston by Samuel Green, Jr., with extracts from two letters from Mather at Deal

ELISHA COOKE

MASS. AGENT 1649

Elisha Cooke, Boston physician, sent to England in 1690 to join Mather as official agent of the colony

the northern frontier. Military defense had been Andros's strong suit, and his removal had resulted in a collapse of the frontier defenses.[73] For another thing, people in New England who did not like the old charter increasingly made their interests known in England. Several merchants were in the council chambers with Andros and were quick to speak out, as soon as it was plain that Andros would be cleared of any wrongdoing.[74]

Francis Brinley and his son Thomas were among the merchants who aligned themselves with Andros. Francis Brinley had lived long in Newport, Rhode Island, where he was elected to the Court of Assistants. The rebellion of April 1689 had seemed to him an open door to anarchy: "Unless some divine providence or human power relieve us, nothing appears but ruine and confusion, property and priviledge (so much talkt of) will be destroyed, and all things else set up that may make a people miserable . . . An oppressive government is to be preferred before . . . anarchy."[75]

By May 1690, it seemed to Mather that everything was lost. "The Earle of Monmouth assured me that the King was offended at New England because they had Imprisoned their Governor and could prove nothing against him, That the Agents had cutt the throat of their Countrey." Mather's supporters in Parliament were "Scandalized," he wrote, "so that I was afraid all my labor had bin lost, and that all the friends whom I had brought into the Interst of New England would desert them." Only his own persistent efforts had prevented the appointment of Andros or another like him. "This I write," Mather went on, "not conjecturally, but as that which is indubitably so."[76]

STALEMATE

The four agents representing Massachusetts could not agree among themselves what strategy to pursue now. Their instructions directed them to obtain the old charter with additional privileges, and Mather and Ashurst knew how unrealistic that was. They wanted to ask William for a new charter and hoped they would be able to include in it the colony's most important privileges. Oakes could see the point. Elisha Cooke stubbornly refused, and stuck rigidly with his instructions to get back the old charter.

The four men argued endlessly until dull-eyed with fatigue, but suddenly it was too late to accomplish anything. William had left with his Protestant army to wage war against the Catholic forces of James in Ireland. The agents had lost their chance to appeal to the king. At the Committee for Trade and Plantations their stock sank lower. Andros prepared a long document showing how much he had spent raising troops and building defenses against the Indians on the New Hampshire and Maine borders, and how the rebellion in Boston had opened the frontier to attack by French and Indian forces. Hurriedly Cooke and Oakes drew up a reply. But although they waited in the anteroom to the committee chambers until late at night, they were never called.[77]

After Andros came Randolph with a meticulously detailed complaint against illegal trade flourishing in Boston after the April 18 rebellion. The Commissioners of the Customs, who backed up Randolph, made even more comprehensive complaints. Under the law all ships leaving Boston with an enumerated commodity, such as tobacco, were to post bond to sail directly to England. Copies of the bonds should have been sent to London. None, however, had arrived, and Elisha Cooke could do no more than argue that the missing papers must have been lost at sea. It seemed a lame excuse.[78]

Over and over again the Massachusetts agents presented themselves at the door to the council chamber, but were denied a hearing. They repeatedly submitted written responses to Andros and Randolph, but the committee did not find time to consider them. Attention was riveted instead on the war in Ireland. At the River Boyne, near Drogheda, William's forces defeated James's army in a bloody battle for survival, James fled to France, and the revolution in England was secured. Protestant English control over Catholic Ireland, however, was far from secure, and the terrible war would continue. William remained in Ireland until the end of August 1690, when he at last broke off the unsuccessful siege of Limerick and returned to London. With the king back in Westminster, the agents girded themselves for another effort. Ashurst, Oakes, and Mather, but not Elisha Cooke, addressed a petition to the king for a new charter.[79] Mather used his old friends to gain an audience, and William seemed to accept the idea. He referred the business to his chief legal officers, the Attorney-General Sir John Treby, the Solicitor-General Sir John Somers, and to the two Lords Chief Justices, Sir John Holt and Sir Henry Pollexfen.[80]

Mather was elated, for he was sure he could work more easily with these men than with the committee and William Blathwayt. The four men assigned to the task met several times during the fall and invited Mather to all of their meetings. They drew up a list of the main heads of a possible royal charter for Massachusetts. Under Mather's influence, and without Blathwayt's meddling, the resulting draft was virtually a repeat of the colony's old charter, although the crown was now given the authority to review Massachusetts laws. When the draft was presented to William, he referred it properly enough to his Privy Council, and that body sent it to its Committee for Trade and Plantations. The agents were back where they had been in June and July of the previous year. The draft was received in the committee not as the work of the crown legal officers, but as a "Proposal offered by the New England Agents."[81]

London was again in the grip of a cold winter. Wan sunlight barely warmed its narrow streets, and on the short winter days the rooms were dark early in the afternoon. By the end of January 1691, Mather's spirits matched the weather. "The affaire of N. E. is not to this day brought to a comfortable issue," he wrote. News came that an attempt in October by Sir William Phips to capture Quebec had been a fiasco. "The consequence," Mather wrote, "is like to be very sad to N. E. Now their enemies everywhere are insulting over them." He had heard nothing from his family for more than a month. He was lonely and anxious. "How it may be with my Family I know not, but am full of Fears and sadness." London, once so bright and glamorous, had its dark side too. In his chamber at Copthall Court Mather spent whole days in prayer. "Keep me," he beseeched his God, "keep me from sinking under the burdens of spirit that do oppress me."[82] The business of New England languished in the committee. Without some spur nothing was likely to happen. William was in Holland, now, warring against France. Mather busied himself with the Nonconformist churches about London. A movement was afoot to effect a union between Congregationalists and Presbyterians, and he was pleased to be asked to participate.

HEADS OF AGREEMENT: DISSENTERS RECONCILED

After years of surviving underground, persecuted by a common enemy, forced to retreat to the bare essence of their religious practices, the Independents and Presbyterians in England had found that there was very little difference between them, certainly not as much as when they were vying for power during the 1650s. Mather's brother Nathaniel was already involved; he had become one of the managers of a common fund for the relief of ministers of either church. The main spirit behind the reconciliation was John Howe, whose friendship with Mather went back to the 1650s. Since then, although Howe had crossed the narrow line to join the Presbyterian party, he remained in close sympathy with the Congregationalists. In January 1691 he drew up proposals for uniting the two churches and recruited Mather to help persuade the other ministers in and about London to agree to it. Negotiations went on during January and February. Increase was in an ideal situation to act as go-between. He was flattered at the attention given him and excited at the role he was able to play in what he believed to be the evolution of the true church. By March most of the Congregational and Presbyterian ministers in London had signed a document called "Heads of Agreement Assented to by the United Ministers in and about London, formerly called Presbyterian and Congregational." [83]

Like any document written to bury differences between people who disagree, the Heads of Agreement could be read in different ways. To Increase Mather it generally affirmed the plan of Congregational churches spelled out in the Cambridge Platform while at the same time approving the wider baptism he had defended in 1675. The Heads of Agreement spoke of the "Catholick Visible Church" made up of "The whole multitude of Visible Believers and their infant-seed." [84]

But how was Congregational autonomy to be squared with the national authority of a Presbyterian system? The Heads went on to describe "particular churches" created out of the general Catholic church by societies of "visible saints," who agreed among themselves to worship together. No particular church was more powerful than any other, and each was to ordain its own pastor. Ordinarily each church fellowship should ask the advice of the neighboring churches about the choice of a pastor, and ordinarily the approval of neighboring churches was required for the ordination of the new man. [85] So far, the Heads of Agreement corresponded to New England practice, although that little word "ordinarily" left the door unlocked against the insinuation of more Presbyterian control over the nomination and ordination of ministers. In this the agreement in London would add to the seemingly irresistible tide in America that removed ministers more and more from the authority of the brethren. The pastors and elders were to "Rule and Govern," the agreement read; the brethren were to "Consent." [86]

Once again Increase found himself more flexible and forward-moving than his older brother. Nathaniel considered the Heads of Agreement unacceptable and refused to sign. [87] Increase, on the other hand, sent a copy back home to Cotton, who quickly and proudly announced it as the wave of the future. Father and son together took pride in the role the father had played in England and in the numerous testimonies of gratitude from English ministers.

In addition to helping the Independents and Presbyterians bury the hatchet, Mather developed his many friendships among leaders of England's Dissenting community. He was now partaking regularly of the Lord's Supper with Dr. Bates at Hackney and frequently preached there. He went with Bates to visit Richard Baxter the day before Baxter's death. Baxter dedicated his last book *Glorious Kingdom of Christ* to Mather.[88] But despite these activities and rewards in the field of religion, it was politics not religion that governed Mather's life in England. Politics shaped his days, determined his society, filled his thoughts, and satisfied his creative needs and ambitions. Mather spent little time at his writing table while in England, and although he preached a sermon every week, the five or six books he published in these years were political books.

THE NEW CHARTER

The draft of a new charter for Massachusetts that Mather had helped the crown's legal officers write in November and December 1690 arrived at the Committee for Trade and Plantations in January 1691, accompanied by more than two hundred pages of supporting documents.[89] The Lords of the committee turned the bundle of papers over to its clerk, William Blathwayt, for analysis and a recommendation, and Blathwayt now squared off against Increase Mather in the final contest over the future government of Massachusetts.

The news of Sir William Phips's disastrous attempt to storm Quebec and of repeated French successes on the land frontier between French Canada and New England gave Blathwayt an immediate advantage. If Massachusetts were to regain her old autonomy, Blathwayt warned, "The damage will not be theirs alone, the blow will reach all the other Plantations which are under his Majesty's Government and have an immediate effect upon the revenue of the customs and manufacturers of England. This I foretold very early, as I foresee greater and irreparable mischief if not prevented by a higher hand, for how can it be otherwise while a mean and mechanical sort of people shall pretend to and abuse the highest acts of royal government under the color of an imaginery charter they have justly forfeited."[90]

Increase Mather worked furiously to line up support for New England. He saw Cooke and Oakes occasionally, but Sir Henry Ashurst was his constant companion as he and Mather sought out the members of the committee. Sir William Phips was now in London, and Mather brought him along as well. Typical of Mather's pursuit of every potential advantage was his arrangement at Court to introduce Phips to the Queen.[91]

On the other side were formidable opponents. Randolph, with his detailed eyewitness reports, the Customs Commissioners, Admiralty, Treasury, all backed Blathwayt. As damaging to Mather's cause as anything else were the letters and petitions from New England asking for more direct royal control. A petition with sixty-three signatures, circulated in November 1690, was licensed for printing in April 1691. Most of these petitioners were men who had not been enfranchised under the old charter. It became increasingly clear that the struggle in London would not be between the old moderate and popular factions, but between those who had been enfranchised under the old charter and those— now the great majority in Massachusetts—who had not.[92]

With the king due back from Flanders in April, Mather did everything he could to get ready. On March 31 he finished a short pamphlet, "Reasons for the Confirmation of the Charters," and circulated it to members of the committee and other potential allies.[93] On April 9, just before the king's arrival, Mather gained an audience with the queen. He urged her to use her influence in Massachusetts's behalf. She was as gracious, and as noncommittal as William himself.[94]

It is surprising that with so much damaging testimony against them Mather and the other agents were able to hold their own in the committee. For a week in April arguments were presented by all parties. The issues boiled down to whether or not the governor of Massachusetts should be appointed by the crown or elected by the people. On this the committee was deadlocked and resolved to go to the king for a decision.[95] The very next day Mather succeeded in obtaining an interview with William in the royal bed chamber. New England, Mather said, was different from the other colonies. "Such a Governor will not suit with the people of New England as may be very proper for the other English plantations." William was polite but cautious and noncommittal. He would see what would be done when the Privy Council next met.[96]

Two days later William attended his Council. Could he, he asked, legally appoint his own governor? Certainly, Chief Justice Sir John Holt told him; the old charter was vacated and the king could impose whatever form of government he wished. In that case, William said, "he believed it would be for the Good and Advantage of his Subjects in that Colony, to be under a Governor appointed by himself." He wished the agents would nominate someone who would meet the approval of the people of Massachusetts. But he did think that at this time the governor must be a military man. Mather wrote that the king agreed at this meeting that the colony's "Charter-Priviledges" should be "Restored and Confirmed to Them."[97] The next day William left once more for Holland. In Whitehall William Blathwayt's office issued an "Order in Council," summarizing the previous day's Council meeting. This summary did not quite agree with Mather's. The Order in Council reported that the king had ordered Massachusetts should have "a Governour of his own Appointing . . . And that the *Massachusetts Colony* should be settled on the same foundation with *Barbadoes* etc." [98]

Mather immediately sensed something dreadfully wrong. The Order in Council said nothing of ancient charter privileges. Instead it spoke of Barbados, where royal governors had traditionally been powerful, even tyrannical, figures. In Massachusetts the governor had always been weak, little more than a presiding officer. The old governor in Massachusetts had had no veto over the actions of the General Court and almost no powers of appointment. Mather hurried to several members of the committee whom he knew to be sympathetic. He explained his fears, but gained no assurance that anything could be done. Mather sent a copy of the Order in Council to Flanders, in case the king could be persuaded to review the matter and make a correction, but no answer came back. The Order in Council would stand. Maybe Elisha Cooke had been right to have nothing to do with a new charter, after all. Mather haunted Whitehall. He ran into Edward Randolph, and the two men exchanged angry words. He met frequently with William Blathwayt, who controlled everything. Finally, in mid-May the Privy Council ordered the attorney general to draft another charter for Massachusetts. [99]

Attorney General Sir John Treby was someone Mather was sure he could work with. "These blessings," he wrote, "call for prayer in a special manner." [100] The next day he was at Treby's door, and in the ensuing weeks he went there often, either conferring with Sir John or with his chief clerk, Mr. Gwillym. It was expensive, of course. Men in government were accustomed to receiving little presents. Mather's were in gold—ten guineas to Sir John today, five to Gwillym tomorrow. That was without mentioning tips to doormen, coaches in bad weather, and pay for scriveners to transform his wretched scrawl into presentable writing. [101] Mather later wrote, "I found it necessarie to gratifie severall persons, some with 20; Some with 30; Some with 40; Some with 50 guineas, etc., as aloe to bestow dayly gratifications—on Servants belonging to persons of Quallitie . . ." [102]

It all paid off, however, and Sir John prepared a draft charter that so closely followed Mather's ideas that when it was presented to the committee on June 8, one of the members scoffed that "by such a Charter as this, the King's Governour would be made a *Governor of Clouts,*" that is to

Courtesy, Perry-Castenada Library, University of Texas at Austin

John Bleau's map of London and Middlesex County, England, 1654, where Mather lived from 1688 to 1692

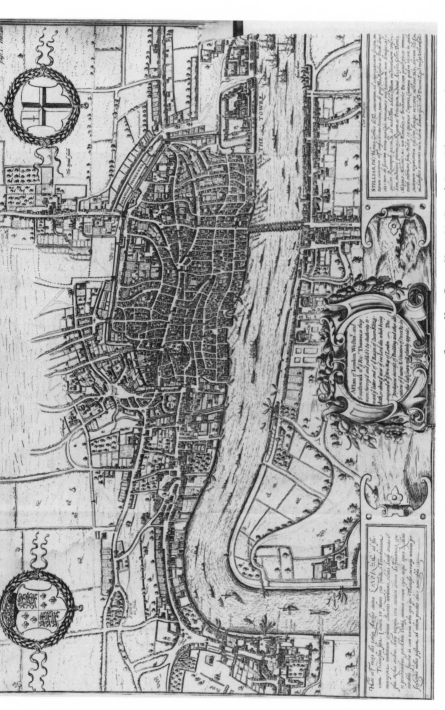

Courtesy, Harry Ransom Humanities Research Center, The University of Texas at Austin

"A plan of London, Westminster, and Southwark north of ye River Thames" around 1600, printed in Edward Hatton's *A New View of London*, 1708

Courtesy, Harry Ransom Humanities Research Center, The University of Texas at Austin

Map of London in the early eighteenth century showing St. Paul's Cathedral (center) and Whitehall palace (to the far left), where Increase Mather met with James II; printed in James Howell's *Londinopolis; An Historical Discourse . . . , 1657*

say, of nothing. Treby's thirty-eight page draft provided for a royal governor appointed by the king but without power in the colony. All appointments of sheriffs and justices and officers of the courts of admiralty and probate, all commissions in the militia, and all legislative power resided in the General Court without veto. The franchise to vote for members of the General Court was vested in freemen, as it had been in the old charter, and not freeholders as in England.[103]

This draft charter did not survive long in the committee. Carmarthen brusquely referred it to Blathwayt for analysis and recommendations. While waiting for that report the committee itself began to reflect a national swing in favor of the Tory party. Mather's allies on the committee attended less and less frequently, so that for the remaining six months of 1691 it would be Carmarthen, Secretary of State Daniel Finch Lord Nottingham, and William Blathwayt who made decisions at the Plantation office.[104] Mather could do no more. "The charter drawn up and presented to the Lords," he recorded in his diary, "is by an old Adversary opposed." He was tired. His thoughts turned more and more towards home. "Bless my Poor Family which I am so farr distant from, and have been so long absent from." He began once again to anticipate the date he might return to Boston. "Shall I go in the vessel now almost ready to go?" he asked himself in prayer.[105]

At the end of June, Blathwayt returned a devastating critique of the attorney-general's draft charter. He recommended fifteen modifications, the most important of which were these: 1) the General Court should be elected by freeholders and everywhere the term "freemen" should be replaced by "freeholder"; 2) assistants or council members should be chosen by the General Court or assembly (and not by royal appointment as elsewhere in royal colonies); 3) the governor should appoint all judges, justices of the peace, and sheriffs, with the advice of this council. A week later the committee followed Blathwayt's suggestions and adopted two more important changes: 4) laws were to be submitted to the crown for review and approval; 5) the governor should have a veto over all the actions of the assembly.[106]

These five propositions, out of many lesser ones, contained the essence of the political change embodied in the new charter. All were wide departures from past Massachusetts government. Mather did his best to keep the committee from approving them. He worked night and day, buttonholing anyone who had a voice: Sir John Somers, the Master of the Rolls Mr. Powle, Secretary of State Nottingham. He spoke to the Archbishop of Canterbury and the Bishop of London, imploring their help. He argued with Blathwayt all one morning, spent an outrageous sum on dinner at Pontack's, and spent the afternoon in the council chamber with the committee.[107]

The seasons had once again come full circle and London sweltered in mid-summer heat. John Evelyn, the diarist, thought it "a most extraordinary hot season." The pace Mather set himself was too severe and his health broke. Feverish and too weak to make his way to Whitehall or to stand long hours in the council chamber, he asked Elisha Cooke to go in his place. Something might come up which would make his being there an advantage to Massachusetts. But Cooke would have nothing to do with this new charter and declined to go. He and Mather had long since parted ways.[108] For a few days Mather was confined to his chambers. On July 21 he was out again and on the twenty-second back at Whitehall to argue with Blathwayt. Mather and Sir Henry Ashurst took Blathwayt to dinner at the Castle Tavern, but Blathwayt was less amenable than Sir John Treby and would not give in. He seemed to win every round.[109]

At last Mather lost his *sang froid.* He burst out to Sir John, "I would sooner part with my life than consent to [Blathwayt's proposals] or any thing else that did infringe any Liberty or Privilege of Right belonging to my Countrey." Losing his temper, however, did no good, and Mather learned yet another valuable lesson, when a noble member of the council rebuked him sharply. "They did not think the *Agents* of *New-England* were *Plenipotentiaries* from another Sovereign State." The fact was, Mather was reminded, the royal will would decide, whether Mather liked it or not.[110]

On July 30 Mather and Ashurst made one more effort to defeat Blathwayt's recommendations. They did accept changing the franchise from freemen to freeholders. That itself would transform the old Puritan government. But they could not accept: 1) that the governor should appoint judges, sheriffs, and justices of the peace; 2) that the council should be appointed and not elected by the people; 3) that the governor should have a veto over the actions of the assembly; 4) that the king should have unlimited time during which he could approve or disapprove of laws passed by the assembly.[111]

Debate in the council was long and stubborn. In the end it came down to two issues: who would appoint the judges, sheriffs, and justices of the peace, the governor or the assembly? And could the governor veto any action of the assembly or only the laws it passed? The council, deadlocked, left the final determination of these points to the king. Secretary Nottingham sent an express packet to Flanders for the answers and told William in no uncertain terms where he and Carmarthen stood.[112]

There now came a much needed break in the business. London was slowly emptying for the summer. Sir John went on vacation. The mood at Whitehall relaxed. Mather, Ashurst, Phips, and Blathwayt all dined together.[113] Mather and his son took a coach out to the country. They did not go far, only about ten miles north of Westminster to the village of Barnet. There they listened to the famous Vincent Alsop preach on Sunday. Mather drank the mineral waters at Barnet Wells. The next day he drove with Francis Charlton, a hot-tempered Whig gentleman, in the latter's calash, to Highwood Hills. Later he moved himself and Sam to rented rooms in Totteridge, a quiet village set amid parks, woods and farm lands, long since swallowed up by metropolitan London.[114]

August 12 Phips came riding out from London with news that the king's answer had come back, and that Massachusetts had lost. William had decided in favor of Blathwayt's and the committee's proposals on every count. Phips and Mather hurried back to London. They dined with Sir Henry Ashurst and pondered what to do now. Mather was wary of a trick and thought they ought to see the king's letter. Beyond that, all agreed that they would lose more than they would gain if they stubbornly refused to accept the king's decision as final. "We then resolved," Mather wrote, "to get as much Good and prevent as much Hurt to the countrey as possible." The next morning Secretary Nottingham showed Mather the royal letter, and there was no getting around it. Ashurst and Mather then went to the queen's secretary, Mons. D'Alonne, and signified that they would accept those points in the charter which had been in dispute.[115]

Mather returned to Totteridge. For the first time in months there was nothing for him to do, nothing he could do. For days he rested, saw no one, entertained himself reading the *Acta Eruditorum*. He seems to have been untroubled by the turn of events. He had worked as hard as was humanly possible. He could have done no more. Although the principal decisions had gone against Massachusetts, he was confident that had he and Ashurst not labored as they had the outcome would have been much worse. And there were many details left unfinished such that he might still accomplish something. The reader of Mather's diary and memoirs, however, cannot fail to sense that the revolutionary fire of the 1660s had gone out. Where was the Puritan zeal now? Where the jeremiads? Where the righteousness? Mather seemed content now to be on easy working terms with the great men of England. When he again returned to White-hall, it was to work with and not against the government on the details of the new charter.

On August 26 Mather was back in London. Blathwayt was in a hurry to complete the charter, now that the main points had been settled, and he sent a peremptory note to the Attorney General, Sir John Treby, to cut short his holidays at Tunbridge Wells and prepare a new draft. Mather haunted the Attorney General's offices and made suggestions every step of the way. At his insistence, for example, the charter guaranteed the land grants and property rights established under the old charter, even though—as had been argued by Andros—the procedures had been il-legal in English common law. [116]

The new Massachusetts charter established a House of Representa-tives elected on the basis of a forty shilling freehold franchise, and a Council, whose members were to be nominated by the Representatives and approved, or not, by the governor. Every other royal council in the American colonies was appointed with no popular or democratic constit-uency at all. Its importance in the Massachusetts charter, however, was magnified by another unusual feature. The governor's broad powers of appointment—officers of all courts, sheriffs, justice of the peace, militia officers—were to be exercised under the new charter "with the advice and consent of the council." [117] The phrase and the purpose behind it first appear in royal instructions to governors in the West Indies, where it had been in the crown's interest to curb the freewheeling and arbitrary behav-ior of the royal governors. [118] Administrative procedures for Barbados seem to have had some standing as a model in the minds of the staff of the Plantation Office since the Order in Council of April 30 had specified that the governor was to have powers "as in Barbados and the other Plan-tations." The idea soon gained acceptance. William Penn incorporated it in 1683 into the Pennsylvania Frame of Government, and the Plantation Office used it in Sir Edmund Andros's commission as Governor-General of the Dominion of New England, 1686. [119] Blathwayt's recommenda-tions for a new Massachusetts charter on July 2, 1691, included the for-mula. [120] Sir Henry Ashurst and Mather, apprently not realizing the advantages to them of the "advice and consent" rule, refused to accept Blathwayt's language. [121] They were overruled by the king.

The fact that the Massachusetts Council was to be nominated by an elected House of Representatives made advice and consent a unique brake on the extensive powers of the governor. In 1787 its use for this same purpose was carried over to the Constitution of the United States.

Therefore, although the royal governor under Massachusetts's new charter had far greater powers than the elected governor under the old charter, the House of Representatives of Massachusetts had greater powers than the lower house in any of the royal colonies. Massachusetts henceforward had a mixed form of government.

The geographical extent of the new charter government was still to be established, and here Mather himself reached as far as he could. The towns of Plymouth had never successfully sued for a royal charter, and Mather was able to bring them within the bounds of Massachusetts. [122] He was frustrated with regard to the New Hampshire towns. Royal government there under Sir Lionel Cranfield had been a shambles, but the committee was persuaded by Samuel Allen, the London merchant who had bought up the Mason family claims to New Hampshire, to keep the region separate from Massachusetts, and when John Usher of Boston, an associate of Allen's, offered to defray the costs of government, he was appointed lieutenant governor. Lands further east were more available. Mather and Sir Henry Ashurst successfully petitioned to have Maine and Nova Scotia included within the charter boundaries. [123]

In April, as an accommodation to Mather's insistent pleadings, William III had said that even though the governor of Massachusetts should be appointed by the crown and should be a military person, the king nevertheless wished to appoint someone who would be acceptable to the colonists. The agents were invited to nominate not only the first royal governor, but the twenty-eight members of the first council. Elisha Cooke would have nothing to do with these nominations. "On the Exchange," Mather wrote, "I spoke to dr. Cooke. I told him Hee might see the draught of the charter for N. E. if he would be at the charges of 9 guineas. He replyed, Hee did not think it worth them." [124]

On September 18, Mather and Ashurst presented nominations for governor, deputy governor and councilors. [125] For governor they named someone who seemed ideal—Sir William Phips, a captain of men, who had already led an expedition to recover Spanish treasure, and been knighted for the exploit by James II, commander of a successful attack on the French fort at Port Royal and the large, if mismanaged, expedition against Quebec. Phips seemed preeminently qualified from the king's point of view. He was also peculiarly within the Mather camp, for he had come to religion late, been brought to the point of regeneration by a sermon of Increase's, and baptized into the North Church by Cotton in 1690. [126] The fact that William Phips had had no experience at all in the fine arts of political leadership seemed to trouble no one. How unsuited he was for the governorship was still to be discovered. For the moment he seemed a fine choice to take the sting out of the fact that Massachusetts could no longer elect its governors.

For council members Mather and Ashurst chose wisely and with an eye to ensuring that the new government would work with and not against the charter. Eighteen of the twenty-eight men named were already serving as elected magistrates. The new members represented by and large the mercantile interests of the larger coastal towns, which is to say that they were predisposed to cooperate with England. The political leaders left out of the new council were those die-hard Puritans who had all along refused to compromise: Elisha Cooke and Thomas Oakes, Thomas Danforth, but also Peter Tilton and John Smith.[127] Tilton, Deputy for Hadley in the 1660s, had been a particular ally of the young Mather and the parting of their ways now highlighted the change in Mather's expectation for New England. For deputy governor the agents nominated William Stoughton, a bleak, narrow-minded Puritan whose future role as a judge in the witch trials would permanently darken his reputation, but who, perhaps not unrelatedly, had a character and view of government acceptable to Massachusetts.

All of Mather's labors in England came to a symbolic climax on October 7, 1691, when the new charter for Massachusetts received the great seal of England. None of the participants, certainly not William Blathwayt or Increase Mather, realized, perhaps, so close were they to the day-by-day events, how significant a watershed was now crossed. The Puritan commonwealth dreamed of and put in place by John Winthrop was no more; the constitutional framework for the pluralistic, secular society that would be inherited by John Adams was now in place. Mather himself had experienced a profound change in his political thinking. He and Henry Ashurst (Mather called him "Sir Harry") discovered in the new charter provisions that made it, in Mather's own words, a "Magna Charta for New England." Not a little irony resides in the turn of mind that permitted him now to take great pride in the charter that contained so many fundamental changes from the old government.

"God has been so gracious to me, as to make me instrumental in obtaining for my Countrey a *MAGNA CHARTA*, whereby Religion and English Liberties, with some peculiar Priviledges, Liberties, and all Men's Properties, are Confirmed and Secured, (Allowance being given for the Instability of all Humane Affairs) to Them and their Posterity for evermore."[128]

The language hides the fact that the terms of the new charter wiped out the political basis of the old colony. A franchise based on church membership and a government elected entirely within the colony gave way to a franchise based on property and a government supervised and directed from London. These new political relationships were appropriate to Massachusetts at the end of the seventeenth century. The old colony itself had changed. The more or less continuous modification of Puritan society, at work from the first settlements, had reached a point where replacing the old political order satisfied far more people than it disturbed. The overwhelming majority of men who petitioned the crown in 1690 for a settlement of government were not freemen under the old charter. The new charter gave legitimacy to changes which the majority of people approved.

Increase Mather himself, for all his religious conservatism, was in the forefront of accommodation to the new circumstances. "By this *New Charter*," he wrote, "great Priviledges are granted to the People in *New-England*, and in some Particulars, greater than they formerly enjoyed." Modern historians have agreed. "The Province Charter of 1691," wrote historian Samuel Eliot Morison, "gave Massachusetts Bay a greater measure of home rule than any other royal or proprietary colony in America enjoyed." [129] Mather went on in a way astonishing in light of his earlier political writings:

For all *English* liberties are restored to them: No Persons shall have a Penny of their Estates taken from them; nor any Laws imposed on them, without their own Consent by Representatives chosen by themselves. Religion is secured; for Liberty is granted to all Men to Worship God after that manner which in their Consciences they shall be perswaded is the most Scriptural way. [130]

The new charter allowed Massachusetts to establish the Congregational church with public funds: "The General Court may by Laws Encourage and Protect that *Religion* which is the general Profession of the Inhabitants there." Even more important was the provision that the governor would appoint judges and justices of the peace only "with the advice and consent" of the council, which itself would be nominated by the elected assembly.

As long as their Principal Magistrates, Judges, Justices of the peace, are such as will encourage Vertue and Piety, and punish Vice, Religion will flourish: And if they have not such, the fault will not be in the *New-Charter*, but in themselves; since no bad Councellor, Judge, or Justice of the Peace can now be imposed on them." [131]

Mather set forth these arguments in a twenty-four-page pamphlet, *A Brief Account Concerning Several of the Agents of New-England,* which he wrote in October after the charter had passed the Great Seal.[132] His language again exhibited an almost total lack of the rhetoric of divine Providence. He wrote instead in the language of English Whiggery.

> I may rationally suppose that an Account of my Negotiation in *England,* where I have been attending the great Affair of *New-England* for more than Three Years, will be expected from me.

> When I began my voyage from *Boston* for *London* (which was in *April,* 1688.) *New-England* was in a very deplorable Condition. He that was then Governour there, acted by an Illegal and Arbitrary Commission; and invaded Liberty and Property after such a manner, as no man could say anything was his own. Wise men believed it to be a necessary Duty to use all Lawful means to obtain some Relief and Remedy against those growing Evils.[133]

The language of English constitutionalism, so treasured later by Americans, had replaced the spiritual language of John Winthrop, John Cotton, Richard Mather, and Increase Mather. Without attempting to justify or call attention to the new perspective, Increase Mather heralded a new era of political thought. The charter of 1691 should be supported because it "secures Liberty and Property, the fairest flowers of the Civil State."[134]

Personally Mather was relieved to have the nerve-wracking business finished. He was convinced that Massachusetts had gotten the best arrangement possible under the circumstances. "What cause have I to prayse the Lord. Hee has preserved me and my Samuel with me, and has kept us alive ever since we have been in E. Hee has blessed my Family in my Absence. Hee has been with my son Cotton very graciously. Hee has prospered my Negotiations for N. E. so as that the Colledge there is secure, and Magna Charta granted whereby Liberty and property is confirmed to all in that Land. Bless the Lord, O my soul."[135]

True, relations with Elisha Cooke and Thomas Oakes were bad. A week after the great seal had been affixed, all four agents met at Ashurst's, a bitter meeting, without reconciliation. What more could we have done? Ashurst asked. There was no answer. All but Ashurst prepared to return to Boston.[136]

Mather had already begun to pack his books. Three years worth of purchases made it a burdensome task. He visited frequently with Nathaniel and the many new friends he had in the nonconformist community. He made several trips to pay large fees to Mr. Gwillym, the Attorney General's clerk, and repay loans. On November 4 the Earl of Nottingham took him in for a last audience with the king, a courtesy call handled graciously by both men. Two days later Nottingham invited Mather to dinner at his own home, where other guests were the Bishop of Norwich and Dr. Bates. Mather luxuriated in the atmosphere of cordial agreement, the Anglican bishop, London's most fashionable Presbyterian minister, and New England's leading Congregationalist divine, all supping together with the Earl of Nottingham, his Majesty's principal Secretary of State.[137]

Departure was uncertain at best and long delays put off the event. Once again the round of leave-taking. On Christmas day Mather took a coach out to Hackney, where he had joined communion so often. He returned that night to pack more chests for the ship. There were more delays, and it was March 1692 before he and Sam left London for good.[138] This time they took the coach to Southampton, a two-day journey. Phips met them there and carried them in a yacht across to the Isle of Wight, where they took passage on a merchantman. They made their way down the Channel, and on March 29, 1691, Increase and Sam stood on deck to watch the south coast of England slip out of sight. Sir William Phips, Massachusetts's new governor, sailed on the man-of-war *Nonesuch*, Captain Short, Commander.[139]

CHAPTER 8

Massachusetts Under the New Charter

[1692-1702]

The long sea voyage gave Mather ample time to ponder the future. Thirty years ago he had fled England as an exile for his religion. Now circumstances were very different, and he was a different person. In the last four years in and around London he had experienced a world of wealth and power beyond anything remotely possible in Boston, and in that larger world he had received recognition and exercised influence to an extraordinary degree. Although he did not know it, Increase Mather was of that first generation of British colonials who would, over the next three centuries, be intoxicated by the wealth and sophistication of the mother country and the metropolis. By comparison his own small home and wooden meetinghouse were rustic. Harvard College was smaller than the school at Newington Green and its students few in comparison. Only in the context of the wilderness and the errand of the first fathers did Harvard and North Church seem significant.

Puritan Massachusetts had in the past invariably turned against and voted out of office its agents who had returned from London. Friends had warned Mather of that and tried to persuade him to stay in England. He had given it careful thought, enough so that Cotton had gotten wind of it and written a hurt and angry letter.[1] But the question was still on Mather's mind as he wondered for the second time in his life about his future on the American frontier. Was he once again going into some kind of exile?

WITCHCRAFT AND CASES OF CONSCIENCE IN SALEM

In Massachusetts he met immediately a suffocating, morbid religious preoccupation that made Massachusetts this summer the greatest possible contrast to the London just left. While Mather had been journeying homeward, three women—Tituba, a half-Indian, half-African slave from the West Indies; Sarah Good, a hard-bitten, slatternly English woman eking out the roughest kind of peasant life; and Sarah Osburne, a propertied, self-reliant farm wife who had long since turned her back on the local church—had been accused of witchcraft and jailed. The accusations were brought by a group of girls and young unmarried women ranging in age from twelve to eighteen. By the time Mather reached Boston, waves of hysterical accusations were radiating out from the poor farming village of Salem. People had been accused of witchcraft before in New England and had been tried and executed, but never before had there been this kind of mass hysteria.

Why did the frenzy over witchcraft, which started in Salem in the early spring of 1692 and quickly spread to other towns nearby, come at this particular time? Scholars have searched for an answer to that question for generations without a complete explanation. Certainly there had always existed in New England the folk culture of witchcraft, magic, charms, incantations, and curses. Most well-to-do families, the better educated, and the ministry accepted intellectually the existence of witchcraft, but they held this culture at arm's length as usually confined to the poorest and most illiterate segments of society. At this moment in the history of Anglo-America, however, witchcraft and society's responses to it burst out like a wicked bloom in the New England garden.[2]

Underneath all the purely local circumstances that contributed to the frenzy lay the fact that for three years, ever since the overthrow of Sir Edmund Andros, New England, and particularly the maritime towns and villages, were in confusion. Legitimate government disappeared with Andros's arrest. Political insecurity was exacerbated by the collapse of the frontier in Maine and New Hampshire under attack from French, Roman Catholic Canada. The birthrate declined, and again as in King Philip's War fleeing refugees straggled along dirt roads leading toward Boston. Massachusetts bravely and naively sent an expedition by sea to capture Quebec in 1690. It struggled homeward miserably defeated, three or four hundred men lost their lives to smallpox, dysentery, and fever directly attributed to the mismanagement of the expedition. After that Massachusetts, waiting for legitimization from England, was bank-

William Stoughton, deputy governor from 1692 to 1701, chief justice at the
Salem witchcraft trial of Bridget Bishop

A FURTHER
ACCOUNT
OF THE
TRYALS
OF THE
𝕹ew=England Witches.
WITH THE
OBSERVATIONS
Of a Perſon who was upon the Place ſeveral Days when the ſuſpe&ed Witches were firſt taken into Examination.

To which is added,

Caſes of ·Conſcience
Concerning Witchcrafts and Evil Spirits Perſonating Men.

Written at the Requeſt of the Miniſters of *New-England*.

By *Increaſe Mather*, Préſident of *Harvard* Colledge.

Licenſed and Entred accozding to Dzder.

London: Printed for **J. Dunton,** at the *Raven* in the *Poultrey* 1693. Of whom may be had the *Third Edition* of Mr.*Cotton Mather's Firſt Account* of the Tryals of the *New-England* Witches, Printed on the ſame ſize with this *Laſt Account,* that they may bind up together.

Cotton Mather's *A Further Account of the Tryals of the New-England Witches,* supporting witchcraft trials, published with Increase Mather's *Cases of Conscience,* 1693; Increase Mather (then president of Harvard) contended, in opposition to his son, "it were better that ten suspected witches should escape, than that one innocent person should be condemned."

The Wonders of the Invisible World.

OBSERVATIONS

As well *Historical* as *Theological*, upon the NATURE, the
NUMBER, and the OPERATIONS of the

DEVILS.

Accompany'd with,
Some Accounts of the Grievous Molestations, by DÆ-
MONS and WITCHCRAFTS, which have lately
annoy'd the Countrey; and the Trials of some eminent
Malefactors Executed upon occasion thereof: with several
Remarkable *Curiosities* therein occurring.

Some Counsils, Directing a due Improvement of the terrible things, lately done, by the Unusual & Amazing
Range of EVIL SPIRITS, in Our Neighbourhood: &
the methods to prevent the *Wrongs* which those *Evil
Angels* may intend against all sorts of people among us;
especially in Accusations of the Innocent.

Some Conjectures upon the great EVENTS, likely
to befall, the WORLD in General, and NEW-EN-
GLAND in Particular; as also upon the Advances of
the TIME, when we shall see BETTER DAYES.

A short Narrative of a late Outrage committed by a
knot of WITCHES in *Swedeland*, very much Resem-
bling, and so far Explaining, *That* under which our parts
of *America* have laboured!
THE DEVIL DISCOVERED: In a Brief Discourse upon
those TEMPTATIONS, which are the more Ordinary *Devices*
of the Wicked One.

By **Cotton Mather**.

Boston Printed, and Sold by *Benjamin Harris*, 1693.

The Wonders of the Invisible World on "operations of the Devils," by
Cotton Mather, 1693

rupt and forced to resort to tax levies undreamed of before. If public insecurity were ever to lead to a manic upwelling of the darker side of life,
now was that time.[3]

Acting quickly, Governor Phips created a special court of oyer and
terminer to call juries and try those already indicted. Deputy Governor
William Stoughton sat as chief justice. The first fatal victim of the hysteria, Bridget Bishop, was brought to trial on June 2. The proceeding
was less a trial than a replay of the hearing which had earlier resulted in
her being jailed. The accusations were so dramatic and the public psychology so overwrought that Bridget Bishop's guilt seemed a foregone
conclusion. The jury found her guilty and the judges sentenced her to
death. They hanged her from the great oak tree on gallows hill in Salem
on June 10, 1692.

That was quick work, but the court would have to be quicker yet,
because the accusations kept pouring in. As more, and more respectable,
people were accused and jailed, some doubts arose in the minds of responsible people. Surely the mere accusation by hysterical adolescent
girls could not itself justify the death penalty. The court went into recess
for the rest of June while responsible men took a longer look at what was
happening. In Cambridge a meeting of the ministers in and around
Boston discussed the question. Samuel Willard, who would soon be one
of the accused himself, was there. So were Increase and Cotton Mather.
The central concern was the way "spectral evidence" was accepted as
proof of guilt. When the frenzied girls accused individuals by name,
they said that the likeness of that person, his or her specter, came to
pinch, bite, and torment them. There was a general belief that the devil
was behind it, but that the devil could only control the specter of a willing accomplice. The girls' testimony was taken as prima facie evidence
that the person whose specter had tormented them was in league with
the devil. God would not permit Satan to use the specter of an innocent
person.

Or was it possible? Could not the devil assume the shape of an innocent person? The ministers meeting at Cambridge thought so, and they
drafted a private memorandum in which they cautioned the judges to use
the greatest care in accepting spectral evidence. Unfortunately, this message was conveyed in a most ambivalent way. The minister who served as
secretary to the meeting and drafted its report was none other than
Cotton Mather, and Cotton by this time was obsessed with a belief that
the devil had begun a last-ditch war for the collective soul of New England. The other ministers, older than he, agreed. The memorandum,

which urged caution in the use of spectral evidence, concluded with a recommendation for a "speedy and vigorous prosecution" of the accused.[4]

At the end of June the court resumed. Chief Justice William Stoughton, a rigid, domineering, and pitiless man, guided it. The court room again was a stage for hysterical adolescent girls and bemused, credulous elders. Men or women accused of being witches were brought face to face with their accusers. As soon as that happened, the victims fell writhing to the floor, tormented by unseen hands. The victims swore that they were pinched and scratched by shapes or specters of the accused, visible only to the victims themselves. Not knowing what other course to take, themselves swept up by the fear of the devil, the court accepted this spectral evidence and convicted the accused. On July 19 five women were hanged together from the gallows tree.

On August 1 the ministerial association met again in the college hall at Cambridge. Only seven of the twenty-two members were present. They agreed among themselves that Increase Mather should compose a statement about the rules of evidence that should be adopted in cases of witchcraft. Going back to his study in Boston, Mather set to work with his usual thoroughness. Looking back on it now, Mather worked with painful, tragic slowness. Later that month four more were executed, three of them men, and on September 16 two more men. The executions quickened but could not catch up with the accusations. More than a hundred were in prison on September 22 when another multiple execution took the lives of six women and two men from a total of six towns, including Boston. At the center of each conviction was the issue of spectral evidence.

Increase Mather was pulled in two directions. At the assembly of ministers he had agreed to write out arguments against using spectral evidence in capital cases. But would there have been any case against the accused if spectral evidence were not used? Like the others, Mather was horrified at the outburst of accusations and the mounting executions. On the other hand, he was deeply troubled at the rising tide of atheism, which was widely thought to be connected to the growing disbelief in the world of spirits. His brilliant son Cotton was obsessed with that invisible world and had no doubt at all that the trials must continue. Cotton too disapproved of spectral evidence but he believed even more that Satan was at war with New England. Cotton's concern was that a statement from his father criticizing the procedures of the court, given the popular dismay at the executions, might bring about a cessation of the war against Satan's witches. Increase Mather weighed these possibilities, and decided with his contemporaries and against his son. He would write against the court's use of spectral evidence.

By the end of September, Mather had composed a carefully reasoned and documented statement of about seventy pages, titled "Cases of Conscience Concerning Evil Spirits." On October 3 he read it to the assembly of ministers. The executions of September had already taken place and five more had been found guilty and were waiting execution. The ministers adopted Mather's paper. Samuel Willard wrote a powerful introduction and fourteen ministers signed to indicate their support. Cotton Mather did not sign, for he had another plan. A handwritten copy was hurriedly given to Sir William Phips.[5] "The First Case that I am desired to express my judgement in, is this," Mather started out, "Whether it is not possible for the Devil to impose on the Imaginations of persons bewitched, and to cause them to Believe that an Innocent, yea that a Pious person dos torment them, when the Devil himself doth it . . . ? The answer to the Question must be Affirmative," Mather wrote.[6]

Satan could indeed impersonate innocent persons. So-called spectral evidence must not be used alone to convict persons of being in league with the devil. "The Second Case which is to come under our Consideration, *Viz.* if one Bewitched is struck down with the Look or Cast of the Eye of another, and after that Recovered again by a Touch from the same person, is not this an infallible proof that the person suspected and Complained of is in League with the devil? . . . *Answer*: It must be owned that . . . This may be ground for Examination, but this alone does not afford sufficient matter for conviction."[7]

Mather gave extended reasons to support both these opinions. He believed that witches did exist and witch trials were justified. But, "The Evidence in this Crime of Witchcraft ought to be as clear as in any other Crimes of a Capital nature," and "There have been ways of Trying Witches long used . . . which the Righteous God never approved of."[8] At the end of his book Mather summed up thus: "It is better that a Guilty Person should be ABSOLVED, than that he should without sufficient ground of Conviction be condemned. I had rather judge a Witch to be an honest woman, than judge an honest woman as a witch."[9]

By October 3 Cotton had nearly finished his own book on the witchcraft trials, one expressly meant to counterbalance the effect of his father's. Cotton believed correctly that the unpopularity of the trials by now was such that, if his father strongly criticized them, they would end. That, he feared, would be a victory for Satan. He wanted to defend the judges, and he wanted to make sure that the defenses of Massachusetts against the devil were kept up. To this end he hurried to complete his own book, which supported and justified what the court had done. Cotton Mather finished his book, *Wonders of the Invisible World*, and had it in press first.[10]

By now all Massachusetts was abuzz over the trials, the many executions, the further accusations, and the men and women still in jail. Popular opinion was running strongly against the whole sorry business, and when *Wonders of the Invisible World* was published in defense of the judges, public opinion turned against Cotton. Cotton Mather was no less sensitive to his good name than his father. To defend himself he persuaded Increase to add a postscript to his own book which would take some of the opprobrium off Cotton. This Increase did: "Some I hear have taken up a Notion, that the Book newly published by my Son, is contradictory to this of mine. 'Tis strange that such Imaginations should enter into the Minds of Men: I perused and approved of that book before it was printed, and nothing but my Relation to him hindered me from recommending it to the World." And why should Increase not have approved it? Both he and Cotton believed in witches and the need to bring them to trial by the best rules of evidence: "The design of the preceding dissertation, is not to plead for witchcrafts, or to appear as an advocate for witches. I have therefore written another discourse, proving that there are such horrid creatures as witches in the world, and they are to be extirpated and cut off from amongst the people of God.

"Nor is there designed any reflection on those worthy persons who have been concerned in the late proceedings at Salem. They are wise and good men, and have acted with all fidelty according to their light. Having therefore so arduous a case before them, pitty and prayers rather than censures are their due."[11]

Phips himself acted promptly after receiving *Cases of Conscience:* The court of oyer and terminer had been in recess and was disbanded. Phips pardoned the five who had been convicted but were still in jail. The sudden storm that had swept over eastern Massachusetts in the summer of 1692 was over as suddenly as it had risen. Some years later, when Mather resumed work on his autobiography, he was able to summarize the episode without suggesting any ambivalence on his part. It is unlikely that the issues had been as plain to him during the crisis. The passage reveals the new climate of opinion and how he wished to be perceived by his children. "I found the Countrey in a sad condition by reason of witchcrafts and possessed persons. The Judges and many of the people had espoused a notion, that the devill could not Represent Innocent persons as afflicting others. I doubt that Innocent blood was shed by mistakes of that nature. I therefore published my Cases of Conscience de Witchcrafts etc—by which (it is sayed) many were enlightened, Juries convinced, and the shedding of more Innocent blood prevented." [12]

POLITICS UNDER THE NEW CHARTER

Except as it persisted in the fervid imagination of a few, the witchcraft hysteria during the summer of 1692 was soon over, a cruel, violent thunderstorm which passed over the land, terrifying at the height of its fury, but leaving behind little of permanence other than a score of ruined lives and a symbol of religious fanaticism later generations of Americans would never lay by. The new charter of 1691 was far different. The new charter brought about fundamental changes in Massachusetts society, and what it did not cause, it symbolized. The royal charter of 1691 was the turning point in the history of Puritan New England. [13]

The laws and institutions under the old charter were now defunct, and 1692 saw a wholesale recreation of the legal framework of society. Prominent among the new legislation was a "Bill for the General Rights and Liberties." This legislation was in effect a bill of rights, and while it established the general design of political rights and liberties as they would develop in America down to the War for Independence, it just as clearly replaced the Body of Liberties which had served Massachusetts in a similar way from 1641. The contrast is as night with day. Whereas the Body of Liberties was infused with the concern to create a religious state, the Bill for the General Rights and Liberties dropped all reference to church and religion. [14]

Perhaps even more dramatic than the thoroughgoing secularism of the new statute was its acceptance by the clergy. Increase Mather led the way with his defense of the new charter in the terms of Whig politics. His son could do no less. In 1692 Cotton Mather preached to the General Assembly a sermon, *Optanda, Good Men Described and Good Things Propounded*, in which, albeit reluctantly, he informed Massachusetts's legislators that their proper sphere was politics and not religion. "A man has a Right unto his Life, his Estate, his Liberty, and his Family," even if he were not a member of a true church. Life, liberty and property, not religion, were the concerns of the government in Massachusetts now. Cotton could not have preached a political sermon more at odds with his father's 1677 *Danger of Apostacy*, yet he was only elucidating the new political order

Increase had just announced in New England's MAGNA CHARTA.[15] Nothing gives clearer evidence that the Mathers, father and son, spoke for a widely-based and fundamental shift in thought than the uniformity of the new political rhetoric. Increase had dropped completely the language of providential Puritanism during his four years in England, but so too did the political writers in Boston who justified or condemned the overthrow of Andros.[16] Assumptions about politics and the relations between state and church had already changed by the time Phips reached Boston with the new charter. The old Puritan state was gone for good.

Governor Sir William Phips may or may not have been sensitive to these shifts in the nature of Massachusetts's government. He was a blunt, uneducated man, more at home on the quarter deck than in the forum. Even Cotton Mather admitted Phips was more likely to use a hatchet than a scalpel. By playing down his own role as governor and giving the initiative in judicial appointments to the House of Representatives whenever he could, Phips did try to carry on the traditional pattern of a weak governor. But an ungoverned temper and a swashbuckling personality were fatal flaws. Early in 1693 Sir William had a furious argument with Captain Richard Short of the royal frigate *Nonesuch*, the ship that had brought him to Boston the previous year and remained on duty off the New England coast. In a rage, Phips attacked the captain and beat him, stripped away his command, and threw him into jail for nine months. Short was eventually able to escape to England.[17] Not long after, Phips fell afoul of the royal collector of customs, a wealthy man from Rhode Island named Jahleel Brenton. Again Boston was treated to the scandalous sight of the governor engaged in a roughhouse on the Town Dock. Before spring was out Phips had bullied and beaten two officers of the crown. His own political support was melting away. Elections to the House of Representatives in May 1693 returned a strong group of Tory-minded merchants, men who had never been part of the old-charter establishment and instead instinctively looked to London as the ultimate fountain of authority. Their spokesman was a merchant named Nathaniel Byfield, who was elected by the town of Bristol although he lived and worked in Boston. Byfield's brother-in-law was Ebenezer Brenton, brother of the Jahleel Brenton whom Phips had attacked and humiliated on the Town Dock. Both Brentons were also elected to the House of Representatives, swelling the ranks of the "Tory" faction. Also elected to the house were supporters of the traditional Puritan government, men ranging all the way from irreconcilables who could not accept the terms of the new charter to supporters of Mather and Phips. Far from being satisfied with the political solution offered by the new charter, the general assembly was full of contention.

Increase Mather tried to quell the dissidents. When he delivered the election day sermon that May, *The Great Blessing of Primitive Counsellors* (Boston, 1693), he itemized the advantages of the new charter (English liberties, property confirmed, no taxes without popular consent) and warned the assembled representatives not to upset it: "There are things which if you sleight or undervalue them, the Most High will doubtless be Offended. Nor is a Murmuring Spirit the right way to obtain *more*. When the children of Israel murmured against those that had been the instruments of their salvation, what did they get by it?"[18] Mather focused on the nominations for council, the first such nominations the assembly would make under the new charter. The charter gave the governor power to appoint judges, but only with the "advice and consent" of the council. This unique arrangement, Mather thought, would save Massachusetts. "Much of the Welfare of the People does consist in their having Able and Upright Judges . . . It cannot but be so in a Government where no Judges are appointed but with the consent of the Council. Good Counsellors will Advise to good Judges, and good Judges will make the Land happy."[19]

For a moment at the very close of this sermon Mather reverted back to the style of the jeremiad: "To be sure the great sin of this Generation is their forgetting the Errand on which their Fathers came into this Wilderness which was not to seek great things for themselves, but to seek the Kingdom of God and Righteousness." But the backbone had gone from the preachment, a disappearance illustrated by Mather's unwillingness now even to itemize what sins he was talking about: "What those sins were I need not say, so much having been spoken concerning that, many Years ago."[20]

Instead, what stands out in this important sermon is a rhetoric unsullied by heavy allusions to a stern God. Consider the irony and sarcasm of this complex passage: "I am not conscious to my self of any hurt or wrong I have done, unless four years hard service, for the preservation of your Liberty and Property, and the procuring of Gifts for you, from Royal and from other Benefactors of greater value than all the Mony I did in that Time Expend on your account, and all this without any the Least Recompence be a wrong to you. *Forgive me that wrong*. You are this day saved from Slavery and Ruine."[21]

After Mather's sermon the House proceeded to nominate members of the Governor's Council. The broad coalition Mather and Ashurst had named the previous year was no longer possible. Several were too old to serve further, others were replaced or absent in England. But the critical change was the nomination against Mather's advice, of Elisha Cooke to the new Council. Cooke had never been reconciled to the new charter. He now became the perennial leader of a Whig opposition to royal government. Phips at once vetoed Cooke's nomination—perhaps on Mather's advice, but there is no evidence of it—and so cut himself off at least temporarily from the Whig leadership after having earned already the full opposition of the Tory royalists. Massachusetts politics was developing quickly into a pattern both new to the Puritan colony and quite beyond Increase Mather's control.

In the summer of 1693, when new nominations were called to replace the rejected Elisha Cooke on the Council, Joseph Dudley presented himself as a candidate. Here was a full turn of the wheel! Dudley, leader of the old moderate faction, who had agreed to head the royal government when the first charter was vacated, and who had been arrested and jailed along with Andros in 1689, was now back and contesting for election. In the intervening years Dudley had been chief justice for the colony of New York. There he had presided over a trial, notorious in New York's history, in which two leaders of New York's 1689 revolution, Jacob Leisler and his son-in-law Jacob Milborne, were tried, convicted, and hanged for treason. After this dramatic example of Tory politics, Dudley returned to his family home in Roxbury. Failing narrowly to be nominated to the Council in Cooke's place, he returned to London in the autumn, accurately foreseeing that in the future the real key to political power in Massachusetts lay not in Boston but in London.[22] There Dudley became a focus for the opposition to Phips from both sides of the political spectrum. Lt. Governor William Stoughton, still smarting at the way Phips had called a halt to the witchcraft trials, wrote to Blathwayt to recommend Dudley for the governorship of Massachusetts. Leaders of the new Tory group did likewise. Captain Short was back in London, as well, lodging his own complaints through the admiralty against the wild man in Boston.

Phips entirely failed to manage the politics of Boston. He dissolved one assembly in the summer, but new elections in November returned a House with an even stronger Tory opposition than before. It elected Nathaniel Byfield its speaker. Phips struck at these political enemies by introducing a bill to require members of the House to be residents in the towns where they were elected. The bill, aimed directly at Byfield and his supporters, squeaked through the House and Council. But even while Sir William was winning these battles in Boston, he was losing in

London. The many accusations brought against him there resulted in a royal order to return to England. William Stoughton was ordered to collect and forward testimony and evidence pertinent to the charges which had been made.[23]

May 1694 elections came and went in a climate of mutual intrigue and recrimination. Nathaniel Byfield and a few others were returned to the House despite the residency requirement. When they brazenly called on the governor to swear them in, Phips came charging downstairs bellowing that he would personally throw them out of the chamber. The election day sermon that year was given by Samuel Willard, who leaned further and further towards the Tory point of view and preached a thinly veiled criticism of the governor.

Willard's 1694 election day sermon, *The Character of a Good Ruler* (Boston, 1694), helps illustrate the changes being wrought in Massachusetts politics by the new charter. Before 1686 the Puritan colony had been governed largely by the magistrates. The governor could neither appoint nor veto. A handful of magistrates, elected at large by the church members, acted as an executive Court of Assistants, a supreme judicial body, and an upper house of legislature. These magistrates, characteristically elected over and over again for years on end, embodied the Puritan ideal of a civil magistrate whose authority came from God and whose responsibility was the welfare of a God-fearing society. They were executive, lawgiver, and judge rolled into one. Under the charter of 1691, all that was changed. Executive, legislative, judicial, and administrative roles were clearly separated. Willard, although making a plea for moral and religious rule, nevertheless abandoned the old pattern and accepted the discrete functions defined in the charter. The structure of the Bay Colony's political life had at a stroke been modernized.[24]

Phips's end was now near. Forced to seek allies in his contest with the Tories, Phips admitted Elisha Cooke to the council. He managed in the fall of 1694 to extract one last weak vote of confidence from the assembly, and, in December, set sail for London. The following spring, word reached Boston that Phips had died of a sudden illness before his case could be properly heard at Whitehall. Massachusetts was left under the immediate leadership of the doughty old William Stoughton.[25] With the immediate source of political turmoil gone, Massachusetts government settled into as close an approximation of the old tenor of life as could be in a rapidly changing world. Stoughton governed much in the spirit of his predecessors before 1686 but the charter of 1691 came to be accepted as the fundamental law of the land.

Mather did not at first seem to recognize how badly Phips had failed. "Wee hear of the death of the Governor Sir Wm Phips," he wrote. "A sore blow to N. E. To the congregation in special; To me in a most particular manner, in that Hee was my friend, neighbor, & by my meanes was made Governor of the Province. The Countrey will want him many wayes: If an ill man should be his successor, it would be a great Judgment to the whole Countrey." [26]

The new charter clearly heralded an end to the old. Disgruntlement on the part of the conservatives continued for years. Elisha Cooke fanned those embers for his own political purposes, since there was no realistic possibility of change, and a growing majority benefited from the new charter anyway. But Increase Mather was caught in a crossfire of criticism, blamed, on one hand, by the Tories for sponsoring Phips and blamed, on the other, by the country Whigs for negotiating the charter. Consequently, although the General Court made good on the loans he had made in London to support his lobbying there, he received nothing for his out-of-pocket expenses or the many small gratuities that had been so often necessary for life in the metropolis. [27]

Increase Mather could tolerate almost anything more easily than personal criticism, and he began to think that he would be better off if he washed his hands of Boston and Massachusetts and returned to England. "Some friends of mine in England who were very willing I should spend the remainder of my days among them, told me that they had been informed that the People of New England were always ungrateful to their public servants. . . . My reply to them was, that. . . . I would go to New England and see, and if I found their prognostications true, I should see (the dear people of Boston concurring with me) my call clear to return to England again." Mather published these remarks and so gave public notice of the possibility that he would leave Boston for England again. [28]

When Increase Mather and Sir William Phips landed at Boston with a new organic law for Massachusetts, a new legal basis for the churches was high in the order of business. The charter declared only that "there shall be a liberty of Conscience allowed in the Worshipp of God to all Christians (Except Papists) . . . " [29] By November 1692 the General Assembly passed an Act for the Settlement and Support of Ministers that required each town to maintain a minister selected by a majority vote of the town meeting. There was not a town in Massachusetts where such a rule would not result in hiring a Congregational minister, although in the southeast near Rhode Island and in the old Plymouth Colony lands, which had now been added to Massachusetts, there were large numbers of Baptists and Quakers. The new law in effect established the Congregational clergy, and it also gave churchgoers who were not communicating members a large voice in choosing the minister. In February 1693 an amendment enabled the membership of each congregation to choose its minister, with their choice to be ratified by a majority of all who attended that meeting, members or not. ("The major part of such inhabitants as do there usually attend on the publick worship of God and are by law duly qualified for voting in town affairs." [30]

For the first time in Massachusetts's history, men other than visible saints and members of the church fellowship had a regular voice in choosing the minister. Isaac Backus, looking back on these milestones, observed that "Formerly the church had governed the world, but now the world was to govern the church, about religious ministers." But not in Boston. Increase used his influence to arrange for the Boston churches to be exempted from the Act for the Settlement and Maintenance, on the grounds that all three Congregational churches there were supported entirely from private contributions and not taxes. [31]

During the four years of Mather's absence, the movement to broaden baptism had gathered momentum. All over Massachusetts the barriers were breaking down. Lay members' opposition to the half-way covenant, almost universal in 1670, was weakening everywhere by 1690. [32] In the years when Increase Mather was in England, Cotton baptized an unprecedented number in the North Church. [33] He sought approval to go beyond the half-way covenant and baptize anyone who came with good recommendations and seemed "openly and seriously to give themselves up to God." Cotton based his arguments in part on his father's published belief, as old as 1675, in the universal church: "Baptism is an Ordinance that belongs to Visible Christians, or those that are visibly of the Catholic Church, before and in order to, their joining a particular." [34] Probably he went further and faster than his father was comfortable with. In December 1692, after Increase had been home for six months, Cotton begged John Richards not to stand in the way of expanded baptism. The son was pulling his father's generation into the future.

Cotton Mather was responsible for another innovation, one which took his father by surprise and which he never fully supported. In October 1690 the ministers from nearby met in the college hall at Cambridge and agreed to form an "Association." In this new undertaking, Cotton had the assistance of Charles Morton, who had had experience with similar ministers' associations in England. The idea that ministers had some standing apart from their particular churches hinted at Presbyterianism. So did the idea that ministers might properly assemble and act separately from the lay brethren. One logical consequence of the separation of ministers and brethren was to substitute ordination of ministers by ministers for the traditional ordination by the church fellowship, and that was what the ministers voted: "not (to) allow the rites of this order to be regularly and conveniently performed by any but such as were themselves of the same order. . . . "[35] When the body of ministers became the licensing authority for membership in the ministry, that was Presbyterian.

Increase himself had unwittingly added authority to this development by helping to bring the Presbyterians and Congregationalists together in London. Cotton seized on the London *Heads of Agreement* as a confirmation of the Cambridge association. The trend of New England Puritan ministers' redefining their role vis-à-vis the gathered churches had already taken a leap forward by the time Increase arrived home.[36]

THE SPIRITUAL WORLD AND THE MILLENNIUM

The four years in England had brought great changes in Increase Mather's family, too. His oldest daughter, Maria, had married Bartholomew Green, a sailor, the year Mather had sailed for England. Twenty-three then, now she was a wife and mother. The family lived in Charlestown, but later moved to Boston's North End. Mather's second oldest daughter, Elizabeth, whom he called his Betty, was twenty-five. Her younger sister Sarah married first, at twenty-one, pleasing her father greatly by marrying the minister at Roxbury, Nehemiah Walter. Roxbury soon became a frequent stop on Increase's circuit of the neighboring towns. Betty was courted by another sailor, William Greenough, a choice that displeased her father. Events soon overcame any resistance when Greenough was captured by Spanish privateers, and for months in 1695 the family worried about Betty's love in a Spanish prison. At last came news that he was alive and well. After he reached Boston in June the next year, the wedding took place within a month. Betty was twenty-nine.[37]

Marriageable daughters, sons-in-law, grandchildren: all this brought new dimensions to Increase Mather's life. His children had homes in Roxbury and Charlestown as well as Boston. Family gatherings took place often and once, on July 1696, Adam Winthrop invited them all to an outing and dinner on Governor's Island. Sixteen of the Mather family were present, including three sons-in-law, one daughter-in-law, and one grandchild, and the three youngest girls, Abigail fifteen, Hannah twelve, and little Jerusha eight.[38]

Although Cotton had taken over the routine duties of the Second Church, Mather found himself busier than ever. When he was in Boston on a Sunday, he divided the morning and afternoon sermons with Cotton. But often Increase preached away. He usually rode or went by water to the towns nearest to Boston: Cambridge, Charlestown, Roxbury, and Dorchester. At Cambridge he would preach in the college hall. In the spring and summer of 1693 he preached twenty-six sermons in eighteen weeks, fifteen of these sermons being out of town. Sometimes he rode from one town to another between morning and afternoon services. Five or six times a month in good weather he took the ferry to Charlestown and rode from there to Cambridge on the college horse.[39] Cotton, working from his father's diaries, wrote of these college visits, "He required a Conforming to the *Statutes* of the College, with a Stedy *Government*, and Faithful *Discipline*. He gave the Students his Directions about their *Studies*! He advised them what *Books* they should chiefly Converse withal, and caution'd them against such as might *Poisen* their Young Minds, and give them a *Taint* which they must sweat out if ever the Churches of GOD had any Real Service from them. He kept alive the *Disputations* of the Batchelours, in which he Moderated; and assigned them especially such *Questions* as led them to an Establishment in the *Truths* which the *Temptations of the Day* rendered most needful to be Defended. He usually *Preached* unto the Scholars every Week, *Sermons* on such Subjects as he thought most useful for them, and in a manner, Calculated for the Instruction of such as would of him Learn to be *True Preachers of the Gospel*. And sometimes he illuminated the *College-Hall* with Elaborate Expositions. It was also a frequent Custom with him, and how worthy of *Imitation!*—to send for the *Scholars* one by one into the *Library*, and there consider with them about their *Interiour State*, and Quicken their Flight unto their SAVIOUR, and invite them into the Dispositions and Resolutions of Serious PIETY; and lay the Solemn Charges of GOD upon them to Turn the Live unto Him; and sometimes bestow *Pious Treatises* upon them . . . Thus Dr. *Mather did continually!*"[40]

The trip by water across to Charlestown and thence to Cambridge by horseback became a favorite time. The ride along the pleasant country roads was an opportunity to muse and dream. "All the way between Charlestown and Cambridge I conversed with God by soliloquies and prayer," he wrote. He fell into a habit of turning that hour's ride into a reverie. More and more in his musing Increase Mather dreamed of re-

turning to England. "I was much melted with apprehensions of my Returning to England again. Strangely perswaded that it would be so."[41]

Long after the witchcraft trials had ended, the world of spirits, whether
demonic or angelic, continued to preoccupy the Mathers, father and son.
As early as November 1692 Cotton was counselling a young woman,
Mercy Short, who seemed to be possessed of evil spirits. By March next
year Mercy was cured, and Cotton had amassed a richly documented case
history.[42] By that time, as if working in tandem, Increase had started to
study and preach about angels. Cotton paid rapt attention to his father's
words. The sermons continued over the summer, and in September Increase, in a reverie, experienced himself what he believed might have
been an angelic visit: "I was inexpressibly melted & that for a considerable Time; & a strange Suggestion that to England I must go. (In this
there was something extraordinary either divine or Angelic.)"[43]

Cotton longed for such direct communication with the spiritual world.
In answer to many prayers and autosuggestion brought on by fasting and
meditation, he had his wish. In his study there appeared before his eyes a
shining, winged angel. It spoke, and Cotton wrote the conversation
down.[44] Authorities as old as St. Paul and as recent as Richard Baxter had
warned against angelic visions, which were all too likely to be imposters
and tricks of Satan. Increase and Cotton were discreet, and Cotton's vision was not trumpeted about town. The next summer, however, the
question of angelic apparitions was raised in the abstract before the Cambridge Association of Ministers, and Increase was asked to write a short
treatise for them on "Whether Angelical Apparitions may in these Dayes
be expected; . . ." A few months later he wrote a hundred-page discourse based on his sermons, added the treatise on apparitions, and saw it
all published as a book, *Angelographia* (Boston, 1696).[45]

The book had had its origin partly in the Salem trials and in Cotton's
persistence about the invisible world of spirits, and partly in the need
Increase felt to defend the very existence of the spiritual world and the
prodigious happenings emanating from it against secularism and atheism. Several times after coming back to Boston he published warnings
and exhortations against "godlessness."[46] With his colleagues in the
Cambridge Association of Ministers, he urged the further collection of
remarkable providences similar to those he had already published in *An
Essay for the Recording of Illustrious Providences*.[47] But the concern that was
to mark his next major contribution to the religious history of New England was something quite different. He took up again in 1693–1694
the conversion of the Jews as a precursor to the thousand-year reign of the

saints. This time he went on to preach not only about the events leading
up to the millennium, but the life of the saints during those glorious
centuries of righteousness. In a dramatic reversal of the mood of the
jeremiads, Mather now focused not on punishment but on "crownes of
everlasting joy."

During Mather's visits in London with Richard Baxter the two men
had discussed Baxter's most recent writing, "Glorious Kingdom of
Christ," in which the older man (Baxter was seventy-six, Mather, fifty-
three) argued that a gradual perfection of life on earth was the correct
interpretation of scriptural prophecy of the millennium. Mather also expected the millennium, but he believed that utopia would come about
through the dramatic, swift, and preternatural return of Christ and the
physical resurrection of the saints. Baxter rejected these literal interpretations; God, he said, would work his redemption through a transformation of human nature.[48] Depite his own disagreement Mather urged
his friend to publish those ideas, and Baxter, liking Mather's candor,
dedicated the book to him: "I therefore direct these lines to you, to intreat you, to write (whether I be alive or dead) your Reasons against any
momentous or dangerous Errour which you shall find."[49]

Before Mather left England, Baxter was dead, and *Glorious Kingdom of
Christ* was published. To write a response seemed in the circumstances
little short of an obligation. He plunged back into the subject he had
treated in his first book, *Mystery of Israel's Salvation* (London, 1669), and
wrote his reply to Baxter, *A Dissertation Concerning the Future Conversion of
the Jewish Nation,* published in London in 1709. In the earlier book he had
focused on the conversion of the Jews, and the text in Romans 11, 26:
"And so all Israel shall be saved." His new book was specifically directed
at "Answering the Objections of . . . Mr. Baxter, and Dr. Lightfoot, and
others. With an Enquiry into the first Resurrection." This, the first
resurrection, rather than the conversions of the Jews, was the "more dis-
putable point, and the one that does meet with a more general Opposition." The central text in the new book is "that famous Text, Revel. 20.
considered and vindicated": "And I saw an angel come down from heaven
having the key of the bottomless pit and a great chain in his hand. And
he laid hold on the dragon, that old serpent, which is the Devil, and
Satan, and bound him a thousand years . . . . " Mather recognized that
generally in Christendom "the Doctrine of the First Resurrection and the
Thousand Years Reign has been condemned for Heresie." Nevertheless,
"The Lord Jesus Christ will appear in Person at the Final Destruction of
Antichrist, then the marriage of the Lamb shall be consumated, and a

New Jerusalem come down from heaven. Which things will be a Thousand Years before the ultimate Resurrection and Judgement."[50]

Mather's literal interpretation of this scripture (following the mid-century Anglican millennialists Joseph Mede and Thomas Goodwin), meant a fundamental revision of the Christian world view traditional since Augustine, for it had been Augustine more than any other who had treated Revelations 20 as an allegory and so removed hopes of a real, earthly utopia from the minds of the faithful.[51] Mather wrote: "If Men allow themselves this Liberty of *Allegorizing*, we may at last Allegorize Religion into nothing but Fancy, and say that the Resurrection is past already. How much safer it is to keep to the Letter of Scripture, when for us to do so is so consistent with the Analogy of Faith?"[52] Keeping to the letter of scripture, Mather looked again, as Mede had done, at the actual words and concluded, "How can a Man then take a Passage of so plain, and ordinarily expressed Words as those about the *First Resurrection* are, in any other Sense than the usual and Literal."[53]

Mather followed up his sermons on the conversions of the Jews and the first resurrection with a lyrical description of the millennium itself, a glorious time when the earth would be ruled by the saints and Christ. "There shall be no more sorrow nor any more pain nor any more crying."[54] Three rhapsodic sermons were in sharp contrast to the dark, foreboding jeremiads of the 1670s. Here was no catalogue of sins, no denunciation of a backsliding people, no threats from a disappointed god, no talk of covenants made and broken. Instead Mather preached of a beautiful time to come, a time when all pain and suffering, even death itself, will disappear from the earth and the elect will live in perfect joy for a thousand years.

Relying largely on texts from the book of Revelation, he built an extended metaphor of the church in terms of the ancient city of Jerusalem. Here is the best example in all of Mather's writings of his use of typology.[55] "There is a double Jerusalem," he said, "the litterall and the spirituall Jerusalem." He used the ancient literal city as the prefiguration or type of the future spiritual city, the "New Jerusalem which comes down from heaven from my god." (Rev. 3.12)[56]

Moving backwards and forwards in time between the past and the future, and moving in and out between the literal and the spiritual cities, Mather created a complex, poetic anticipation of the coming time when afflictions of the faithful would cease and their greatest dreams come true. The New Jerusalem will be the church of God on earth. The church will come down from heaven to earth when the first resurrection, the resurrection of the elect, takes place. Then all will return to earth and be

THE
MYSTERY
O F
Israel's Salvation,

EXPLAINED and APPLYED:
O R,
A DISCOURSE

Concerning the General Converfion of the
I S R A E L I T I S H   N AT I O N.

Wherein is Shewed,

1. *That the Twelve Tribes fhall be faved.*
2. *When this is to be expected.*
3. *Why this muft be.*
4. *What kind of Salvation the Tribes of* Ifrael *fhall partake of (viz.)* A Glorious, Wonderful, Spiritual, Temporal *Salvation.*

Being the Subftance of feveral S E R-
MONS Preached

By INCREASE MATHER, *M. A.*
Teacher of a Church in *Bofton* in *New England.*

Hear the word of the Lord O ye Nations, and declare it in the Ifles afar off, and fay, he that fcattered Ifrael will gather him, and keep him as a fhepherd doth his flock, Jer. 31 10.

And then fhall appear the fign of the Son of Man, and then fhall all the Tribes (τῆς γῆς) of the Land mourn, and they fhall fee the Son of Man coming in the clouds of beaven with Power and great Glory, Matth. 24 30

In the days of the voice of the feventh Angel, when he fhall begin to found, the Myftery of God fhall be finifhed, as he hath declared to his Servants the Prophets, Rev. 10.7.

London, Printed for *John Allen* in *Wentworth-ftreet*, near *Bell-Lane*, 1669.

The Mystery of Israel's Salvation on the conversion of the Jews, published in 1666 and printed in London, 1669

A
DISSERTATION

Concerning the

Future Conversion

OF THE

Jewish Nation.

Answering the Objections of the Reverend and
Learned Mr. *Baxter*, Dr. *Lightfoot*, and others.

With an Enquiry into the first Resurrection.

By INCREASE MATHER, President
of *Harvard-Colledge*, at *Cambridge*, in
New-England.

*Hear the Word of the Lord, O ye Nations, and declare it
in the Isles afar off, and say, He that scattered Israel
will gather him*, Jer. 31. 10.

LONDON:

Printed by *R. Tookey* for *Nath. Hillier*, at the *Prince's Arms* in
Leaden-hall-street. M DCC IX.

Mather's *Dissertation Concerning the Future Conversion of the Jewish Nation,* disagree-
ing with Richard Baxter's interpretation of the millennium; printed in London in
1709

clothed in new bodies, "celestiall bodies."[57] *"In the new Jerusalem, all the unhappy effects of sin are removed.* . . . There will be no more misery there, no more affliction there. . . . It is all day and no Night there, no night of any affliction whatsoever."[58]

Each of you, Mather assured the members of his church, each of you will enjoy the glories of the new city. Jesus knows exactly who are the elect. "He hath a particular knowledg of every one that belongs to him, there is not any one that belongs to the new Jerusalem but christ knowes them by name." Extending the metaphor, "as in a great citty there is a book wherin the names of those that are free men, that are Denisons of the citty are Registered. Others may not pretend to the priviledges of the citty, of the corporation. Even so, christ hath names of those that are cittizens of the heavenly Jerusalem . . . "[59]

"When the citizens of the new Jerusalem shall sitt Upon thrones: It will be the most august glorious day, that ever was since the creation, and wee may not think that it will be *a show only*, that shall be over againe as soone as It doth appeare."[60]

The Day of Judgment itself will be a glorious day: "Know ye not that saints shall Judge the world? Men have mistaken notions generally concerning the day of the Judgment. They think that thereby is intended only vengeance and the execution of Judgment on the wicked, and that is one thing Intended; it will be a day of perdition unto ungodly men, but another thing intended thereby, is *the power of Judicature* shall be putt into the hands of the saints of god."[61]

To be sure, in his ecstasy Mather did not lose sight of the fact that not all people, but only the faithful, would inhabit the new Jerusalem. "There are vast multitudes that never had nor ever shall have that glorious name written upon them. When the new Jerusalem coms downe from heaven, there are many that shall not have an entrance given to them into the citty of god." Outside *"are dogs and whoremongers and liars.* No prophane person, no hypocrite shall have admission into that citty. . . . Whoever shall dye in a state of sin, shall dye in his prophaness, shall dye in his hypocrisie, shall dye in his unregeneracie will never come within that glorious citty."[62]

Calvin had not expected a better life on this earth. In the early part of the seventeenth century, Joseph Mede and Thomas Goodwin re-examined scripture and predicted the coming of good times on earth. The extremism of the Fifth Monarchy movement and then the collapse of the Commonwealth greatly reduced such expectations, and Richard Baxter expressed a more common attitude, when, in the 1660s, he cast doubts on the possibility of a utopia. By the 1690s, however, Baxter had changed his mind. He and Mather disagreed not on whether the earthly millennium would be, but what it would be like.[63] The difference of opinion was important. In the course of time, Jonathan Edwards would advance ideas similar to Baxter's, and they would enter the mainstream of American millennial thought. Increase Mather's expectations would become a minority view and be taken up by the Millerites of the nineteenth century and literalists of the twentieth.[64] Both interpretations replaced the medieval, Augustinian view of history in which the meek would inherit a heavenly city with a millenarian expectation of an earthly world of joy.

Mather wanted to publish all these books in London, and he prepared several packets of manuscripts to go by sea.[65] He dedicated *Angelographia* to Hugh Boscawen, and *Dissertation Concerning the Future Conversion of the Jewish Nation* to Sir John Hartopp, men who had been helpful to him during his four years in and near London. The manuscripts were lost at sea. First he heard that they had fallen into the hands of a French privateer; then that they had been thrown overboard, so they would not fall to the French.[66] He set to work to make new transcriptions.[67] In the end *Angelographia* was published in Boston, *Dissertation Concerning the Future Conversion of the Jews* in London, but not until 1709, and *Discourse Concerning . . . the New Jerusalem* was not published at all during Mather's life. *Two Plain and Practical Discourses*, ready for publication in 1695, came out in London, but not until 1699. After this hard experience Increase Mather satisfied himself with publishing in America.

THE STRUGGLE OVER A CHARTER FOR HARVARD

Mather wanted more than anything else royal confirmation of a charter for Harvard College. As soon as he reached Boston in May 1692 he drafted a charter, and it passed the General Court that spring and was signed into law by Phips on June 27. The new charter created a corporation of ten men with virtually unlimited control over the affairs of the college. The old board of Overseers was dropped. Mather himself was President and John Richards Treasurer. Mather named eight fellows. Two were John Leverett and William Brattle, the teaching fellows he had selected in 1685. They had been in charge for the four years he had been out of the country. The other fellows, non-resident and unsalaried, were neighboring ministers: Samuel Willard and James Allen from Boston's First and Third churches; Nehemiah Hobart from Newton; Daniel Gookin from Cambridge; and Increase's son Cotton and his son-in-law Nehemiah Walter.[68]

The privileges conferred by the charter were substantial. Real and personal estates of the president and fellows were exempt from public taxes. Three of the President's personal servants were exempt from militia service. Mather wrote a new set of college laws to make provision for granting new degrees, and at its second meeting the newly constituted Harvard Corporation conferred the degree of Doctor of Divinity on Mather himself, and then the degree of Bachelor of Divinity on Leverett and Brattle.[69] Mather had taken considerable satisfaction from being introduced in London as the president of the college and even gave that title precedence on the title pages of his books: "President of Harvard College at Cambridge, and Teacher of a Church at Boston in New England." (*Cases of Conscience Concerning Evil Spirits*, Boston, 1692.) His dreams for the college were becoming inseparable from his dreams for honor and dignity for himself. The restructuring of the college occupied a large part of his attention in the summer of 1692 during the height of the Salem witchcraft trials.

But all was not well. Inevitably the college and his control of it intermingled with the political controversies of the decade. Mather's political enemies attacked at the one place he was vulnerable to politics: his presidency of Harvard. Elisha Cooke, Thomas Oakes, and Nathaniel Byfield, for example, persuaded many that Mather should be blamed for the colony's failure to get the old charter restored. Everything people disliked about the new charter could be laid at his feet: royal appointment of the governor, freehold property rather than church membership a basis of the franchise, judicial appeals to England, and royal authority to disallow legislation. Cooke and Byfield made a strong party in the House, and at the very next session of the General Court, the Court voted that the president of the college must reside at Cambridge. The Council, hand-picked by Mather and still under Phips's sway, did not concur,[70] but the handwriting was on the wall: as long as Mather was president his enemies within the House would use the college to attack him. It was a strange reversal from earlier days, when the Deputies had been his strength and the Magistrates the enemy.

In the summer of 1695 Phips was gone and Mather's support in the assembly at a low ebb. Motions were again made for the college president to reside in Cambridge. Mather longed to return to England, but typically he must wait on a call, a visible sign of God's will.[71] "For several dayes, I have been extremely dejected in my spirit, fearing that all my

Faith de an opportunity and advantage to be put into my hands to glorify God and Christ in England was only phansy and delusion but this morning, as I was praying in my study, I had a strange perswasion that Tidings was coming to me from E. that would revive me, I did with Tears and wonderful meltings believe it. So did my sadness of spirit vanish."[72]

He was so sure he would return to England that he rode jubilantly to Cambridge and told his colleagues on the Harvard Corporation that he was "not free to be any longer concerned for the college." They should start, he told them, to search for a new president.[73] Each day Increase and Samuel (who also set his sights on returning) searched the bay for incoming ships which might bear an invitation. Even though he distrusted dreams, Increase could not help but believe when he dreamed he would surely be called back.[74] It was possible now that he would go to England as an agent for the colony. Mather prayed on his knees for such a mission, and in the same breath insisted that he could only go if the call were clear. "If Hee calleth me to so great & hazardous an undertaking, Hee can cause those that have bin against an Agency to be for it, & that have bin against my being so improved, now to be for it, and then I should be satisfyed that his hand was in it, . . . otherwise not; I was exceedingly melted before the Lord, & perswaded that God heard me, and would give me to see a special Answer to prayer."[75]

A week later, all his hopes for England were ruined. "Yesterday," he wrote in his diary, "the Representatives in the General Assembly voted that a Committee should draw up Reasons for sending an Agent to England. This day they voted that they would send none. This sudden change is unaccountable. There is a signal hand of God in it. Thus has Hee again strangely prevented my going to E. Gods Time is the best. The bias on the spirits of the Council last year is unaccountable. So on the deputies this year. . . . It is good to wait.[76] A little later when the winter storms were kicking up seas in the North Atlantic, "God has mercifully prevented my being sent thither again this winter."[77]

Did Increase feel some twinges of guilt at wanting to leave New England? His desire to return to England was pitted against his belief that the people of New England were God's chosen people and Massachusetts itself the place to which the New Jerusalem would come down from heaven. He spent hours rationalizing his position. When he experienced a period of lameness, he wondered if it were a punishment: "Is it to Rebuke me for my being willing to Return to England . . . ? No: for I am very willing to stay where I have Riches enough, and honor enough. I desire not one grain more of those things to be bestowed on me. I can not think of going from my Relations here, without much Reluctancy. So that if I Return to England it must be purely and only to do greater service for Christ, than in New England I am capable of." These pangs of conscience were overcome each time they arose. "The perswasions which have been in my Heart . . . ," he wrote, "I can not help. They were wrought in me when Fasting and praying before the Lord." [78]

There were changes at the college. Both tutors decided to leave. Probably Increase Mather's constant presence for the last three years helped them make up their minds. Mather, besides being old enough to be their father, was opposed to some of their modern ideas, although there were no doubt other considerations. Both young men (they were Cotton Mather's age) chose to marry within the year.

William Brattle was called by the Cambridge church. In a demonstration of his ecclesiastical modernism, he insisted that his ordination be by ministers with no laying-on of hands by the lay members of the congregation. Mather preached the ordination sermon. The older and more conservative members did not like the reversal of Congregational tradition, but in this new day, when "the world rules the church," there was little they could do. Increase Mather also could say little, since his son Cotton in matters such as this was already a modernist himself. [79] John Leverett left the tutoring of Harvard undergraduates to go into law and politics. In 1696 he was elected to the House of Representatives by the voters of Cambridge and began a swift rise to a position of political power. Within three years he was Speaker of the House, which itself proved only a stepping-stone to higher office.

While Brattle and Leverett were preparing to leave the college after ten years, word arrived from London on July 12, 1696, that the Privy Council had disallowed the college charter passed in 1692! The reason, the crown had not been given the right of visitation. Suddenly the presidency, corporation, college laws, and new degrees were all without legal foundation. Worse, Mather was no longer in a position to dictate the terms of a new charter. In the general assembly a Tory council and a Whig house battled each other over a new draft. The council's bill stripped Mather and his colleagues on the corporation of most of their power. It greatly enlarged the corporation, gave the governor and council the supervisory power of "Visitors," required the president and fellows to reside at the college, took away their tax exemptions, and removed the protection of college servants against military service. [80]

The ministers who composed the corporation were incensed. On December 11, 1696, Mather stormed in to tell the representatives that the present corporation would apply directly to the king for a royal charter, and that he himself would go to London to get it. Angered at the threat, the council rushed its bill through and sent it to the representatives, where it passed. Stoughton signed the new charter into law on December 17. The very next day Increase Mather, Samuel Willard, James Allen, and Cotton Mather—the clergy of Boston—all resigned.[81] Samuel Sewall recorded in his diary, "I doe not know that ever I saw the Council run upon with such a height of Rage before. . . . The Ministers will go to England for a charter, except we exclude the Council from Visitation." A few days later all the ministers on the corporation, except Brattle and Leverett, asked that their names not appear in the new charter. Angry as they were, the council backed down and its charter was withdrawn.[82]

In January Increase Mather set his hand to drafting a compromise that might satisfy all parties.[83] He accepted the council's much enlarged corporation, eighteen members instead of ten. He restored the tax exemption of lands occupied by the president and the fellows. He restored exemption from military service for one of the college's servants and three of the president's. He compromised on the question of residency: the president and teaching fellows would be required to live on the campus, but only after the charter of incorporation had been approved by the king in England. For the time being, at any rate, Mather would be free from political motions to force him to Cambridge. As for royal visitation, that too was a compromise. The governor, representing the crown, and council "shall be the Visitors of the said College as there shall be occasion for it."[84] This new draft was passed by both houses and sent with the other assembly laws to England for confirmation.

Mather's uncertainties and frustrations over the college charter produced momentarily a mood of utter despair, so that in at least one sermon that spring Mather questioned his image of a New England Israel. Preaching a funeral sermon for two undergraduates drowned while skating on the late spring ice at Cambridge, Mather said, "There is cause to fear lest *suddenly* there will be no *Colledge* in *New England*; and this is a sign that ere long there will be no churches there. I know there is a blessed day to the Visible Church not far off; but it is the Judgement of very Learned Men, that in the Glorious Times promised to the Church on Earth, *America* will be Hell."[85] Only the college elicited such deep, pessimistic feelings.

Meanwhile, that spring of 1697, Mather preached a sermon at Cambridge which seemed to some to be aimed directly at the modernizing tendencies of the outgoing tutors. Leverett and Brattle were still in residence and would not actually leave until the following October. Mather preached about the old issue of church admissions. It was important, he said, to examine candidates for admission and to be satisfied of their sainthood. He preferred the old method, where the candidate was expected to give a public account of his or her spiritual growth. This was the same issue he had argued over with Stoddard in the winter of 1679–1680. Friendship with Richard Baxter had now made Mather more lenient than he had been then. Baxter had admitted that "I neither know the day nor the year when I began to be sincere," and Mather, who had been wont to treat his own and his father's conversions as the standard, relaxed far enough to accept some fuzziness in people's accounts. But it was important not to abandon the examination altogether. "Beware of the other extream of laxness in admission unto the Lord's holy table."[86] He emphasized, as earlier, that the brethren as well as the minister are responsible for admissions.[87]

He closed his sermon speaking directly to the college students in the audience. As in days of old he spoke of the beginnings of the colony. Warning against "Pelagian and Arminian principles" he resurrected some of the spirit and even patches of rhetoric from the jeremiad: "Do not think it is enough, if you be orthodox in the *fundamental points* of religion. It was not (I can assure you) on any such account that your fathers followed Christ into this wilderness, 'when it was a land not sown.' If you degenerate from the 'order of the gospel,' (as well as from the 'faith of the gospel') you will justly merit the name of *apostates* and of *degenerate plants*." He continued in the pattern of the jeremiad, God will punish his own children more than others: "And such degeneracy in the children of New-England, and most of all in *you*, will be worse than any children in the world."[88] Cotton Mather published the sermon that year as the "epistle dedicatory" to his biography of Jonathan Mitchell.[89]

That Pelagian and Arminian principles were being discussed at Harvard there was no doubt. Both the tutors were spokesmen for new trends from across the Atlantic. One of their early pupils, Henry Newman (Harvard 1687) wrote much later: "Two of my three Correspondents at Cambridge have made more Proselytes to the Church of England than any two men ever did that liv'd in America, . . . These Gentlemen are Mr. Leveret the President of the College (after 1707) and mr. Brattle the Minister of Cambridge who have had the Government of the College there in whole or in part for about thirty years past. . . . 'Tis above 25 years since I had the happiness to be Mr. Leverett's Pupil and then I can bear him and Mr. Brattle witness the only Tutors at that time in the College that they recomment to their Pupils the reading of Episcopal authors as the best books to form our minds in religious matters and preserve us from those narrow Principles that kept us at a Distance from the Church of England."[90]

Admiration for those "Episcopal authors" had reached Boston and the Harvard campus on the wings of the latitudinarian movement that infused the Church of England after the Restoration. But there was more to Harvard liberalism than that. Episcopalian authors would also have included the Cambridge Platonists, represented by Henry More, Nathaniel Culverwell, and Ralph Cudworth, who had as one of their chief goals the reconciliation of Christian and Platonic ethics. John Leverett thought enough of them to make a handwritten précis of More's *Enchiridion Ethicum* for use as a textbook and was directly responsible for putting this branch of ethics into the curriculum. Pagan ethics taught along with scriptural ethics troubled Mather, but it was difficult to oppose this trend directly inasmuch as a prominent and prolific Dissenter in England, Theophilus Gale, who left his very large personal library to Harvard College, had been engaged in a similar endeavor.[91]

The latitudinarian movement encompassed a wide spectrum of English writers, ranging from Joseph Glanville to Archbishop Tillotson and Bishop Gilbert Burnet. Glanville, whose work Mather was eager to cite in defense of a spiritual world, was nevertheless a spokesman for the new spirit of reason and compromise, as evidenced in his 1676 essay, *The Agreement of Reason and Religion.* The new mood replaced the older English Calvinism with a tolerance for diverse opinions compounded with a quiet assurance that religion must be reasonable. Archbishop Tillotson's writings were probably the most widely read books, after scripture, in the American colonies. The men most responsible for introducing Tillotson (as well as Henry More) to Harvard were John Leverett and Benjamin Colman.[92] The temper of the latitudinarian movement, and among English Dissenters it was more a movement of temperament than an attack on doctrine, was cool, complacent, agreeable. The difference between it and the jeremiad style of the 1670s can be epitomized by a remark of Joseph Glanville: "To be confident in opinions is ill manners and immodest. . . . This is that spirit of immorality that saith unto dissenters, 'Stand off, I am more orthodox than thou art'; a vanity more capital than error."[93]

Increase Mather's relationship to the movement was of necessity complex and paradoxical. To the degree that the latitudinarians defended the spiritual world against the inroads of materialistic atheism, they were allies. But the idealism of the Cambridge Platonists was tied to pagan writers whom Mather suspected. When in England he had been only too glad to obtain the help of both Bishop Burnet and Archbishop Tillotson in his campaign for the Massachusetts charter.[94] In 1695 he acknowledged that the high clerics of England were a far cry from the bishops who had silenced his father and driven him out of England. "Had the Sees in England, fourscore years ago," Mather wrote, "been filled with such Arch-Bishops and Bishops as those which King William . . . has preferred to Episcopal Dignity, there had never been a New-England."[95] When one considers the venom with which Mather and others wrote of the English king and bishops as Antichrist in the 1660s, when members of the first generation were alive and the regicides were hiding in the New England countryside, this statement in 1695 is itself a remarkable illustration of the changed, moderate temper of the times. Nevertheless, Mather did not want to see the unique order of New England churches changed, and because he increasingly came to see Harvard undergraduates as the only source of church leadership in the coming years, their attitudes were particularly important to him.

Increase Mather must have been happy to see the two tutors whose attitudes were so much more tolerant and broad-minded than his own go. The question then came, who would succeed them? Leverett and Brattle stayed on until mid-October.[96] On November 15 the members of the Harvard Corporation gathered at Mather's house to make a final choice for replacements. The two men chosen were Ebeneezer Pemberton and Jabez Fitch, both of them graduates and students at Harvard, both pupils of the retiring tutors. Fitch was acceptable to Mather, but not Pemberton, who seemed heavily influenced by Leverett and a man of violent and disrespectful temper. Willard must have backed Pemberton, for the next day Mather was still so angry at the choice that he told his old friend he would never go to his house again until Willard apologized. Two weeks later President Mather summoned the students together at the college and announced the new tutors.[97]

All the summer and fall of 1697, Increase Mather was expecting to return to England. Most often he believed that he would be sent as an agent of the colony with the specific mission to lobby for royal approval of the college charter. In the Council and in the House of Representatives the votes for and against Mather's going were evenly divided. On June 7 the Corporation recommended to the Council that Mather be sent, and two days later the representatives agreed, but on June 15 the representatives reversed their vote.[98] Mather was himself ambivalent about his role at the college and frequently spoke of relinquishing the presidency. Every time he proposed to resign, the Corporation persuaded him not to.[99] He was busy with the college all year, preaching to students, moderating disputations, counselling some individually about their "spiritual state," or simply meeting there with the ministers' association. Always he sustained the belief that he would return to England: "Surely this Lords day the spirit of the Lord melted my Heart when I had hope that Hee has work for me to do in England, & that there I shall glorify the Lord Jesus Christ, & do service for his Name, Interest, & Kingdom in the world."[100] For all his desire to go to England, Mather was unwilling to act on his own initiative. He had been called to the North Church; he must be called away from it. It seems to have been inconceivable to him that he might move to England on his own. He waited for Providence. This awkward and unsatisfying situation continued unresolved through the first half of the next year.

In May 1698 there came about a dramatic alteration in his prospects. A new royal governor had at last arrived in America. Richard Coote, Earl of Bellomont, went first to New York. So eager were Mather and the Harvard Corporation to resolve the question of the college charter, that they sent one of their members down to New York to ask Lord Bellomont's opinion what to do. He sent back word that because the charter of 1697 gave powers of visitation to the Massachusetts Council as well as the king's governor, it was improbable that it would be approved. Bellomont's letter circulated between the Council and the House of Representatives, and a few days later the proposal from the Harvard Corporation that Increase Mather go to England to lobby for the charter was again, and seemingly finally, turned down.[101] Mather continued "in secret Communion with God" to have "soul-melting Hope that the Lord has work for me to do for his Name in England."[102] Secondhand reports of the debate in the Council told him what he already knew: "Troubled at what I was told yesterday, that I had bin much reflected on in the Council. And that some said I deserved a years Imprisonment. Is this my Reward for taking so much pains to serve and save N.E.!"[103] "What is the meaning of providence that when that matter has come to the birth there has not bin strength to bring forth?" and "The Lord direct me what to do as to a Resignation of my Relation to the Colledge: And be with me on the Commencement approaching."[104]

Far from being sent back to England, Mather suddenly found himself called, more insistently than ever, to move to Cambridge. The Corporation itself recommended to the assembly that a vice-president be appointed to reside at the college, "under the continuall assistance and Countenance of the Reverend President (the continuance of whose relation to the Colledg is on all Accounts needfull) and in his absence, to have the full power of the President." [105] This time a grand committee, which included the Speaker of the House, Nathaniel Byfield (an enemy), Samuel Sewall from the Council (an old friend), Isaac Addington, the Secretary of the Colony, and others from both houses, came to visit Mather in his home. Dark had already fallen; the candles were lit and a fire blazed in the great hearth as they pleaded and argued with Mather to take up residence on the campus. Byfield assured him that every member of the House wished it. Sewall gave probably the most persuasive arguments: "I told him of his Birth and education here; that he look'd at Work rather than Wages, all met in desiring him, and should hardly agree so well in any other." [106]

A week later, on December 16, Mather sent his answer in writing to Lieutenant Governor Stoughton. As to the salary of £200, he said, he had no objection, although it is less than he had in Boston. But if he were to move, he would needs leave off his public ministry. "Should I leave preaching to one thousand five hundred souls (for I suppose that so many use ordinarily to attend in our congregation), only to expound to forty or fifty children . . . ?" He was nearly sixty years old and a younger man would be better. "One reason for my retaining my relation to the College this long has been, because it was thought that would facilitate its charter settlement. Could I see that done, I could with great joy give way to another President." His church, Mather wrote, would not let him go. "They well know, that I have had a strong bent of spirit, to spend (and to end) the remainder of my few days in England, and that the thing that keeps me here, now the Gospel has a free passage there, is my love to them; for which cause they will not consent to my being discharged. . . ." Finally, "I neither will nor have I obstructed the settlement of the College in a better hand. I have often (as your Honor well knows) desired to resign my relation to that society; and, if it will not be grievous to you, I shall tomorrow (if you please) deliver a resignation of the president-ship to the Senior Fellow of the Corporation. . . ." [107]

This did not put an end to it. The issue dragged on into the following spring. The Council, House of Representatives, and even the Corporation were so evenly divided that no resolution was reached. Certainly some were furious at Mather and suspected his offers to resign were insincere. Samuel Torrey (minister from Weymouth, Fellow on the Corporation) said as much in a meeting with the Council: "Only mr Torrey said all I said was nothing. Hee said to me that my pretending to Resign was but a flourish." The next day Mather reported he had "discourse with mr Torrey who desired me not to Resign the presidentship. Professed entire respect to me etc."[108] Nothing had changed.

BOSTON AT THE CENTURY'S END

In the eight years 1692–1700 Massachusetts went through an extraordinary transformation. War with France had begun in 1689 and spread to a cruel, intermittent forest warfare on the northern and eastern frontiers of New England. Refugees straggled back along dirt roads leading towards Boston. Increase wrote sadly, "At the eastward some poor people live upon the broth of Horses which they kill for meat, and have no bread."[109] Food was scarce throughout the colony and an embargo was put on the export of peas and wheat. Mather grimly recorded from time to time the lives lost and captives taken in the Indian war, fifteen at Billerica, twelve at Pascataway, thirty at Haveril.[110]

In 1697 came a brief respite in the war. Family concerns were often on Mather's mind. Maria had a difficult birth; the son was christened Mather Green. Little Jerusha, his youngest daughter, now entering adolescence, was weak and seemed emotionally unstable. Hannah, on the other hand, was too healthy, and although engaged to John Oliver, got herself involved in a scandal; Mather wondered if the wedding would take place.[111] Much worse was the news of Maria's brother John Cotton. After the scandal in Boston in 1664, John Cotton had ministered to the church in Plymouth for thirty years. Now after all that time the same fatal weakness: another scandal involving two women members of the Plymouth church. John Cotton fled again, this time to South Carolina. He died there before his wife and children could join him.[112]

There were other personal tragedies. Samuel Willard and Mather for twenty years had led the Boston clergy and from Boston, all New England. Age, changing circumstances, losses in their families began to take their toll. Willard's church chose young Simon Bradstreet, grandson of the old governor, as an assistant for him. Bradstreet was one of the Harvard liberals. He believed, for example, that the church covenant was unscriptural, a human invention. Willard did not want any part of him, but Bradstreet was popular with the younger people. Willard was exasperated beyond measure to discover that he must put up an exhausting fight to avoid being saddled with an unwanted assistant.[113]

That same summer Willard's thirteen-year-old son Richard accidentally drowned in Cambridge. The boy had gone there to enroll in college, and afterwards had walked down to the river that hot afternoon in late June to swim, but he tripped and went in fully clothed. His college admission papers were in his pocket when they pulled the body out.[114]

Maria, Mather's wife, became very sick and "full of pain." All about him Mather saw men and women of his generation passing on. The next month, December 1697, a ship from England brought news of his brother Nathaniel's death. That evening friends crowded into the small house across from the North Church to comfort Mather in his grief. He was the only one of the five brothers, four of them ministers, still living. The sense of his own mortality was strong. That week in his own church he surrendered the pulpit to his sons, Samuel preaching in the morning and Cotton in the afternoon. "Both my sons are employed in the worke of the Lord, my eyes seeing it, and my ears hearing it!"[115] He hardly guessed he would live another quarter century.

The winter of 1697–1698 was a bitter one in eastern Massachusetts. Boston was beset with epidemics of colds and coughs. In January, with Maria still weak, and his sons Samuel and Cotton confined to bed, Increase preached both morning and afternoon as he had in the old days. One night that same month, with a heavy freeze settling over Boston, he married his daughter Hannah, only seventeen, to John Oliver.[116]

The heavy snows and freezing temperatures were worse than anyone could remember. Mather's was not the only family beset with sickness. Willard was up and down. Captain Joshua Scottow was buried without a minister present because of the cold weather. The water in the bay froze solid, and one Wednesday early in February Mather walked across to Charlestown on the ice.[117] He paid for his adventure the next day with an attack of what he called the gout. First it struck one foot, which swelled so he could neither stand nor get his shoe on. Then the pain attacked the other knee and Mather was confined to his bed for a week. He tried what remedies and prescriptions he could glean from his wide reading:

A Special Medicine for the Gout Take so many raisins of the sun as will make a plaister for the Grief. Pound them like mortar. Then plaister there. If the Grief be extreme mix some opium therewith

For Sciatica: Boyle a pint of old Malmsey with Lib. 1 of butter out of the churn unsalted. Let them boil untill it come to a salve. Therewith anoint the grief warm. Use it for any other pain.

If the warm blood of the patient be included in the shell and white of an egg, which exposed to a gentle heat, and mixed with bite of flesh you shall give with the blood to a hungry dog or swine, the disease shall instantly pass from you into the dog and thereby leave you. Thus the Dropsy, gout, Jaundice is cured. Helmont of Magnetic Cure of Wounds. p. 12[118]

Mather was housebound for three weeks before the siege was past. "I bless God I can read, though I can not go." His sons managed services in the church. By the time Mather was out of the house again, a thaw had set in and the town fathers had set a guard at the ferry landing to prevent people from going out on the ice.[119]

Later that year Samuel Mather managed to return to England. The young man had wanted to ever since he and his father had come back to Boston in 1692. For a time it had seemed that he would end up with a congregation in Barbados, but fortunately arrangements for England were completed first. With his father's words of love in his ears, Samuel boarded the frigate *Orford* at the end of June 1698. He carried with him a bundle of his father's manuscripts for the London press. "The Lord be with him," Mather prayed, "and when God shall bring him to London, there open a door for service to him."[120] Samuel would indeed find service in London and a church near Oxford. He would not return to Boston, nor would father and son meet again.

Boston continued to grow, despite the hard economic times. Negroes now replaced Indians as house servants. "In my family a Negroe servant has done wickedly and is run away," Mather noted in his diary, a reason for humiliation.[121] At an afternoon service in 1698 Cotton Mather baptized two adult Negroes and two Negro children. "A Comfortable and a glorious sight," Increase wrote, "to see Negros professing Repentance and Faith in Christ, and so baptised with their children into his Name."[122]

Simon Bradstreet, turned down by Willard at Boston's Third Church, accepted a call from Charlestown. The church there decided to let all in the town have a say in choosing the minister. Increase and Cotton Mather wrote a letter, which their congregation approved, admonishing the Charlestown saints "for betraying the Liberties of the Churches, in their late putting in the Hands of the whole Inhabitants, the choice of a minister."[123] The Charlestown church asked the Mathers, father and son, to join them on the day of Bradstreet's ordination, but they wrote back they could not countenance the ordination of a man who did not believe in the church covenant. They stayed away.[124] The younger generation of ministers was getting established nevertheless: Brattle at Cambridge, now Bradstreet at Charlestown. Willard's church was evenly divided in trying to choose between the Harvard tutors, liberal Ebeneezer Pemberton or traditional Jabez Fitch.

It was usual in the 1690s for a church to call a council of neighboring churches to help resolve differences of opinion. In the years after 1695 Mather was often in demand for this duty. Sudbury, Watertown, Chebaco all called in church councils on which Increase Mather sat. They required long horseback rides and nights away from home listening to the disputants, then often successive meetings of the council in Boston.[125] The use of church councils was both a symptom of changing religious patterns and the forerunner of a tighter organization of the clergy, a move toward the Presbyterian style.

In November 1698 another public execution took place, the spectacular mixture of popular entertainment and reinforcement of social mores. As before, official Boston made the most of the opportunity. Twice the convicted person was brought to the North Church to hear sermons by Increase Mather, by now a past-master at exciting the emotions of the crowd. Sarah Threeneedles had been convicted of murdering her illegitimate infant after the young man she said was the father, the socially prominent Thomas Savage, Jr., denied any responsibility. Sex, violence, and the execution of a young woman all contributed to the excitement of the occasion. The final sermon, on execution day, was held in the large Third Church. Cotton Mather preached and thought it the largest crowd ever, four or five thousand. The church was so filled he had to climb over the pews to reach the pulpit. Increase Mather, perhaps uncomfortable in the crush, stayed at Willard's house next door. His two sermons were soon published, the attempt of two booksellers to capitalize on the occasion, New England's version of the popular press.[126]

DEFYING THE PLATFORM: THE BRATTLE STREET MANIFESTO, 1699

By 1698 tensions within the religious community in and around Boston had reached the breaking point. A group of modernists, inspired by the latitudinarian spirit of England, plotted a change. The five ringleaders were Brattle, then at the Cambridge church; Leverett, Speaker of the House of Representatives; Simon Bradstreet, at the Charlestown church; Ebeneezer Pemberton, the liberal teaching fellow at Harvard; and Thomas Brattle, William's older brother, whom Mather had named College Treasurer to succeed John Richards. Two of them, Leverett and Bradstreet, were grandsons of former governors of Massachusetts. All were innovators in church matters and had already drawn Mather's and Willard's fire.

Mather, Willard, and James Allen were the old men now. They had together ruled Boston's three churches since the 1670s, Mather at the North Church since the 1660s. Mather was sixty years old in 1699 and the others within a year of two of him. All had graduated from Harvard before the younger men were born and had dominated the intellectual life of Massachusetts. Mather and Willard between them accounted for eighty percent of all the published sermons in Massachusetts during these years. Mather's prestige was enormous after his four years in England. Who else had talked personally to kings and queens? Who else had friendships with the great officers of state at Whitehall and the most famous Dissenters in England? Together, Allen, Mather, and Willard dominated the established church in Boston and suffocated dissent.

Around the young conspirators coalesced a larger group, most of them men of business. In January 1698 they raised £250 to purchase from Thomas Brattle a piece of land in the heart of Boston. Their plan was to form a new church that would reflect their own modern views, and where they could escape from the stultifying control of the older generation. The ringleaders invited a college friend, Benjamin Colman, to come from England to take on the job of minister. Benjamin Colman's parents had come from England in 1671 and eventually joined Mather's North church. Benjamin was born in 1673 and grew to adulthood hearing Mather's sermons. He later attended Harvard with Bradstreet and Pemberton and joined the North Church after graduating. As soon as he earned his M.A. degree in 1695 Colman left for England. Slim, pale, with high color in his cheeks, Benjamin Colman was exquisite. Many people noted it. He quickly won favor among the leading Dissenters in London, and the Presbyterian board found him a church in Bath, a favorite watering place of English gentry. There Colman formed a lasting attachment to two Dissenting poets, Elizabeth Singer Rowe, "Philomela," and Isaac Watts. The relationships had singular influence on Colman's preaching and thence on the religious sensibilities of New England.[127]

Colman was in Bath when the letters came from his classmates asking him to come back to Boston. If he agreed to come, they advised him to have himself ordained in England, for there was sure to be opposition from the ministers in Boston. So Colman was ordained by the Presbyterians in London, and when he stepped ashore at Boston, he brought a new elegance of language into the old Puritan city. Two weeks later Colman published to the world a "Manifesto" of the principles that would guide the new church on Brattle Street.[128]

The minister, he wrote, would read passages of scripture without com-

QUÆSTIONES,

Quas pro modulo

DISCUTIENDAS

Sub Clariſſimo VIRO,

D. CRESCENTIO MATHERO,

Academiæ HARVARDINÆ,

quæ eſt CANTABRIGIÆ Nov-Anglorum,

PRÆSIDE Literatiſſimo ;

Die Comitiorum Proponunt Inceptores'

in ARTIBUS.

Die Tertio Quintilis. M DC XC V.

A *N Detur in non-Renatis Liberum Arbitrium ad*
(*bonum Spirituale* ?
Negat Reſpondens BENJAMIN COLMAN.

An Sola Fides, quatenus apprehendit Chriſti Merita, et
(*Illis innititur, Juſtificet* ?
Affirmat Reſpondens EBENEZER WHITE.

An Gentes ex Naturæ Lumine Salutem poſſint Conſequi ?
Negat Reſpondens JOHANNES MORS.

An Pontifex Romanus ſit Ille Antichriſtus, Quem futurum
(*Scriptura prædixit* ?
Affirmat Reſpondens CALEB CUSHING.

Harvard College Quaestiones for 1695 graduating class under Mather's presidency; among those listed, Benjamin Colman, future minister of Brattle Street Church, Boston

Benjamin Colman, minister of Boston's Brattle Street Church from 1699 to 1747

Samuel Willard, minister of South Church and acting president of Harvard after
Mather, from 1701 to 1707

THE
CHARACTER
Of a GOOD
RULER.

As it was Recommended in a
SERMON

Preached before his Excellency the
GOVERNOUR, and the Honourable COUNSELLORS, and Assembly of the REPRESENTATIVES
of the Province of *Massachusetts-Bay*
in *NEW-ENGLAND.*

On *May* 30. 1694.

Which was the Day for Election of
COUNSELLORS for that Province.

By *Samuel Willard*, Teacher of a
Church in *Boston.*

Boston Printed by *Benjamin Harris,* for
Michael Perry, under the *West End*
of the *Town House.* 1694.

The Character of a Good Ruler, 1694 election day sermon, by Samuel Willard

ment or explanation, in the manner of the Anglican church. ("Dumb reading" the Puritans had called it in earlier times.) Baptism would be offered to any child. The minister would admit to the Lord's Supper whomever he judged to be proper, and candidates for admission need only be examined by him, if they wished, and could dispense with a statement of their religious experience to the whole church. Election of future ministers in the "Manifesto Church" would be by everyone, including women, who contributed to its upkeep, not only the communicating members. There was more, all of it, point by point, departing from the traditions of a gathered church of the brethren.[129] To be sure, the "Manifesto" acknowledged the Westminster Confession. There was to be no innovation in the doctrines of grace or redemption. The walls being breached were the practices of Congregational worship hammered out fifty years before and enshrined in the Cambridge Platform, not the doctrine of the Savoy Confession.

At first the three senior ministers in Boston made a solid front against the innovators. It was soon apparent, however, that many respectable churchgoers were ready to let the young men try their wings. Willard gave in first, succumbing to arguments from within his own congregation. His Third Church, born in the controversy over the half-way covenant, had always been more liberal than either of the other two churches. Willard, also, was by temperament a more open man than Allen or Mather. They refused through December to have anything to do with the innovators.

But they could not stop what was happening. Sober people realized that controversy more than the new church threatened religion in Boston. Peacemakers were soon at work to mediate between the warring parties. William Brattle, who among the ringleaders was closest to Increase Mather, drew up a statement that modified the blunt prose of the "Manifesto" and offered a compromise. Benjamin Colman, whose very nature was that of a peacemaker, persuaded his church members to approve it, and Increase caved in. A ceremonial fast day was set for the end of the week.[130]

On January 31, 1700, a great crowd came to witness the reconciliation. Sewall was there and noted down the sequence: "Mr. Colman reads the Writing agreed on. Mr. Allin Prays, Mr. Colman preaches, prays, blesses. P.M. Mr. Willard prays, Mr. I. Mather preaches, Mr. Cotton Mather prays, Sing the 67 psalm without reading. Mr. Brattle sets Oxford Tune. Mr. Mather gives the Blessing. His Text was, Follow peace with all men and Holiness. Cot. must follow peace so far as it consists with Holiness. Heb. 12.14." [131]

Despite the show of harmony, Boston's older church community was deeply divided. Lay members in Massachusetts had always been far more conservative than their ministers. They came to Increase Mather now in puzzlement and for reassurance, and Mather, who had seen the innovations starting little by little at the college and then in the nearby churches, set out to reaffirm in print the traditional New England way of Congregational churches, as it had been worked out by the first-fathers and as it had always been in his lifetime. The task did not take long. Every point was as familiar to him as if it had just been hammered out in synod. Within two months, by March 1700, he finished a short book, *The Order of the Gospel*, which addressed one by one the seventeen points of the "Manifesto."

"If we Espouse such principles as these," he wrote, "Namely, that Churches are not to Enquire into the Regeneration of those whom they admit unto their Communion. That the Admission to Sacraments is to be left wholly to the prudence and Conscience of the Minister. That Explicit Covenanting with God and with the Church is needless. That Persons not Qualified for communion in special Ordinances shall Elect Pastors of Churches. That all Professed Christians have right to Baptism. That Brethren are to have no Voice in Ecclesiastical Councils. That the Essence of a Ministers call is not in the Election of the People, but in the Ceremony of Imposing hands. That Persons may be established in the Pastoral Office without the Approbation of Neighboring Churches or Elders; We then give away the whole Congregational cause at once, and a great part of the Presbyterian Discipline also." [132]

Mather at least would hold firm to the vision in the Cambridge Platform of the gathered church of God's elect. "It is not my own Cause," he wrote to the people of Massachusetts, "but Yours, which I have here undertaken and plead for. Did I say Yours? Nay, it is Christ's cause." [133]

Men joining the Brattle Street church did not care a fig for "old Mather's" *Order of the Gospel*, or rather they did care, for they were flushed with excitement at what they were accomplishing and wanted to exult over the vanquished. Some of them—probably not Colman or William Brattle, for it was not Colman's nature and Brattle continued his admiration of Increase—composed a rude, satirical reply. They called it *Gospel Order Revived* and took the manuscript that summer to Bartholomew Green to be printed anonymously. [134]

There took place then one of those curious side-plays of history unimportant in itself but revealing about the society in which it happens. Green, who had printed many a book for Increase Mather, and Cotton Mather, too, said he would not print this one anonymously, unless he first got the approval of the Lieutenant Governor. No one thought that the Lieutenant Governor, William Stoughton, famous as the presiding judge in the witchcraft trials, would smile on this jejune ridicule of Boston's most prestigious ministers. The authors expostulated with printer Green, and when he stood firm, they took their manuscript to New York, where they had it printed with an additional "Advertisement" that the "press" in Boston would not print it for fear of retaliation from Increase Mather and his friends.

The incident raises questions about Boston's lively book trade. Did Mather really exert an informal censorship over the Boston press? Why did the authors of *Gospel Order Revived* not take their manuscript to another Boston printer? Or did they? There are supposed to have been as many as seven printers in Boston at this time. Almanac writers in the 1690s, including William Brattle, continued their war over astrology and had their works printed.[135] Were there liberal and conservative printers?

Bartholomew Green was furious when he read the aspersions made against him in *Gospel Order Revived*. He printed a handbill, Cotton Mather wrote a pithy little paragraph for it denouncing the secret authors, and before long the affair grew to large proportions. Thomas Brattle, John Mico (a wealthy merchant), and Zechariah Tuttle at one time or another swore out depositions about their dealings with Green. He in turn gave counter depositions and was generally backed up by the two journeymen printers in his shop. Before it was over Green, who after all had the power of the press at his disposal, printed the relevant documents. As a by-product they tell us more about printing contracts, pricing, and press runs, than do any other earlier documents.[136]

Some support for the suggestion that the Mathers, father and son, controlled the Boston press comes from the fact that in that same year 1700 Solomon Stoddard published in London a book, *Doctrine of Instituted Churches* (London, 1700), which argued for a national church along Presbyterian lines and for using the Lord's Supper as a means to grace. As soon as Stoddard's book reached Boston, Cotton Mather hurried a rebuttal into print, in which he wrote, "We," meaning Cotton and his father, "We told him Seven Years before the publication of it, that if it came abroad, we would as publickly animadvert upon it."[137] Did Stoddard publish in London because no one in Boston would print a book the Mathers disapproved?

Cotton's rebuttal to Stoddard's Presbyterianiam was indirect. *Order of the Gospel* had already appeared, and Cotton wrote that it fortuitously served as an answer to Stoddard as well as to the Brattle Street manifesto. He reprinted John Quick's *Young Man's Claim*, an old standby of English Independency, added his own preface, "A Defence of Evangelical Churches," and persuaded eight other ministers to lend their names to the enterprise. It seems probable that Cotton, perhaps in collaboration with his father, who had preached in Quick's London church in 1690, was already planning to publish a Boston edition of *A Young Man's Claim* and used it as an opportunity to reply at once to Stoddard. It seems impossible, given the publication dates, that Stoddard could have written *Doctrine of Instituted Churches* after the appearance of Increase Mather's *Order of the Gospel* and still have it published in London and copies available in Boston soon enough for Cotton to publish "Defence of Evangelical Churches" all in 1700, as is sometimes suggested. [138]

So the new century began with a new church in Boston and renewed desertion of the Platform by the maverick Stoddard in Northampton. Of the two, the Brattle Street Church seemed to be the more telltale sign that times had changed.

CHAPTER 9

The Last Puritan

[1703-1723]

HARVARD LOST

Lilacs were blooming in Boston in the spring of 1699, when the city learned that England had rejected another batch of Massachusetts laws, including the 1697 version of the Harvard charter. Once again the now tiresome business of seeking a new charter for the college had to be addressed. The problem was that the crown insisted the king have oversight over the college. A new draft was prepared which gave the crown exclusive right of visitation. At the same time, and also for the first time in the history of the college, the draft included a religious test: "no person shall be chosen, and continued President, Vice-President, or Fellow, of said Corporation, but such as shall declare and continue their adherence unto the principles of Reformation, which were espoused and intended by those who first settled this country, and founded the College, and have hitherto been the profession and practice of the generality of the churches of Christ in New England." [1]

Both the Council and the House approved the innovation. Governor Bellomont did not. He wrote to the Lords of Trade in London that the paragraph would exclude forever "all members of the Church of England" from being on the college's governing board and vetoed the proposed charter, and they were back at the beginning, as far as the college charter was concerned. [2]

It was another summer before a new draft charter was again thrust into the legislative mill. This time the Council persuaded Governor Bellomont to give his approval to powers of visitation held by the king through his governor and the Council jointly. There would be no religious test. Mather, deep in his efforts to counteract the influence of the Brattle Street Church—he sent the manuscript of *Order of the Gospel* to the printer that March—went so far as to speculate if it might not be better not to have a charter at all: "Is it not much more eligible to have the Colledge turned into a school for Academical Learning without priviledge of Conferring degrees, as in Geneva it has bin where many Eminent divines have had their education, than to consent to such fatal alterations in the government of the Colledge, as some would have?"[3] Nothing came of that idea, nor is there any evidence that Mather even raised it publicly. On another point, however, the new draft charter was explicit: "The President of the said Corporation, as also all The Fellows and Tutors, thereof receiving salary shall reside at the Colledge. . . ."[4] Mather's political enemies had triumphed.

The General Assembly asked him to call a church meeting that very evening, and a delegation from the assembly went to explain and cajole the membership. The next day the following vote passed the brethren: "Being under the sense of the great benefit we have long enjoyed by the labor of our pastor, the Rev. Increase Mather, among us, it must needs be unreasonable and impossible for us to consent that his relations to us, and our enjoyment of him and them, should cease.

"Nevertheless, the respect we have to desire and welfare of the publick does compel us to consent that our good pastor may so remove his personal residence to the Colledge at Cambridge as may be consistent with the continuance of his relation to us, and his visits to us, with his publick administrations, as often as his health and strength may allow it."[5]

The language was clouded, but the meaning was plain. Mather must try to live in Cambridge despite everything. He moved there in the summer, leaving Maria at home in Boston. Every day Mather walked the short distance along hot, dusty lanes to the college buildings situated at the edge of the town common. An imposing new dormitory, Stoughton College, had been completed the year before. It was a good match in height and length to Old Harvard Hall and offered students amenities unheard of half a century before. Students in Stoughton College could, for example, rent space in the cellar to keep wine during term. The bricks to build the new hall had come from the long unused Indian College, where the early presses had printed Mather's first books.

Mather went each day to Old Harvard Hall. In the cool shade of the large central room he lectured to the students. His subjects on alternate weeks were taken from the Old Testament (Genesis 1 and 2) and the New (Matthew 1 and 2). Other days he climbed the narrow stairs to the library directly above. If there was a consolation for leaving his wife and home, it lay here, a collection of books even larger than his own. In the long summer days Mather summoned the students one by one to discuss their studies and their spiritual life. He spent hours reading in the light from the large windows overlooking the yard. On Sundays he preached in William Brattle's church to the Cambridge congregation.[6]

This was village life with a vengeance. Increase nearly died from boredom. In the fall, with summer passing and the days shortening, life became intolerable. By mid-October he groaned aloud as he faced long evenings in a lonely rented room already uncomfortably cold. The thought of longer, darker, colder months ahead crushed his spirit. "This has been the most uncomfortable three months that ever I saw. . . . ," he wrote. "I shall not refuse to take care of the college (which I have done these nineteen years past) for this winter. Only then I desire that another president may in the mean time be thought of." "Nor dare I," he wrote, "(lest I be guilty of the sixth commandment) continue any longer at Cambridge."[7] He could see little need for his presence there. That October Mather returned to Boston, welcoming the salt wind off the bay, the big North Meetinghouse, the busy streets and his own bed. In March 1701 he reluctantly agreed to return to Cambridge until commencement. He was resigned now to leaving the presidency and the turmoil which surrounded it: "I must entreat my friends not to be grieved or troubled at me if I now earnestly desire that another president may be thought of, that so I may enjoy that repose which my age infirmities and approaching death makes necessary for me."[8] Once more and finally Mather moved to Cambridge, but now with a clear end in sight.

It had not been easy for this outspoken champion of an older and far more strict Puritan generation to win the hearts of Harvard's undergraduates at the turn of the century. The strain told on Mather and found expression at the end of his farewell sermon to the students on June 29, 1701. Having cast himself in the role of parent, Mather concluded with the formula he had learned from his own father and would use with his own children.

"And now, *My Children,* what shall I say more unto you? I hope, that as to *many* of you, (*Oh! That it might be All of you!*) I shall meet you with Joy, at the right hand of CHRIST, in the *Great Day of His Appearing and His Kingdom,* when both you and I shall Rejoice, that ever He brought and placed me among you. But, if any of you, who are the Students in the *College,* prove so Miserable, as to *Dy in your Sins,* and in a *Christless Condition,* I earnestly Protest unto you *this Day,* that I shall testify against you before the Lord JESUS CHRIST in *that Day,* that I have called upon you both Publickly and Privately, to make sure of an Interest in Him.[9]

The thought was familiar, a ritual required of parent to child even in this metaphorical scene. Yet there was a stridency in Mather's language which suggests how difficult it must have been for him to preach to these young men at the dawn of a new century and how relieved he was to lay down the responsibility. He concluded his sermon: "I am now Pure from the Blood of your Souls; If any of you (which *Mercy Prevent!*) shall *Dy in your Sins,* your Blood will be upon your own Unhappy Heads. *I have done the part of a Faithful Father to you!*"[10]

In July 1701, as soon as commencement exercises were complete, he returned to Boston for good. His long presidency was over. By the narrowest possible margin, eleven to ten, the Council voted to replace him with Vice-President Samuel Willard. A similar vote squeaked through the House after Mather loyalists almost blocked it. The issue of residency at Cambridge was then shown to have been the sham Increase Mather had always thought, a device to oust him. Willard, no more willing than Mather to leave a large, wealthy Boston church for the doldrums of village life, agreed to spend one or two nights each week at Cambridge. The political faction was satisfied.[11]

The unfairness of that settlement outraged Mather and brought about another serious break with his old friend. What made Willard's acceptance particularly galling was that he "readily accepted of the offer without so much as once consulting with me about it."[12] In his bitterness Mather did not hesitate to belittle Willard's qualifications. Cotton Mather lost his temper entirely. One day encountering Samuel Sewall, a member of the Council that had accepted the new arrangement, in a book shop near the Town House he burst out against the Council's action, abusing Sewall so loudly that passersby in the street stopped to listen. Sewall sent Increase a haunch of venison to smooth things over, but demanded an apology from the son. It was a week before his sense of propriety was satisfied.[13]

The surrender of the presidency was a turning point in Increase Mather's life. At first he was angry and bitter. Philistines had captured the Ark of New England. That November he preached two sermons that reflected his feelings. The text of the first is from I Samuel 4.21:. God allowed the Philistines to crush the Israelite army and capture the Ark. When the news came, Eli's daughter-in-law gave premature birth to a son. She named him Ichabod, saying the glory is departed from Israel for the Ark of God is taken. The text of the second sermon is from Ezekiel 9.3:, "And the glory of the God of Israel was gone up from the cherub." The prophet tells of a moment just before the destruction of Jerusalem, when all are about to be killed except those few faithful who have been marked for salvation. "If the Fountain should fail," Mather preached, "I mean the Colledge, which has been one of the glories of New England; if that should fail, . . . the glory is like to be gone from these churches in less than one generation." [14]

Ichabod, or A Discourse Shewing what Cause there is to Fear that the Glory of the Lord is Departing New England (Boston, 1702) are the most pessimistic sermons Mather had preached since the days of King Philip's War. In them are passionate rehearsals of those themes of New England's beginnings which he had first developed in the biography of his father. But nowadays Increase Mather no longer carried the country with him. He was out of step with the times. The jeremiad had become a distinctly American form of sermonic and literary expression. Rooted in the prophetic language of the Old Testament, it would long outlast the men who planted it in Anglo-American culture. The jeremiad was not, however, the characteristic expression of New England after 1700. The Addisonian style of Benjamin Colman more clearly filled that role.

There is, therefore, some irony in the fact that *Ichabod* marks a further development of the Boston book trade, in the use of engravings. No fewer than four of the surviving copies of *Ichabod* contain engraved prints of Mather's portrait, two by R. White, an English engraver who made his plate in 1688, two from an engraving made in 1701 in America by Thomas Emmes, apparently copied from White's. The Emmes portrait, the first copperplate engraved in New England, was added to a sermon of Mather's published in 1701, but as an afterthought, after the fascicles had been sewn. The four volumes of *Ichabod* published with portraits established the beginnings of a new and more ostentatious era in book production. The innovator in Boston was yet another bookseller-publisher, Nicholas Boone, who was also the publisher of Boston's first news weekly. [15]

JOSEPH DUDLEY: IMPERIAL GOVERNOR

After Sir Williams Phips's death in 1695, William Stoughton served as governor in Boston until 1699. The choice of a governor under the new colonial charter was up to London. Joseph Dudley had already gone there in search of the office. He allied himself with the Tory faction, however, and so lost when the Whigs recovered power. Richard Coote, Earl of Bellomont, an impecunious Irish peer, was appointed instead. As an experiment in imperial administration Coote was appointed Governor General of New York and Massachusetts together.

Bellomont was not particularly interested in Massachusetts. He went first to New York and did not visit Massachusetts until May 1699. He arrived just in time for the annual May nominations to the Council. The election sermon would be a great state occasion, and Mather was chosen to deliver it. He was mild and ecumenical: "A man whose heart honours God, . . . Suppose him to be *Episcopalian, Congregational, Presbyterian, Antipedobaptist,* in his Opinion, if he is a Godly man, he honours Godliness wherever he seeth it." [16] If Mather hoped to win the governor's favor, he was disappointed, for Bellomont thought him a proud, selfish, and pedantic person. [17]

Increase Mather, suffering his first summer at Cambridge, hoped Bellomont would back him in seeking a royal charter for Harvard College. Bellomont, however, gave him no help and returned to New York in July 1700. Mather was left to suffer defeat in his struggle over the college. The next spring Bellomont died, so that quite suddenly the succession to the governorship was open again. Joseph Dudley, still in London, now revived his candidacy. Since losing his earlier bid, Dudley had ingratiated himself with Tory and Church of England magnates. As a client of Lord John Cutts, Dudley served as Lieutenant Governor and member of Parliament from the Isle of Wight. He joined the newly-formed Society for the Propagation of the Gospel in Foreign parts, whose aim was to bring New England Dissenters back into the fold of the Anglican church. [18] Dudley also had a powerful and broad base of support in Massachusetts. Lt. Governor Stoughton, now deceased, had supported his candidacy for governor ever since 1692, and by 1700 there was a "Dudleian" party in both the Council and the House. Secretary Addington, Nathaniel Byfield, and John Leverett were all Dudley men. So was John Higginson, minister at Salem and descendent of Salem's first minister. "If we should have a high Church of England-man," he wrote, "or some Huffing Hectoring Blade . . . or if any hungry courtier or any Stranger that knows not N. E. (as Exodus 1.8) and will not reguard the Interest of these Churches, But the contrary, it may be a great affliction to us. . . . Therefore I do humbly and earnestly recommend . . . this Honoured Gentleman Mr. D." [19] Increase and Cotton Mather both wrote letters to England in August of 1701 in support of Dudley's candidacy. Dudley had written a persuasive letter to Cotton in which he seemed genuinely to regret the past: "Absence has given Mee a true Vallue of My country and the Religion and Virtue that dwells in it. . . ." [20] So father and son were taken in by the honeyed words and joined the broad coalition of New England men urging the crown to make Joseph Dudley their next governor.

Early in 1702 the House of Representatives chose Increase to deliver the election sermon again. His lackluster performance reflected his discouragement at being forced out of Harvard College. He hammered away on two public themes: the advantages of the 1691 charter and the need to preserve the traditional order of church worship. Both houses voted to have the sermon published, although in a much smaller press run than the previous year's election sermon by Joseph Belcher. Mather dedicated the published sermon to the House. [21]

Two weeks later, on a warm June afternoon, Dudley landed with a great entourage at Scarlett's Wharf in the North End. As they passed Mather's church the new clock over the front portico struck five o'clock. Escorted by an honor guard and with much pomp, Dudley crossed the rickety bridge over Mill Creek, skirted the boat basin, and came into view of the crowd waiting at the Town House. As many as could squeezed inside. When he took his oath of office, Dudley kissed the Bible in the Anglican way. Increase asked the Lord's blessing nevertheless. A huge feast was served to the crowd. Volleys of shot were fired by the honor guard. Cotton offered a public prayer of thanks. Then the new governor-general was handed into Charles Hobby's coach, to be drawn by six horses to his home in Roxbury. [22] In Boston the old Puritan style had given way to an era of pomp.

With the arrival of Dudley the political life of Massachusetts began for the first time truly to reflect the transfer of English political patterns to New England. Phips and Stoughton had thought of themselves in the way of the old charter governors, [23] and Bellomont had concentrated his attention on New York and left Massachusetts pretty much alone. Dudley was different. Like Phips and Stoughton, he was a native son. Trained for ten years in the politics of England, however, he was ready to employ the lessons learned there to establish his power in Massachusetts. He would, for example, use the church for political purposes. Because he lived on his family lands in Roxbury, he joined the Congregational church there, but he simultaneously supported and attended Episcopal services at King's Chapel in Boston. His pragmatic approach to the church as a political institution would have been incomprehensible in the old Boston.

Equally revealing of the new politics was Dudley's frank use of patronage. The new charter gave the governor many new appointments which under the old charter had been made by the General Court. Mather had always insisted, however, that the new charter protected the people, because the governor would need the "advice and consent" of the Council, for his appointments, and the House had a voice in choosing the Council. But Dudley did what was then customary in England and used appointments to build his own political party. No sooner had he arrived than he presented to his Council a long list of judicial appointments. The Council prepared to pass around slips of paper for a secret vote on each, but Dudley stopped them short and forced a voice vote. By such intimidation of the Council Dudley was soon able to gain "consent" for many unpopular or questionable appointments, so much so that his tactics were talked about in the coffee shops of London. Appointments of Jahleel Brenton and his brother to judicial posts showed which way the wind blew. Dudley also appointed his own son Paul to the positions of Attorney General, Justice of the Peace for Suffolk County, and probate registrar for Suffolk County.[24] Adding insult to injury, Paul Dudley, who had been known to Mather since he had admitted him into the college, now joined Colman's Brattle Street Church. When Governor Dudley arrived in Boston, Mather nervously added a second dedication to his election sermon, which was already in press, hinting at an old fear: "You have (I am well assured) that *Greatness of Soul in you,* as to disdain any thought of revenge."[25] But in July Mather ruefully acknowledged in his diary, "the Governor newly come nominates very ungodly men to be in place of power, and the Council has consented contrary to express Scripture."[26]

The weather turned hot and sultry. Smallpox was bad again. Mather grew more depressed. Samuel Willard conducted the commencement at Harvard and for the first time in twenty years, except when out of the country, Mather had no part to play in it. Willard, moreover, was Dudley's brother-in-law and, therefore, seemed likely to have more influence over the new governor than Mather. It was galling. Mather was more disaffected from Boston than he had been for years, but strangely, he had no particular enthusiasm now for going to England. Instead he withdrew into a shell.

"These are the *last Lecture Sermons* Preached, or intended to be Preached by me," he wrote that summer regarding the Thursday mid-week lectures. "The other work incumbent on me, and the advances of Age which have now overtaken me, and the ill treatment which I have had from those from whom I had reason to have expected better, have discouraged me from being any more concerned on such Occasions." [27]

AN AGING INDIAN COMMISSIONER

The war in Europe between England and France was renewed in 1702 and quickly spread to North America and the long-troubled eastern frontier. The tangled skein of Indian diplomacy, punctuated by sudden raids, brutal assaults, and treachery on both sides, was tangled further by new French strategies. With the use of snowshoes and sleds, Dudley managed to put the Abenaki on the defensive, and they fell back to the positions of their French allies and persuaded the governor of New France, Vandreuil, to attack western Massachusetts. [28] In the first weeks of February 1704 a large force of several hundred French and Indian soldiers travelled undetected across the snow and ice from Montreal to the Connecticut River Valley to attack at dawn the fortified garrison town of Deerfield. They overran the town's defenses and carried off almost a hundred prisoners—men, women, and children—forcing them all to start back on the long march to Montreal.

"Among [the prisoners] is my Cousin Williams, & his wife & children," Mather wrote in his diary. "His wife was my brother Eleazars daughter. His children my brothers grandchildren. 3 of them killed. The rest (5 of them) are expected captives." [29] His niece, the wife of John Williams, died in the first few days after falling while crossing an ice-filled stream. Two of his grand-nieces and nephews were killed when they could not keep up the pace of the march. Increase followed what little news filtered back and tried not to brood about their chances: He wrote in his diary on March 18, "A very cold night Freezing within doors. The Lord pity poor captives" [30]

Mather was at this time one of the "Indian Commissioners" responsible for managing the affairs of the New England Company, which was the one organized effort of the Puritans to Christianize the American Indian. The company itself, more formally known as the Society for the Propagation of the Gospel in New England, had been organized in 1649. From then until the Massachusetts charter was lost in 1684, the Commissioners of the United Colonies administered the company's affairs in America. [31] They financed John Eliot's translations of the Bible into Algonquian, printed the "Indian Library," and supported a handful of men, like Daniel Gookin, an assistant in the General Court for many years, in missionary work among Indian communities. King Philip's War virtually destroyed the communities of Christian Indians, and the company's activity fell to a low ebb. By 1688 when Mather got to England, both Eliot and Gookin were dead. In England the company was moribund, but by 1692 it experienced renewed life. Major Robert Thompson, with whom Mather had stayed in Newington Green, was elected governor of the company, followed in 1695 by the even more active Sir Henry Ashurst.[32] In America the company's affairs were managed by five or six Indian Commissioners. William Stoughton, who had served the company since 1685, was now assisted by Sir William Phips, Charles Morton, John Richards, Wait Winthrop, and Increase Mather. But the American Commissioners did little, and their meetings were poorly attended. In 1698 Mather wrote Sir William Ashurst that all of them were dead or dying but Stoughton, Winthrop, and himself. On Mather's recommendation Ashurst appointed six additional commissioners, including Samuel Sewall and Cotton Mather. Sewall, more than any other, now became the mainstay of the work in America.[33] Mather himself wrote frequently to Ashurst about the work, but he seems never to have gone into the field or preached to Indians.

In 1698, a young man in the employ of the company, Samuel Danforth, translated four of Increase's sermons into Algonquian.[34] It was a contribution to the Company's Indian Library, but did little to influence the course of events. When personal tragedies like the abductions from Deerfield brought warfare close to home, Mather had no constructive remedy.

Persistent frontier warfare set heavy odds against a humane policy towards the Indian. Mather's brother-in-law Solomon Stoddard, for example, wrote to Governor Dudley in 1703 that soldiers might "be put into a way to Hunt the Indians with dogs . . . as they doe Bears . . . They are to be looked upon as thieves and murderers, they doe acts of hostility, without proclaiming war. They don't appear openly in the field to bid us battle, they use those cruelly that fall into their hands. They act like wolves and are to be dealt with all as wolves."[35] Mather never talked like that. Nevertheless, twenty-five years after his espousal of Indians in King Philip's War his energies on their behalf were at a low ebb.

Increase Mather was feeling the vulnerability and fragility of old age. Twice earlier in his life he had been sick and near death, once in 1669–1670 and again at the crux of the reform movement in 1679–1680. This was different. He was not stricken with a life-threatening illness, but harassed year after year by painful, debilitating complaints. Sometimes he would be kept from work for weeks at a time. In February 1704 he suffered a light stroke, "My memory quite gone for near an hour."[36] That summer, nearing sixty-five and aware "that my opportunities and abilities for service are in a manner gone," Mather began plans to choose his successor in the church. "When I am gone there will be need of such."[37] These adjustments to old age made him afraid, not of death but of old age and decline. What if he were left to live out his years in wracking pain? He suffered from kidney stone. "Continual motions to urin; & gravel came with it. H. coloured as if bloody. Oh that God would prepare me for another world, & (if it be his will) give me an easy and speedy passage into his Kingdom."[38]

The new mood brought with it an unexpected sentimentality and a maudlin concern over life and death. "Is this the first day of that year in which I am to dye, & to go into the eternal world . . . If I dy quickly, some few will lament my death. Whereas if I live a while longer I shall be useless. It is a great mercy for a minister not to outlive his work."[39] More and more stricken by gout, growing corpulent, troubled by arthritic pain in his hands, Mather worried most that old age would rob him of his memory and the power of his intellect. A portrait painted sometime in the 1700s, understood by oral tradition to have been a "likeness," shows the ravages of time and age.[40]

In the days before modern medicine there was little an aging person could do. "Much pain in the night," Mather wrote in 1705. "About noon pain in the small of my back, and my urine cutting and painful to me. I endeavored (as well as I could) to prepare for the Sabbath. But broken and shattered." The next day Mather could not get across the street to his church. "Thus does the Lord rebuke me, and make me like a broken vessel."[41] Medical science could not provide much help. Mather tried one nostrum after another: "Garlik, oyle of Turpentine in Sugar. Syrup of marshmellows"; "I think the Liquor of Azam was blessed for the removal of my paine"; "Spirit of Lavender (60 drops) with a mouthful of gingerbread recovered me"; "Took Bateman's purging . . . Syranam Gumm to my knee (for gout)"; "An ill fitt of the cholic . . . Used Tea made with Alehoof and syrup of marshmellows"; "I could not attend my studies this day, because of pain in my Jaws. Found relief by Fetherfew with Rum"; "Some ease by applying parsley with Salt to my Left ear."[42]

Maria was growing older too. Their fortieth wedding anniversary came in March 1702. Increase wrote in 1705, "My wife has been ill with a Rheumatism these diverse weeks past," and later, praying to the Lord, "Especially in that my wife continues ill still, having not bin able to go or stand for more than 6 weeks." In May Maria was back on her feet, although their youngest child, Jerusha, still living at home, was "weakly."[43]

The warm summer weather of 1705 tempted Mather to a trip to the hot springs at Lynn, where he had been going off and on for thirty years. He planned a working vacation during which he could transcribe some sermons for the press while enjoying a change of scene. One Wednesday in August he rode horseback up to the seaside village. He stayed with his colleague, Jeremiah Shepard, for two weeks, worked, dined out, visited the hot spring "where meditated," preached for his host both Sundays, and rode back to Boston much refreshed.[44]

Mather had stopped preaching regularly at churches outside Boston. He now spent more time than ever in his study, occasionally staying up until midnight or after.[45] He no longer was obsessed with the thought of returning to England and on reflection found this change in his feelings "strange." The House of Representatives was about to take up again the question of sending an agent to England about the college charter. Increase hoped they would not ask him. "I was formerly very desirous to have gone to E. again," he wrote in his diary. "But of late years have left praying about it, as Supposing it to be a thing improbable. And I am now not desirous to remove because of my old age, but would rather go to be with Christ. Nevertheless, the discourse of that matter being revived, it is my duty to pray about it. I therefore set this day apart humbly to cry to God that I may not be sent to England again."[46]

COLMAN, STODDARD, AND THE PRESBYTERIAN MOVEMENT

Despite his years and the aches and pains that went with them, Increase Mather rode horseback through the May woods in 1705 to sit on an ecclesiastical council at Sudbury and reurned home the next evening, a five-hour horseback ride each way.[47] Such assignments on church councils were both more frequent and more difficult than before. The homogeneous character of Puritan society was disappearing. The new colonial charter gave the franchise to anyone with property, and in every town but Boston the unchurched had a say in who would be ordained minister. Something else was happening, too. The ministers increasingly believed they had a special role in society, a role separate from each man's office in a particular church. This tendency among ministers towards a professional understanding of their status had been growing for fifty years. Now, as townsmen began to participate in choosing men for ordination,

Ichabod.

OR

A DISCOURSE,

Shewing what Caufe there is to Fear that the

GLORY

Of the *Lord*, is Departing from

NEW-ENGLAND.

Delivered in Two SERMONS,

By Increafe Mather.

Pfal. 78 60, 61. So that He forfook the Tabernacle of Shiloh; the Tent which be placed among men; And delivered His Strength into Captivity, and his Glory into the Enemies hand.
Ezek. 20. 49, Then faid I. Ah Lord God, they fay of me, Doth he not fpeak Parables?

Bofton, Printed for *N. Boone* at the Sign of the BIBLE. 1729.

Mather's sermons, *Ichabod* of 1702, lamenting the spiritual decline of New England

ministers were beginning to think of ways they could organize as a body to control the process.

In May 1704 twenty-three ministers from all parts of Massachusetts assembled in Boston at their annual convention. Increase Mather was prostrate from a kidney stone and could not be present.[48] Samuel Willard moderated. Those in attendance agreed unanimously to measures designed to increase church membership throughout the colony. Among other things, they hoped all ministers would organize themselves into local associations like the Cambridge Association, which Charles Morton and Cotton Mather had started in 1690. A few months later, the Cambridge Association, Samuel Willard again moderating, sent a circular letter to local associations proposing that they enter into regular correspondence with one another. This time, too, Increase was absent.[49]

The next year Benjamin Colman went further; he proposed the formation of standing councils in which ministers would have an "equal vote" with laymen. Ministers, Colman argued, should not be overruled by the brethren, since ministers "may be modestly supposed to be the superiors in knowledge and grace."[50] His proposal meant that two recommendations would be on the next agenda: one, to form regional associations of ministers; the other, to form a standing council of delegates from those associations.

Five associations of ministers in eastern Massachusetts sent representatives to Boston in September 1705. This time Increase was present. A committee working paper, "Question and Proposals," urged that ministers everywhere form associations to advise (and admonish) their members, examine new candidates for ordination, and help churches choose new ministers.[51] Increase Mather approved these associations. They were, he wrote in 1716, "not only lawful, but absolutely necessary for the Establishment of these churches."[52] The second part of the proposals had been formulated by Colman. He recommended a standing or permanent council consisting of all ministers who belonged to the regional associations and of lay delegates from each of their churches, chosen annually by the lay brethren. In this plan a majority of the ministers would be required to pass any vote, and conversely a majority of the ministers would have veto power in the council. Colman's proposal for greater ministerial power had a frankly Presbyterian flavor.

Mather was flatly opposed. He put his objections in writing, "Answer to the Proposals." The ministers under such an arrangement, he wrote, would "consult, contrive and determine how to make themselves such lords in their churches that no brother should dare to wag his tongue

QUÆSTIONES
PRO MORE SOLITO,
AGITANDÆ,
SUB REVERENDO
D. D. Johanne Leverett,
ACADEMIÆ HARVARDINÆ,
QUÆ EST, NUTU DIVINO,
APUD NOVI ORBIS Cantabrigienses
PRÆSIDE,

In Comitiis Publicis, a Laureæ Magiftralis Candidatis :

Quinto Nonarum Quintilium, M. D C C. X V I I.

AN Concedendo cuivis Chriftiano judicium Difcretionis, privatus fpiritus fiat judex Controverfiarum ?

Negat Refpondens THOMAS FOXCROFT.

An Textus Hebraicus Veteris Teftamenti fit adeo ab omni corruptela immunis, ut fit Norma completa, ad quam omnes verfiones conformari debeant ?
Affirmat Refpondens JONATHAN PIERPONT.

An Terra fit Centrum Univerfi ?
Negat Refpondens SAMUEL THAXTER.

An præter fimplicis intelligentiæ et vifionis, Statuatur in DEO *Scientia quædam Tertia et Media ?*
Negat Refpondens NEHEMIAS HOBART.

An Radii Luminofi fint Corporei ?
Affirmat Refpondens SAMUEL ANDREW.

An Juftitia inhærens, fit caufa formalis fidelium juftificationis coram DEO ?
Negat Refpondens SAMUEL ASPINWALL.

An Ecclefia Invifibilis fit Idea Platonica ?
Negat Refpondens ENOCH COFFIN.

An Sol fit flamma ?
Affirmat Refpondens ADAM CUSHING.

An Virtus confiftat in Mediocritate ?
Affirmat Refpondens JOB CUSHING.

An cuique Animæ humanæ immediate poft mortem fit locus et ftatus proprius a DEO *affignatus, prout bene aut male fe gefferant in præfenti feculo ?* *Affirmat Refpondens* EBENEZER GAY.

An Decretum tollat libertatem ?
Negat Refpondens JOHANNES BROWN.

His Succedit Oratio Gratulatoria.

Harvard College Quaestiones for 1717 graduating class under the presidency of John Leverett

A Prospect of the Colledges in Cambridge in New England

Harvard College, 1726, drawn by William Burgis; colleges from left to right:
New, Stoughton, Massachusetts

against anything." Mather argued that in practice in a standing council
the lay delegates would not have been instructed by their churches on any
particular issue, and so would not be able to represent the laity vis-à-vis
the ministers. Even more objectionable was the veto power the ministers
would hold. It was never the practice, Mather wrote in 1716, "that one
half of the Pastors in Synods should have a Negative on the Whole Council, nor Asserted That Pastors have a greater Authority than Ruling
Elders." It was fundamental to Mather's understanding of the indepen-

dent, Congregational churches that the minister act in a synod only as a delegate and not as an ordained person.[53]

Mather's opposition killed the standing council. The proposal to form regional associations was adopted the next May (1706) by the annual convention of ministers meeting in Boston. The proposal for a standing council was never enacted by statute or practice. Cotton wrote later, "There were some very considerable persons among the ministers as well as of the brethren, who thought the liberties of particular churches to be in danger." Benjamin Colman was more specific: "Under the Doctor's frowns, and the stiffness of some churches, it is come to nothing."[54]

Benjamin Colman, himself enjoying a Presbyterian ordination, had tried to move Massachusetts in that direction and failed. Mather's cousin Solomon Stoddard made more radical Presbyterian proposals. In his book *The Doctrine of Instituted Churches,* which was printed in England and arrived in Massachusetts in 1700, Stoddard argued for a national church, with open communion as a converting ordinance, and church government by ministers and ruling elders at the expense of the brethren. This book brought forth a rebuttal, "Defence of Evangelical Churches," written by Cotton Mather and signed by both the son and his father. Stoddard's reforms were more drastic than Colman's, and if anything, the appearance of Stoddard's book brought Colman and the Mathers a little closer in opposition to the greater enemy.[55] *Instituted Churches* had no lasting effect in New England, and by 1707 even Stoddard had abandoned it.[56] In his new book, *The Inexcusableness of Neglecting the Worship of God* (Boston, 1708), Stoddard abandoned the idea of a national church and retreated to his opinion of 1685 that the sacraments, while not converting ordinances, might help some prepare for God's grace.[57]

Solomon Stoddard, perhaps more than any other figure among New England Puritan leaders, felt imprisoned by a stubbornly conservative society. His church in Northampton had refused before to go along with his plans to use the sacraments as converting ordinances, and towards the end of his life Stoddard was outspoken in his criticism of the ignorance and hard-headedness of the brethren.[58] When he wrote *The Inexcusableness of Neglecting the Worship of God* in 1708, his frustration was evident: "It may possibly be a fault and an aggravation of a fault, to depart from the ways of our Fathers; but it may also be a virtue, and an eminent act of Obedience to depart from them in some things. Men are wont to make a great Noise that we are bringing in Innovations, and depart from the Old Ways."[59]

Increase Mather was happy that his cousin had given up his most radical ideas. Mather defended the traditional way, that is, to keep the Lord's Supper free from all but the truly regenerate, but at the same time he announced his respect for Stoddard as a man of God: "Nothwithstanding his Errors (for so I must account them) in the Controverted Questions, I esteem him a Pious Brother, and an Able Minister of the New Testament, a Serious Practical Preacher, in his Ministry designing the Conversion and Edification of the Souls of men; and as such I do, and shall Love and Honour him: and hope that we shall in the Lord's time, meet where Luther and Zwinglius differ not in their Opinions." [60]

Mather did not make the mistake of confusing his stepbrother's ministry with the catholic spirit at the Brattle Street Church or at Harvard. Superficially, both Stoddard and the latitudinarians were alike in opening the communion table to the unregenerate. But what characterized the latitudinarian position was a softening of piety, a loosening of commitment, an inclination to let hopefulness substitute for certainty. Conviction strong enough to justify forcing others to toe the line was no longer polite in those circles. The men who started Brattle Street Church admired a cool, disengaged, tolerant approach to religion and church worship. Mather's piety had always been hot and passionate, and he recognized in Stoddard the same Puritan quality. Stoddard's maverick behavior came from his passion not from the cooling breezes of reasonableness. That the two men disagreed on points of church discipline was far less important to Mather than their equal commitment to soul saving. In their old age both were increasingly evangelical preachers. Isaac Backus, himself a great Baptist leader and even more stubborn than Mather on the question of admission to the sacrament, concluded: "Neither of them could convince the other, though they were two of the most able ministers in the land." [61]

JOSEPH DUDLEY AND THE CRISIS OF 1707

During the first ten years of Joseph Dudley's governorship the most important political issues in Massachusetts grew out of the new war with France, Queen Anne's war, 1702–1713. The French attack on Deerfield introduced a new set of conditions. Henceforward English captives would be exchanged for French soldiers and sailors captured on the Maine and Nova Scotia coasts, and prisoner exchange became a major issue for both governments. But prisoner exchange was soon entangled with secret efforts on the part of the English to spy out the military defenses of Quebec, and paradoxically to engage at the same time in illegal trade.

When several Englishmen were convicted in 1706 of trading with the enemy, Governor Dudley was implicated in their scheme. The prisoner exchange was completed that autumn, and all but one of the Deerfield prisoners came home, but Dudley remained under suspicion.[62] Several New England merchants petitioned the Queen for his removal. Some merchants in London did the same. Cotton Mather, indiscreet and characteristically voluble, threw himself into the fray by collecting affidavits against Dudley. He sent this material to Sir Henry Ashurst, and it all appeared that summer in an anonymous publication, *A Memorial of the Present Deplorable State of New England* (London, 1707).[63] Late in October 1707, copies of the petitions and Mather's book arrived in Boston.

In an accidental conjunction of events Samuel Willard had died the previous month. For thirty years he and Increase Mather had been the most important ministers in the colony, their churches the most influential. Politics had tended to draw them apart, for Willard had disliked Governor Phips and was allied to Dudley by his sister's marriage to him. But Mather's and Willard's common interests far outweighed their disagreements, and even after Willard had become acting president of Harvard, the two senior men of God lived amicably and their paths crossed frequently. Willard was a year younger than Mather. As Increase led the funeral procession, he felt more alone than ever.[64] Willard's death meant a search for a new college president, and on October 28 the Corporation met to cast its votes: one vote for William Brattle, one for Cotton Mather, three for Increase Mather, and eight for John Leverett.[65] The Corporation vote was dispatched to the General Court, where a final decision would be made. The election of Leverett would mean the triumph of latitudinarian religion at Harvard.

Two issues, the choice of a new president for Harvard and the accusations against Governor Dudley, were now stirred together into the political pot. On November 1, 1707, Dudley confronted his Council with the petition for his removal and without allowing any debate won from the Council a unanimous vote of support. Samuel Sewall was one of those who yielded to Dudley's insistence, and not until later that day was he able to read Cotton Mather's collection of evidence against the governor; he at once began to have second thoughts.[66] Dudley now turned his attention to the House. Gaining its support would be more difficult. On November 20 he made a long speech in which he made much of the Council's unanimous vote. The next day the Representatives voted nevertheless not to concur with the Council. At this, in the Council, tempers flared, Cotton Mather was blamed for the Governor's troubles and men shouted that Mather's book ought to be burned in public.[67] Sewall, how-ever, changed sides and marching up to the governor, told him so: "Skrewing the Strings of your Lute to that height," he told Dudley, "has broken one of them; and I find myself under a Necessity of withdrawing my Vote."[68]

During these same weeks campaigning began for the college presi-dency. John Leverett's allies circulated a letter in favor of his nomination and collected thirty-nine signatures from ministers across the colony, many of them old students of Leverett's.[69] Cotton Mather started his own letter-writing campaign to persuade members of the House of Represen-tatives to vote against Leverett.[70] On November 28 the General Court divided, the Council voting to approve Leverett, the House against him.[71] Twice in one month the House of Representatives had rebuffed Governor Dudley, and each time Cotton Mather was at the heart of its action. This time Dudley found the key to his problem. He proposed to reinstate the Harvard charter of 1650. The House had always been senti-mental about the old days, and the appeal of putting the college back under its earlier form of government proved too much for them. On De-cember 6 the House reversed itself and concurred with the Council on the choice of John Leverett for president of Harvard. Dudley's political fortunes began to mend from that time. He was able to fend off the hos-tile petition for removal, and in the spring the Privy Council in London dismissed all charges against him as "frivolous."[72]

On January 14, 1708, Governor Dudley installed John Leverett at Cambridge. The road from Boston was dotted with carriages. Others went by sleigh across the ice on the Charles River. The ceremonies began upstairs in the great library so dear to Increase Mather, with Dudley im-plementing the old charter of 1650 by reducing the number of corpora-tion members to seven, as it had specified. Then the ceremonies moved downstairs into the great hall, where Dudley, his back to a "noble fire," bestowed on John Leverett the symbols of office: College Records, Char-ter, Seal, and Keys. Then came short speeches in Latin, prayers, singing of a psalm, and a fine dinner laid out on several tables. Neither Increase nor Cotton was there. Several others were also conspicuous by their ab-sence: James Allen and Thomas Bridge, ministers at the First Church, Major General Wait Still Winthrop, Colonel Elisha Hutchinson, and others who sided with the Mathers.[73]

The Mathers, father and son, were bitter over what had happened. They blamed Dudley most of all. The hurt over losing the college was too sharp to bury, and they decided that they must at least confront Dudley openly. A week after the ceremonies, on January 20, 1708, each wrote a letter to the governor. For the older man it was a difficult letter to write, one touched with bitterness and the memory of a long relationship. He recalled how he had long ago considered asking Dudley to be his assistant at the North Church, and how in those days Dudley had treated Increase as his spiritual father. Assuming that role now, Increase rehearsed succinctly the public outcry against Dudley's conduct of the governorship: accusations of bribery, conspiracies to undermine the charter in Whitehall, his failure to seek a royal charter for Harvard, his role in the 1691 trial and execution of Jacob Leisler and Jacob Milborne, his habit of spending Sunday afternoon with Anglicans rather than with his church in Roxbury. "I am under pressure of conscience," Increase wrote, "to bear public testimony without respect of persons." He would live with a clear conscience that at least the governor knew how his old friend and sometime spiritual advisor felt. There would be no room for misunderstanding between them.[74] Oddly, Mather made no mention of John Leverett, but, in regard to the college, only Dudley's failure to pursue a royal charter.

Cotton wrote, too, dating his letter the same day as his father's, and like his father he studiously avoided any mention of Leverett. Where Increase had been blunt and direct, the son was elaborate, mannered, circuitous, and allusive. His relationship with Dudley had never had the intimacy of his father's. Cotton expounded in six pages what his father had written in two.[75]

Dudley responded with one letter to both, giving as good as he got, charging them with being "insufferably rude towards one whom divine Providence has honoured with the character of your Governour." At the end Dudley alluded to the real reason for the Mathers' break: the appointment of Leverett to Harvard's presidency. "I desire you will keep your station, and let fifty or sixty good ministers, your equals in the province, have a share in the government of the college, and advise thereabouts as well as yourselves and I hope all will be well.

"I am an honest man, and have lived religiously these forty years to the satisfaction of the ministers in New England," Dudley went on. "Your wrath against me is cruel, and will not be justified. But now . . . the college must be disposed against the opinion of all the ministers in New England, except yourselves, or the Governour torn in pieces. This is the view I have of your inclination."[76]

This exchange of letters describes as well as anything the arrival of a new political culture in eastern Massachusetts. Just as John Leverett, grandson of one of Massachusetts's fiercest Puritan governors, established the latitudinarian spirit at Harvard College, so did Joseph Dudley, also son of an early Puritan governor, establish eighteenth-century English political culture at Boston. Cotton Mather's letter makes it plain that the bribery which characterized the machinery of English government at London was foreign and shocking to the Puritan tradition. It was, nevertheless, there to stay. Although Increase and Cotton Mather continued to lead prominent lives in Boston, much admired and listened to, after 1708 two institutions, the provincial government and the college, were beyond their reach.

PUBLISHED SERMONS, 1703–1712

With that letter to the governor Increase Mather ended twenty years of direct involvement in provincial politics. It had been an exhilarating and sometimes dismaying experience. The letter to Dudley was a bittersweet ending. If it meant his resignation from political life, it also meant he could turn once more to his ministry and his study, where he had always found the greatest consolation. The tenor and content of Mather's sermons had changed over the years. Most obvious now was a simple evangelism based on Christ. He urged that belief in Christ was the one, single recipe for salvation. "Is it not a marvellous thing," he wrote, "that any man should undertake to give an answer to that most serious question [What shall we do to be saved?], and forget Apostle Paul's Answer, 'Believe on the Lord Jesus Christ and thou shalt be Saved.'"[77] Simultaneously with this shift of emphasis he spoke less often to a corporate audience, a New England Israel. Instead he addressed himself to single souls whom he hoped to bring to God.

Mather continued to use the old, plain style and defended it against the more felicitous prose styles wafting across from England. "I have observed," he wrote in 1703, "that Plain, Practical Sermons, the design whereof is to promote conversion and Holiness, do the greatest Good."[78] On a companion theme he wrote the next year that "Books which have done the greatest good, have not been Learned, and Elaborate, but Plain, Practical Discourses."[79] Over and over again during these years Mather returned to that theme of simplicity. "The Plain Scriptural Sermon" was the tool God uses to convert sinners. He eschewed wit and elegance: "The Reader will not find any Studied Fine Phrases, nor a Gingling with Latin, Greek, and Hebrew Sentences. . . . So much Latin is so much Flesh in a Sermon."[80]

The three sermons published together in 1710 under the title *Awakening Truths Tending to Conversion* illustrate Mather's plain style and diction. Towards the close of the second sermon, when Mather called upon sinners to pray to save themselves, he told the story of Jonah:

"As Jonah's Mariners when they were in extreme danger of being cast away in a Storm at Sea, how they did Pray and Cry to God! *We beseech thee, O Lord, we beseech thee, let us not Perish.* And when Jonah was a sleep, they waked him, saying, *What meanest thou, O Sleeper, arise, call upon thy God, if so be God will think upon us that we perish not.* Thou unconverted Sinner art like to perish in a Storm of Divine Vengeance, thy Soul is like to be lost in a Sea of Wrath, and wilt thou not Cry to God to Convert & Save thee." [81]

These simply told stories were a stock in trade. As he always had, Mather often used direct discourse in recounting them. Consider this tale from the last sermon in this collection:

A famous Writer speaks of one, that when he was in danger of being devoured by a wild Beast, Cried out for help; 'O come and help me,' (said he). 'I am yet alive! I am yet alive!' So go Cry to God, and say, Lord, Come and save me, 'I am yet alive; my Body is on this side of the Grave, & my Soul on this side of Hell; I know the Lord can, and I hope and pray that he will Save me.' [82]

Such language now sounded old-fashioned to many ears in Boston. In 1707 Benjamin Colman published two sermons which set new standards for elegance and politeness, *The Government and Improvement of Mirth* and *A Practical Discourse upon the Parable of the Ten Virgins.* Typical adjectives in Colman's vocabulary were serene, gradual, moderate, tolerable, tolerant, irenic, conciliatory, discreet, humane, affable, courteous, obliging, free, open, sincere, and graceful. Form as well as rhetoric was changing. Colman thought the old-fashioned sermon artificial, "as we in Sermons first propose a doctrine, and then explain its forms and then produce arguments for its proof." [83] With sentences such as these, "There's not necessity of being Immodest or Profane, Idle and Impertinent, in order to be Merry," and religion need not be "*dull and heavy, sad and disconsolate, sour and morose.* Not only does Religion *Allow,* but it obliges unto cheerfulness with Sobriety," Colman's *The Government and Improvement of Mirth* would have been puzzling if not outrageous to earlier Puritans. [84]

More than style was at stake. The integration of the pagan philosophy of Greece and Rome with traditional Judaeo-Christian religion was gaining in England and France, and now in Boston too. [85] After 1700 Mather often belittled this trend. We have lately seen, he wrote, "many Small Books pretending to promote Devotion and Religion. But there is little of the Spirit of the *Gospel* or of Real *Christianity* to be found in some of them. Only such *Morality* as taught by *Socrates, Plato, Aristotle, Epictetus, Plutarch, Cicero, Seneca,* and other Gentiles, who *knew not the only true God. . . ."*[86]

One cannot observe Increase Mather railing against Latin and Greek tags and elaborate, witty sentences without remembering that the writer who stood above all others in this regard was his own son. What did Increase think of Cotton's rococo style? His overweening use of Latin and Greek quotation? His puns, alliterations, neologisms, and allusions? And what did the son think of the father's condemnation of it all?

Mather emphasized, in addition to a simple dependence on Christ and an insistence on plain, scriptural sermons, the approaching millennium. His *Dissertation Concerning the Future Conversion of the Jewish Nation,* written before 1695 and lost at sea, was printed at last in London in 1709. In this small, forty-page essay Mather insisted, against the English Baxter and Lightfoot, that the millennium was still ahead. However unfashionable in the new century, he continued to preach the chiliad.[87] In 1707 and every year afterwards Mather returned to the subject in sermons which either insisted on the near approach of the millennium or explored in detail again the life of the saints to come.[88]

Perry Miller considered one of these, *A Discourse Concerning Faith and Fervency in Prayer,* "the finest of his Chiliastic hymns."[89] In language rising to pitches of ecstasy Mather promised his listeners and then his readers "that before the consummation of all things, the World will be in an happier State than ever yet it has been since mans Apostacy from God."[90] "When this Kingdom of our Lord Jesus Christ shall come and prevail over the World, *There will be Peace and Tranquility throughout the Earth.* Psal. 72.7 . . . Not only Peace, but *abundance of Peace.* Such happy tranquility as the like was never yet known in the World. One of Christs glorious Titles is, *The Prince of Peace,* Isai. 9.6."[91] *A Discourse Concerning Faith and Fervency in Prayer,* a volume of about one hundred pages, was a publishing enterprise of at least five Boston booksellers, each of whom had a separate title page printed for it. It was printed also in London in 1713 and again in Ireland in 1820.[92]

It was fashionable at the turn of the century to write devotional manuals which spiritualized everyday occurrences as aids to private devotions. Cotton was particularly adept at it. Increase did not write manuals as such, but between 1704 and 1712 at least seven of his volumes of published sermons contained guides for spiritualizing nature, for example, *The Voice of God in Stormy Winds* (1704) or *Seasonable Meditations*

both for Winter and Summer (1712).[93] Nature's more dramatic events, however, continued for Increase Mather to be what they had always been,
certain signals from God, the meaning of which was left for man to interpret. When Boston shook with an earthquake in 1705, he returned to
his old theme, and now there was a hint of irritation towards a younger
generation whose understanding of the natural world failed to incorpo-
rate the old providential world view. "There never happens an Earthquake but God speaks to men on the Earth by it: And they are very
stupid if they do not hear His Voice therein."[94]

COSMOPOLITAN BOSTON IN THE EIGHTEENTH CENTURY

Perhaps one reason why Increase Mather no longer wanted to return to
England was that Boston grew more like London with every passing
year. The great dynamic for change was war, war between England and
France, in 1689–1696 and 1702–1713. Unlike King Philip's War,
these were worldwide wars for empire into which both England and
France threw their national resources of treasure and armies. In America
most of the fighting was over the Sugar Islands of the Caribbean. Though
of lesser strategic importance, the forest frontier between northern New
England and Canada, and the seacoasts from northeast of Boston to the
shores of the St. Lawrence were the scenes of sporadic and sometimes
desperate fighting. The impact of European armies on Puritan New England was devastating. Frontier towns took the brunt of the punishment. The result was a profound disruption of community life. The
grim realities of war, smoking ruins, burned barns, killed livestock, and
the dead and maimed were constant fears from the coast to the Connecticut River Valley. Whole villages were abandoned, the eastern frontier
collapsed towards Boston, crops went unattended, the birth rate dropped.
A general economic depression settled on the eastern region. Mather
noted in his diary that families there had taken to eating horsemeat.[95]

Boston was transformed into a great port serving as the northern base of
English sea power. Starting in 1696, when Admiral Sir Francis Wheeler
brought his fleet north from the West Indies, Boston was seldom free
from the effects of the navy. The last arrival was in the early summer of
1711, when an armada arrived for the conquest of Quebec and the invasion of Canada. Another British admiral, Sir Hovenden Walker, had
sixty ships under his command. The transports carried five thousand soldiers, more than the adult population of Boston. The inner harbor, between Boston's wharves and Bird Island, was jammed with warships.

The Names of the STREETS, Lanes & Alleys,

Within the Town of *Boston* in *New-England*.

At a Meeting of the Free-holders and other Inhabitants of the Town of Boston, *duely Qualified & Warned according to Law, being Convened at the Town-house, the 22d. day of* September, Anno Domini. 1701.

Voted, That the Select-men of this Town are impowered to Assign & Fix Names, unto the several Streets and Lanes within this Town, as they shall judge meet & convenient.

At a Meeting of the Select-men of the Town of Boston, *the 3d. day of* May, Anno Domini, 1708.

Ordered, That the Streets, Lanes and Alleys, of this Town, as they are now (by the said Select-men) Named and Bounded, be accordingly recorded in the Town Book, and are as followeth, *viz.*

1. THE broad Street or Way from the Old Fortification on the Neck, leading into the Town as far as the late Deacon *Eliot*'s corner. **Orange Street.**

2. The Way below the late Deacon *Eliot's* Barn, leading from Orange Street Easterly by the Sea Side. **Beech Street.**

3. The Way leading Easterly from the said Deacon *Eliot's* corner, passing by the late Deacon *Allens*, extending to Wind-mill point. **Essex Street.**

4. The Way leading from the late Elder *Ransfords* corner in Essex Street, extending Southerly into Beech Street, and so down to the Sea. **Ransfords Lane.**

5. The Way leading from the late Capt. *Frayes* corner Westerly, to the bottom of the Common, with the return Southerly down to the Sea. **Frogg Lane.**

6. The Street from the corner of the House now in the Tenure of Capt. *Turfrey*, nigh Deacon *Eliots* corner, leading Northerly as far as Dr. *Oakes*'s corner. **Newbury Street.**

7. The New Alley between Mr. *Blyns & Durants* in Newbury Street, leading Westerly into the Common. **Hogg Alley.**

8. The Street leading Easterly from *Wheelers* corner in Newbury Street, passing by the Towns Watering place, as far as Capt. *Dyers* Barn. **Pond Street.**

9. The Way leading from *John Ushers* Esq. his Barn Southerly into Essex Street. **Short Street.**

10. The Way leading from the lower end of Pond-street, North-Easterly into Church Green, by Summer Street. **Blind Lane.**

11. The Way from *Cowels* corner in Newbury Street, leading Westerly into the Common. **West Street.**

12. The Way from *Ellise's* corner nigh the upper end of Summer Street, leading Westerly into the Common **Winter Street.**

13. The Street leading Easterly from Dr. *Oake's* corner in Newbury Street, passing by the House of Capt. *Timothy Clark*, extending to the Sea. **Summer Street.**

14. The Street from *Baxters* corner in Summer Street, leading Southerly by the late Deacon *Allens*, extending down to the Sea. **South Street.**

15. The Way from *Bulls* corner at the lower end of Summer Street, leading Southerly to Windmill point. **Sea Street.**

16. The Street leading from *Penemans* corner at the upper end of Summer Street, passing by the South Meeting-house, to Mr. *Haugh's* corner. **Malborough Street.**

17. The Way leading from *Brisco's* corner in Marlborough Street passing by Justice *Bromfields* into the Common **Rawsons Lane**

18. The Way leading from the South Meeting-house, passing by Mr. *Borlands*, and so down to the Sea by *Mr Halaways*. **Milk Street.**

19. The Alley leading Southerly from *Southers* corner in Milk Street, to Capt. *Clarks* corner in Summer Street **Bishops Alley.**

20. The Lane leading South-Easterly from Mr. *Borland's* corner in Milk-Street to *Beards* corner in Cow Lane. **Long Lane.**

21. The Street where Mr. *Daniel Oliver* dwells, passing from Milk-Street up to Fort-Hill **Oliver Street.**

22. The Way leading Southerly from Fort-Hill to *Mercy's* corner in Summer Street. **Cow Lane.**

23. The Way from the lower end of Summer Street, leading North-Easterly by the Sea Side, with the return up to the Rope Walk. **Flownder Lane.**

24. The Alley by *Whartons* house in Cow-lane, leading Easterly into *Harrisons* Rope Walk. **Crooked Alley.**

25. The Way from *John Roberts*'s house in Cow Lane, leading Easterly by Capt *Bonners*, into the Rope walk. **Gridley's Lane.**

26. The Way from the upper end of Cow Lane on Fort Hill leading Easterly, passing by *Mr. Joseph Hubberts* down to the Sea. **Gibbs's Lane.**

27. The Way leading from the Northerly Side of Fort Hill passing down Easterly by the Old Brew-house into Battery March. **Sconce Lane.**

28. The Way leading from *Hallaway's* corner by the end of Milk Street, passing by the Battery, extending to the lower end of *Gibbs*'s Lane. **Battery March.**

29. The Way leading Southerly from *Gibbs's* Lane on Fort Hill, passing by *Drinkers* to the Rope-walk. **Belchers Lane.**

30. The Way from Mr. *Haugh's* corner, leading Northwesterly by the Latin School, extending as far as Mrs. *Whetcombs* corner. **School Street.**

31. The Way leading from Mrs. *Whetcombs* corner westerly through the upper side of the Common, and so down to the Sea. **Beacon Street.**

32. The Way leading from Beacon Street, on the upper side of the Common unto Mr. *Allens* Orchard. **Davies Lane.**

33. The Way leading from Beacon Street, between Capt *Alfords* and Madam *Shrimptons* Pasture, up to Centry Hill **Centry Street.**

34. The Street from the lower end of School Street, leading Northerly as far as Mr. *Clarks* the Pewterers Shop. **Corn-Hill.**

35. The Way leading from a Tenement of Capt. *Clark's* nigh the lower end of School Street, to Mrs. *Winslows* corner in *Joyliffs* lane. **Spring Lane.**

36. The Street leading from *Cox* the Butchers Shop in Corn-hill, passing by Major *Walleys*, as far as the corner of *Mr. Olivers Brick Ware-house*. **Water Street.**

37. The Alley leading from the end of Water-Street, through Mr. *Olivers* Land by *Odell's* into Milk Street. **Coopers Alley.**

38. The Way leading from Water Street, passing between Major *Walley*'s and Mr. *Bridghams* Lands into Milk Street. **Tanners Lane.**

39. The Lane passing from Water Street into Milk Street, according to the Name by which it hath been formerly known. **Joyliffs Lane.**

40. The Way passing Round the Old Meeting-House. **Church Square.**

41. The Way leading from Corn Hill, including the Wayes on each side of the Town House, extending Easterly to the Sea. **King Street.**

42. The Street leading from Mr. *Derings* corner in Corn Hill to *Houchen's* corner at the upper end of Hanover Street. **Queen Street.**

43. The Way leading from the Mansion House of the late *Simon Lynde* Esq. by Capt. *Southacks*, extending as far as Col. *Townsends* corner. **Trea Mount Street.**

44. The Way leading from *Melyen*'s corner near Col. *Townsends*, passing through the Common along by Mr. *Sheafs* into Frog Lane. **Common Street.**

45. The Alley leading Easterly from the Common, on the North side of Madam *Ushers* House. **Turn again Alley.**

46. The Way leading from the Exchange in King Street, passing by Mrs. *Phillips*'s into Water Street. **Pudding Lane.**

47. The Way leading from King Street, by the House of *Isaac Addington* Esq. with the Return into Pudding Lane. **Half-square Court.**

48. The Way leading from Mr. *Mackarty*'s corner in King Street to Elder *Bridghams* Ware-House in Water street. **Leveretts Lane.**

49. The way leading from Justice *Dummers* corner in King-street, passing over the Bridge as far as Mrs. *Dafforns* corner in Milk-street. **Mackeril Lane.**

50. The way leading from the House formerly the Castle-Tavern in Mackeril-lane, passing by Mr. *Halaways* wharffe to the Sea. **Crabb Lane.**

51. The way leading from the Sign of the Orange Tree, passing by Mr. *Stephen Minots* to the Mill Pond, and from thence to the lower end of Cold-lane **Sudbury Street.**

52. The way leading from *Emmons's* corner passing by Justice *Lynde*'s Pasture, extending from thence westerly to the Sea. **Cambridge Street.**

53. The way passing on the Northerly side of Livery-stable, in Justice *Lynds*'s Pasture, to Mr. *Allens* Farm-house. **Green Lane.**

54. The way from Mr. *Pownings* corner by Dock-square, leading *Southerly* into King-street. **Crooked Lane.**

55. The square from the House of *Eliakim Hutchinsons* Esq. to Mr. *Pembertons* corner on the one side, and from *Kenny*'s Shop to Mr. *Meers*'s corner on the other side. **Dock Square.**

56. The way leading from Major *Savage*'s corner in Dock-square, to Madam *Shrimptons* corner in King-street. **Shrimptons Lane**

57. The way leading from Mr *Meers*'s corner along by the side of the Dock, as far as the corner of the Ware-House, formerly Major *Davis*'s. **Corn Market.**

58. The Alley leading from Mr. *Mountforts* in Corn Market, to Capt. *Fitch*'s corner in King-street. **Pierses Alley.**

59. The way leading from Justice *Palmers* Ware-House in Corn-market, up to *Mr. Moorcocks* buildings. **Corn Court.**

60. The way leading from Mrs. *Butlers* corner, at the lower end of King-street, to the Swinging Bridge, & from thence to the lower end of *Woodmansies* Wharffe. **Merchants Row.**

61. The way leading from *Platts*'s corner, passing Northwesterly by the Sign of the Dragon to the Mill Pond. **Union Street.**

62. The Street from between *Houchens*'s corner and the Sign of the Orange Tree, leading Northerly to the Mill Bridge. **Hanover Street.**

63. The way leading from Mr. *Pembertons* corner at the end of Dock-square, to Justice *Lyde's* corner in Hanover-street. **Wings Lane.**

64. The way leading from *Wings* Lane to Mr. *Colmans* Church, and from thence the two ways, *viz. Southerly* to Queen-street, and *Easterly* to Dock-square. **Brattle Street.**

65. The new way leading from Mr. *Pollords* corner in *Brattle*-street, thro' Mr. *Belknaps* Yard into Queen-street **Hilliers Lane.**

66. The way leading Northwesterly from Mr. *Harris*'s corner in Hanover-street, down to the Mill Pond. **Cold Lane.**

67. The way leading from Capt. *Ballantines* corner nigh the Mill-bridge, to the corner of Capt. *Fitches* Tenement in Union Street. **Marshalls Lane.**

68. The way leading from *Brooks's* corner in Marshalls Lane, passing by Mr. *Bulfinches*, to Scottows Alley. **Creek Lane.**

69. The way leading from Creek Lane to Capt. *Lows* corner, in Union Street. **Salt Lane.**

70. The way leading from Creek Lane, to Mr. *Webbs* corner in Union *Street*. **Marsh Lane.**

71. The way leading from the sign of the *Star* in Hanover Street passing Northerly behind Capt. *Evertons* house **Link Ally.**

72. the way from the Conduit in Union Street, leading Northerly over the Bridge to *Ellikons* corner, at the lower end of Cross Street. **Anne Street.**

73. The way from Mr. *Antrams* corner nigh the Conduit, leading North-easterly by the side of the Dock, as far as Mr. *Winsors* Ware-house. **Fish Market.**

74. The New way from Union Street, passing Southwesterly between the buildings of the late Capt. *Christopher Clark* deceased. **Minots Court.**

75. The Alley by Capt. *Abijah Savages* in Anne Street, leading Northwesterly to Creek Lane. **Scottows Alley.**

76. The way between Capt. *Winsors* and Mrs. *Pembertons*, in Anne Street, leading to the Wharfes by the *Swinging* Bridge. **Swingbridge Lane.**

77. The Street from Mount-joys corner at the lower end of Cross Street, leading Northerly to the *Sign* of the *Swan* by Scarlets Wharfe. **Fish Street.**

78. The way leading Northwesterly from Mr. *Thomas's* corner in Anne Street. **Paddeys Alley.**

79. The Street leading from the Mill Bridge Northerly, as far as Mr. *Jonas Clarks* corner at the end of *Bennet Street*. **Middle Street.**

80. The way leading Northerly from *Stanburys* corner nigh the Mill Bridge, as far as Mr. *Gees* corner in Prince-street. **Back Street**

81. The way leading from the Mill Pond *South-Easterly*, by the late Deacon *Phillips*'s Stone-house, extending down to the *Sea*. **Cross Street.**

82. The way from the *North-westerly* end of *Cross Street* passing by *Verings* house *Northerly* nigh the Mill Pond. **Old Way.**

83. The Lane leading from *Middle Street*, passing by the House of the late Capt. *Timothy Prout*, into *Fish Street*, and so down to the Sea. **Wood Lane.**

84. The way from *Wales*'s corner in *Middle Street*, leading North-westerly into Back-street. **Beer Lane.**

85. The Alley leading from *Anne Street*, between the late Capt. *Lakes* and *Nanneys* buildings, to Mr. *Indecotts* shop in Cross-street. **Elbow Alley.**

86. The Alley leading from *Fish Street* between the Lands of *John Clark* Esq and the successors of Mr. *Samuel Gallop* Deceased, into Middle-street. **Gallops Alley.**

87. The *Street* leading Northwesterly from *Marvels* corner in Middle-street, passing by the House formerly the sign of the Black Horse, extending to the *Sea* at Ferry-way **Prince Street**

88. The *Street* leading Northerly from the end of *Bennet Street*, nigh Mr. *Jonas Clarks*, extending to the Sea. **North Street.**

89. The Street leading *South-Easterly* from *Williams's* corner, nigh Mr. *Jonas Clarks* down to the Sea, by *Scarletts Wharffe*. **Fleet Street.**

90 The Alley leading *North-Westerly* from the North Meeting-House into Middle-street. **Bell Alley**

91. The Square lying on the Southerly side of the North-Meeting-House, including the ways on each side of the Watch-House. **Clarks Square.**

92. The Way leading South Easterly from the North Meeting-House into Fish Street. **Sun Court.**

93. The Way leading from the North-Meeting-House Northerly by Capt. *Tho. Barnards* into Fleet Street. **Moon Street.**

94. The Way leading Northerly from Mrs. *Winsleys* corner between Col. *Foster's* and Mr. *Frizzel's* into Fleet Street. **Garden Court.**

95. The Street leading Northerly from *Mr. Everton's* corner, nigh *Scarlet's Wharfe*, to the North Battery. **Ship Street.**

96. The Way leading North-Westerly from the North-Battery, to the Ferry way by *Hudson's* Point. **Lyn Street.**

97. The Way leading Westerly along the shore from *Hudson's* Point to the Mill Stream by Mr. *Gee's* Ship yard. **Ferry Way.**

98. The Street leading North-Westerly, from Mrs. *Ransford's* Corner in North Street towards the Ferry Point at *Charles Town*. **Charter Street.**

99. The Way leading from *Carwithys* Corner in Prince Street, to Mr. *Phips*'s Corner in Charter Street. **Salem Street.**

100. The Way leading Northerly from *Travis's* Corner in Prince Street, to the end of Ferry-way by *Hudsons's* Point. **Snow Hill.**

101. The Way leading South Easterly from Snow Hill to Salem Street. **Hull Street.**

102. The Way leading North-westerly from Mr. *Jonas Clarks* Corner to Salem Street. **Bennet Street.**

103. The Way leading N. westerly from Capt. *Stevens's* Corner in N. Street, with the return into Bennet Street. **Love Street.**

104. The Alley leading from the Burying place in Charter Street to *Adkins*'s Lime Kiln in Lyn Street. **Lime Alley.**

105. The Alley leading from Charter-street down by *Benj. Williams*'s in Lyn-street. **Sliding Alley.**

106. The Way leading from Charter-street down by Mrs. *Buckley*'s into Lyn-street. **Henchmans Lane.**

107. The Alley Leading from Charter-street down through Mr. *Greenoughs* Ship Yard into Lyn-street **Greenoughs Alley**

108. The Alley leading from North street down by the Salutation into Ship-street. **Salutation Alley.**

109. The Alley leading from North-street along by *Mr. Will. Parkmans* into Ship-street near the North Battery. **Battery Alley.**

110. The Alley leading from North-street down to Capt. *Richards*'s corner in Ship-street. **White Bread Alley.**

BOSTON: Printed by *Bartholomew Green*, in Newbury Street: Sold by the Booksellers. 1708. *Price 3d.*

Courtesy, Massachusetts Historical Society

1708 broadside naming and bounding the streets, lanes, and alleys of Boston to be recorded in the Town Book

Samuel Sewall, merchant, bookseller, and judge. Oil painting by John Smibert

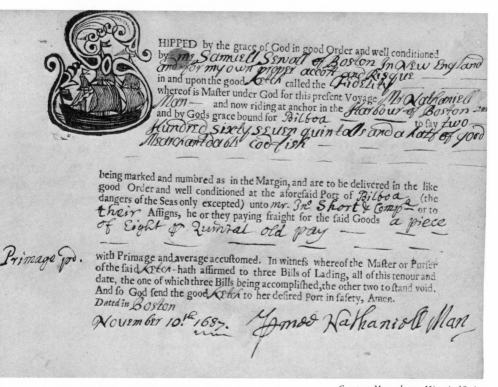

SHIPPED by the grace of God in good Order and well conditioned by *ms Samuell Sewall of Boston In New England and for my own proper accott and Risque* in and upon the good *Ketch* called the *Fidelity* whereof is Master under God for this present Voyage *Mr Nathaniell Man* and now riding at anchor in the *Harbour of Boston* and by Gods grace bound for *Bilboa to say two hundred sixty seven quintalls and a half of good Merchantdable codfish*

being marked and numbred as in the Margin, and are to be delivered in the like good Order and well conditioned at the aforesaid Port of *Bilboa* (the dangers of the Seas only excepted) unto *mr. Jno Short & Compa* or to *their* Assigns, he or they paying fraight for the said Goods *a piece of Eight ℈ Quintal old pay*

Primage God. with Primage and average accustomed. In witness whereof the Master or Purser of the said *Ketch* hath affirmed to three Bills of Lading, all of this tenour and date, the one of which three Bills being accomplished, the other two to stand void. And so God send the good *Ketch* to her desired Port in safety, Amen. Dated in *Boston* November 10.th 1687.   *James Nathaniell Man*

Samuel Sewall's shipping manifest of November, 1687, recording a load of codfish bound for Bilbao aboard the ketch, "Fidelity"

Merchantmen and coasters had to thread their way through to discharge at the wharves. Most of the fleet anchored in the outer harbor, east of Castle Island. A tent city went up on Noddle Island, where troops were quartered ashore, and small boats busily plied back and forth across the bay.[96]

These fleets destroyed old, Puritan Boston once and for all. Officers of the army and navy strained the town's meagre resources for entertainment and society, bringing with them gold braid, brilliant uniforms, and all the arrogance and mannerisms of Europe's military caste. Joseph Dudley, who held the rank of colonel, encouraged pomp and protocol. Sewall remembered finding Lieutenant Governor William Stoughton stripped to the waist, mowing his own hayfield. Not so Dudley. Sewall recorded Dudley's arrival on April 25, St. George's Day, 1706. "Govr. comes to

Old Feather Store in Dock Square built in 1680, from oil painting of 1820

Town guarded by the Troops with their Swords drawn; dines at the (Green) Dragon, from thence proceeds to the Townhouse, Illuminations at night. Capt. Pelham tells me several wore crosses in their Hats; which makes me resolve to stay at home." [97] That same St. George's day some wag fixed a cross to a dog's head and turned him loose in the streets. A drunken boatswain from the fleet struck at the dog, then went into the shop and knocked down an innocent bystander. Sewall noted laconically "pretty much blood was shed by means of this bloody Cross, and the poor Dog a sufferer." [98]

With the military officers came behavior that was loud, boisterous, uninhibited, swashbuckling, often sacrilegious, drinking and swaggering about town. Lower ranks and common sailors and soldiers also brought their own culture into the city, like their superiors creating a demand for places of public entertainment. In 1691 Boston had thirty-two taverns, alehouses, and grog shops; in 1710 there were eighty-one. Cases of adultery and bastardy steadily increased. Prostitution became common and by 1710 bawdy houses were a regular business. In the same

King's Head Tavern, corner of Fleet and North streets, near Scarlet's Wharf and several blocks from Old North Church

years a wave of petty crime hit the city with many episodes of shoplifting, housebreaking, and theft. Silver, silks, and fine linens were most often stolen. Without much evidence some accused the increasing numbers of country peddlers of fencing the stolen goods. Boston seemed to have acquired many aspects of a metropolis.[99]

The arrival of a fleet and troops created an instant if irregular market demand for provisions. Shortages occurred. Boston had become the entrepôt for the entire New England coast. From it now radiated cart roads in all directions, where before only rough tracks and forest trails existed. The New England economy was being integrated into the North Atlantic economy. A harvest failure in Europe in 1711 increased the demand for flour exports from Boston. Bread riots protested the export of grain and flour, leading to a boost in local prices. A mob cut away the rudder of a ship laden with grain to keep it from leaving the harbor. Dudley was forced against his will to place an embargo on food exports.[100]

The rich became richer and the poor poorer. In sharp contrast to

Advertifement.

THefe are to give Notice to all Perfons where thefe Papers
fhall come; that a Servant Man belonging to *Hannah Bof-*
worth of *Hull*; Whofe Name is *Matthew Jones*: He is a *Tay-*
lor by Trade, a Man of a middle ftature, and pretty flender, a-
bout *twenty fix* years of age, in good Apparel, a grey Cafter Hat
with a Clafp on it, a *Periwig of bright brown Hair*, in a clofe Coat
& Breeches of a *brownifh colour*, cloth Serge: Wolfted Stockins,
and French Falls or Wooden heel'd Shoes: Ran away from his
Miftrifs the 22d. of *February* 1682. If any Perfon will fecure this
Runaway he fhall be well fatisfied for his pains; and whofoever
fhall bring him to *George Elifton* Shop keeper in *Bofton* fhall
have forty fhillings in Money. There was a tall young man a
Bellows-maker that worked in *Bofton* in company with this *Taylor*,
his Name is *Benjamin Smeed*.

March 6. 1683. /4

Courtesy, Massachusetts Historical Society

1683 notice offering 40 shillings for finding runaway slave, a tailor named
Matthew Jones, Boston. Blacks were replacing Indians as household servants by
the eighteenth century.

the economic depression on the frontier, Boston experienced a steady
new construction. After 1700 most of the city streets that had been dirt
lanes in the 1660s and 1670s were now paved with cobblestones, with
drainage channels of paving stones laid down the center. The first underground drain was built in 1704, financed by the families in the neigh-
borhood it served. In 1700, the largest buildings were the churches, all
still constructed of clapboards, but more and more wealthy merchants
were building two- and three-story brick houses. Merchants, increasingly prosperous from a world at war, put up luxurious homes. [101]

The North End around Mather's church became the center of this
building boom. In 1711 William Clark bought open land in front of
Increase Mather's church and built what was then the most opulent of
Boston homes, a three-story brick dwelling with twenty-six rooms. On

John Bonner's map of Boston, printed in 1722 and sold at the Town House "where may be had all sorts of Prints, Maps &c"

Courtesy, New York Public Library

Boston's North End, 1722, detail from John Bonner's map. Old North Church, Increase Mather's church, (B), built in 1650 and rebuilt after the fire in 1676, is in Clarke's Square; New North (H), built in

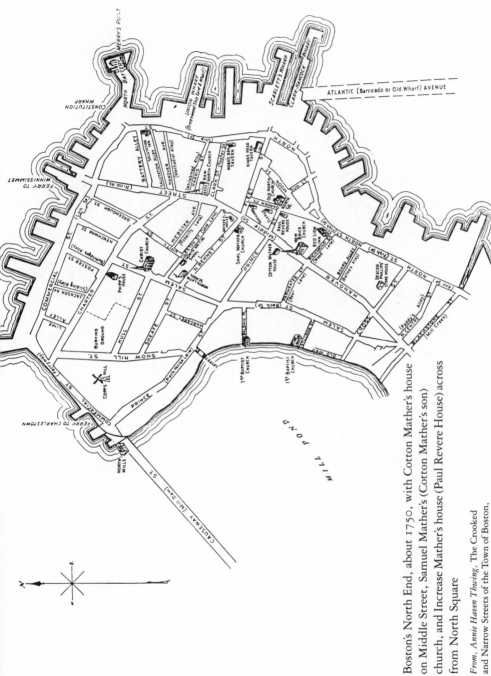

Boston's North End, about 1750, with Cotton Mather's house on Middle Street, Samuel Mather's (Cotton Mather's son church, and Increase Mather's house (Paul Revere House) across from North Square

From, Annie Haven Thwing, The Crooked and Narrow Streets of the Town of Boston, 1630–1822, *Boston, 1925*

Increase Mather's house (Paul Revere House), built after fire of 1676, as it was in the nineteenth century when it was a Scandinavian boarding house

Mather's other side lived Col. Thomas Hutchinson. Mather had married Hutchinson and Sarah Foster in 1703 in what Samuel Sewall called "a very great wedding." Here was born in 1711 Thomas Hutchinson, who would be governor of Massachusetts during the Stamp Act Crisis, and would remember listening as a child to sermons by old Dr. Mather, who lived next door.

One sharp October evening in 1711 a fire started in the center of town. The blaze engulfed houses on both sides of Cornhill. It swept north, taking in the First Church and then the Town House. A group of sailors scaled the roof of the First Church to rescue its bell and plunged to their deaths when the roof collapsed in a volcano of sparks. Desperately the authorities blew up buildings on both sides of the street; the explosions hurled bricks and splintered timbers into the crowd, killing several. More than a hundred buildings were destroyed. Sailors fifty miles at sea could see the flames reflected from the clouds.[102]

Destruction of the old central part of town cleared the way for fresh building, largely of brick, with many substantial, three-story homes and businesses replacing the original unpainted wooden buildings. The rebuilt First Church, known as the "New Brick Church," was a large, solid, three-story structure with a belfry in the center and soon a clock face over the front door. The new Town House, also of brick, was even more imposing, topped by a three-tiered, square bell tower and a copper weather vane.

The waterfront was also transformed. Earlier the town dock and boat basin had been protected by an old wharf, running parallel to the shore across the mouth of a shallow cove and long in disrepair; now it was replaced by Long Wharf. An extension of King Street, Long Wharf ran 1600 feet straight out into the bay. Tons of rubble left from the fire were used as fill. By 1713 it was complete. Warehouses were built end to end along the north side and as many as thirty ships at a time, including the largest then in the trade, were able to tie up broadside against the south side.[103]

Society adopted refinements of social intercourse. On one day in 1718 Samuel Sewall could rent a hackney coach to carry him along Boston Neck to Roxbury. He put up the horses at the Gray Hound Inn and started a round of visits. He called at the home of the minister, Nehemiah Walter, Increase Mather's son-in-law, but found him out. Sewall went on to Governor Dudley's, but he was out too. Next he stopped at the home of Mrs. William Denison, a wealthy widow and a relation by marriage. He stayed for dinner and on parting left Mrs. Denison small gifts, two knife and fork sets, one with tortoise shell handles, the other in ivory, a pound of raisins and almonds. Sewall, intent on the social graces, often carried with him gifts for people he visited or even met casually on the street. After dinner Sewall made another call in Roxbury, then picked up his coach at the Gray Hound and was carried back to the city in the twilight of a long July evening, much satisfied with life.[104]

Samuel Sewall became a wealthy merchant; he was appointed to the Superior Court, then to Governor Dudley's Council. His son, Samuel, Jr., married the governor's daughter Rebecca. Despite his steady rise in social status and wealth, Sewall remained conservative in dress and manners, almost ascetic. He detested the loud tipsy manners of the new century and especially the fashion of shaving the head and wearing a wig.

Eighteenth-century Boston was a blend of old Puritan simplicity and a new elegance. Periwigs came into Boston with royal governors and army officers. Increase Mather preached that "novelty and singularity in fashions are the badge of a vain mind." He singled out the periwig: "some Church Members indulge themselves in the wearing of (periwigs) which make them resemble the Locusts that come out of the bottomless Pit." [105] The anger evident in such a remark suggests the frustration of a man who sees his way of life insulted or ignored and is powerless to do anything about it.

When Daniel Neal visited Boston in 1719 he found the crowded inner harbor not unlike the Thames at Wapping. He admired Long Wharf, jammed with ships and warehouses. Nothing in London could match it. Walking the half-mile up King Street to the Town House and Exchange, Neal found five printers in business and no fewer than nineteen bookshops. In the city as a whole he estimated there were three thousand houses, of which about a third were now of brick. The streets were paved and named. In the homes of the wealthier merchants he found furniture and table settings as elegant as in London. Boston had become the largest and wealthiest city in British North America and second only to London in the British empire. [106]

FAMILY AND CHURCH

It was early spring, 1714, and Maria Mather was nearing the end of her life. As with virtually every other woman of her era, her influence on public affairs had been indirect, through her husband and her children. Like other women, Maria Mather was not permitted to vote in political elections or in church affairs. She neither wrote books nor spoke in public, although she did follow a routine of meditation and kept a journal. Her sphere was the home; there she shared her husband's spiritual struggles and nurtured their children. The Mather household, a large and complex establishment, was left entirely to her management. In 1714 Maria had kept house for fifty-two years. It had been thirty years since the birth of her youngest. Together she and Increase had raised nine children and lost only one in infancy. In recent years they had seen deaths in the family as often as births. Both knew how lucky they were to have survived together so long a time. The two youngest daughters were already dead. Only one of their daughters was still married to her first husband. Three others had by now been widowed and quickly remarried.

Their son Cotton lost his first wife in 1702 and just last year, in 1713, lost his second.

Families in Massachusetts then had numerous children, although many did not live to adulthood, as all but one of the Mathers' children did. Cotton had fourteen children in twenty-seven years, including one pair of twins. Occasionally a woman died unmarried or childless. Although the woman was spoken of as barren, the lack might instead have been with her husband. Elizabeth, for example, Maria's second oldest daughter, married William Greenough, a sailor, in 1696, when she was twenty-nine. He was often away at sea and the family frequently anxious for his life. When Greenough died Elizabeth was still without children. She married again, this time an older man, Josias Byles, who already had had two wives and raised a large family. Byles was a saddler by trade, and marriage into the Mather family was a step upwards in society. Elizabeth bore her first and only child four years later, when she was forty-one. She named the boy Mather Byles. Of all Maria and Increase's grandchildren, Mather Byles would become the most famous. [107]

Sarah was the only one of Maria's daughters to marry a minister. In 1714 she was living in Roxbury as the wife of the minister there, Nehemiah Walter, a native of Ireland and educated in strict Congregational ways. His parents had moved to Boston in 1679 and joined the North Church, so that Sarah and Nehemiah had known each other since childhood. At Harvard Nehemiah was a brilliant student of languages, but a semi-invalid all his life. Towards the end of his life he would need to read his sermons instead of preaching from memory as his famous father-in-law still did. Nehemiah was respected as a man of God. His reputation may have been partly a reflection of the fame of his father-in-law, but it was also helped by old John Eliot, who had been minister of the Roxbury church and missionary to the Indian for many years when he brought Walter in to be his assistant. When Eliot ordained the young man, he combined the traditional offices of Teacher and Pastor in one. After the ceremony he told him, "Brother, I ordained you a Teaching Pastor. But don't be proud. I always ordain my Indians so." [108] Nehemiah Walter's church at Roxbury had the distinction of having Governor Joseph Dudley, whose family farm was in Roxbury, as a member. Nehemiah was loyal to his father-in-law on the public issues of the day. After Increase had been ousted from the presidency of Harvard College, Nehemiah refused to attend meetings of the Corporation. They named their second son Increase Walter. "Cresy" Walter graduated from Harvard in 1711,

VIVERE, EST
COGITARE

Samuel Mather, Increase Mather's younger son, who returned to live in England in
1698, becoming a Dissenting minister in Witney, Oxfordshire; he died there in
1732. Oil portrait by unknown artist

received an M.A. degree in 1713, and wanted to practice medicine. He died in Jamaica in 1718.[109]

In her later years Maria saw more of Cotton, her first born, than her other male children. Nathaniel died when he was nineteen; Samuel had gone back to England and was settled there. Cotton, with his brilliant mind and incredible energy, was Increase's mainstay at the North Church. Seldom did two days pass together that he was not in the house. In a funeral sermon Cotton quoted from his mother's "Private Papers" of her concern for her children's spiritual wellbeing: "Lord, Let me not be Guilty of the Blood of their *Souls*. I know, I take much . . . Care of their *Bodies*, But, Lord, I pray, that I may take much more Care of their Neverdying Souls."[110]

In Puritan New England the household tended to be nuclear—husband, wife, and children—but the extended family had great importance, performing many of the functions that later centuries expected from other institutions, such as schools, employers, and professional organizations. Such was the pattern in the Mather family. Maria's two brothers were dead in 1714, but their children survived. Both had named their oldest sons after the boys' grandfather, John Cotton; both boys attended Harvard College during Increase's presidency, and both considered Maria's house as a second home. John Cotton, the son of Maria's oldest brother, Seaborn Cotton, was a Harvard classmate of her son Cotton, and the two young men later joined the North Church together. John married Anne Lake, the daughter of John Lake, the wealthy member of the congregation whose early support had been so vital to Increase Mather. Anne Lake Cotton bore him eight children in nineteen years. In Dorchester, Increase's older brother Timothy had raised six children on the original family farm. Of them all only one, Samuel, graduated from Harvard. He became a minister in the church at Windsor, Connecticut.[111] Timothy had never joined his father's church in Dorchester or any church at all, for that matter, nor did most of his children, although as young adults several were baptized under the half-way covenant. Most people in Massachusetts after 1660 or 1670 did not join churches, even though they went to services, and the gathered church of visible saints became, proportionately, smaller and smaller.

Out west in the Connecticut River Valley lived more members of the extended Mather family. Increase's brother Eleazar had had three children by his wife Esther before he died. A son, Warham, was a minister. One daughter, Eunice, married John Williams, who became the minister at Deerfield. Eunice was killed by Indians in 1704, and a daughter, also named Eunice, was carried to Canada as a small girl along with the other children and the father. All were ransomed or exchanged but for Eunice, the youngest. Her Indian parents refused to give her up, and by 1714 Eunice Williams had grown up as a Canawaugh Indian. She married and by her own choice lived the rest of her life with her tribe in Canada.[112] Eleazar's widow, Esther, had married again, this time to Solomon Stoddard. Just as Increase would take his summer vacation at Lynn, Stoddard took his in Boston, and when he came, he preached at Increase's church, perhaps staying in their house. With Stoddard Esther had twelve more children, all nephews and nieces of Maria and Increase. Esther would outlive all the others of her generation and die at ninety-one.[113] So the extended family grew. Early death of one spouse was frequent, but so was quick remarriage of the survivor. The supply of children more than made up numerically for the rapid loss of life. New England couples were exceptionally fertile, and because the entire population of New England was rather small at the beginning, the interconnections of family increased rapidly.

Maria Mather died on a Sunday in April 1714. The next Sunday her husband preached a funeral sermon for his partner of over half a century, its title reflecting some essence of the Puritan understanding of life and death: *Concerning Obedience and Resignation to the Will of God in Everything* (Boston, 1714). Increase published the sermon with a gentle, tender preface to his children, expecting them to be "as much in prayer" for *their* children as their mother had been for them. The next year, at age seventy-six, Increase re-married. It was the ordinary thing to do. His own father and Maria's mother had married late in life. This time, he stayed within the family, marrying Anne Lake Cotton, the forty-eight-year-old widow of Maria's nephew John Cotton. Perhaps he felt he was too old to go out of the family. Perhaps it was the appeal of the famous Cotton name. That same year Cotton Mather also married again for the third time, another widow.

Solomon Stoddard wanted to do something to comfort his brother after Maria's death. He asked Increase to write an introduction to his new book *Guide to Christ* (Boston, 1714). It was a book Stoddard knew Increase would like, because it explained the importance of evangelical preaching and how utterly necessary it was that the preacher himself be a converted person.[114] Mather was indeed pleased and offer a public olive branch to his old theological opponent. "It is known," Mather wrote in his preface to the book, "that in some points (not Fundamentals in Religion) I differ from this beloved Author; Nevertheless, (as when there was a difference of Opinion between Jerome and Austin) Jerome said for all that, I cannot but love Christ in Austin; so do I say concerning my Brother Stoddard. And I pray the Lord bless this, and all his holy labours, for the Conversion, and Salvation of many of God's elect." [115]

That same year Increase Mather also made his peace with Joseph Dudley. Queen Anne had died, and there was the possibility that a new monarch could be persuaded to appoint a new governor. Cotton Mather joined a faction in the House which sought a replacement, but Increase lobbied to have Dudley kept on. "I believe," he wrote Sir Henry Ashurst, "the generality of the people had rather have him continued than to have one sent from England especially one whose sentiments in Religion shall differ from what is the general profession of this Country. . . . Whether he has bin guilty of such Notorious Bribery as some say is none of my business to enquire. Since his estate is here, it is in his Interest to Seeke the welfare of the Country." [116]

CHURCH ESTABLISHMENT

Increase Mather's acceptance of Joseph Dudley climaxed a major swing of mood away from his anger and dejection in the early years of the century. Relieved from contentions of politics and returning to his true sphere of work, his ministry, Mather was feeling remarkably good about himself. He was grateful to all those who had prayed for him over the years; God "has made my Old Age to be a Good Old Age," he had written in 1711 in the preface to a book of sermons. [117] That same summer, on his seventy-second birthday, Increase had written in his diary and later transferred to his autobiography a long reflection on his life, beginning with his "godly parents and Ancestors." The essay is a spontaneous thanksgiving from the pen of a man whose characteristic mood had been one of humiliation and self-reproach. He looked back over his life now in wonder and admiration. He wrote of his service at Cambridge fondly with no mention of his forced resignation or of Leverett's appointment to the presidency. So too, he described his service in England without reference to the subsequent disappointments. He wrote of his family, his wife and children, his great library, and his still sound mind. "I have enjoyed much health therein, and bin kept from painfull diseases. Some touches of the gout several times I have bin afflicted with, but they have bin very gentle ones, and not of long continuance. . . . If ever there was a man in the world that had cause to be thankfull, I am Hee." [118]

One reason for the steady improvement of Mather's mood was the clear evidence that Colman's innovations at the Brattle Street Church, and Leverett's latitudinarian rule at the college, had not brought about a transformation of the Massachusetts churches after all. The Cambridge Platform and traditional New England Calvinism continued to be the outward measure of the ministry and brethren. In Boston, especially, appointments of new ministers after 1700 went entirely Mather's way.[119] In 1705 Thomas Bridge, a staunch conservative, had joined Benjamin Wadsworth at the old First Church, itself always reliably orthodox. No new ministerial appointment was made after that in Boston until September 1713, when the unpredictable and often innovative Ebeneezer Pemberton at Willard's Third Church was joined by Joseph Sewall, son of Mather's trusted ally Samuel Sewall and a man Increase had considered recommending to be his own successor.[120] Joseph could be trusted; there would be no radical religion at the Third or South Church.

That same year Mather single handedly, to hear the victim himself tell it, blocked the ordination of Colman's closest ally. He was John Barnard, whom Increase had admitted to Harvard in 1696 and then seen join the North Church in 1701. A personable and talented young man, Barnard seemed to have a bright future in Boston. Then came one of those "scandalls," the recollection of which hangs like an albatross around the memory of Puritan New England. In 1707 Barnard was appointed chaplain to Massachusetts troops sent to attack the French fortress at Port Royal. Besides acquitting himself well under fire, Barnard engaged in a game of cards with some of his comrades. His church, the North Church, Mather's church, threw it in his face as a sin, and although he was restored to good standing after his confession and repentance, he never forgot that "cruel" treatment.[121] Benjamin Colman defended the young man, and they became friends. In 1709–1710 Barnard went to England, where he was popular and adopted many fashions of society as well as the catholic spirit of the English church. When he returned to Massachusetts, he had no difficulty finding pulpits to preach from. In fact he was much in demand. Yet when it came down to a permanent appointment, one possibility after another fell through, for this reason or that.

Barnard dearly wanted to stay in or near Boston, and his best chance came in 1713. The North Church was overcrowded. A group within the church wanted to form a new congregation and build a new meetinghouse. The church approved this hiving off in January 1713, and all went well until Increase flew into a temper when they chose a site for the new meetinghouse only a block from the existing meetinghouse at

Clarke's Square. ("I am persuaded that a blasting from God will be upon them first or last.")[122] When Mather learned that Colman's great friend Johnny Barnard might be called to this "New North" church, he set to work to block the call. According to Barnard, Mather closeted himself with each of the fourteen founders, one after another, to stop a call to Barnard. In the end the choice went to another man, John Webb. Webb had received his Harvard M.A. that year and was if anything more conservative and fundamentalist in his reading of scripture than Mather himself.[123] So John Barnard, Colman's most obvious catholic imitator in these years, failed to get a Boston church and found himself exiled to Marblehead, then a rank fishing village on the north shore.[124]

Two years later the Brattle Street Church ordained a brilliant but orthodox assistant to Colman himself, and the threat that the old "Manifesto" of 1699 would destroy the New England way seemed to be over. To clinch this enduring ecclesiastical conservatism, both the old First Church and Willard's Third Church added orthodox ministers in the next few years.[125] With such apparent victories, it is understandable that Increase Mather felt pleased the way things were going. He was able, too, for better or for worse, to frustrate Benjamin Colman's every effort to pull the Massachusetts ministers into a Presbyterian-like organization. In 1705 Cotton Mather had helped promote standing councils, although Increase Mather's opposition prevailed. Perhaps because the arguments had continued to be put forward, Increase Mather and John Wise developed the counter arguments in print over the next several years.

John Wise was the pastor of a small church at Chebaco near Ipswich, and the leader of Ipswich's opposition to Sir Edmund Andros in 1688. He sent his satirical blast against the Proposals of 1705, *The Churches Quarrel Espoused* (1713), to New York to be published, perhaps because he expected, like the anonymous authors of *Gospel Order Revived*, that it would be hard to do so in Boston. But a second edition was published in Boston in 1715. Cotton Mather, recognizing himself as one target of the satire, called Wise's book "a foolish libel against some of us, for presbyterianizing too much in our Care to repair the deficiencies in our churches."[126] Increase, on the other hand, was hailed by Wise as "that Faithful and Noble Friend to these Churches, the famous and learned *Increase Mather* . . ."[127] Father and son were once again on opposite sides. Despite the gulf that separated Increase Mather and Wise—Mather a brilliant and conspicuous public figure in Boston, Wise a little-known and seldom read country parson at "Ipswich Farms"—they agreed wholeheartedly on the fundamental importance of the lay fellowship in the gathered church as against the organized ministry. In 1716 and 1717 both published in defense of the gathered churches.

In *Disquisition Concerning Ecclesiastical Councils,* published in Boston in 1716, Increase Mather set out to prove that "not only Pastors but Brethren delegated by the Churches, have equally a right to a decisive Vote in such Assemblies." "It has been objected," he wrote, "that this Principle will make way for Ignorant Mechanicks to carry it in synods against their Learned Pastors." The argument against an equal vote was the old class-conscious one which had been used against the Puritans in England at the beginning of the movement. Should the born-again brethren, in the nature of things uneducated, control their own worship? "But why not?" Mather asked. ". . . The name of Mechanicks, altho' it is Contemptible with us, is not so in all Nations. It was not so among the *Jews* . . . It is not then enough to *Unqualify* a Man for a Synod, that he is a Mechanick. . . . Popery came in at this door, of Pastors assuming more to themselves than belongs to them, and the Fraternities readiness to part with what was theirs."[128]

Wise's second book, *A Vindication of the Government of New England Churches,* came out the next year. He went beyond the single question of councils to defend the entire system set up by the Cambridge Platform. He used Increase Mather's *Order of the Gospel* as a convenient summary. The remarkable feature of his book, however, was his use of natural rights political philosophy to make his point. "To gratifie my own Curiosity . . . ," Wise wrote, "I shall proceed to Inquire into the Natural Reason of the Constitution of those Churches we have been comparing. . . ." He knew he was on fresh ground: "I shall go out of the Common Road, and take into an unusual and unbeaten Path. . . . For to me it seems most apparent, that under Christ the reason of the Constitution of these and the Primitive Churches, is really and truly owing to the Original State and Liberty of Mankind, and founded peculiarly in the Light of Nature."[129]

In 1716–1717 Increase Mather and John Wise stood at a watershed in western thought. Each wrote to justify the New England churches as described in the Cambridge Platform. Mather did so looking backward at centuries of traditional biblical and ecclesiastical scholarship. Wise did so looking forward toward the age of reason and natural rights. He frankly used political philosophy to explain his thoughts of church government. For both men the power and authority of the brethren lay at the heart of the true church. Wise was explicit in referring to this as "Democracy." The contribution of Puritanism to the eventual development of political democracy in English America is nowhere more clear.

Still, it would be wide of the mark to see the Congregational churches as democratic institutions. Boston's population grew much faster than church membership, and although many came to worship, few joined. In the first two decades of the century, 1700–1719, 341 members were added to Mather's North Church; 193 were women, 148 were men.[130] Neither Increase nor Cotton kept a record of how many full members there were at any one time, although Cotton did essay to record deaths, dismissals, excommunications, readmissions, etc. Only the brethren, not the sisters, voted in church affairs, and the circle of people who handled decisions remained small. On important votes in Mather's church around 1720 only fifty brethren cast votes.[131]

Colman deplored the refusal of the Massachusetts churches to adopt Presbyterian forms of church discipline, and as late as 1720 he still identified Increase Mather as the sole opponent: "The Aged Dr. Mather alone opposing it [a synod] we could not obtain one."[132] Yet this long-lasting disagreement between Boston's two outstanding churchmen, so different in age and outlook, was not allowed to disturb the ordinary functions of the churches. On the surface the ministers presented a united front. At ordinations, funerals, and other public ceremonies, Increase Mather and Benjamin Colman were amicably present. Colman officiated on occasion at Mather's meetinghouse. Nevertheless, the differences were real, as was made apparent with double irony in 1718, when the tiny, struggling Baptist congregation, whose meetinghouse was on the edge of Mill Pond, asked the neighboring ministers to assist in the ordination of a new pastor.

This was the same congregation which had its beginning back in 1665, and which had survived the steady and often acid criticisms of Mather and Willard in the 1670s and 1680s. Under the new charter there was no question of the government moving against the Baptists, but more than that, a general acceptance of religious toleration (for Protestants only) characterized the new century. As Colman and others adopted church practices verging ever closer to those of the Anglican church, the gathered fellowship of the Baptists seemed increasingly attractive to Increase. Cotton Mather announced himself a friend of toleration as early as the 1690s, and by 1710 more or less, Increase too was openly friendly to the one Baptist meeting in Boston.

Increase, Cotton, and John Webb accepted the invitation to the ordination of the new Baptist minister. Increase was the more willing to bury the hatchet because the candidate, Elisha Callender, was a Harvard College graduate.[133] The connection with Harvard was important, because Thomas Hollis, the wealthy London Baptist who was one of Harvard College's most important early benefactors, was so encouraged that in 1720 he made a major gift to the college.[134] Benjamin Colman had received the same invitation, but he declined it when he learned that the Baptists would not admit members of his congregation to worship with them. "I tho't the Inconsistency great," Colman wrote, "and so excused my selfe."[135] Thus the catholic spirit of the new century persuaded Increase Mather to welcome an old enemy, while its messenger, Colman, found excuses to stay aloof.

Colman's letters to a correspondent near Glasgow—the Rev. Robert Wodrow, also a correspondent of Cotton Mather's and, on rare occasions, of Increase's—make it clear that the innovations of the Brattle Street Church, so earnestly announced in the "Manifesto" of 1699, had not spread elsewhere in twenty years. In Boston, except for Brattle Street, ministers were still chosen by the communicants only. In Massachusetts generally a written relation of spiritual growth and conversion to Christ was still read aloud to the church membership for its consent to the admission of a new member. Likewise in the colony as a whole except for Brattle Street "and a few other Congregations," there was no public reading of scripture in the service.[136] Old-fashioned Congregational church polity still reigned supreme, to Colman's chagrin.

Suddenly in 1719 an uproar with the dimensions of a religious earthquake shook the orderliness of the Boston churches as nothing else had done since the schism in the First Church over Davenport fifty years before. This time it all took place in the North End. With Increase and Cotton Mather at the old North Church and the Rev. John Webb at the New North not a hundred yards off, all seemed serene. In the spring of 1719 a committee of New North proposed hiring an assistant to John Webb and nominated Peter Thacher. Thacher was ten years Webb's senior, and had received his B.A. and M.A. from Harvard under Mather in the 1690s. He had a great reputation for piety. For twelve years he had been pastor of the church at Weymouth, and for the past several years had longed to get out of that village and back to Boston, where he had many friends and admirers. After a great deal of badgering, Thacher persuaded the Weymouth church to give him a letter of dismissal in February 1719.

Church people in Boston either liked Peter Thacher and found his leaving the Weymouth church acceptable, or they did not like him and frowned at his breaking his spiritual bond with his church. As Colman put it a year later, "a great many of our people think the Relation between pastor and flock to be like that between husband and wife." [137] The Mathers and Webb liked Thacher and asked him to preach in their North End churches. Colman was critical from the first. Before long, a sizeable part of Webb's church voted to bring in Thacher as a second minister. Thereupon a large minority protested because of the way Thacher had treated the Weymouth church, and asked the neighboring ministers to form an advisory council, a time-honored procedure in Massachusetts, and one long defended by Increase Mather. Church councils, wrote Mather, were "not only lawful, but absolutely necessary for the Establishment of these churches." [138] But church councils proved too weak in 1719, as they had been in Davenport's day. Despite unanimous urging against it by other ministers, Webb went ahead with Thacher's installation. Increase and Cotton Mather belatedly joined their colleagues and advised a cooling off period, but to no avail. None of the ministers in Boston would participate in Thacher's installation. Webb invited two from out of town. On the day of installation the dissenting members of New North gathered in the street outside Webb's house to prevent Thacher from going to the meetinghouse, but were foiled when he was slipped out a back door and around the block. Finally, to the "perpetual disgrace of all," both parties crowded into the New North meetinghouse. The din and clamor were too great for any prayers or ordinary installation services at all, so that at last a minister called out from the pulpit, "does the majority still vote for Thacher?" and, declaring that motion carried, Webb and his out-of-town colleagues escaped. [139]

This travesty of an ordination turned Increase Mather from Webb, his own protégé. Such a ceremony, he wrote angrily, "is a Nullity and no Ordination, but a heinous Transgression of the Third Commandment. . . . a Scandal and Dishonour to *New-England*. . . . Neighbouring churches have just cause . . . to admonish, and to renounce Communion with a Church that has acted so Scandalously, except they Repent." [140] The affair had the effect of uniting the Boston ministers, at least in the short run, against Webb and Thacher and behind the dissenters from New North. These, about forty in all, at once laid plans to go their own way, and a third church for the North End was organized. They raised a substantial building fund and quickly built a handsome brick meetinghouse—Colman said it cost over £4000—even closer to Clark Square than New North. On May 10, 1721, Increase, a trembling eighty-two years, opened services there, followed by his son, then both Cooper and Colman from Brattle Street, and Wadsworth from the First Church. The

"New Brick" (some called it the "Revenge Church") received its im-
primatur from all parties. Increase had already announced in print his
satisfaction with this show of support; he wrote about the ministers in
Boston, "I say, *My Brethren,* and not, *My sons,* tho' I am the Natural Father to the Eldest of them [Cotton]; and in some Sense a Father to the
Two Next Eldest of them [Wadsworth and Colman], who were my Academical Children, when Students at the College Thirty Years ago. I rejoyce that I have such Brethren, and that when I am just going out of the
World, I shall Leave Ministers in *Boston,* who, I trust, will defend the
churches, when I shall Sleep with my Fathers." [141] Benjamin Colman reasoned the entire uproar would have been avoided but for Mather's encouragement of Thacher, in the first place, and the lack of a sound system of
Presbyterian church government, in the second. [142]

PUBLISHED SERMONS, 1715−1720

New South was organized in 1717. Boston now had six orthodox congregations. By coincidence, the same year as the opening of the New
South, Ebeneezer Pemberton died after serving in Willard's Old South
Church for seventeen years. Three days later, William Brattle in Cambridge also died. Both had been leaders in the liberal church movement
at the turn of the century. Increase Mather suddenly became aware that
he was outliving not only his own generation of ministers, but the next
generation, as well.

If his body weakened with age, his mind did not. Increase Mather
went on and on, to the dismay of his opponents and the wonder and admiration of his supporters. Between his seventy-fifth and eighty-second
birthdays (1715−1721) he published eight major books in addition to
works already mentioned and numerous prefaces to books of his colleagues. By 1717 Increase's diaries give plain evidence of an aged, trembling hand which could guide the quill pen only with difficulty. He
stopped writing his autobiography altogether, and the diary was reduced
to a few perfunctory words each day, a mere matter of habit. In 1718 a
woman in the congregation came to his rescue. She was able first to take
Increase's sermons down in shorthand and then to transcribe them in a
way suitable to him and for the press. Three of Mather's last books—one
of three hundred pages, comprising sixteen sermons—were written this
way. Mather found it remarkable for a woman to be so skilled. [143]

Increase no longer stood first among the New England ministers in
the writing of books. The prodigious Cotton was far out in front in both

quantity and originality. Then came Benjamin Colman, champion of the Addisonian style, and close behind Colman, Benjamin Wadsworth at the First Church, whom Colman thought to be of poor intellectual merit, but who nevertheless, after Leverett died in 1724, accepted the presidency of Harvard College, as Colman and Joseph Sewall would not.[144] Mather continued to view Colman's rhetorical style as a threat to true religion. Thus in 1715 he repeated more emphatically than ever his adherence to plain style: "incorruptness, Gravity, Sincerity, and sound Speech" were to be preferred over "a Modish Way of Preaching." Dissenters in England, he wrote, "so they might be thought to be *florid,* they affect a *drammatick* style . . . and bring over our Playhouse Phrases into the Language of the Pulpit."[145]

He made more exact his beliefs about rational or natural religion in *Discourse Concerning The Existence . . . of God* (1716). At the outset Mather agreed with the rationalists that nature itself reveals the existence of a Creator: "It is as clear to The Understanding of a Rational Creature, as the Light of The Sun at Noon, that none but One who is Eternal, and whose Power is Infinite could be The Maker of The World." And, "atheism is the most unreasonable Thing that possibly can be."[146] Nevertheless, "Men cannot from the Light of Nature know that there is a Christ, or that the Son of God is become a Man, and has died, that thro him the World might be saved; these are Gospel Mysteries, not known but by supernatural Revelation."[147] The year before, Cotton Mather, a more thorough student of natural science than his father, expressed the same conclusion in his *Christian Philosopher.*[148] Father and son agreed on the limits of reason and natural religion.

Turning his back on the tribalism of the 1670s, Increase in 1721 told the new rising generation that their parents' faith could not help them, they were on their own. In 1678 he had preached, "Now God hath seen good to cast the line of election . . . for the most part through the lives of the Godly Parents. There are, it is true, Elect Children who are not born of Elect Parents, but there are few (if any) Elect Parents without Elect Children."[149] Now he preached, "It is not in the power of Parents to give Grace to their Children. They give them what they have in this world, but that is all. . . . A Godly Man can no more make his Children Godly than he can Raise the Dead from their graves."[150]

Was there a hint of disillusionment here? Mather no longer preached as if New England were a New Israel. He still used typology to interpret scripture: the Old Testament Jews were a type of the present-day elect. But he did not speak of New England's errand or the first fathers. In-

Several REASONS

Proving that Inoculating or Tranfplant-
ing the *Small Pox*, is a Lawful Practice,
and that it has been Blelfed by GOD
for the Saving of many a Life.

By *Increafe Mather,* D.D.

Exod. XX. 13. *Thou fhalt not kill.*
Gal. I. 10. *Do I feek to pleafe Men? if I pleafe Men,
I fhould not be a Servant of* CHRIST.

It has been Queftioned, Whether *Inoculating*
the *Small Pox* be a Lawful Practice. I incline
to the Affirmative, for thefe Reafons.

I. **B**Ecaufe I have read, that in *Smyrna, Con-
ftantinople,* and other Places, Thoufands of Lives have been faved by
Inoculation, and not one of Thoufands has
mifcarried by it. This is related by Wife &
Learned Men who would not have impofed on
the World a falfe Narrative. Which alfo has
been publifhed by the *Royal Society*; therefore a
great Regard is due to it.

    II. WE hear that feveral *Phyficians* have
Recommended the Practice hereof to His *Majefty,* as a Means to preferve the Lives of his
Subjects, and that His Wife and Excellent *Majefty King GEORGE,* as alfo his *Royal Highnefs*
the *Prince* have approved hereof, and that it is

Essay by Mather defending inoculation against smallpox, 1721

stead, he appealed to individuals to separate themselves from a sinful world, a tacit recognition that pluralistic, eighteenth-century Boston was no longer Immanuel's land. "So then," he wrote in 1720, "we must not do as the greatest part of the World do. . . . If there is a proud, foolish fashion, if many take it up, others take it up and think they do well. Why? Everybody does it. But what says the Scripture, Exod. 23.2, Thou shalt not follow a multitude to do evil. . . . Christians must be singular Persons, it becomes them to have an holy singularity, they must not do as others do." [151] Three sermons in the spring of 1720 all spoke of the sense of isolation: "Many are Called, who are not Effectively Called," "Men May be of the Visible Church, and Yet Not be of the Lord's chosen," and "The Chosen of God are comparatively but Few." [152] History had gone full circle, and as had been the case before there was a New England, it was necessary again to call the faithful to separate themselves from a sinful world.

In 1718 Mather published a book on the beatitudes, which he had covered in fifteen separate sermons over the preceding three or four years. Here is an unexpected contrast to the man who had once decided not to smile in public and who had become famous for his jeremiads. At the end of this series he added a sixteenth sermon, "Concerning Assurance of the Incomprehensible Love of Christ." "There are some Christians," he preached, "who think they may not come to the Lord's Supper before they have Assurance, which is a great mistake. For one reason why that Ordinance has been Instituted, is, That so Believers might have their Faith confirmed and strengthened to an Assurance. It is a Sealing Ordinance." [153] This three hundred page book sold so well a second edition appeared after three years.

The closest Increase Mather came to preaching a work ethic à la Richard Baxter's *Christian Directory* came in 1719, and it was not very close. In the last pages of a sermon encouraging people to pray for Christ's intercession Mather reflected on the poverty among Boston's growing population of poor laborers. "Alas! Sinful *Boston*, does thou not see, that Poverty is coming on thee like an armed Man, and that many of thy Houses will be forsaken and left desolate." One explanation, he said, was idleness: "There is not that Industry among us as ought to be. How many spend their Time in Taverns; if they spent their Time Industriously, they might live comfortably." [154] The passage bears little relationship to the moral injunctions of Baxter cited by Max Weber as evidence of the growth of a work ethic. Mather began this passage with a general observation of the economic life of Boston vis-à-vis the rural hin-

CRESCENTIUS MATHERUS.
Ætatis Suæ 85. 1724.

Engraving of Increase Mather by John Stuart, after 1688 painting by van der Spriett

Increase Mather. Painting of the 1700s by an unknown artist

terland: "The Merchant Oppressing the People in the Country, the People in the Country Oppressing the People in *Boston*: but who does the Oppression chiefly fall upon? Not so much the Rich, as upon the poor; the poor are like to be crushed to death." [155] From this expression of class sympathy Mather at once branched out to a short catalogue of sins: sexual immorality ("Many in Boston are guilty of the Sins of Sodom;") pride ("Poor People will go beyond their rank, and beyond their ability, which is a great iniquity and very provoking to God;") gluttony ("Fullness of bread, and of drink, great abuse that way;") and idleness. [156]

As a catalogue of sins, it hardly bears comparison to Mather's "Provoking Evils" of 1675 and 1679. In truth, times had changed, and with them the way men, even men as conservative as Mather, thought about the world. Aware of the many proposals in these new times about land banks, paper money, and other economic policies, Mather made a brief reference to strategies which might "bring money into the Country, and save the Land from ruine," but then dropped it: "That is a matter out of my Province to meddle with." Instead he fell back on the old formula, Repent and Pray. "If you do that, I can assure you in His Name, He will deliver you out of your distress." [157] It all seems a dry, truncated, emotionally empty and formal return to a formula that had once dominated the sermons in Boston. He did not say that industry was a moral good in itself or that prosperity was evidence of salvation.

THE END OF TIME

Earlier in life, Increase Mather had often enough complained that visitors or public engagements took up too much time and in particular took him away from his study. Now towards the end of his life he complained even more. His son Samuel admitted that Increase paid so few pastoral visits "that he has sometimes been complained of." [158] Increase became increasingly testy over lost time. In 1717 he grumbled that even dining out with the governor, Samuel Shute, was now a waste of precious time. "Time miserably lost by visitors. . . . Time lost by Impertinent visitors." [159]

Mather's mind continued to function remarkably well, and he was in great demand to baptize children, including now his great-grandchildren, and to participate in the ordinations of new ministers who were sometimes themselves young enough to be his grandchildren. He wrote and preached, not infrequently exchanging pulpits with other ministers in Boston. In a letter to Sir William Ashurst in August 1717, he wrote, "As to my-selfe, I am now aged being in my 79 year, yet through the wonderfull goodness of God, able to preach in the largest meeting house in N.E., sometimes to near upon two thousand [souls?] and to continue . . . in my sermon without any use of notes: People tell me they can hear me as well as they could 40 years ago." In the next sentence, though, Mather had to admit the weakness of age. "Nonetheless," he wrote, "I find a difference between 40 and almost fourscore and hope it will not be long before I shall rest from my Labors." [160]

The next year he made out a last will and testament, afraid that if he did not do it now, when his head was clear, he might not be able to at the end. He was, he wrote, still made anxious by the dreams and nightmares ("ephialtes") which had frightened him in 1670. There was not much of an estate, outside his library and the house. "It has bin thought that I have bags by me, which is a great mistake. I have not twenty pounds in silver, or in Bills." He gave the loyal Cotton his greatest treasure, "all my manuscripts, and the one halfe of my Library." Cotton, who was named executor, was also to receive all the cash, and the few items of special value in Mather's house: a watch, a clock, "my silver tanckard." In the North End where opulent merchant homes were going up, Increase had led the ascetic life he preached. Except for books. The other half of his library he left to his son Samuel in England and to the two grandchildren in America, Mather Byles and Thomas Walter, who seemed destined for the ministry. The house and its furnishings went to the four daughters. Increase had already agreed with his second wife that their estates should not intermingle. As an afterthought, in a postscript, Increase wished "that my Negro servant . . . shall not be sold after my decease, but I do then give him his liberty and let him then be esteemed a Free Negro." [161]

Fate had one last great public cause for the aging minister. On May 12, 1721, he wrote in his diary, "The small pox in Town." That summer an epidemic swept the city, and Increase, immune by virtue of his own smallpox in 1657, was swept up in it, visiting the sick, worrying about his children and their families, and supporting the new method of inoculation after his son's championing had led to a public furor. [162]

Cotton Mather, acting on a judgment he had made five years earlier, first proposed inoculation. Only Zabdiel Boylston among the town physicians would try it, however, and soon there was a popular outcry against it, led by Dr. William Douglass, a Scot immigrant and the only man in Boston with an earned medical degree. [163] Most Boston ministers

A FATHER Departing.

A SERMON

On the DEPARTURE of the

Venerable and *Memorable*.

Dr. Increase Mather,

Who Expired *Aug.* 23. 1723.

In the EIGHTY FIFTH Year of his Age.

By One *who, as a* SON *with a* FA-
THER, *ferved with him in the*
Go*ſpel*.

---

2 Chron. XXIV. 15, 16.

*He was full of Days, when he died ;— And
— He had done Good in Iſrael.*

Parer Obiit !—— PIETAS Vivit, aliequi eſt
fareor, undé perpetuo mæſtus fis   *Pernach.*

BOSTON:

Printed by *T. Fleet*, for *N. Belknap*, at his
Shop near *Scarlet*'s Wharf, 1723.

"A Father Departing," sermon by Cotton Mather, written August 23, 1723, after
Increase Mather's death at 85

Courtesy, Massachusetts Historical Society

Cotton Mather in 1728, the year of his death. Mezzotint by Peter Pelham

backed Cotton Mather. Colman wrote a long letter in support of inoculation, signed by both Mathers, Prince, Webb, Colman, and Cooper and published in *The Boston Gazette,* July 27 to 31, 1721.[164] Probably most people in Boston, and certainly the majority of physicians, were opposed. The town selectmen ordered Boylston to stop. Boylston refused. A fused bomb was thrown into Cotton Mather's house. It fortunately failed to explode, thus preserving the message that went with it, "Cotton Mather, You Dog, Dam You: I'll inoculate you with this, with a pox to you." James Franklin, starting up *The New-England Courant,* sided against inoculation and before long the struggle for public approval was taking place in the pages of the *Courant* and *The Boston Gazette.* A new era had begun in the history of print in English America.

Increase came to the public support of inoculation in November, 1721, when he joined Cotton in a broadside, *Several Reasons Proving that Inoculating . . . is a Lawful Practice.* "My Sentiments, and my son's also, about this matter are well known," he wrote; "Also we hear that the Reverend and Learned Mr. Solomon Stoddard of Northampton concurs with us; so doth the Reverend Mr. Wise of Ipswich, and many other younger Divines . . ."[165] It is ironic that Mather chose to single out the two men whom later historians have most often called his antagonists. Mather's next publication about smallpox came in the form of a letter to the *Gazette* in January 1722. He criticized the *Courant* and its editor, James Franklin, for its stand against inoculation. "Those who have known what New-England was from the beginning, can but pity poor Franklin, a young man."[166] Finally, on the last day of January 1722, Increase published another broadside, *Some further Account of the Small Pox,* in which at Cotton's suggestion he summarized a paper presented eight months earlier (April 1721) to the Royal College of Physicians in London, in which inoculation was strongly recommended.[167] By now the epidemic had largely run its course and the public controversy died away. Colman later collected and sent to England statistics showing that 5,742 persons had contracted smallpox "in a Natural Way," of whom 841 or fourteen percent died; 147 were inoculated, of whom three, or two percent, died.[168] What a paradox it was that the Boston ministers encouraged inoculation and the practicing physicians opposed it. The seed of that contradiction had been sown forty years before with books about comets and with the Boston Philosophical Society.

Six months later, June 1722, Mather painfully wrote out the preface to his last book of sermons, *The Dying Legacy of a Minister to His Dearly*

Beloved People. "Old Age has so Debilitated me," he wrote, "that I have no Hopes of Preaching another Sermon. Besides my Right Hand is become Paralitical, and shakes after that manner that I cannot Write any Long Discourses." [169] After this, the man who had led the way for so many years in preaching and writing preached and wrote no more, except for one or two brief prefaces in others' books. [170]

On September 27, 1722, Mather blacked out for a few minutes. ("He fell into an Apoplectic sort of Deliquium . . . out of which he Recovered in a few Minutes.") "It so enfeebled him," Cotton wrote, "that he never went abroad any more." [171] During the ensuing eleven months his general condition deteriorated, so that Cotton, who was in daily attendance, wrote of his "Complicated Maladies." About the first of August 1723, just as in the case of his father, Increase's bladder ceased to function, and within three weeks of increasing pain, he died in his son's arms. [172]

A week later the funeral was held. Governor William Dummer, President of the College John Leverett, Chief Justice Samuel Sewall, and three ministers from the three oldest churches were pallbearers. On the short route to Copp's Hill Burrying Place in the North End a hundred and sixty Harvard graduates led the way. Following after the pallbearers came fifty ministers, more or less, and a crowd of spectators beyond counting. For weeks afterwards memorial sermons were preached in New England on the passing of this man whose life and works encompassed so much of the history of the colony. [173]

The insistent voice from the North Church was stilled, the great library upstairs soon dispersed. [174] The next year Cotton Mather published a biography of his father, as Increase had done of his. Cotton titled his book, *Parentator: Memoirs of Remarkables in the Life and Death of the Ever-Memorable Dr. Increase Mather. Who Expired, August 23, 1723.*

Looking back at Mather's life during its eighty-four years when the face of Boston and indeed all New England had changed so much, we find it appears surprisingly large. Increase Mather filled a large space in Massachusetts's history. While he was alive he was, of course, primarily a churchman, a minister of God, a preacher of sermons. Early Puritanism, the original, intense, plain, ascetic, pietistic, judgmental Puritanism of the providential world and the gathered church, had passed in Massachusetts before Mather died, although he himself, its greatest American exemplar, remained true to the very end. Had he been no more than a churchman, his place in New England's history would have been large enough.

Mather, however, filled other spaces. The political arena was one. He was proud of the new colonial charter, the one that brought "advice and consent" into the Anglo-American political constitution, although in fact he fought rearguard actions on all its major points. He called it a charter of liberties, but it destroyed the political structure which had supported Puritanism, and there were always critics in Massachusetts. In 1721 the colony's agent to London, Jeremy Dummer (Harvard, 1699) wrote, "the new charter . . . is not much more than a shadow of the old one." Dummer suggested "mismanagement" in the negotiations.[175] Forty years later, on the eve of independence, John Adams wrote that "there is less to be said in excuse for it than for witchcraft, or hanging the Quakers."[176] New England traditions die hard.

Mather's life was filled with ironic reversals. He was a profoundly conservative man, yet all his life his driving energy pushed out in new directions, as with the Boston press, or reinvigorated failing institutions, as with Harvard College. His adoption of the rhetoric of Whig politics during the years in London gave impetus to a new and secular way of thinking in Massachusetts, even though he himself reverted to the earlier plain style and in his late millennial writings employed a rhetoric as biblical as any from the previous century. His most enduring influence on the culture of his region and his country was his contribution of those images of the "First Fathers of N.E.," who ventured on "that unparallell'd Undertaking, even to Transport themselves, their Wives and Little ones, over the rude Waves of the vast Ocean, into a Land which was not sown." The greatest irony, Mather's own life has been used to represent the worst in America's Puritan beginnings.[177]

Mather's images of those beginnings originated with his biography of his father. He was diffident then about writing a biography and published it anonymously, because English Puritan culture frowned on biography's potential for exaggerating the role of the human person. ("Put not your trust in princes, nor in the son of man." Psalms 146:3.) His reason for writing the biography nevertheless serves well all biographers: "Nor is it to be doubted," Increase wrote, "but that there have been many famous in their Generations, whose Memories are buried in the dust, for want of some one to undertake this office, whereby their Names might have been perpetuated to Posterity."

Vixere fortes ante Agamemnona
Multi: Sed illachrymabiles
Urgentur ignotiq, longâ
Nocte; Carent quia vate Sacro.

"Many brave men lived before Agamemnon, but all are overwhelmed in unending night, unwept for, unknown, because they lack an inspired poet."[178]

Notes

ABBREVIATIONS

AAS, American Antiquarian Society
CSM, Colonial Society of Massachusetts
MHS, Massachusetts Historical Society

1. The Legacy, Birth, and Education of a Puritan

1. Cotton Mather, *Parentator. Memoirs of Remarkables in the Life and Death of the Ever-Memorable Dr. Increase Mather* (Boston, 1724), 5. This is Cotton Mather's biography of his father, published a year after Increase Mather's death and three years before his own. Cotton imitated his father, who wrote a biography of *his* father. Cotton's own son, Samuel, wrote his life in 1729. It was the fourth family biography and the third generation to write one.

2. Increase Mather, *The Life and Death of that Reverend Man of God, Mr. Richard Mather* (Cambridge, 1670). Facsimile edition, William J. Scheick, ed. (Bainbridge, N.Y.: York-Mail Print, Inc., 1974), 29–33.

3. Charles E. Hambrick-Stowe, *The Practice of Piety. Puritan Devotional Discipline in Seventeenth-Century New England* (Chapel Hill: University of North Carolina Press, 1982), 27.

4. Perry Miller, "Marrow of Puritan Divinity," in *Errand into the Wilderness* (Cambridge: Harvard University Press, 1956; N.Y.: Harper & Row, 1964), 82. See also Norman Petit, *The Heart Prepared: Grace and Conversion in Puritan Spiritual Life* (New Haven: Yale University Press, 1966), 78–79.

5. Hambrick-Stowe, *Practice of Piety*, 43.

6. Thomas Shepard, quoted in Ibid. Shepard, who died early at age 44, was among the half-dozen ministers who most directly shaped Massachusetts religious culture in Richard Mather's time.

7. Ibid., 44.

8. Increase Mather, *Life and Death*, 34.

9. Ibid., 35.

10. Ibid., 36–37.

11. Ibid., 37–38. Stephen Foster, "English Puritanism and the Progress of New England Institutions, 1630–1660," in *Saints and Revolutionaries. Essays on Early American History*, ed. by David D. Hall, John M. Murrin, and Thad W. Tate (N.Y.: W. W. Norton, 1984), 22.

12. For example, Thomas Shepard's account in Michael McGiffert, ed., *God's Plot: the Paradox of Puritan Piety. Being the Autobiography and Journal of Thomas Shepard* (Amherst: University of Massachusetts Press, 1972), 49.

13. Increase Mather, *Life and Death*, 42.

14. John Winthrop, "Reasons to be Considered and Objections with Answers," quoted in Edmund Morgan, ed., *Founding of Massachusetts* (N.Y.: Bobbs-Merrill, 1964), 175–182.

15. Richard Mather, "Arguments tending to prove the Removing from *Old-England to New*," in Increase Mather, *Life and Death*, 43–54.

16. See David D. Hall, "Understanding the Puritans," in Herbert J. Bass, ed., *State of American History* (Chicago: Quadrangle Books, 1970), 330–349.

17. Winthrop, "A Modell of Christian Charity," in Morgan, ed., *Founding of Massachusetts*, 190–204.

18. Hambrick-Stowe, *Practice of Piety*, 48.

19. Ibid., 49.

20. Ibid., 100.

21. Max Weber, *The Protestant Ethic and the Spirit of Capitalism,* trans. by Talcott Parsons, (N.Y.: Scribner's Sons, 1930, 1958), 105–121.

22. Cambridge Platform, in Williston Walker, *Creeds and Platforms of Congregationalism* (N.Y.: Scribner's Sons, 1893; Boston: Pilgrim Press, 1960), 204.

23. Richard Barry Burg, *Richard Mather of Dorchester* (Louisville: University of Kentucky Press, 1976), 26–27.

24. John Norton, *Answer to the Whole Set of Questions of the Celebrated Mr. William Apollonius* (London, 1648), translated by Douglas Horton (Cambridge: Harvard University Press, 1958).

25. William Wood, *New-England's Prospect* (London, 1634), The English Experience, No. 68 (N.Y.: Da Capo Press, 1968), 37.

26. Quoted in Edmund Morgan, *Visible Saints. The History of a Puritan Idea* (N.Y.: New York University Press, 1963), 100. Burg, *Richard Mather,* 33–34. Foster, "English Puritanism," 19–20.

27. Morgan, *Visible Saints,* 80–108.

28. Increase Mather, *Autobiography,* Michael G. Hall, ed. (Worcester, Mass.: American Antiquarian Society, 1962), 278.

29. Here, as elsewhere below, biographical facts of the Mather family are pieced together from a variety of sources, of which the most important are, Increase Mather, *Life and Death;* Cotton Mather, *Parentator;* Increase Mather, *Autobiography;* Increase Mather's family Bible record, printed in Chandler Robbins, *History of the Second Church, or Old North in Boston* (Boston, 1852), 215; Increase Mather diaries; Samuel G. Drake, "Pedigree of the Family of Mather," in Cotton Mather, *Magnalia Christi Americana* (London, 1702), Samuel G. Drake, ed., 2 vols. (Hartford, Conn., 1853); John S. Sibley, *Biographical Sketches of Graduates of Harvard University,* 3 vols. (Cambridge, 1873–1885); Clifford K. Shipton, *Biographical Sketches of Those Who Attended Harvard College, Sibley's Harvard Graduates,* vols. 4, 5, and 6 (Cambridge: Harvard University Press, 1933–1942).

30. Increase Mather, *Life and Death*, 30–31.

31. Richard Mather, *A Farewell Exhortation to the Church and People of Dorchester* (Cambridge, 1657), 8–11.
32. Increase Mather, *Life and Death,* 37.
33. Quoted in Francis J. Bremer, *The Puritan Experiment: New England Society from Bradford to Edwards* (N.Y.: St. Martin's Press, 1976), 109–110.
34. Burg, *Richard Mather,* 49–52, 57–62.
35. Bremer, *Puritan Experiment,* 116, 120.
36. Quoted in Walker, *Creeds and Platforms,* 169.
37. Burg, *Richard Mather,* 108–110.
38. Quotations from the Platform are taken from Walker, *Creeds and Platforms,* 194–237.
39. For the law of 1636 see Morgan, *Visible Saints,* 101.
40. Darrett B. Rutman, *Winthrop's Boston: Portrait of a Puritan Town, 1630–1649* (Chapel Hill, N.C.: University of North Carolina Press, 1965), 267–268.
41. Burg, *Richard Mather,* 110–111. On the issue of opposition between ministry and laity, see Foster, "English Puritanism," 7–12, 28–29.
42. Scenes of Harvard College are drawn from Samuel E. Morison, *Harvard College in the Seventeenth Century,* 2 vols. (Cambridge: Harvard University Press, 1936).
43. Ibid., 5–6, 562–563.
44. Ibid., 107.
45. *Autobiography,* 278. Steward's Book, Harvard University, *Harvard College Records,* III, CSM, *Publications,* 31 (1935), 139.
46. *Autobiography,* 279.
47. Increase Mather, *Life and Death,* 62.
48. Carl Bridenbaugh, *Cities in the Wilderness: the First Century of Urban Life in America* (N.Y.: Ronald Press, 1938), 9, 15, 17–18.
49. Robbins, *History of the Second Church,* 6–9.
50. North Church Petition to Magistrates and Deputies, Sept., 1653, and Magistrates' reply, Sept. 13, 1653, 10:82, 83. Massachusetts State Archives. Salem Church Objections, nd, Ibid., 84. Michael Powell to Court, Aug. 22, 1654, Ibid., 86, 87. North Church petition to ordain Powell, nd [1654], Ibid., 88. For other cases of the General Court's interference in the choice of ministers, Oct. 20, 1658, to Aug. 24, 1664, Ibid., 92–97. John Farnum is discussed in Chapter Two below. For Preston's words and the class implications, see Christopher Hill, *Puritanism and Revolution: Studies in Interpretation of the English Revolution of the Seventeenth Century* (N.Y.: Schocken Books, 1964), 217–218.
51. *Autobiography,* 279–280.
52. Ibid., 281.
53. Nathaniel Mather to John Rogers (?), London, Dec. 23, 1651, *Mather Papers,* MHS, *Collections,* 4 ser., 8 (1868), 5.
54. Francis J. Bremer, "Increase Mather's Friends: the Trans-Atlantic Congregational Network of the Seventeenth Century," AAS, *Proceedings,* 94, pt. 1 (1984), 64–74, 82–83.
55. R. Tudur Jones, *Congregationalism in England, 1662–1962* (London: Independent Press, 1962), 32. For an overview of returned Puritans in England, see William Sachse, "Harvard Men in England, 1642–1714," CSM, *Publications,* 35 (1951), 119–144.

56. A. G. Matthews, *Calamy Revised, Being a Revision of Edmund Calamy's Account of the Ministers and Others Ejected and Silenced, 1660–1662* (Oxford: Clarendon Press, 1934), 343–344.

57. Ibid., 344.

58. *Autobiography*, 281. The ensuing account of Increase's movements until leaving England in 1661 is taken largely from *Autobiography*, 281–286.

59. Samuel Mather to Increase Mather, April 20 and Sept. 10, 1659, MSS American 1502, Boston Public Library.

60. For the history of the English Congregationalists in the declining years of the Commonwealth, Jones, *Congregationalism in England*, 33–62.

61. Ibid., 44–45.

62. *Autobiography*, 284.

63. Jones, *Congregationalism in England*, 48–58.

64. In addition to *Autobiography*, 284–286, Nathaniel Mather to Increase Mather, from Rotterdam, Dec. 1661, *Mather Papers*, 5–6.

2. The Struggle for Identity

1. *Autobiography*, 286; Cotton Mather, *Parentator*, 23.

2. *Autobiography*, 286.

3. Ibid., 285.

4. Ibid., 286.

5. Thomas J. Holmes, *Increase Mather: A Bibliography of His Works*, 2 vols. (Cleveland, 1931), 478.

6. Nos. 233–234, 227–228, VI; no. 170, X, Suffolk County Court Deeds, MHS.

7. *Autobiography*, 359.

8. The most authoritative genealogy is Mather's own, printed in Robbins, *Second Church*, 216–217.

9. Julius H. Tuttle, "The Libraries of the Mathers," AAS, *Proceedings*, 20 (1910), 280–290. Kenneth Ballard Murdock, *Increase Mather, the Foremost American Puritan* (Cambridge: Harvard University Press, 1925), 75–78.

10. Diary, Aug. 5, 1665.

11. Diary, 1665–1667, passim.

12. Diary, May 3, 4, July 26, 1664; May 8, 17, 22, 24, Aug. 1, Oct. 20, 1665; Oct. 29, 1666. George Emery Littlefield, *Early Boston Booksellers* (Boston: Club of Odd Volumes, 1900; N.Y.: Burt Franklin, 1969), 65–77, 95–96.

13. E.g., diary, June 11, Aug. 7, 1666. For the network of correspondents, see Bremer, "Increase Mather's Friends: The Trans-Atlantic Congregational Network of the Seventeenth Century," 59–96.

14. Increase Mather to John Davenport, June 2, 1662, *Mather Papers*, 188–189.

15. "Letters and Papers Relating to the Regicides," Ibid., 122–225.

16. Increase Mather to Davenport, June 2, 1662, *Mather Papers*, 188.

17. Brooks Holifield, *The Covenant Sealed: the Development of Puritan Sacramental Theology in Old and New England* (New Haven: Yale University Press, 1974), 179–182. A good introduction to typology is Erich Auerbach, *Scenes from the*

Drama of European Literature (N.Y.: Meridian, 1959), 50–56. For the background to the synod of 1662, see Robert G. Pope, *The Half-Way Covenant: Church Membership in Puritan New England* (Princeton: Princeton University Press, 1969), 13–42.

18. Quoted in Edmund Morgan, *The Puritan Family: Religion and Domestic Relations in Seventeenth-Century New England* (N.Y.: Harper & Row, 1966), 106.

19. Isabel M. Calder, *The New Haven Colony* (New Haven: Yale University Press, 1934), 1–49. For the contrast between Richard Mather and John Davenport, see Steven Foster, "English Puritanism," 21–23.

20. Robert Middlekauf, *The Mathers. Three Generations of Puritan Intellectuals. 1596–1728* (N.Y.: Oxford University Press, 1971), 121–122. Holifield, *Covenant Sealed,* 180–181.

21. Pope, *Half-Way Covenant,* 49–55. Walker, *Creeds and Platforms,* 267–269. Increase Mather to John Davenport, Oct. 21, 1662, *Mather Papers,* 205–206.

22. Charles Chauncy, *Anti-Synodalia Scripta Americana* (London, 1662), endorsed by Eleazar and Increase Mather and John Mayo. John Davenport, *Another Essay for Investigation of the Truth* (Cambridge, 1663), with Increase Mather, "An Apologetical Preface." John Allin, *Animadversions upon the Antisynodalia Americana* (Cambridge, 1664). Richard Mather and Jonathan Mitchell, *Defence of the Answer and Arguments of the Synod* (Cambridge, 1664). Michael G. Hall and William L. Joyce, "The Half-Way Covenant of 1662: Some New Evidence," AAS, *Proceedings* 87, pt. 1 (1977), 97–110.

23. Robbins, *Second Church,* 12.

24. *Autobiography,* 287.

25. Diary, Mar. 7; Apr. 8, 11, 12, 1664.

26. Increase Mather's narrative account, 3, III, Second Church Records, MHS. Robbins, *Second Church,* 21–22.

27. Diary, May 13, 1664. Richard Mather and Jonathan Mitchell, *A Defence of the Answer and Arguments of the Synod* (Cambridge, 1664).

28. Diary, May 14, 18, 1664.

29. Diary, June 21, 1664.

30. Diary, Mar. 29, 1664.

31. Diary, Apr. 21, 27, May 12, 1664.

32. Diary, May 8, 1664.

33. Diary, May 19, 1664.

34. Diary, Apr. 18, 19, 1664.

35. *Diary of Samuel Sewall. 1674–1729,* M. Halsey Thomas, ed. (N.Y.: Farrar, Straus and Giroux, 1973), 379, n. 14. Diary, May 3, 1664.

36. Diary, June 11, 1664.

37. Sewall, *Diary,* 379, n. 14.

38. Diary, Apr. 28, 1664.

39. Diary, Apr. 25, 26, 27, 1664.

40. Diary, May 13, 1664.

41. Diary, May 21, 1664.

42. Diary, May 25, 26, 27, 1664.

43. John Hull, *Diaries of John Hull,* AAS, *Transactions and Collections* 3 (1857), re-

printed in *Puritan Personal Writings: Diaries*, Sacvan Bercovitch, ed., Library of American Puritan Writings: Seventeenth Century, vol. 7 (N.Y.: AMS Press, 1982), 211–212.

44. Diary, May 30, 1664.
45. Diary, June 22, 1664.
46. Diary, June 28, 30, July 1, 9, 11, 12, 13, 16, 29, Sept. 17, 22, 23, 1664.
47. Diary, June 30, 1664.
48. Diary, July 4, 5, Aug. 20, 1664.
49. Diary, Dec. 6, 7, 1664.
50. Diary, Jan. 24, July 6, Aug. 3, 8, 15, 24, Nov. 1, 1664.
51. Diary, Aug. 20, 1664.
52. Diary, Oct. 29, 30, 31, 1664.
53. Diary, Nov. 5, 1664.
54. Diary, Dec. 19, 1664.
55. Diary, Dec. 10, 1664.
56. 5–9, III, Second Church Records, MHS.
57. Quoted in William G. McLoughlin, *New England Dissent, 1630–1833. Baptists and the Separation of Church and State* (Cambridge: Harvard University Press, 1971), 57.
58. Diary, Apr. 12, 1664.
59. McLoughlin, *New England Dissent,* 51–59. William G. McLoughlin and Martha Whiting Davidson, eds., "Baptist Debate of April 14–15, 1668," MHS, *Proceedings,* 76 (1964), 91–133.
60. Diary, Aug. 15, 1665.
61. Direct discourse between Mather and Farnum is excerpted from Mather's longer account, 20–24, III, Second Church Records, MHS, later printed in Samuel Willard, *Ne Sutor Ultra Crepidam. Or Brief Animadversions Upon the New-England Anabaptists Late Fallacious Narrative* (Boston, 1681) and again in Robbins, *Second Church,* 291–295.
62. Diary, Dec. 11, 1665.
63. McLoughlin and Davidson, eds., "The Baptist Debate of April 14–15, 1668," 109.
64. Ibid., 116, 128.
65. Ibid., 133.
66. Ibid., 95.
67. Legal papers relating to the arrest and trials of the Baptists, April 28, 1666, to March 5, 1672. fols. 214–230, XX, Massachusetts State Archives.
68. Dates on which Mather heard examinations are Diary, Jan. 30, Mar. 3, Apr. 14, 28, July 21, Dec. 22, 1665; Jan. 17, Apr. 13, Aug. 29, 31, Sept. 14, 1666; Jan. 18, 1667.
69. Diary, Feb. 16, 1665.
70. Diary, Mar. 26, 1666.
71. Diary, Jan. 6, 1667.
72. Diary, Aug. 25, 1665.
73. Diary, Oct. 17, 1664.
74. Diary, Feb. 8, 1665.
75. Diary, June 26, 1665.

76. Diary, July 13–14, 1665; Mar. 29, 1666.

77. Papers relating to the royal commissioners' negotiations with the General Court, *Records of the Governor and Company of the Massachusetts Bay in New England,* Nathanel B. Shurtleff, ed., 5 vols. (Boston, 1853–1854), IV, 157–273.

78. Diary, Apr. 25, May 8, 19, 1665.

79. Diary, May 25, 1665.

80. Diary, May 16, 1665.

81. Diary, Mar. 11, 1666.

82. Diary, Sept. 6, 1666.

83. Diary, Oct., 1665–May, 1667, passim.

84. Diary, Aug. 16, 21, 1665.

85. Diary, June 6–9, 1665.

86. Burg, *Richard Mather,* 27–30.

87. Diary, June 10–23, 1665.

88. Diary, July 4, 1664.

89. Diary, Jan. 3, 1665.

90. Diary, Feb. 24, 26, 1665.

91. Diary, Mar. 2, 6, 1665.

92. Diary, Apr. 3, 1665.

93. Diary, Apr. 27, 1665.

94. Diary, June 2, 1666.

95. Gershom Scholem, *Sabbatai Sevi: The Mystical Messiah, 1626–1676* (Princeton: Princeton University Press, 1973), 521–549.

96. Diary, Feb. 12, 1666, and Feb.–July, 1666, passim.

97. Diary, Aug. 6, 1666. Cotton Mather, *Parentator,* 61–62.

98. Diary, Aug. 19, 1666.

99. Diary, July 5, 25, 28, 31, Aug., 4, 10, 12, 17, 22, Nov. 25, 27, 28, 1665.

100. Diary, Aug. 31, Sept. 2–7, 11, 13, 18, 19, Oct. 4, 5, Nov. 3, 9, 10, 20, 28, 1665. Cotton Mather, *Parentator,* 58.

101. Diary, May 3, 6–8, 10–14, 16, 20–23, 29, 30, June 3, 1667.

102. Increase Mather, *The Mystery of Israel's Salvation* (London, 1669), Davenport's "Epistle," 4.

103. Cotton Mather, *Parentator,* 61–65.

104. Quoted in Mason I. Lowance, Jr., *The Language of Canaan. Metaphor and Symbol in New England from the Puritans to the Transcendentalists* (Cambridge: Harvard University Press, 1980), 315, n. 51.

105. Benjamin Colman, *Prophet's Death* (Boston, 1723), quoted in Kenneth Silverman, *The Life and Times of Cotton Mather,* (N.Y.: Harper & Row, 1984), 7.

106. The narrative and documentation of these events and their sequel appear fully in Hamilton Hill, *History of the Old South Church (Third Church) Boston, 1669–1884,* 2 vols. (Boston, 1890), I, 1–159.

107. Ibid., 21–22.

108. Ibid., 36.

109. Ibid., 48.

110. Ibid., 60.

111. Increase Mather, *Life and Death,* 65–66.

112. Hill, *Old South Church*, 88–89.

113. *Autobiography*, 287–288.

114. Ibid., 289.

115. Ibid., 290.

116. Ibid., 288–289.

117. "This winter 1671–1672, I sent to London, a Discourse on Math. 24–30 which is entitled, Diatriba de Signo Filii Hominis. . . . For some reason I chose to write it in Latin. I sent it to Mr. Caryl, Mr. Lee, and some other friends. If they publish it, give me your judgement on it also." Increase Mather to Samuel Petto, Mar. 28, 1672, Misc. Bound Mss, MHS.

118. Kenneth B. Murdock, *Literature and Theology in Colonial New England* (Cambridge: Harvard University Press, 1949), 117; Perry Miller and Thomas H. Johnson, *The Puritans* (N.Y.: Harper and Row, 1963), II, 461; Cecelia Tichi, "Spiritual Biography and the 'Lord's Remembrancers'," *William and Mary Quarterly* 3 ser., 28 (Jan. 1971), 69; William J. Scheick, "Introduction" in Increase Mather, *Life and Death*, 7. For a general discussion of Puritan biography, William Haller, *Rise of Puritanism* (N.Y.: Columbia University Press, 1938; Harper & Row, 1957), 94–116.

119. William J. Scheick first drew attention to the pervasive theme of father and son in his introduction to the 1974 facsimile reprint of *Life and Death*, 7–21.

120. Increase Mather, *Life and Death*, 30–31.

121. Ibid., 80.

122. Increase Mather, *The Mystery of Christ, Oppened and Applyed* (Boston, 1686), 15.

123. Increase Mather, *Life and Death*, 42–43.

124. Middlekauf, *Mathers*, 98.

125. David Leverenz, *Language of Puritan Feeling. An Exploration in Literature, Psychology, and Social History* (New Brunswick, N.J.: Rutgers University Press, 1980), 197.

126. Edward Johnson, *Wonder-Working Providence of Sion's Saviour in New England* (1652), quoted in Philip F. Gura, *A Glimpse of Sion's Glory. Puritan Radicalism in New England* (Middletown, Conn.: Wesleyan University Press, 1984), 214. See also Gura, *Sion's Glory*, 229–232.

127. Leverenz, *Language of Puritan Feeling*, 265: "Second generation preachers covered their filial sense of inadequacy and competition with a grandiloquent myth of the first generation and a magnified sense of group failure."

128. Quoted in Pope, *Half-Way Covenant*, 173.

129. Eleazar Mather, *A Serious Exhortation To the Present and Succeeding Generation in New England* (Cambridge, 1671), 15.

130. Ibid., 17.

131. Ibid., 14.

132. *Autobiography*, 291.

133. Hambrick-Stowe, *Practice of Piety*, 26, 27.

134. Family record, Robbins, *Second Church*, 216. Stephen J. Roper, "The Early History of the Paul Revere House," CSM, *Publications* 51, *Architecture in Colonial Massachusetts* (Boston, 1979), 8–9. Plan of Hanover Street and Vicinity in George Emery Littlefield, *The Massachusetts Press* (Boston: Club of Odd Volumes, 1907), 11.

135. *Autobiography,* 291. Here, as in many later instances, Mather transcribed into his autobiography from a diary which has since been lost.

136. Ibid., 296.

137. Ibid., 297.

138. Ibid., 300.

139. Increase Mather, *Some Important Truths About Conversion* (London, 1674), ix, 14, 20, 51, 176. For the dating of these sermons see Holmes, *Increase Mather,* 529.

140. Increase Mather, *Some Important Truths About Conversion,* v–vi.

3. God's Agent On Earth

1. Increase Mather, *Some Important Truths,* xxi.

2. Cotton Mather, *Parentator,* 40. Max Weber found this perpetual self-control and denial of spontaneity to be at the heart of Puritan asceticism. Weber, *Protestant Ethic,* 119.

3. Hambrick-Stowe, *Practice of Piety,* 228–229.

4. Diary, Mar. 25, 1675.

5. Examples from 1671–1672 are printed in *Autobiography,* 293–300.

6. *Autobiography,* 297–298.

7. Ibid., 299.

8. Roper, "Revere House," 6–9.

9. Diary, Apr. 5–7, 1675.

10. Diary, Apr. 9, 1675.

11. Diary, Apr. 10, 1675.

12. Diary, Apr. 10–13, 1675.

13. Diary, Aug. 12, Sept. 1, 1675; May 5, 9, June 29, 1676.

14. David Levin, *Cotton Mather: The Young Life of the Lord's Remembrancer, 1663–1703* (Cambridge: Harvard University Press, 1978), 10–11. Silverman, *Cotton Mather,* 13–15.

15. Levin, *Cotton Mather,* 30–32, 317. Silverman, *Cotton Mather,* 15–17. Cotton Mather's son Samuel wrote that his father had a speech impediment from birth: Samuel Mather, *The Life of the Very Reverend and Learned Cotton Mather* (Boston, 1729), 26.

16. *Autobiography,* 301.

17. Sibley, *Harvard Graduates,* I (1873), 228–233.

18. Hull, *Diary,* 238.

19. Levin, *Cotton Mather,* 28–32; Morison, *Harvard College,* 390–408.

20. Diary, Apr. 16, 19, 26, May 28, 1675. *Diary,* Belknap transcript, March 11–Nov. 28, 1675, MHS, *Proceedings* 13 (1855–1858), 318–319.

21. Diary, June 18, 1675.

22. Diary, June 22, 1675.

23. Diary, Nov. 27, 1675.

24. Increase Mather, *The Day of Trouble is near* (Cambridge, 1674).

25. *Geneva Bible,* facsimile edition (Madison, Wisc.: University of Wisconsin Press, 1969), Ezek 7, 7.

26. Increase Mather, *Day of Trouble,* Preface.

27. Ibid., 22–23.
28. Ibid., 23.
29. Ibid, 25.
30. Ibid., 26.
31. Ibid., 26. Hambrick-Stowe, who calls this "the finest seventeenth-century jeremiad," gives a somewhat different reading of this passage, *Practice of Piety*, 247. See also Sacvan Bercovitch, *American Jeremiad* (Madison, Wisc.: University of Wisconsin Press, 1978), 60. For a radically different interpretation, see Leverenz, *Language of Puritan Feeling*, 197.
32. Increase Mather, *Day of Trouble*, 27–28.
33. Leverenz, *Language of Puritan Feeling*, 176, 185.
34. Increase Mather, *Mystery of Christ*, 151. The importance of these sermons was first developed by Emory Elliott, *Power and the Pulpit in Puritan New England* (Princeton: Princeton University Press, 1975), 133–134.
35. Increase Mather, *Mystery of Christ*, 139.
36. Ibid., 144–148.
37. Ibid., 117.
38. Ibid., 140.
39. Holmes, relying on Mather's preface to *Mystery of Christ*, dated these sermons from the 1670s, Holmes, *Increase Mather*, 352. Confirmation exists in Oakes's foreword, inasmuch as Oakes died in 1681, and in Mather's statement that the second sermon in this collection of eight was delivered when he was preaching on Rev. 2. That was in 1672: sermon books, Mather MSS, AAS. The important point is that these messages of assurance and comfort were preached contemporaneously with the jeremiads and do not represent a different, gentler, and more evangelical period. Mather's diary during the 1670s, particularly for Sabbath days, reveals the same mood of comfort and assurance from "Jesus the Mediator of the new Covenant," quoted in *Autobiography*, p. 317. Furthermore, it was in 1675 that Mather, in a polemical dispute with Habakuk Glover, insisted on the redeeming power of Christ's sacrifice: Michael G. Hall and William L. Joyce, "Three Manuscripts of Increase Mather," AAS, *Proceedings* 86, pt. 1 (1976), 117–119.
40. Leverenz, *Language of Puritan Feeling*, 198–199. Elliott, *Power and the Pulpit*, 125–135.
41. Increase Mather, *A Brief History of the War with the Indians of New-England*, (Boston, 1676), reprinted in Richard Slotkin and James K. Folsom, *So Dreadfull a Judgment: Puritan Responses to King Philip's War* (Middletown, Conn.: Wesleyan University Press, 1978), 87.
42. Benjamin Church, *Entertaining Passages Relating to Philip's War* (Boston, 1716), reprinted in Slotkin and Folsom, *So Dreadfull a Judgment*, 398.
43. Ibid., 398–412. Douglas Leach, *Flintlock and Tomahawk: New England in King Philip's War* (N.Y.: Norton, 1958), 45–72.
44. Increase Mather, *Brief History*, 102–103.
45. Leach, *Flintlock and Tomahawk*, 88–89.
46. *Massachusetts Records*, V, 49–50.
47. Diary, Oct. 14, 1675.
48. Increase Mather, *Brief History*, 105.

49. *Massachusetts Records,* V, 59–63. Mather recorded in his diary that the Deputies passed the bill on November 9, but the Magistrates, "pretending they had not time," delayed a week: "A sore rebuke . . . Alas that Reformation should stick at the head." *Diary,* Belknap transcript, Nov. 9–15, 1676, MHS, *Proceedings,* 2 ser. 13 (1899, 1900), 401.

50. Pp. 30, 37–38, 39, III, Second Church Records, MHS. Increase Mather, *Wo to Drunkards. Two Sermons . . .* (Cambridge, 1673): "The Lord has set me as a Watchman in this great town and charged me to blow the trumpets, that sinners may have warning of their danger," i–ii.

51. Weber, *Protestant Ethic,* 156–158. Increase and Eleazar, on the other hand, thought business activity itself was a waste of time, because it diverted man's attention. "Oh consider, the time was when less of the world, but was there not more of Heaven? less Trading, Buying Selling, but more Praying. . . ." Eleazar Mather, *A Serious Exhortation,* 9.

52. Diary, Nov. 10, 1675.

53. For the Great Swamp fight see Leach, *Flintlock and Tomahawk,* 128–135, and Church (who was wounded there), *Entertaining Passages,* 413–417.

54. Diary, Dec. 5, 1675.

55. Rutman, *Winthrop's Boston,* 268.

56. Diary, Jan. 27, 1676.

57. Leach, *Flintlock and Tomahawk,* 46–47, 148–151.

58. Diary, Feb. 4, 1676.

59. Mary Rowlandson, *The Sovereignty and Goodness of God . . . A Narrative of the Captivity and Restauration of Mrs. Mary Rowlandson.* (Cambridge, 1682), reprinted in Slotkin and Folsom, *So Dreadfull a Judgment,* 323–324.

60. Diary, Feb. 17, 24, 1676.

61. Diary, Feb. 24, 1676.

62. Rowlandson, *Sovereignty of God,* 349. Samp was a gruel made with ground corn.

63. Hull, *Diary,* 241.

64. Rowlandson, *Sovereignty of God,* 354.

65. Ibid., 352.

66. Ibid., 360–361.

67. William Hubbard, *The Happiness of a People in the Wisdom of their Rulers* (Boston, 1676), 38, 54–56, 58. See Anne Kusener Nelsen, "King Philip's War and the Hubbard-Mather Rivalry," *William and Mary Quarterly,* 3rd series, 27 (1970), 615–629.

68. Diary, May 8–16, 1676.

69. Auerbach, *Scenes from the Drama of European Literature:* "In the figural system the interpretation is always sought from above; events are considered not in their unbroken relation to one another, but torn apart, individually, each in relation to something other that is promised and not yet present. . . . In the figural interpretation the fact is subordinated to an interpretation which is fully secured to begin with" (p. 59). "In this way the individual earthly event is not regarded . . . as a link in a chain of development . . . but viewed primarily in immediate vertical connection with a divine order which encompasses it. . . ." (p. 72).

70. Increase Mather, *An Earnest Exhortation* (Boston, 1676), reprinted in Slotkin and Folsom, *So Dreadfull a Judgment*, 173.

71. Ibid., 174. Increase Mather's use of Old Testament history to interpret events of his own day is not the same as typology. Mather assumed that God, outside time, would mete out similar punishments for similar offenses, regardless of historical circumstances. Used conservatively, typology argued that events in the Old Testament foreshadowed specific events that happened later and were recounted in the New Testament. See Auerbach, *Scenes from the Drama of European Literature*, 50–54. This was the sense in which Increase's brother Samuel understood typology when he wrote his important book on the subject. (See Chapter 5) Samuel Mather's book probably acted as a brake on any tendency Increase might have had to broaden the application of typological method to include events in New England as the fulfillment (antitypes) of earlier events in scripture. By and large, when Increase compared recent history to biblical times, such as his father's crossing the Atlantic to Moses' crossing the Red Sea, or New England as New Canaan or New Jerusalem, he spoke metaphorically, not typologically. In practice, however, the differences between metaphor and typology were often indistinct, and probably the climate of opinion in Massachusetts in the seventeenth century attracted many preachers to an expanded use of typology. Modern scholars have generally focused their attention on this enlarged application of typological method.

72. Increase Mather, *Earnest Exhortation*, 174.

73. Ibid., 182.

74. Ibid., 176.

75. Diary, June 5, 1676.

76. Increase Mather, *Earnest Exhortation*, 186.

77. Ibid., 187. See also *Diary*, Belknap transcript, May 9, Aug. 7, 1676, MHS, *Proceedings*, 2 ser., 13 (1899, 1900), 403.

78. Increase Mather, *Earnest Exhortation*, 189.

79. Ibid., 190.

80. Ibid., 190. *Earnest Exhortation* was published together with *Brief History*, where the engraving is printed, 102.

81. Ibid., 196.

82. Ibid., 179–180.

83. Ibid., 197–198.

84. Increase Mather, *Brief History*, 82.

85. Ibid., 83.

86. Ibid., 139.

87. "To the Reader," *Earnest Exhortation*, 167.

88. Increase Mather, *Brief History*, 81. See Holmes, *Increase Mather*, 71–72, for a discussion of these accounts.

89. Diary, May 1, 2, 1676.

90. Diary, June 6, 15, 27, July 1, 3, 7, Aug. 2, 9, 14, 21, 1676.

91. Increase Mather, *Brief History*, 81.

92. Richard Chiswell to Increase Mather, London, February 16, 1677, *Mather Papers*, 575–576.

93. William Hubbard, *A Narrative of the Troubles with the Indians in New-England* (Boston, 1677).

94. John Cotton to Increase Mather, Mar. 19, Apr. 14, 1677, *Mather Papers,* 232–235.

4. Spiritual Leadership

1. Increase Mather to John Cotton, Dec. 13, 1676, Mather Papers, AAS. *Diary,* Belknap transcript, Nov. 27, 1676, MHS, *Proceedings,* 2 ser., 13 (1899, 1900), 404. *Autobiography,* 303; Suffolk County, Massachusetts, *Records of the Suffolk County Court, 1671–1680,* CMS, *Publications,* 29–30 (Boston, 1933), II, 272–283.

2. Diary, Nov. 27, 1676.

3. Diary, Nov. 28, 1676.

4. Increase Mather to John Cotton, Dec. 13, 1676, Mather Papers, AAS.

5. Ibid.

6. Ibid.

7. Two illustrations exist, one on the Bonner Map of Boston, 1722, and one a nineteenth-century drawing reproduced in Silverman, *Cotton Mather,* opposite p. 306.

8. No. 170, Aug. 29, 1677, X, Suffolk Deeds, MHS.

9. No. 278–279, Oct. 5, 1677, X, Suffolk Deeds, MHS. Sewall, *Diary,* July 1, 1676, mentions a "Jethro, his Niger," who was captured by Indians in the war and later released. That Jethro was apparently the servant or slave of a man killed in the war.

10. "A Catalogue of Books I had by the great bounty of Madam Usher," dated Dec. 5, 1676. 29, II, American MSS, 1502, BPL.

11. *A Discourse Concerning the Danger of Apostasy,* published as the second sermon in Increase Mather, *A Call From Heaven to the Present and Succeeding Generations* (Boston, 1679), p. 56.

12. Ibid., 57.

13. Hull, *Diary,* 238; Sewall, *Diary,* Dec. 18, 1676.

14. *Danger of Apostasy,* 75–77.

15. Ibid., 78.

16. Ibid.

17. Ibid., 84.

18. Petit, *Heart Prepared,* 78–79, 90, 133–134.

19. Quoted in Edmund S. Morgan, *American Slavery, American Freedom,* (N.Y.: Norton, 1975), 187.

20. Murdock, *Increase Mather,* 106.

21. Lawrence C. Wroth and Marion W. Adams, *American Woodcuts and Engravings, 1670–1800* (Providence, R.I.: John Carter Brown Library, 1946), 6.

22. Printed in Hubbard, *Narrative of the Troubles.* Richard Holman, "Foster's Woodcut Map of New England," *PAGA: Printing and Graphic Arts,* 8 (1960), 53–92.

23. Wroth and Adams, *Woodcuts and Engravings,* 6.

24. Increase Mather, *Diary,* Belknap transcript, Dec. 25, 1674, MHS, *Proceedings,* 2 ser., 13 (1899, 1900), 398, 399. A sketch of Foster's life and work is Samuel A. Green, *John Foster, the Earliest American Engraver and First Boston Printer* (Boston: MHS, 1909).

25. Increase Mather, *The Wicked Man's Portion,* preached Mar. 18, 1674, and *The Times of Men are in The Hand of God,* preached May 4, 1675. *Wicked Man's Portion* was the second execution sermon published in New England, establishing a minor genre begun with Samuel Danforth, *Cry of Sodom Enquired Into* (Cambridge, 1674). See Ronald A. Bosco, "Lecture at the Pillory: the Early American Execution Sermon," *American Quarterly,* 30 (1978), 156–176.

26. The portrait is illustrated as item 437 in Boston Museum of Fine Arts exhibit catalogue, *New England Begins: The Seventeenth Century,* 3 vols. (Boston, 1982), III, 462.

27. Littlefield, *Early Massachusetts Press,* II, 6–10.

28. Hambrick-Stowe, *Practice of Piety,* 49. The study of the Massachusetts press begins with Charles Evans, *American Bibliography* vol. I, 1639–1729 (Chicago: Charles Evans, 1903) and Roger P. Bristol, *Supplement to Charles Evans' American Bibliography* (Charlottesville, Va.: University Press of Virginia, 1970).

29. Increase Mather's Preface to Davenport's *Another Essay* (1663), was unsigned. *Life and Death* (1670) was published anonymously. *Mystery of Israel's Salvation* and *Some Important Truths* were published in London. Increase Mather's first signed publication in New England was his preface to Eleazar Mather, *A Serious Exhortation.* Prefaces in several of Increase Mather's early works reveal uncertainty about the propriety of his putting himself in the public eye through published works. See for example *Brief History,* 81–82, or *Times of Men,* iv. Even in this Increase followed in his father's footsteps. Richard published the first extant collection of sermons in New England: Foster, "English Puritanism," 33, n. 72.

30. Thirteen of Mather's bound sermon books are in the Mather Papers, AAS.

31. Increase Mather, *Life and Death,* 71.

32. Increase Mather, *Wicked Man's Portion,* i.

33. Increase Mather, *Some Important Truths,* xviii, xxi.

34. Increase Mather, To the Reader, in Samuel Torrey, *An Exhortation unto Reformation* (Cambridge, 1674) sig. Az, quoted in Hambrick-Stowe, *Practice of Piety,* 248.

35. Increase Mather, *Discourse Concerning Baptism* (Cambridge, 1675), 3.

36. Ibid., 9.

37. David D. Hall, *The Faithful Shepherd: a History of the New England Ministry in the Seventeenth Century* (Charlotte, N.C.: University of North Carolina Press, 1972), 225–6. Holifield, *Covenant Sealed,* 183–4.

38. Nathaniel Mather to Increase Mather, Feb. 26, 1676, *Mather Papers,* 7–8.

39. Ibid., 7–32.

40. Increase Mather, *Divine Right of Infant Baptism* (Boston, 1680).

41. Nathaniel Mather to Increase Mather, Mar. 2, 1681, *Mather Papers,* 31.

42. Nathaniel to Increase Mather, Mar. 28, 1682, Ibid., 35.

43. Pp. 11, III (Book No. 1 1/2), Second Church Records, MHS.

44. Ibid.

45. Pp. 63–82, I; pp. 1, 5–9, 15, III (Book No. 1 1/2), same volume, reversed pagination, 8–12, Second Church Records, MHS.

46. Increase Mather, *Pray for the Rising Generation* (Cambridge, 1678), 11.

47. Quoted in *Autobiography*, 315.

48. Ibid., 317–318.

49. Ibid.

50. Increase Mather, *Pray for the Rising Generation*, 12.

51. "For if they shall soe doe (which God forbid) then in such Case I hereby testify unto them, that their Father . . . and their mother . . . will rise up against them. . . ." Richard Mather, Last Will and Testament, Oct. 16, 1661, *New England Historical and Genealogical Register*, 20 (1866), 248–255.

52. Increase Mather, *Pray for the Rising Generation*, 22.

53. Increase Mather, *Wicked Man's Portion*, 18.

54. Ibid., 19.

55. *Geneva Bible* 2 Samuel 18 : 33.

56. Ibid.

57. Increase Mather, *Wicked Man's Portion*, Preface. Leverenz offers a Freudian interpretation, *Language of Puritan Feeling*, 205–206.

58. Cotton Mather to John Cotton, November, 1678, *Mather Papers*, 384. Increase Mather kept tally of the sick and the dead, *Diary*, Belknap transcript, MHS, *Proceedings*, 2 ser. 13 (1899, 1900), 406–407.

59. Ibid. Hull, *Diary*, 244; Stannard estimates 20% of the Boston population died, David E. Stannard, *The Puritan Way of Death: a Study in Religion, Culture and Social Change* (N.Y.: Oxford University Press, 1977), 53–54.

60. Increase Mather, To The Reader, in Thomas Thacher, *A Fast of God's Chusing* (Boston, 1678), 3–4.

61. Petition of the ministers, May 28, 1679, excerpted in Williston Walker, *Creeds and Platforms*, 414–415.

62. Thomas Jollie to Increase Mather, Apr. 2, 1677, *Mather Papers*, 317–319.

63. Jollie to Increase Mather, Jan. 18, 1678, Ibid., 320.

64. Hambrick-Stowe, *Practice of Piety*, 131–132, 248–252. David Hall, *Faithful Shepherd*, 244.

65. Burg, *Richard Mather*, 50. Richard Mather, *An Apologie for the Churches in New England* (London, 1643) and Richard Mather, *Church Government and Church Government Discussed* (London, 1643) were both written to justify covenants.

66. James A. Goulding, "The Controversy between Solomon Stoddard and the Mathers: Western versus Eastern Massachusetts Congregationalism," Ph.D. diss., Claremont Graduate School, 1971, 350–351. Pope, *Half-Way Covenant*, 253.

67. Goulding, "Controversy," 400–407.

68. Thomas Cobbet to Increase Mather, Nov. 12, 1678, *Mather Papers*, 289.

69. Seymour Van Dyken, *Samuel Willard, 1640–1707* (Grand Rapids, Mich.: Erdman Publishing, 1972), 39; Hambrick-Stowe, *Practice of Piety*, 250.

70. Peter Thacher's Journal of the Synod proceedings, printed in Walker, *Creeds and Platforms*, 417–419.

71. Ibid.

72. Increase Mather's corrected manuscript copy of the actions of the Synod,

Mather Papers, AAS. See Hall and Joyce, "Three Manuscripts of Increase Mather," 114–116.

73. Cambridge Platform, Chapter XII, in Walker, *Creeds and Platforms*, 221–222.
74. Increase Mather, "An Answer to Mr. Stoddard's 9 Arguments . . . ," printed in Everett Emerson and Mason I. Lowance, Jr., "Increase Mather's Confutation of Solomon Stoddard's Observations Respecting The Lord's Supper 1680," AAS *Proceedings*, 83, pt. 1 (1973), 29–65. The disagreements between Increase Mather and Solomon Stoddard were once among the most vague and hypothetical issues in American historiography. The early disagreements, c. 1670–1690, are now thoroughly documented. See the above and William L. Joyce, "Note on Increase Mather's Observations Respecting the Lord's Supper," Ibid., pt. 2 (1973), 343–344; Thomas M. Davis and Jeff Jeske. "Solomon Stoddard's 'Arguments' Concerning Admission to the Lord's Supper," Ibid., 86, pt. 1 (1976), 75–111. Stoddard had not relaxed his belief in human depravity or the necessity of a thorough conversion. His disagreements with Mather were over less important things. See James W. Jones, *The Shattered Synthesis: New England Puritanism Before the Great Awakening* (New Haven: Yale University Press, 1973), 106–116.
75. *Autobiography*, 305.
76. *Necessity of Reformation* (Boston, 1679), in Walker, *Creeds and Platforms*, 423.
77. Ibid., Article I, 427.
78. Ibid., Article X, 431.
79. Ibid., e.g., Article V, 429; Article VIII, 430.
80. Ibid., Question I, 426.
81. Ibid., 427.
82. Ibid., Question II, 433–437, passim.
83. Ibid., Question II, Article XI, 437.
84. *Massachusetts Records*, quoted in Walker, *Creeds and Platforms*, 419–420.
85. The new church covenant for the North Church is printed at the end of Increase Mather, *Returning Unto God the Great Concernment of a Covenant People* (Boston, 1680).
86. Hambrick-Stowe. *Practice of Piety*, 250–252.
87. *Autobiography*, 305.

5. New Worlds of Science and Hope

1. *Autobiography*, 305–306.
2. Diary, Sept. 6, 1680.
3. Diary, 1680–1681, passim.
4. Diary, Sept. 6, 1680.
5. *Diary*, Belknap transcript, March, 1679, MHS, *Proceedings* 2 ser. 13 (1899, 1900), 407.
6. McLoughlin, *New England Dissent*, 75, 83, 104–05.
7. Diary, Jan.–Feb., 1681, passim. Increase Mather, To The Reader, Nov. 4, 1681, in Willard, *Ne Sutor Ultra Crepidam* (Boston, 1681).
8. Increase Mather, To The Reader, in Willard, *Ne Sutor Ultra Crepidam*, 2–4.

9. Simon Bradstreet to Increase Mather, Apr. 20, 1681, *Mather Papers,* 477–479; Thomas Corbet to Increase Mather, Dec. 13, 1681, Ibid., 291–293.

10. John Russell to Increase Mather, Mar. 28, 1681, Ibid., 83.

11. Ibid., 82.

12. John Foster, *MDCLXXXI. An Almanack* (Boston, 1681). Morison, "The Harvard School of Astronomy in the Seventeenth Century," *New England Quarterly,* 7 (1934), 21.

13. Florian Cajori, trans. and ed., *Sir Isaac Newton's Mathematical Principles,* 2 vols. (Berkeley: University of California Press, 1934), II, 516–518; Marion Barber Stowell, *Early American Almanacs, the Colonial Weekday Bible* (N.Y.: B. Franklin, 1977), 53–54, 288 note 23.

14. Moses Coit Tyler, quoted in David Hall, "On Native Ground," AAS *Proceedings,* vol. 93, pt. 2 (1983), 323.

15. John Richardson, "The Countryman's Apocrypha" and "A Perpetual Calendar, fitted for the Meridian of Babylon, Where the POPE is elevated 42 Degr," *1670. An Almanac* (Cambridge, 1670).

16. See in this connection Robert K. Merton, "Puritanism, Pietism and Science," in *Social Theory and Social Structure* (N.Y.: Free Press, 1968), 628–660.

17. John Sherman, *1674. An Almanac; 1676. An Almanac; 1677. An Almanac* (Cambridge, 1674, 1676, 1677).

18. Cotton Mather, *Magnalia,* I, 515–516.

19. Littlefield, *Early Massachusetts Press,* II, 12–13.

20. The gravestone is illustrated in Museum of Fine Arts, Boston, *New England Begins,* II, 321.

21. Ibid., 322.

22. Diary, June 30–July 10; July 27, Aug. 2, 8; 18, 1682; Epistle in Increase Mather, *Practical Truths Tending to Promote the Power of Godliness* (Boston, 1682).

23. Increase Mather, *The Latter Sign Discoursed* (Boston, 1682), 6.

24. Michael G. Hall, "Introduction of Modern Science into 17th Century New England: Increase Mather," *Ithaca,* 26 VIII–2 IX (Paris: Hermann, 1962), 262–264.

25. Diary, Sept. 12, 1682.

26. Martha Ornstein, *Role of Scientific Societies in the Seventeenth Century* (N.Y.: Columbia University, 1913), 198–205.

27. Diary, April 23, 30, May 10, June 25, July 23, Sept. 3, Dec. 10, 1683. Otho T. Beall, Jr., "Cotton Mather's Early 'Curiosa Americana' and the Boston Philosophical Society of 1683," *William and Mary Quarterly,* 3 ser., 18 (1961), 362–367.

28. Increase Mather, *Kometographia, Or a Discourse Concerning Comets* (Boston, 1683), 7.

29. Maxine Van de Wetering, "Moralizing in Puritan Natural Science: Mysteriousness in Earthquake Sermons," *Journal of the History of Ideas,* 43 (1982), 417–418.

30. Increase Mather, *Kometographia,* vi.

31. John Norton, *Abel Being Dead, Yet Speaketh: or the Life and Death of . . . John Cotton* (London, 1658), 47.

32. Increase Mather, *Kometographia,* 130.

33. Increase Mather, Ibid., 132–133.

34. Ibid., 136.

35. Ibid., 136.

36. Ibid., 137.

37. Ibid., 139.

38. Ibid., 141.

39. Diary, Jan. 30, 1683.

40. Quoted in Middlekauf, *Mathers,* 145.

41. Basil Willey, *Seventeenth Century Background* (London, 1934; Grove City, N.Y.: Doubleday, 1953), 195–203.

42. Diary, 1683 passim.

43. Holmes, *Increase Mather,* 238. Increase Mather, *An Essay for the Recording of Illustrious Providences* (Boston, 1684), with all its complexities and paradoxes of thought has been a favorite of later centuries, frequently reprinted and often the subject of scholarly analysis: Holmes, *Increase Mather,* 232–249; Middlekauf, *Mathers,* 143–148; Miller, *Colony to Province,* 142–145.

44. Sermon Book, 1682–1685, Mather Papers, AAS. Diary, May 6–10, June 11–13, 16–17, 1684.

45. Increase Mather, *Doctrine of Divine Providence* (Boston, 1684), 53.

46. Ibid., 46.

47. Ibid., 7.

48. Ibid., 23.

49. Ibid., 12.

50. Ibid., 41–42.

51. Printers File, AAS, Library. Littlefield, *Early Massachusetts Press,* 44–45.

52. Diary, July 26, 28; Aug. 8, 9, 1681.

53. Diary, Aug. 19, 22, 24, 25, Sept. 6, 8, 16, Oct. 3, 15, 17, 27, 1681.

54. Diary, June 13, Oct. 3, 10, 1681; Aug. 1, Sept. 12, Oct. 18, Nov. 31, Dec. 26, 1682.

55. Henry J. Cadbury, "Harvard College Library, and the Libraries of the Mathers," AAS, *Proceedings,* n.s. 50 (1940), 21–22.

56. Diary, Nov. 7, Dec. 5, 13, 30, 1681; Jan. 5, 19, 25–26, Mar. 20, 27, Apr. 10, 1682.

57. Diary, Apr. 10, 1682.

58. Levin, *Cotton Mather,* 52–53.

59. Silverman, *Cotton Mather,* 37.

60. Levin, *Cotton Mather,* 88–91; Silverman, *Cotton Mather,* 24–33.

61. Quoted in Hambrick-Stowe, *Practice of Piety,* 34.

62. Sewall, *Diary,* Jan. 28, 1686.

63. Increase Mather, *Practical Truths Tending to Promote the Power of Godliness* (Boston, 1682), Preface.

64. Silverman, *Cotton Mather,* 45–46.

65. Diary, June 27, 1681.

66. Diary, June 30–July 10, 1682; July 31–Aug. 13, 1683.

67. Increase Mather to Abraham Kick, Nov. 20, 1683, *Harvard College Records,*

CSM, *Publications*, 49 (1975), 149–150. Mather also asked for two scholarly works about comets.

68. Samuel Bache to Increase Mather, 1684, Jamaica, 83, V, American MSS 1502, BPL.

69. Nathaniel Mather to Increase Mather, Feb. 20, 1676–Feb. 26, 1687, *Mather Papers*, 1–68. "For I am perswaded Comets doe no more portend than Eclipses, and Eclipses no more than the constant conjunctions of the sun & moon, that is, just nothing at all . . . ," Ibid., 49. For the lost portrait of Nathaniel see Frederick L. Weis, "Checklist of the Portraits in the Library of the American Antiquarian Society," AAS *Proceedings*, 56, Pt. 1 (1947), 92–93.

70. Samuel Mather, *Figures or Types of the Old Testament*, Mason I. Lowance, Jr., ed. (N.Y.: Johnson Reprint, 1969), xii.

71. Nathaniel Mather to Increase Mather, Aug. 13, 1683–Dec. 31, 1684, *Mather Papers*, 47–61.

72. Samuel Mather, *Figures or Types*, xii–xx.

73. Increase Mather, "Preface," *Practical Truths Tending to Promote the Power of Godliness*.

74. John Higginson to Increase Mather, Aug. 22, 1682, *Mather Papers*, 282.

75. Diary, Nov. 7, 1682.

76. Increase Mather, *Practical Truths Tending to Promote the Power of Godliness*, 99.

77. Ibid., 132–133.

78. Ibid., 120.

79. Ibid., 218.

80. See above pp. 102–103.

81. Increase Mather, *Mystery of Christ*, 1, 6.

82. Increase Mather, *Practical Truths Tending to Promote the Power of Godliness*, 136.

83. Increase Mather, *The Greatest Sinners Exhorted and Encouraged to Come to Christ* (Boston, 1686), i.

84. Membership Lists, 63–82, I; 15, III, Second Church Records, MHS. Farnum's readmission, Sept. 1683, Ibid., 43.

85. Richard Mather wrote his diary or autobiography to age 39. Increase drew on it for the early part of his father's biography: *Life and Death*, 28. Shepard's autobiography has been published several times, most recently by Michael McGiffert, ed., *God's Plot: The Paradoxes of Puritan Piety, Being the Autobiography and Journal of Thomas Shepard* (Amherst, Mass.: University of Massachusetts Press, 1972). Increase Mather's autobiography was first published in 1961, *The Autobiography of Increase Mather*, M. G. Hall, ed., AAS, *Proceedings*, 71 (1961).

86. Increase Mather, *Autobiography*, p. 277.

87. Ibid., 277.

88. Ibid., 294. Daniel B. Shea, Jr., *Spiritual Autobiography in Early America* (Princeton: Princeton University Press, 1968), 157–161.

89. Increase Mather, *Autobiography*, 286–287.

90. Ibid., 310.

91. Ibid., 287–300.

92. Ibid., 313–314.

93. Ibid., 316.

6. Dominion of New England

1. For a recent summary of Massachusetts's economic developments after 1660, see Richard R. Johnson, *Adjustment to Empire: The New England Colonies, 1675–1715* (New Brunswick, N.J.: Rutgers University Press, 1981), 11–22.

2. J. M. Sosin, *English America and the Revolution of 1688* (Lincoln, Neb.: University of Nebraska Press, 1982), 57–61.

3. J. M. Sosin, *English America and the Restoration Monarchy of Charles II* (Lincoln, Neb.: University of Nebraska Press, 1980), 264–280.

4. Theodore B. Lewis, "Land Speculation and the Dudley Council of 1686," *William and Mary Quarterly*, 31 (1974), 255–272.

5. Kenneth A. Lockridge, *A New England Town: the First Hundred Years* (N.Y.: Norton, 1970), 9.

6. Philip Greven, Jr., *Four Generations: Population, Land, and Family in Colonial Andover, Massachusetts* (Ithaca, N.Y.: Cornell University Press, 1970), 58–62.

7. Quoted in Demos, "Notes on Life in Plymouth Colony," *William and Mary Quarterly*, 3 Ser., 22 (1965), 266.

8. Statistical information supplied by David Odell Damerall, based on *Report of the Record Commissioners of the City of Boston*, I (Boston, 1876), 68–76, 91–127, 158–170.

9. For the development of English policy towards New England 1675–1685, see Johnson, *Adjustment to Empire*, 27–56; and Sosin, *English America and the Restoration Monarchy*, 276–301.

10. Michael G. Hall, *Edward Randolph and the American Colonies, 1676–1703* (Chapel Hill, N.C.: University of North Carolina Press for the Institute of Early American History and Culture, 1960), 1–20.

11. Sosin, *English America and the Restoration Monarchy*, 289.

12. Diary, Jan. 6, 1681.

13. Randolph to Robert Southwell. Mar. 12, 1681, quoted in Hall, *Edward Randolph*, 64.

14. Increase Mather to Joseph Dudley, Jan. 20, 1708, MHS, *Collections*, 1 ser., III (1794, reprinted 1810), 126–127.

15. John Richards to Increase Mather, Aug. 21, 1682–Apr. 20, 1683, *Mather Papers*, 494–502.

16. Diary, Mar. 8, 26, 1683. Sosin, *English America and the Restoration Monarchy*, 266–270. Hall, *Edward Randolph*, 76.

17. Hall, *Edward Randolph*, 79–97. Sosin, *English America and the Restoration Monarchy*, 278–293.

18. *Autobiography*, 307; Diary, Nov. 30, 1683. An unsigned document printed in MHS *Collections*, 3 ser., I (1825), 74–81, is thought by some to have been written by Mather. I believe it was not, because its language and argumentation are unlike any authentic Mather papers of this period.

19. Peter Bulkeley to William Blathwayt, Dec. 7, 1683, quoted in Hall, *Edward Randolph*, 80.

20. Sosin, *English America and the Restoration Monarchy*, 271.

21. *Autobiography*, 308.

22. Diary, Feb. 4, 27, 1684.

23. Sosin, *English America and the Restoration Monarchy*, 271. Jeremy Belknap, *The History of New Hampshire*, 2 vols. (Dover, N.H.: 1812; N.Y.: Johnson Reprint, 1970), I, 106–107.

24. Edward Randolph to Simon Bradstreet, Sept. 4, 1684; Simon Bradstreet to Edward Randolph, Dec. 8, 1684. Robert N. Toppan and Alfred T. S. Goodrick, eds., *Edward Randolph; Including His Letters and Official Papers*, 7 vols. (Boston: Prince Society, 1898–1909), III, 322–323, 338–339.

25. Randolph to Samuel Shrimpton, July 18, 1684, Ibid., 310.

26. Sosin, *English America and the Restoration Monarchy*, 296.

27. Diary, July 16, 1684. *Autobiography*, 309.

28. *Autobiography*, 310.

29. Ibid., 311.

30. The letter is printed in *Mather Papers*, 104–107, and *Randolph Letters*, III, 312–316.

31. Randolph to Simon Bradstreet, Sept. 4, 1684, *Randolph Letters*, III, 322.

32. Mather to Dudley, Nov. 10, 1684, *Randolph Letters*, III, 327–331; *Mather Papers*, 100–104.

33. *Autobiography*, 310.

34. Ibid., 318.

35. Sosin, *English America and the Restoration Monarchy*, 299–300.

36. Sewall, *Diary*, Nov. 12, 1685.

37. *Autobiography*, 319.

38. Holmes, *Increase Mather*, 23–24.

39. Increase Mather, *Arrow Against Profane and Promiscuous Dancing* (Boston, 1685), 1–2, 24–25, quoted in Holmes, *Increase Mather*, 24–25.

40. Chester Noyes Greenough, "John Dunton's Letters from New England," CSM, *Publications*, 14 (1913), 213–257. For more on John Dunton, Bonamy Dobrée, *English Literature in the Early Eighteenth Century*, Oxford History of English Literature, vol. 8 (N.Y.: Oxford University Press, 1959), 346–348.

41. Holmes, *Increase Mather*, 479–487.

42. *Harvard College Records*, 4, CSM, *Publications* 49 (1975), 145–151. Diary, Aug. 8, 1682; June 26, Aug. 14, Sept. 12, 1683; Jan. 3, 1684.

43. Morison, *Harvard College*, 452–465.

44. *Harvard College Records*, 4, CSM, *Publications* 49 (1975), 145–151. *Autobiography*, 313. Morison, *Harvard College*, 472–473.

45. Morison, *Harvard College*, 423–430, 473, 476–477. The 1686 College Laws are printed, *Harvard College Records*, 2, CSM, *Publications*, 16 (1925), 848–850. The new college laws are misleadingly called the "Dudley Laws." They were drafted by Mather and, like the new tutors, put in place during his acting presidency.

46. Increase Mather written directive, n.d., 13, no. 32, Coll. P., I, Harvard College Archives.

47. Norman Fiering, *Moral Philosophy at Seventeenth-Century Harvard. A Discipline in Transition* (Chapel Hill, N.C.: University of North Carolina Press for the Institute of Early American History and Culture, 1981), 36–40.

48. To The Reader in John Flavel, *England's Duty* (London, 1689), quoted in Holmes, *Increase Mather*, 586–587.

49. Morison, *Harvard College,* 236–249. *Compendium Physicae,* in CSM, *Publications,* 33 (1940) with commentary by S. E. Morison and Theodore Hornberger. See also I. Bernard Cohen, "The *Compendium Physicae* of Charles Morton," *Isis* 33 (June, 1942), 659–660.
50. Students to Increase Mather, May 4, 1685, Prince MSS, MHS.
51. Nathaniel Mather to John Cotton, July 21, 1685, Prince MSS, MHS. Kenneth Silverman kindly supplied me with a copy and transcript of this letter. *Autobiography,* 313.
52. *Autobiography,* 313; Morison, *Harvard College,* 504–505.
53. Morison, *Harvard College,* 475–476.
54. Nathaniel Mather to John Cotton, July 21, 1685, Prince MSS, MHS.
55. Ministers to General Court, July 22, 1685, MHS, *Proceedings,* 12 (1871), 105–107; Sosin, *English America and the Revolution,* 66–67.
56. Sewall, *Diary,* Nov. 13, 18, 20, Dec. 4, 1685, and note 32, p. 84.
57. Ibid., Jan. 23, 1686.
58. Ibid., Jan. 28, 1686.
59. Ibid., Apr. 13, 15, May 12, 1686.
60. Ibid., May 12, 1686.
61. Ibid., May 17, 1686.
62. Ibid., May 17, 21, 1686.
63. Ibid., May 21, 1686.
64. John Tulley, *An Almanack* (Boston, 1687, 1688, 1689, 1690). Stowell, *American Almanacs,* 58–59.
65. *Diary,* Belknap transcript, Sept. 27, 1687, MHS, *Proceedings,* 2 ser. 13 (1899, 1900), 411. Sewall, *Diary,* 1687–1688, passim.
66. Morison, *Harvard College,* 476–477.
67. Holmes, *Increase Mather,* 46–63.
68. Sosin, *English America and the Restoration Monarchy,* 244–252; Sosin, *English America and the Revolution,* 12–22. For an account of Andros's rule, see Richard Johnson, *Adjustment to Empire,* 74–82.
69. Sosin, *English America and the Revolution,* 74.
70. Ibid., 73; David S. Lovejoy, *The Glorious Revolution in America* (N.Y.: Harper & Row, 1972), 184–185.
71. *Autobiography,* 320.
72. Sosin, *English America and the Revolution,* 25–26.
73. *Autobiography,* 320.
74. Sewall, *Diary,* Jan. 25, 1688.
75. *Autobiography,* 320. Two drafts of the address to James II are printed, *Mather Papers,* 697–698. They are quite dissimilar. One is in Willard's handwriting. The other, less unctuous, is more like Mather.
76. *Autobiography,* 321.
77. Ibid. Sewall, *Diary,* Jan. 31, 1688. Papers relating to the trial are in Massachusetts Archives, 129, no. 320.
78. *Autobiography,* 322. Sewall, *Diary,* Mar. 22, 1688.
79. *Autobiography,* 322–323. Diary, Mar. 27–Apr. 7, 1688. Sewall, *Diary,* Apr. 7, 1688. Cotton Mather to John Cotton, Apr. 11, 1688, Mather Papers, Alderman Library, University of Virginia.

7. Representing Massachusetts in London

1. *Autobiography*, 323–324; Diary, Apr. 8–May 16, 1688.

2. Diary, May 16–25, 1688; Expense account in Diary, May 16–24, 1688. John Evelyn, *Diary of John Evelyn*, E. S. de Beer, ed. (London: Oxford University Press, 1959), 879.

3. Kellaway, *New England Company*, 77–78; Fiering, *Moral Philosophy at Harvard*, 280.

4. Matthews, *Calamy Revised*, 344.

5. Diary, May 30, 1686; *Autobiography*, 325–326. Identification of "Mr. Pen" as the proprietor of Pennsylvania is in Cotton Mather, *Parentator*, 114.

6. *Autobiography*, 326.

7. Diary, June 1, 1686; *Autobiography*, 329–330.

8. Diary, June 2–30, 1686.

9. Evelyn, *Diary*, 883.

10. Diary, June 21, 1688.

11. Diary, July 2, 1688; *Autobiography*, 330. Draft memorial of grievances, n.d., Petition for Harvard College, n.d., *Mather Papers*, 113–115; Petition of Mather, Nowell and Hutchinson to the king, n.d., *Mather Papers*, 699–702. Sosin, *English America and the Revolution*, 76–77, notes 24 and 25.

12. J. M. Sosin, *English America and the Revolution*, 77–78, notes 26, 27.

13. Diary, Aug. 10, 11, 1688. Petition of Mather, Nowell, and Hutchinson to Committee for Trade, n.d., *Mather Papers*, 116.

14. Diary, Aug. 29, 31, Sept. 11, 12, and passim Aug.–Sept.–Oct. 1686. Bond of Mather, Nowell, and Hutchinson to pay Mason £200 plus interest, Aug. 30, 1688, no. 31, Box 7, Mather Papers, AAS.

15. Diary, Sept. 26, Oct. 16, 1688.

16. Diary, June–Aug. 1688, passim; Feb. 4–5, 1689; To The Reader in John Flavel, *England's Duty* (London, 1689), quoted in Holmes, *Increase Mather*, 347–348.

17. Diary accounts, May 17, 23, 24, June 28, 1688; Diary, July 3, 5, Aug. 2–4, 1688. Murdock, *Mather*, 270.

18. Holmes, *Increase Mather*, 546–562. Diary, Aug. 1, Sept. 5, Dec. 11, 1688. John Leusden to Increase Mather, Jan. 18, 1689, *Mather Papers*, 678–680.

19. Diary, Aug. 1, 1688.

20. Diary, Oct. 16, 18, Nov. 1, 1688.

21. Joshua Moody to Increase Mather, Oct. 4, 1688, *Mather Papers*, 366.

22. Ibid., 366–367.

23. Nathaniel Mather to Cotton Mather, Aug. 31, 1688. *Mather Papers*, 673.

24. John Cotton to Increase Mather, Sept. 10, 1688, *Mather Papers*, 257.

25. Quoted by Increase Mather, Apr. 5, 1714, in *Sermon Concerning Obedience and Resignation*, iv–v, and in Holmes, *Increase Mather*, 478.

26. Joshua Moody to Increase Mather, Feb. 8, 1689, *Mather Papers*, 369.

27. Evelyn, *Diary*,, 894–895.

28. *Diary*, Dec. 3, 1688. Nathaniel Mather to Cotton Mather, Aug. 14, 1688, *Mather Papers*, 672.

29. Diary, Dec. 26, 1688.

30. Diary, Dec. 4, 1688. Manuscript summary, Various 1664–1796, Mather Papers, AAS. Diary, accounts for January 16, 1689.
31. Bremer, "Friends of Increase Mather," 70.
32. Sosin, *English America and the Revolution,* 147–149.
33. *Autobiography,* 341; Diary, Jan. 29, 1689.
34. Diary, Jan. 9, 1689. *Autobiography,* 331–332. Evelyn, *Diary,* 896.
35. Diary, Jan. 31, 1689.
36. Manuscript summary, Various 1664–1796, Mather Papers, AAS. Diary, Jan. 1689, passim.
37. Diary, Feb. 2, 1689.
38. Johnson, *Adjustment to Empire,* 144–150.
39. [Sir Robert Southwell ?] to Earl of Nottingham, Mar. 23, 1689, in Hall, Leder and Kammen, *Glorious Revolution in America,* 67.
40. Diary, Mar. 14, 1689. *Autobiography,* 332.
41. [Sir Robert Southwell ?] to Earl of Nottingham, Mar. 23, 1689, Hall, Leder, and Kammen, *Glorious Revolution in America,* 67.
42. Johnson, *Adjustment to Empire,* 150–157; Sosin, *English America and the Revolution,* 128–129.
43. Quoted in Johnson, *Adjustment to Empire,* 161. For the Corporation Bill, see Ibid., 160–169.
44. For the progress of the bill and Increase Mather's lobbying, see R. C. Simmons, "The Massachusetts Charter of 1691," in *Contrasts and Connections: Bicentennial Essays in Anglo-American History,* H. C. Allen and Roger Thompson, eds. (London: Bell and Sons, 1974), 72–76.
45. Major documents in this war of words are reprinted in William H. Whitmore, ed., *Andros Tracts,* 3 vols. (Boston: Prince Society, 1868–1874), II and III. Whitmore ascribed the fifty-page pamphlet, *A Vindication of New England,* to Increase Mather. Holmes does not include it in his bibliography, and I agree with Holmes. *A Vindication of New England* does not seem to me like Mather's work. Holmes, on the other hand, does include *A Further Vindication of New England,* which Whitmore did not see. See the thorough discussion of these tracts in Holmes, *Increase Mather* 272–276, 357–369, 373–376.
46. For a short summary of these and the opposition pamphlets, Johnson, *Adjustment to Empire,* 164–166.
47. Diary, Jan. 23, Feb. 2, 19, Mar. 12, 1689.
48. Sewall, *Diary,* Mar. 28–Apr. 7, 1689.
49. Diary, Feb. 7–8, 1689; Sewall, *Diary,* Apr. 29–30, 1689.
50. Sewall, *Diary,* June 27–28, 1689.
51. Diary, Sept. 13, 1688. Sir Robert Thorner to Increase Mather, March 14, 1689, *Mather Papers,* 677–678, and note 677. Morison, *Harvard College,* 485–486.
52. Sewall, *Diary,* June 28, 1689.
53. *Autobiography,* 332–333.
54. Ibid.
55. Johnson, *Adjustment to Empire,* 158. *Autobiography,* 339.
56. Johnson, *Adjustment to Empire,* 158–159.
57. Ibid., 167.

58. *Autobiography,* 339.

59. Ibid., 339; Sewall, *Diary,* Aug. 14–Sept. 15, 1689.

60. *Autobiography,* 340.

61. Ibid., 340.

62. Whitmore, ed., *Andros Tracts,* II, 15–18.

63. R. Johnson, *Adjustment to Empire,* 168–169.

64. *Autobiography,* 342, quoting Diary for Jan. 18, 1690. Increase Mather, *A Brief Account Concerning Several of the Agents of New England* (London, 1691), in Whitmore, ed., *Andros Tracts,* II, 276. Johnson, *Adjustment to Empire,* 168–169. For a discussion of the bill's chances, if Parliament had not been dissolved, see Johnson, *Adjustment to Empire,* 169–170; Simmons, "Massachusetts Charter," 75.

65. Johnson, *Adjustment to Empire,* 170–171.

66. Sosin, *English America and the Revolution,* 93–96, 140 note 36. Johnson, *Adjustment to Empire,* 90–120.

67. Randolph to Bishop of London, Oct. 25, 1689, *Randolph Letters,* IV, 305; Sosin, *English America and the Revolution,* 96–97.

68. Massachusetts's charges against Andros, Dudley, et al., *Andros Tracts,* I, 149–173, reprinted in Hall, Leder, and Kammen, *Glorious Revolution in America,* 56–62.

69. Johnson, *Adjustment to Empire,* 117 note 107.

70. Increase Mather's notes, and Thomas Brinley to Francis Brinley, May 28, 1690, in Theodore B. Lewis, "Sir Edmund Andros's Hearing Before the Lord's of Trade and Plantations, April 17, 1690," AAS, *Proceedings,* 83, pt. 2 (1973), 244–250. Elisha Cooke to Simon Bradstreet, Oct. 16, 1690 in Hall, Leder, and Kammen, *Glorious Revolution in America,* 69–75. Increase Mather, *Autobiography,* 340. Johnson, *Adjustment to Empire,* 171–176.

71. Elisha Cooke to Simon Bradstreet, Oct. 16, 1690, in Hall, Leder, and Kammen, *Glorious Revolution in America,* 71–72. Thomas Brinley to Francis Brinley, May 28, 1690, in Lewis, "Sir Edmund Andros's Hearing," 247–250.

72. Increase Mather's notes, in Lewis, "Sir Edmund Andros's Hearing," 244. *Autobiography,* 340. Johnson, *Adjustment to Empire,* 173 note 89. Sosin, *English America and the Revolution,* 132 note 10.

73. Johnson, *Adjustment to Empire,* 191–194. Sosin, *English America and the Revolution,* 94, 97–98.

74. Johnson, *Adjustment to Empire,* 183–190. Sosin, *English America and the Revolution,* 132–133.

75. Quoted in Sosin, *English America and the Revolution,* 100.

76. *Autobiography,* 340–341.

77. Elisha Cooke to Simon Bradstreet, Oct. 16, 1690, in Hall, Leder, and Kammen, *Glorious Revolution in America,* 72–73.

78. Ibid., 73–74.

79. Increase Mather wrote "three of the Agents" signed the petition, *Brief Account,* 276. See Johnson, *Adjustment to Empire,* 179, for a discussion of which three.

80. Increase Mather, *Brief Account,* 276–277. Simmons, "Massachusetts Charter of 1691," 76.

81. Increase Mather, *Brief Account*, 277. Johnson, *Adjustment to Empire*, 180–181. Simmons, "Massachusetts Charter," 76.

82. Diary, Jan. 31, 1691.

83. Walker, *Creeds and Platforms*, 441–446. Diary, Jan. 14, 15, 27, 29, Feb. 3, 4, 6, 19, 28, Mar. 2, 1691. A copy of the Minutes of the General Assembly of United Ministers of Devon, John Flavel, Moderator, June 23, 1691, as appendix to the Diary for 1691. *Autobiography*, 338.

84. "Heads of Agreement," printed in Walker, *Creeds and Platforms*, 457.

85. Ibid., 457–458.

86. David Hall, *Faithful Shepherd*, 224–226.

87. Walker, *Creeds and Platforms*, 451 note 3.

88. Diary, passim, and Dec. 7, 1691. *Autobiography*, 338. Murdock, *Mather*, 266 and 262–277, passim.

89. Johnson, *Adjustment to Empire*, 180 note 107.

90. Quoted in Johnson, *Adjustment to Empire*, 207.

91. Diary, Mar. 7, and Jan.–Mar., 1691, passim.

92. Johnson, *Adjustment to Empire*, 186, 187–188, 207.

93. Diary, Mar. 31, 1691; Increase Mather, *Brief Account*, 227; Johnson, *Adjustment to Empire*, 208 note 58. *Andros Tracts*, II, 225–229.

94. Diary, Apr. 9, 1691; *Autobiography*, 333–335.

95. Johnson, *Adjustment to Empire*, 209–211.

96. Diary, Apr. 28, 1691; *Autobiography*, 335–336.

97. Increase Mather, *Brief Account*, 280.

98. Ibid.

99. Increase Mather, *Brief Account*, 280–281; Diary, May 7, 9, 18, 20, 1691. Johnson, *Adjustment to Empire*, 212.

100. Diary, May 20, 1691.

101. Diary, May–June, 1691, passim; Diary accounts, Apr.–June 1691.

102. Kenneth B. Murdock, "Increase Mather's Expenses as Colonial Agent," CSM, *Publications*, 27 (1932), 203. Johnson, *Adjustment to Empire*, 213 note 68.

103. Simmons, "Massachusetts Charter," 77.

104. Johnson, *Adjustment to Empire*, 213–214.

105. Diary, June 17, 1691.

106. Journal of Lords of Trade, July 2, 1691, *Calendar of State Papers, Colonial Series, America and West Indies, 1689–1692*, W. Noel Sainsbury, ed. (London: Public Record Office, 1901), #1606, 1631. Johnson, *Adjustment to Empire*, 214–216. Simmons, "Massachusetts Charter," 78–79.

107. Diary, July, 1691, passim. Frequent attendance at the Committee for Trade and Plantations is indicated in *Cal. of State Papers, Colonial, A&WI, 1689–1692*, #1631, 1650, 1665.

108. Diary, July 17, 1691. Evelyn, *Diary*, 913.

109. Diary, July 22, 1691.

110. Increase Mather, *Brief Account*, 281. Diary, July 24, 1691.

111. Johnson, *Adjustment to Empire*, 222–223.

112. Journal of Lords of Trade, July 29, 1691, *Cal. of State Papers, Colonial, A&WI, 1689–1692*, #1669–1670, 1675. Sosin, *English America and the Revolution*, 136–138.

113. Diary, Aug. 6, 1691.

114. Diary, Aug. 8–26, 1691.

115. Diary, Aug. 12–14, 1691. Increase Mather, *Brief Account*, 283. Johnson, *Adjustment to Empire*, 224.

116. *Cal. of State Papers, Colonial, A&WI, 1689–1692*, #1710, 1711, 1724 SS, 1737, 1738, 1758, 1759. Increase Mather, *Brief Account*, 283–284. Sosin, *English America and the Revolution*, 138.

117. Massachusetts Charter of 1691, Francis Newton Thorpe, *Federal and State Constitutions, Colonial Charters, and Other Organic Laws of . . . the United States of America*, 7 vols. (Washington, D.C.: Government Printing Office, 1909), III, 1879.

118. Leonard W. Labaree, ed., *Royal Instructions to British Colonial Governors, 1670–1776*, 2 vols. (N.Y.: Appleton-Century for the American Historical Association, 1935), I, 82–83, 371–372, 396–397.

119. Thorpe, *Federal and State Constitutions*, III, 1863–1869; V, 3066.

120. *Cal. of State Papers, Colonial, A&WI, 1689–1692*, #1606, 1631.

121. Ibid., #1669, 1670.

122. Johnson, *Adjustment to Empire*, 180; George D. Langdon, Jr., *Pilgrim Colony: A History of New Plymouth, 1620–1691* (New Haven: Yale University Press, 1966), 234–240.

123. Johnson, *Adjustment to Empire*, 217–220, 227. For Mather's almost daily attendance at the Attorney-General's office and Plantation Office, see Diary, Sept. 1691, passim.

124. Diary, Sept. 17, 1691.

125. *Cal. of State Papers, Colonial, A&WI, 1689–1692*, #1772. Johnson, *Adjustment to Empire*, 228–230.

126. Cotton Mather, *Magnalia*, I, 181–182.

127. Johnson, *Adjustment to Empire*, 229–230.

128. Increase Mather, *Brief Acoount*, 296.

129. Increase Mather, *Brief Account*, 288. Morison, *Harvard College*, 484.

130. Increase Mather, *Brief Account*, 288.

131. Ibid., 289.

132. Diary, Oct. 3, 5, 6, 13, 1691.

133. Increase Mather, *Brief Account*, 273.

134. Quoted in T. H. Breen, *The Character of the Good Ruler: Puritan Political Ideas in New England, 1630–1730* (New Haven: Yale University Press, 1970), xii. Others have remarked on the new political rhetoric, e.g., Perry Miller, *From Colony to Province*, 157, and Johnson, *Adjustment to Empire*, 392–393.

135. Diary, Sept. 30, 1691. Samuel Mather had already been awarded his Harvard B.A. degree *in absentia*, Sewall, *Diary*, July 2, 1690.

136. Diary, Oct. 13, 1691.

137. Diary, Sept. 23, 24, 29, Oct. 17, 23, Nov. 4, 6, 1691; Expenses, Sept. 22 and Oct.–Dec., 1691, passim.

138. Diary, Dec. 25 and passim, 1691. *Autobiography*, 337.

139. *Autobiography*, 343–344. Samuel Mather, *Memoirs of the Life of the Late, Reverend Increase Mather, D. D.* (London, 1725), 57.

8. *Massachusetts Under the New Charter*

1. Increase Mather, *Great Blessing of Primitive Counsellors* (Boston, 1693), 7. Silverman, *Cotton Mather*, 78.
2. John Putnam Demos, *Entertaining Satan: Witchcraft and Culture of Early New England* (N.Y.: Oxford University Press, 1982), describes the place of witchcraft in New England culture. Histories of the Salem trials abound. See Marion L. Starkey, *The Devil in Massachusetts: A Modern Enquiry into the Salem Witch Trials* (N.Y.: Knopf, 1949; Anchor Books, 1969) or Paul Boyer and Stephen Nissenbaum, *Salem Possessed, the Social Origins of Witchcraft* (Cambridge: Harvard University Press, 1974).
3. See Johnson, *Adjustment to Empire*, 196–204, for an enlargement of this explanation.
4. Levin, *Cotton Mather*, 208–210; Levin, "Did the Mathers Disagree about the Salem Witchcraft Trials?" AAS, *Proceedings*, 95, pt. 2 (1985), 4.
5. Holmes, *Increase Mather*, 108–138. Middlekauf, *Mathers*, 150–155.
6. Increase Mather, *Cases of Conscience Concerning Evil Spirits* (Boston, 1692), 1.
7. Ibid., 1, 43.
8. Ibid., 52.
9. Ibid., 67.
10. Levin, *Cotton Mather*, 216–221; "Did The Mathers Disagree?" 5–9.
11. Increase Mather, *Cases of Conscience*, 70 and postscript.
12. *Autobiography*, 344.
13. The political narrative can be followed in Johnson, *Adjustment to Empire*, 278–288, and Sosin, *English America and the Revolution*, 225–226.
14. Breen, *Character of a Good Ruler*, 164–167.
15. Ibid., 200–201.
16. Ibid., 152–155.
17. Sosin, *English America and the Revolution*, 226.
18. Increase Mather, *Great Blessing of Primitive Counsellors*, 3–4.
19. Ibid., 16.
20. Ibid., 21.
21. Ibid., 8.
22. Johnson, *Adjustment to Empire*, 282.
23. Damerall, "The Modernization of Massachusetts: the Transformation of Public Attitudes and Institutions, 1689–1715," Ph.D. diss., University of Texas at Austin, 1981, 226–232.
24. Breen, *Character of the Good Ruler*, 196–197. Damerall, "Modernization of Massachusetts," 3–20.
25. Johnson, *Adjustment to Empire*, 285–289.
26. Diary, May 18, 1695.
27. Increase Mather's Expense Account submitted to House of Representatives, June 7, 1694, printed in Murdock, "Increase Mather's Expenses as Colonial Agent," 202–203.
28. Increase Mather, *Great Blessing of Primitive Counsellors*, p. 7.
29. Thorpe, *Federal and State Constitutions*, vol. 3, 1881.
30. Susan Martha Reed, *Church and State in Massachusetts, 1691–1740* (Urbana, Ill.: University of Illinois Press, 1914), 22–26 and n. 17. Isaac Backus,

Church History of New England from 1620 to 1804 (Philadelphia, 1853), 127.

31. Isaac Backus, *Church History,* 127.
32. Pope, *Half-Way Covenant,* 185–205.
33. Pp. 63–82, I, Second Church Records, MHS.
34. Cotton Mather to John Richards, Dec. 14, 1692, *Mather Papers,* 397–401. David Hall, *Faithful Shepherd,* 207, 224. Holifield, *Covenant Sealed,* 185.
35. David Hall, *Faithful Shepherd,* 221.
36. Ibid., 198–220, 223.
37. References to the Mather children are scattered through the Diary. For Betty's fiancee and marriage, Diary, June 15, 29, 1695; June 13, 27, July 11, 1696.
38. Diary, July 28, 1696.
39. Diary, Apr.–June 1693, passim.
40. Cotton Mather, *Parentator,* 172–173; *Autobiography,* 345; Morison, *Harvard College,* 499, n.2.
41. Diary, Sept. 3, Oct. 29, 1693.
42. Levin, *Cotton Mather,* 223–232; Silverman, *Cotton Mather,* 120–124.
43. Diary, Sept. 3, 1693; Silverman, *Cotton Mather,* 129.
44. Silverman, *Cotton Mather,* 125–128. I follow the dating of Cotton's angelic vision given in Kenneth Silverman, "A Note on the Date of Cotton Mather's Visitation by an Angel," *Early American Literature,* 15 (1980), 82–86.
45. Silverman, *Cotton Mather,* 125, 135–136; Records of the Cambridge Association, August 6, 1694, MHS, *Proceedings,* 17 (1879–1880), 272. Holmes, *Increase Mather,* 11–17.
46. Increase Mather, Preface in J.S., *Second Spira* (Boston, 1693), 4; *Solemn Advice to Young Men* (Boston, 1695), 3–4; *Two Plain and Practical Discourses* (London, 1699), quoted in Holmes, *Increase Mather,* 612–615.
47. Records of Cambridge Association, Nov. 6, 1693, Mar. 4, 1694, MHS, *Proceedings,* 17 (1879–1880), 271.
48. Ernest Lee Tuveson, *Redeemer Nation: the Idea of America's Millennial Role* (Chicago: University of Chicago Press, 1968), 36–38.
49. Quoted in Holmes, *Increase Mather,* 198.
50. Increase Mather, *Dissertation Concerning the Future Conversion of the Jewish Nation* (London, 1709), 14, 17, 18, 21, 23.
51. Tuveson, *Redeemer Nation,* 12–17. For a wider discussion of these Puritan ideas, see Peter Toon, ed., *Puritans, The Millennium and the Future of Israel: Puritan Eschatology 1600–1660: A Collection of Essays* (Cambridge, Eng.: James Clarke, 1970).
52. Quoted in Mason I. Lowance, Jr., and David Watters, "Increase Mather's 'New Jerusalem': Millennialism in Late Seventeenth-Century New England," AAS *Proceedings,* 87, Part 2 (1978), 349.
53. Ibid.
54. Increase Mather, "A Discourse Concerning the Glorious State of the Church on Earth under the New Jerusalem," Mason I. Lowance, Jr. and David Watters, eds., AAS *Proceedings,* 87, pt. 2, (1978), 386. I now believe these sermons were preached in 1692 or 1693. See Ibid., note 5, p. 363.
55. Ibid., 355–359.
56. Ibid., 364–365.
57. Ibid., 381.

58. Ibid., 385–386.
59. Ibid., 389–390.
60. Ibid., 393.
61. Ibid., 405.
62. Ibid., 406.
63. Tuveson, *Redeemer Nation*, 35–36.
64. Ibid., 27–30, 55–57.
65. Diary, Oct. 5, 18; Nov. 2, 1695.
66. Diary, June 13, Aug. 8, 1696.
67. Diary, Sept. 5, Oct. 3, 1696.
68. Morison, *Harvard College*, 490. The 1692 charter is printed here, 654–656. Josiah Quincy, *History of Harvard University*, 2 vols. (Cambridge, Mass.: 1840), I, 69–70.
69. Morison, *Harvard College*, 491.
70. Quincy, *History of Harvard*, I, 73–74; Morison, *Harvard College*, 498–499.
71. Diary, June 29, July 13, 1695. For similar expressions, see *Autobiography*, 345–347.
72. Diary, July 27, 1695. *Autobiography*, 348.
73. Diary, Aug. 5, 1695. Morison, *Harvard College*, 509, n.2.
74. Diary, Nov. 7, 1695.
75. Diary, Nov. 30, 1695. *Autobiography*, 349.
76. Diary, Dec. 6, 1695. *Autobiography*, 349.
77. Diary, Jan. 16, 1696.
78. *Autobiography*, 350.
79. Sewall, *Diary*, Nov. 25, 1696; David Hall, *Faithful Shepherd*, 219–220.
80. Morison, *Harvard College*, 511. Quincy, *History of Harvard*, I, 82–85.
81. Diary, Dec. 11, 1696. Morison, *Harvard College*, 511.
82. Sewall, *Diary*, Dec. 19, 1696. Morison, *Harvard College*, 511–512. Quincy, *History of Harvard*, I, 128.
83. Diary, Jan. 4, 5, 1697.
84. Charter of 1697, Morison, *Harvard College*, 656–658. Quincy, *History of Harvard*, I, 87, implies John Leverett's name was left out of this charter by Mather. Morison, *Harvard College*, 513, n.1, concludes that if it had been left out, Mather put it back. Leverett and Brattle, although resigning as tutors, were both named as fellows in the 1697 charter.
85. Increase Mather, *Discourse Concerning the Uncertainty of the Times of Men* (Boston, 1697), quoted in Holmes, *Increase Mather*, 182.
86. Increase Mather, "Epistle Dedicatory," in Cotton Mather, *Ecclesiastes*, in *Magnalia*, II, 68.
87. Ibid., 76.
88. Ibid., 79.
89. Ibid., 66.
90. Morison, *Harvard College*, 505–506.
91. Fiering, *Moral Philosophy*, 251–252, 280.
92. Fiering, *Moral Philosophy*, 323–330; Norman Fiering, "The First American Enlightenment: Tillotson, Leverett, and Philosophical Anglicanism," *New England Quarterly*, 54 (1981), 323–330; Teresa Toulouse, *The Art of Prophesying: New England Sermons and the Shaping of Belief* (Athens, Ga.: University of

Georgia Press, 1987), 49–74; Larzer Ziff, *Puritanism in America. New Culture in a New World* (New York: Viking, 1973), 272–278.

93. G. R. Cragg, *From Puritanism to the Age of Reason: A Study of Religious Thought within the Church of England, 1660–1700* (Cambridge: Cambridge University Press, 1966), 66, 81, 224; Toulouse makes clear that substantive issues as well as style were at stake: *Art of Prophesying,* 48–50, 61–62, 68–74.

94. *Autobiography,* 327–328.

95. Increase Mather, To The Reader in *Johannes in Eremo* in *Magnalia,* I, 248.

96. Morison, *Harvard College,* 507, n.4.

97. Diary, Nov. 15, 30, 1697. Sewall, *Diary,* Nov. 20, 1697; Perry Miller, *The New England Mind: From Colony to Province* (Cambridge: Harvard University Press, 1953), 447.

98. Diary, June 7, 9, 12, 15, 1697.

99. Diary, July 17, Aug. 7, 12, Sept. 4, 15, 1697.

100. Diary, Sept. 26, 1697.

101. Sewall, *Diary,* June 10, 1698; Diary, June 11, 14, 1698.

102. Diary, June 26, 1698.

103. Diary, June 28, 1698.

104. Diary, July 2, 1698.

105. Morison, *Harvard College,* 521–522.

106. Sewall, *Diary,* Dec. 8, 1698.

107. Quincy, *History of Harvard,* I, 499–500.

108. Diary, Feb. 23, 1699.

109. Diary, Mar. 20, 1697.

110. Diary, Aug. 10, 1695, July 11, 1696, Mar. 20, 1697.

111. Diary, July 17, Aug. 7, 1697, Jan. 21, 29, Feb. 4, 1699.

112. Diary, July 3, Sept. 4, Oct. 30, 1697. Sewall, *Diary,* Sept. 30, 1697, and p. 378, n.14.

113. Sewall, *Diary,* Jan. 28, Feb. 8, 1697.

114. Sewall, *Diary,* June 28, 29, 1697.

115. Diary, Nov. 27, Dec. 10, 19, 22, 1697. Sewall, *Diary,* Dec. 10, 1697.

116. Diary, Jan. 22, 23, 28, 1698.

117. Sewall, *Diary,* Jan. 12–Feb. 21, 1698. Diary, Feb. 2, 1698.

118. Diary, Mar. 1698–Feb. 1699, appendix.

119. Diary, Feb. 2–27. Sewall, *Diary,* Feb. 28, 1698.

120. Diary, July 29, 30, 1698.

121. Diary, Dec. 30, 1693.

122. Diary, Nov. 13, 1698.

123. Diary, Apr. 4, 1697. Book No. 2 (1689–1717), unpaged, Apr. 4, 1697, Second Church Records, MHS.

124. Mather to Charleston Church July 2, 1698, *Mather Papers,* 119–121.

125. Salem: Diary, Apr. 24, 1695. Watertown: Diary, July 16, 1695; Sept. 4, 1697. Sudbury: Diary, July 23, Aug. 2–4, Sept. 1, Oct. 1, 6, 13, Nov. 1, 1698. Chebaco: Diary, Aug. 6, Sept. 3, 5–7, 12. Nov. 10, 1698; Jan. 12, 1699.

126. Increase Mather, *The Folly of Sinning Opened and Applyed* (Boston, 1699); Sewall, *Diary,* Nov. 17, 1698; p. 400, n.19.

127. Shipton, *Sibley's Harvard Graduates,* IV (1933), 120–123. Clayton H. Chap-

man, "The Life and Influence of Benjamin Colman, D.D.," Ph.D. diss., Boston University, 1947, 1–221; Toulouse, *Art of Prophesying,* 57–63; Ziff, *Puritanism in America,* 275–277.

128. Chapman, "Benjamin Colman," 23–25.
129. *A Manifesto or Declaration of Faith Set Forth by the Undertakers of the New Church Now Erected in Boston in New-England, November 17, 1699* (Boston, 1699).
130. Sewall, *Diary,* Jan. 24–25, 1700. Despite William Brattle's modernism in church matters, he and Increase Mather remained lifelong friends and admirers. See Mather to Speaker of the House [October, 1707], *Harvard College Records* 4 (1975), 195–196, and William Brattle to Mather, May 8, 1707, Ibid., 217–218. The text of Brattle's watered-down statement has not been found.
131. Sewall, *Diary,* Jan. 31, 1700.
132. Increase Mather, *Order of the Gospel* (Boston, 1700), 8.
133. Ibid., 9.
134. *Gospel Order Revived, Being an Answer to a Book lately set forth by the Reverend Mr. Increase Mather* (N.Y., 1700). For conjecture about the authors see Holmes, *Increase Mather,* 394–395.
135. William Brattle, *1694. An Almanack* (Boston, 1694); John Tulley, *An Almanack* (Boston, 1694); Christian Lodowick, *1695. The New England Almanack* (Boston, 1695).
136. Bartholomew Green, *Printer's Advertisement,* (Boston, 1701). Reprinted in Thomas, *History of Printing in America,* AAS, *Transactions and Collections,* 2 vols. (Albany, N.Y., 1874), I, 415–422.
137. Cotton Mather, *Preface,* in John Quick, *Young Man's Claim unto the Sacraments,* (Boston, 1700), 22.
138. Holmes, *Increase Mather,* 9, 343.

9. *The Last Puritan*

1. Morison, *Harvard College,* 524.
2. Ibid., 524–525. Murdock, *Increase Mather,* 354–355.
3. Morison, *Harvard College,* 527.
4. Ibid., 530.
5. Records of North Church in Robbins, *History of the Second Church,* 297.
6. Extract and draft of letters from Increase Mather to Lt. Governor Stoughton, Oct. 17, 1700; Mar. 4, 1701, *Harvard College Records,* IV, 179–180, 188–189.
7. Ibid.
8. Ibid.
9. Increase Mather, "Farewell Sermon," in Cotton Mather, *Parentator,* 178.
10. Ibid.
11. *Autobiography,* 351. Resolution of General Court, Sept. 6, 1701, *Harvard College Records,* IV, 191–192. Morison, *Harvard College,* 533–534.
12. *Autobiography,* 351.
13. Sewall, *Diary,* Oct. 18–Oct. 24, 1701. Morison, *Harvard College,* 534–535.
14. Increase Mather, *Ichabod, or a Discourse Shewing What Cause there is to Fear that the Glory of the Lord, is Departing from New-England* (Boston, 1702), 46.

15. Holmes, *Increase Mather,* 36, 302–305.

16. Increase Mather, *The Surest Way to the Greatest Honour* (Boston, 1699), 15–16.

17. Earl of Bellomont to Samuel Sewall, Aug. 14, 1700, quoted in Johnson, *Adjustment to Empire,* 340 n.76.

18. Ibid., 332–335, 337.

19. Higginson to John Howe, nd, quoted in Ibid., 338–339.

20. Dudley to Cotton Mather, Aug. 25, 1701, quoted in Ibid., 340.

21. Increase Mather, *The Excellency of A Publick Spirit* (Boston, 1702), 5. Holmes, *Increase Mather,* 249–254.

22. Sewall, *Diary,* June 11, 1702.

23. Damerall, "Modernization of Massachusetts," 4–8.

24. Ibid., 240–242. Johnson, *Adjustment to Empire,* 385–386.

25. Quoted in Holmes, *Increase Mather,* 252.

26. Diary, July 1, 1702.

27. Quoted in Holmes, *Increase Mather,* 254.

28. Damerall, "Modernization of Massachusetts," 127–132, 190–191.

29. Diary, Mar. 11, 1704.

30. Diary, Mar. 18, 1704.

31. Kellaway, *New England Company,* 62–80.

32. Ibid., 145–166.

33. Ibid., 203–205.

34. *Masukkenukeeg Matcheseaenuog* (Boston, 1698), a translation of Increase Mather, *Greatest Sinners Exhorted* (Boston, 1686).

35. Quoted in Kellaway, *New England Company,* 206–207.

36. Diary, Feb. 12, 1704.

37. Diary, June 17, 1704.

38. Diary, May 31, 1704.

39. Diary, Jan. 1, 1704. Mather here adopted January 1 instead of Lady Day, Mar. 25, as the beginning of the new year.

40. Frederick L. Weis, "Checklist of Portraits in the Library of the American Antiquarian Society," 89–90.

41. Diary, Jan. 6–7, 1705.

42. Diary, Jan. 6–7, Apr. 7, 14, June 13, 14, 1705.

43. Diary, Feb. 10, Mar. 10, June 2, 1705.

44. Diary, July 28, Aug. 22–Sept. 4, 1705.

45. Diary, Aug. 31, 1702; Apr. 3, 1704.

46. Diary, Aug. 18, 1705.

47. Diary, May 22–23, 1705.

48. Diary, May 31–June 3, 1704.

49. "Records of The Cambridge Association," MHS, *Proceedings,* 17 (1880), 252. Signatures of those present are printed in Walker, *Creeds and Platforms,* 484.

50. Quoted in J. William T. Youngs, Jr., *God's Messengers. Religious Leadership in Colonial New England, 1700–1750* (Baltimore: Johns Hopkins University Press, 1976), 70.

51. Walter, *Creeds and Platforms,* 486–490.

52. Increase Mather, *Disquisition Concerning Ecclesiastical Councils* (Boston, 1716), 35.

53. Increase Mather, Answers to the Proposals, nd, Mather Papers, AAS, quoted in

Youngs, *God's Messengers*, 72. Increase Mather, *Concerning Ecclesiastical Councils*, 7. Goulding, "Stoddard and the Mathers," 637–638, 733–734.

54. Colman to Robert Wodrow, Boston, Jan. 23, 1719, in "Some Unpublished Letters of Benjamin Colman," Niel Caplan, ed., MHS, *Proceedings*, 77 (1966), 114. Youngs, *God's Messengers*, 72; Damerall, "Modernization of Massachusetts," 57.

55. Holmes, *Increase Mather*, 343.

56. Paul Lucas, "'An Appeal to the Learned': the Mind of Solomon Stoddard," *William and Mary Quarterly*, 3 ser., 30 (1973), 272.

57. Ibid., 266–277.

58. Ibid., 284.

59. Stoddard, *Inexcusableness of Neglecting the Worship of God* (Boston, 1708), preface.

60. Increase Mather, *Dissertation Wherein the Strange Doctrine . . . is Examined and Confuted* (Boston, 1708), 4.

61. Backus, *Church History*, 136–137. The modern history that Increase Mather and Solomon Stoddard were at loggerheads stems mostly from Perry Miller's article "Solomon Stoddard," *Harvard Theological Review*, 34 (1941), 277–320 and his influential book *New England Mind: From Colony to Province*, 277–285. Paul R. Lucas, in "'An Appeal to the Learned': The Mind of Solomon Stoddard" has greatly improved our understanding. See especially pages 259–261. Mather and Stoddard did disagree. They also thought of themselves as relatives, friends, and colleagues in the ministry, who after 1708 no longer let their disagreements override their common commitments.

62. Damerall, "Modernization of Massachusetts," 191–200.

63. Thomas James Holmes, *Cotton Mather, A Bibliography of His Works*, 3 vols. (Cambridge: Harvard University Press, 1940), 664–672.

64. Sewall, *Diary*, Sept. 15, 1707.

65. Ibid., Oct. 28, 1707.

66. Ibid., Nov. 1, 1707.

67. Ibid., Nov. 20–24, 1707.

68. Ibid., Nov. 25, 1707.

69. Morison, *Harvard College*, 551–552.

70. Ibid., 552–554.

71. Sewall, *Diary*, n.21, p. 574; Nov. 28, 1707.

72. Ibid., Nov. 25–Dec. 6, 1707. Morison, *Harvard College*, 555–556, Johnson, *Adjustment to Empire*, 344–345.

73. Sewall, *Diary*, Jan. 14, 1708.

74. Increase Mather to Dudley, Jan. 20, 1708, MHS, *Collections*, 3 (1794, reprinted 1810), 126–128.

75. Ibid., 128–134.

76. Ibid., 135–137.

77. Increase Mather, *Practical Truths Tending to Promote Holiness*, (Boston, 1704), 3–4. See also Increase Mather, *The Blessed Hope, and the Glorious Appearing of the Great God our Saviour, Jesus Christ* (Boston, 1701).

78. Increase Mather, *Soul-Saving Gospel Truths* (Boston, 1703), 4–5.

79. Increase Mather, *Practical Truths Tending to Promote Holiness*, 1–2.

80. Increase Mather, *Awakening Truths Tending to Conversion* (Boston, 1710), iv.

81. Ibid., 88.

82. Ibid., 120.

83. Quoted in Miller, *From Colony to Province,* 270.

84. Colman, *The Government and Improvement of Mirth* (Boston, 1707) A2, A4.

85. Fiering, *Moral Philosophy,* 293.

86. Increase Mather, *Practical Truths Tending to Holiness* (Boston, 1704), 2–3. For similar comments see *Awakening Truths* (1710), iv; *Plain Discourse Shewing Who Shall, and Who Shall Not, Enter . . . Heaven* (Boston, 1713), iv.; To The Reader in Nehemiah Walter, *Discourse Concerning the Wonderfulness of Christ* (Boston, 1713), i–ii.

87. Holmes, *Increase Mather,* 197.

88. Increase Mather, *Meditations on Death* (Boston, 1707). Appendix to *Dissertation Wherein the Strange Doctrine* (1708). *Discourse Concerning Faith and Fervency in Prayer* (Boston, 1710). *Meditations on the Glory of the Heavenly World* (Boston, 1711).

89. Miller, *From Colony to Province,* 188.

90. Facsimile reprint in Holmes, *Increase Mather,* 163.

91. Quoted in Lowance and Watters, "Increase Mather's 'New Jerusalem'," 351.

92. Holmes, *Increase Mather,* 161–165.

93. Hambrick-Stowe, *Practice of Piety,* 275–277.

94. Increase Mather, *A Discourse Concerning Earthquakes* (Boston, 1706), 8.

95. Diary, Mar. 20, 1697.

96. 1711 Survey of Boston Harbor, reproduced in Nathaniel B. Shurtleff *Topographical and Historical Description of Boston* 3rd ed. (Boston, 1890), 61. Johnson, *Adjustment to Empire,* 244–247. Bridenbaugh, *Cities in the Wilderness,* 204. Thomas Hutchinson, *The History of the Colony and Province of Massachusetts Bay,* Lawrence Shaw Mayo, ed. (Cambridge: Harvard University Press, 1936), 50–154, is the best account of the war.

97. Sewall, *Diary,* Apr. 23, 1706.

98. Ibid.

99. Bridenbaugh, *Cities in the Wilderness,* 220–226.

100. Ibid., 179–196.

101. Ibid., 146–171.

102. Sewall, *Diary,* Oct. 18, 1711. Bridenbaugh, *Cities in the Wilderness,* 210–211.

103. Bridenbaugh, *Cities in the Wilderness,* 171–172.

104. Sewall, *Diary,* July 25, 1718.

105. Increase Mather, *Burnings Bewailed* (Boston, 1711), 23.

106. Bridenbaugh, *Cities in the Wilderness,* 292.

107. Increase Mather, Record of children's births, printed in Robbins, *History of the Second Church,* 216–217. Shipton, *Sibley's Harvard Graduates,* 7 (1945), 464–493.

108. Sibley, *Graduates of Harvard,* 3 (1885), 296–297.

109. Shipton, *Sibley's Harvard Graduates,* 5 (1937), 587.

110. Cotton Mather, *Maternal Consolations* (Boston, 1714), 41–42.

111. Samuel J. Barrows and William B. Trask, eds., *Records of The First Church at Dorchester in New England, 1636–1734* (Boston, 1891), passim. Sibley, *Graduates of Harvard,* 2 (1881), 364–368.

112. Sibley, *Graduates of Harvard, 3* (1885), 256.
113. Sibley, *Graduates of Harvard, 2* (1881), 116−117.
114. Lucas, "Solomon Stoddard," 288.
115. Increase Mather, To The Reader, in Stoddard, *Guide to Christ* (Boston, 1714), xii. For a different interpretation of Mather's preface, see Jones, *Shattered Synthesis,* 117−121.
116. Increase Mather to Ashurst, Nov. 22, 1714, quoted in Johnson, *Adjustment to Empire,* 350−351.
117. Increase Mather, *Meditations on the Glory of the Heavenly World,* v.
118. *Autobiography,* 355−358.
119. Miller, *From Colony to Province,* 452.
120. *Autobiography,* 358.
121. John Barnard, "Autobiography of the Reverend John Barnard," MHS, *Collections,* 3 ser., 5 (1836), 177−243. Shipton, *Sibley's Harvard Graduates,* 4 (1933), 504−505.
122. *Autobiography,* 359.
123. Shipton, *Sibley's Harvard Graduates,* 5 (1937), 466.
124. Barnard, "Autobiography," 214−217.
125. Miller, *From Colony to Province,* 451.
126. Quoted in George Allen Cook, *John Wise, Early American Democrat* (N.Y.: Columbia University Press, 1952), 126.
127. John Wise, *Churches Quarrel Espoused* (N.Y.: 1713), George A. Cook, ed. (Gainesville, Fla.: Scholars' Facsimiles and Reprints, 1966), 42.
128. Increase Mather, *Disquisition Concerning Ecclesiastical Councils,* title page, 17, 19.
129. John Wise, *A Vindication of the Government of New-England Churches* (Boston, 1717), Perry Miller, ed., (Gainesville, Fla.: Scholars' Facsimiles and Reprints, 1958), 29−30.
130. List of new members, 1663−1741, 63−82, I, Second Church Records, MHS.
131. For example, the vote on Oct. 22, 1722, to elect a successor to Increase Mather, V (unpaged), Second Church Records, MHS. Forty-nine brethren present, thirty-four voting.
132. Colman to Robert Wodrow, Boston, Nov. 17, 1719, "Letters of Benjamin Colman," 116.
133. Increase Mather, Preface in Cotton Mather, *Brethren Dwelling together in Unity* (Boston, 1718), the ordination sermon. Backus, *Church History,* 137−138; Shipton, *Sibley's Harvard Graduates,* 5 (1937), 512−513.
134. Backus, *Church History,* 138−139.
135. Colman to Robert Wodrow, Jan. 23, 1719, "Letters of Benjamin Colman," 113.
136. Colman to Robert Wodrow, Jan. 23, 1719, Ibid., 110−112. Colman's published letters to Wodrow on this subject should be supplemented by Patrick Erskine to Robert Wodrow, Oct. 5 and Dec. 20, 1718, nos. 14 and 18, vol. 20, Quarto, Wodrow Letters, National Library of Scotland.
137. Colman to Robert Wodrow, Boston, Mar. 1, 1720, Ibid., 118.
138. Increase Mather, *Disquisition Concerning Ecclesiastical Councils,* 34−35; Result of the Synod of 1662, Question II, in Walker, *Creeds and Platforms,* 337−339.
139. Robbins, *History of the Second Church,* 170−174. Shipton, *Sibley's Harvard*

Graduates, 4 (1933), 305–306; Colman to Robert Wodrow, Boston, Mar. 1, 1720, "Letters of Benjamin Colman," 111.

140. Increase Mather, *Further Testimony Against the Scandalous Proceedings of the New-North Church in Boston* (Boston, 1720), 1–2.

141. Increase Mather, *A Seasonable Testimony to Good Order* (Boston, 1720), Preface. Several documents signed by Mather during the controversy were printed in *Account of the Reasons* (Boston, 1720), a collection of documents published by supporters of the New Brick church.

142. Colman to Robert Wodrow, Boston, Mar. 1, Dec. 7, 1720, "Letters of Benjamin Colman," 117–122.

143. Increase Mather, *Sermons Wherein those Eight Characters . . . Commonly Called the Beatitudes, are Opened and Applyed* (Boston, 1718), iii. Increase Mather, *Five Sermons on Several Subjects* (Boston, 1719), Preface.

144. Colman to Robert Wodrow, Boston, May 26, Dec. 7, 1724, June 27–July 3, 1725, "Letters of Benjamin Colman," 133–139.

145. Increase Mather, *Several Sermons Wherein is Shewed that Jesus Christ is a Mighty Saviour* (Boston, 1715), ii. It seems probable that Mather had Colman and his English models in mind when he wrote this veiled criticism. See Toulouse, *Art of Prophesying*, 50–74. Colman remained orthodox in doctrine: James W. Jones, *The Shattered Synthesis. New England Puritanism before the Great Awakening* (New Haven: Yale University Press, 1973), 93–100.

146. Increase Mather, *Discourse Concerning the Existence and Omniscience of God* (Boston, 1716), 6, 65.

147. Ibid., 30–31.

148. Middlekauf, *Mathers*, 303–304.

149. Increase Mather, *Pray for the Rising Generation* (1678), 11.

150. Increase Mather, *Advice to the Children of Godly Ancestors* in Cotton Mather, *A Course of Sermons on Early Piety* (Boston, 1721).

151. Increase Mather, *Awakening Soul-Saving Truths* (Boston, 1720), 73–77, 87–88.

152. Ibid., title page and preface.

153. Increase Mather, *Sermons Wherein those Eight Characters* (1718), 294.

154. Increase Mather, *Five Sermons* (1719), 126.

155. Ibid.

156. Ibid.

157. Ibid., 127.

158. Samuel Mather, *Memoirs of the Life of . . . Increase Mather*, 74.

159. Diary, Jan. 8, March 1, June 25, 1717. Time lost by "visitors" was more frequent, e.g. Jan. 15, Feb. 27, Apr. 9, 22, 24, 26, 1717.

160. Increase Mather to Sir William Ashurst, Boston, Aug. 12, 1717, *Harvard College Records*, IV (1975), 265. Mather repeated these very phrases two years later in a letter to Robert Wodrow, Nov. 11, 1719, no. 21, vol. 20, Quarto, Wodrow Letters, National Library of Scotland. Cotton wrote of his father's "wonderful performances" and how he "treats vast Assemblies of people with a Vigorous and Brightness in his public ministrations, which everyone wonders at. . . ." Cotton Mather to Robert Wodrow, Dec. 4, 1717; Oct. 6, 1718, nos. 12, 15, Ibid.

161. Increase Mather, "Last Will and Testament," *New England Historical and Genealogical Register,* 54 (1851), 445–447.
162. Diary, May 12, June 8, 9, 18, 26, July 7, 13, Aug. 4, 13, Sept. 1, 29.
163. This account of the smallpox inoculation episode is based on Raymond P. Stearns, *Science in the British Colonies of America* (Chicago: University of Illinois Press, 1970), 417–426.
164. Holmes, *Increase Mather,* 377.
165. Printed in facsimile in Ibid., 502.
166. Ibid., 377.
167. Printed in facsimile in Ibid., 518.
168. Stearns, *Science in the British Colonies of America,* 444.
169. Increase Mather, *Dying Legacy of a Minister to His Dearly Beloved People* (Boston, 1722), 2.
170. "Testimony Finished," dated Nov. 10, 1722, was published over Increase Mather's name in *Elijah's Mantle* (Boston, 1722), a small collection of documents probably edited by Cotton Mather. "Testimony Finished" is a précis of Increase's life written in the first person. It is beautifully written and touches all Mather's important concerns: the errand into the wilderness, scriptural revelation, grace, pure churches, examination for admission to churches, Harvard College, the rising generation, punishment for apostasy. Because it is so carefully wrought, and contains language unlike Increase's own style, I believe it was written by Cotton and not by his failing father. See Holmes, *Increase Mather,* 575–578. Cotton Mather reprinted "Testimony Finished" in *Parentator,* 203–206.
171. Cotton Mather, *Parentator,* 201.
172. Ibid., 209–210.
173. Ibid., 211–212.
174. Tuttle, "The Libraries of the Mathers," 269–356; Cadbury, "Harvard College Library and the Libraries of the Mathers," 20–48.
175. Quoted in Simmons, "Massachusetts Charter," 83.
176. Ibid., 84.
177. E.g., Vernon Louis Parrington, *Main Currents in American Thought:* vol. 1, *The Colonial Mind* (N.Y.: Harcourt, Brace, 1927, 1930), 98–101.
178. Horace, *Odes,* IV.9.25–28. Identification and translation are by William J. Scheick, "Introduction and Notes," *Life and Death,* 85.

Bibliography

A Guide to the Sources Used
in this Work

I. MANUSCRIPT COLLECTIONS

American Antiquarian Society: Mather Family Papers, Curwin Family Papers.
Boston Public Library: Prince Collection (Am. Ms. 1502).
Harvard University: Harvard College Archives.
Massachusetts Historical Society: Miscellaneous Bound MSS; Second Church Records; Suffolk Deeds; Belknap, Colman, and Saltonstall Papers.
Massachusetts State Archives: Volumes 26, 29, 35–37, 57–58, 112–113, 129.
National Library of Scotland: Robert Wodrow Collection.
University of Virginia, Alderman Library: Mather MSS.

II. GUIDES TO PRINTED PRIMARY SOURCES

Bristol, Roger P. *Supplement to Charles Evans' American Bibliography.* Charlottesville, Va.: University Press of Virginia for the Bibliographical Society of America, 1970.
Evans, Charles. *American Bibliography* Vol. 1, 1639–1729. Chicago: Charles Evans, 1903.
Holmes, Thomas J. *Cotton Mather: A Bibliography of His Works.* 3 vols. Cambridge: Harvard University Press, 1940.
———. *Increase Mather: A Bibliography of His Works.* 2 vols. Cleveland, Ohio: 1931.
———. *The Minor Mathers. A List of Their Works.* Cambridge: Harvard University Press, 1940.

III. PRINTED PRIMARY SOURCES

Allin, John. *Animadversions upon the Antisynodalia Americana.* Cambridge, 1664.
Barnard, John. "Autobiography of the Reverend John Barnard." In MHS, *Collections.* 3rd ser., 5 (1836): 177–243.
Barrows, Samuel J. and William B. Trask, eds. *Records of the First Church at Dorchester in New England, 1636–1734.* Boston, 1891.

Baxter, Richard. *Autobiography*. Abridged by J. M. Lloyd Thomas. London: Dent, 1931.

Brattle, William. *1694. An Almanack*. Boston, 1694.

Cambridge Association of Ministers. "Records of Cambridge Association of Ministers," MHS, *Proceedings* 17 (1880): 262–281.

Chauncy, Charles. *Anti-Synodalia Scripta Americana*. London, 1662.

Church, Benjamin. *Entertaining Passages Relating to Philip's War*. Boston, 1716. Reprinted in Richard Slotkin and James K. Folsom, *So Dreadfull a Judgment: Puritan Responses to King Philip's War, 1676–1677*. Middletown, Conn.: Wesleyan University Press, 1978.

Clarke, Samuel. *The Lives of Sundry Modern English Divines*. London, 1651.

Colman, Benjamin. *The Government and Improvement of Mirth*. Boston, 1707.

———. *A Manifesto or Declaration Set Forth by Undertakers of the New Church Now Erected in Boston, in New-England, November 17, 1699*. Boston, 1699.

———. *The Prophet's Death Lamented and Improved*. Boston, 1723.

———. "Some Unpublished Letters of Benjamin Colman." Edited by Niel Caplan. MHS, *Proceedings* 77 (1966): 101–142.

Danforth, Thomas. *The Cry of Sodom Enquired Into*. Cambridge, 1674.

Evelyn, John. *The Diary of John Evelyn*. Edited by E. S. De Beer. Oxford Standard Authors Edition. Oxford: Oxford University Press, 1959.

Foster, John. *1675. An Almanac*. Cambridge, Mass., 1675.

———. *1676. An Almanac*. Cambridge, Mass., 1676.

———. *MDCLXXXI. An Almanac*. Cambridge, Mass., 1681.

Geneva Bible. Geneva, 1560. Facsimile edition. Madison: University of Wisconsin Press, 1969.

Gospel Order Revived, Being an Answer to a Book Lately Set Forth by the Reverend Mr. Increase Mather. New York, 1700.

Great Britain. *Calendar of State Papers, Colonial Series, America and West Indies, 1689–1692*. Edited by W. Noel Saintsbury. London: Public Record Office, 1901.

Green, Bartholomew. *Printer's Advertisement*. Boston, 1701.

Harvard University. *Harvard College Records*. 5 vols. In CSM, *Publications* 15–16 (1925), 31 (1935), 49–50 (1975).

Hevel, Johan. *Cometographia: totam naturam cometarum . . . exhibens*. Danzig, 1668.

Hubbard, William. *The Happiness of a People In the Wisdome of their Rulers*. Boston, 1676.

———. *A Narrative of the Troubles with the Indians in New-England*. Boston, 1677.

Hull, John. *Diaries of John Hull*. In AAS, *Transactions and Collections* (1857). Reprinted in *A Library of Puritan Writings: the Seventeenth Century*. Edited by Sacvan Bercovitch; vol. 7, *Puritan Personal Writings: Diaries*. N.Y.: AMS Press, 1982.

Hutchinson, Thomas. *The History of the Colony and Province of Massachusetts Bay*. Edited by Lawrence Shaw Mayo. 3 vols. Cambridge: Harvard University Press, 1936.

Labaree, Leonard W., ed. *Royal Instructions to British Governors, 1670–1776*. 2 vols. N.Y.: Appleton-Century for the American Historical Society, 1935.

Lodowick, Christian. *1695. The New-England Almanack*. Boston, 1695.

McLoughlin, William G. and Martha Whiting Davidson, eds. "The Baptist Debate of April 14–15, 1668." In MHS, *Proceedings* 76, 1965: 91–133.

Mather, Cotton. "Defence of Evangelical Churches." In John Quick, *Young Man's Claim*. Boston, 1700.

―――. *Ecclesiastes; the Life of the Reverend and Excellent Jonathan Mitchell*. Boston, 1697.

―――. *Magnalia Christi Americana*. London, 1702. Edited by Samuel G. Drake. 2 vols. Hartford, Conn., 1853.

―――. *Maternal Consolation*. Boston, 1714.

―――. *Parentator. Memoirs of Remarkables in the Life and the Death of the Ever-Memorable Dr. Increase Mather*. Boston, 1724.

Mather, Eleazar. *A Serious Exhortation to the Present and Succeeding Generation in New-England*. Cambridge, 1671.

Mather, Increase. *Advice to the Children of Godly Ancestors*. In Cotton Mather, *A Course of Sermons on Early Piety*. Boston, 1721.

―――. *Angelographia*. Boston, 1696.

―――. "An Answer to Mr. Stoddard's 9 Arguments against Examinations concerning a Work of Grace. . . ." Edited by Everett Emerson and Mason I. Lowance. AAS, *Proceedings* 83, pt. 1 (1973): 29–66.

―――. *An Apologetical Preface to the Reader*. In John Davenport, *Another Essay*. Cambridge, 1663.

―――. *An Arrow against Profane and Promiscuous Dancing*. Boston, 1684.

―――. *Autobiography*. Edited by Michael G. Hall. Worcester, Mass., 1962.

―――. *Awakening Soul-Saving Truths*. Boston, 1720.

―――. *Awakening Truths Tending to Conversion*. Boston, 1710.

―――. *The Blessed Hope, and the Glorious Appearing of the Great God our Saviour, Jesus Christ*. Boston, 1701.

―――. *A Brief Account Concerning Several of the Agents of New-England*. London, 1691.

―――. *A Brief Discourse Concerning the Unlawfulness of the Common Prayer Worship*. Cambridge, 1686.

―――. *A Brief History of the War with the Indians of New-England*. Boston, 1676.

―――. *A Brief Relation of the State of New England*. London, 1689.

―――. *Burnings Bewailed*. Boston, 1711.

―――. *A Call from Heaven to the Present and Succeeding Generations*. Boston, 1679.

―――. *Cases of Conscience Concerning Evil Spirits*. Boston, 1693.

―――. *The Day of Trouble is near*. Cambridge, 1674.

―――. [Diary.] "A Few of Dr. Belknap's Extracts" from a lost diary of 1674–1687. MHS, *Proceedings* 3 (1855–1858): 317–320.

―――. [Diary, 1675–1676.] MHS, *Proceedings*, 2 ser., 13 (1899–1900): 337–374.

―――. [Diary.] Belknap extracts not printed previously. MHS, *Proceedings*, 2 ser., 13 (1899–1900): 397–411.

―――. *Diatriba de Signo Filii Hominis, et de Secundo Messiae Adventu*. Amstelodami, 1682.

―――. *A Discourse Concerning Baptism*. Cambridge, 1675.

―――. *A Discourse Concerning Earthquakes*. Boston, 1706.

―――. *A Discourse Concerning Faith and Fervency in Prayer*. Boston, 1710.

―――. *A Discourse Concerning the Existence and Omniscience of God*. Boston, 1716.

―――. "A discourse Concerning the glorious state of the church on earth under the New Jerusalem." Edited by Mason I. Lowance and David Watters. AAS, *Proceedings* 87, pt. 2 (1977): 362–408.

———. *A Discourse Concerning the Uncertainty of the Times of Men*. Boston, 1697.

———. *A Discourse Proving that the Christian Religion is the only True Religion*. Boston, 1702.

———. *A Disquisition Concerning Ecclesiastical Councils*. Boston, 1716.

———. *A Dissertation Concerning the Future Conversion of the Jewish Nation*. London, 1709.

———. *A Dissertation Wherein the Strange Doctrine . . . is Examined and Confuted*. Boston, 1708.

———. *The Divine Right of Infant Baptism*. Boston, 1680.

———. *The Doctrine of Divine Providence*. Boston, 1684.

———. *A Dying Legacy of a Minister to his Dearly Beloved People*. Boston, 1722.

———. *An Earnest Exhortation to the Inhabitants*. Boston, 1676.

———. Epistle Dedicatory. In Cotton Mather, *Ecclesiastes*. Boston, 1697.

———. *An Essay for the Recording of Illustrious Providences*. Boston, 1684.

———. *The Excellency of a Publick Spirit*. Boston, 1702.

———. "Fare-wel Sermon." June 29, 1701. Excerpted in Cotton Mather, *Parentator,* 174–179.

———. *The First Principles of New-England*. Cambridge, 1675.

———. *Five Sermons on Several Subjects*. Boston, 1719.

———. *The Folly of Sinning Opened and Applyed*. Boston, 1699.

———. *Further Testimony Against the Scandalous Proceedings of the New-North Church in Boston*. Boston, 1720.

———. *A Further Vindication of New-England*. London, 1689.

———. *The Great Blessing of Primitive Counsellours*. Boston, 1693.

———. *The Greatest Sinners Exhorted . . . to Come to Christ*. Boston, 1686.

———. *Heaven's Alarm to the World*. Boston, 1681.

———. *An Historical Discourse Concerning the Prevalancy of Prayer*. Boston, 1677.

———. *Ichabod or a Discourse Shewing what Cause there is to Fear that the Glory of the Lord, is Departing from New-England*. Boston, 1702.

———. *Kometographia, Or a Discourse Concerning Comets*. Boston, 1683.

———. *The Latter Sign Discoursed*. Issued with the second printing of *Heaven's Alarm to the World*. Boston, 1682.

———. *The Life and Death of that Reverend Man of God, Mr. Richard Mather*. Cambridge, 1670. Facsimile edition, edited by William J. Scheick. Bainbridge, N.Y.: York-Mail Print, 1974.

———. *Masukkenukeeg Matcheseaenvog*. An Algonkian translation of *The Greatest Sinners Exhorted*. Boston, 1698.

———. *Meditations on Death*. Boston, 1707.

———. *Meditations on the Glory of the Heavenly World*. Boston, 1714.

———. *The Mystery of Christ Opened and Applyed*. Boston, 1686.

———. *The Mystery of Israel's Salvation*. London, 1669.

———. *A Narrative of the Miseries of New-England*. London, 1688.

———. *The Necessity of a Reformation*. Boston, 1679.

———. *New-England Vindicated*. London, 1689.

———. *The Order of the Gospel*. Boston, 1700.

————. *Plain Discourse Shewing Who Shall, and Who Shall not, Enter . . . Heaven.* Boston, 1713.

————. *Practical Truths Tending to Promote Holiness.* Boston, 1704.

————. *Practical Truths Tending to Promote the Power of Godliness.* Boston, 1682.

————. *Pray for the Rising Generation.* Cambridge, 1678.

————. Preface. In J. S., *Second Spira.* Boston, 1693.

————. Preface. In Cotton Mather, *Brethren Dwelling Together in Unity.* Boston, 1718.

————. *The Present State of the New-English Affairs.* Boston, 1689.

————. *Reasons for the Confirmation of the Charters belonging to the Several Corporations in New-England.* London, 1691. Reprinted in *Andros Tracts,* 2:225–229.

————. *A Relation Of the Troubles which have hapned in New-England, By reason of the Indians there.* Boston, 1677.

————. *Renewal of Covenant the Great Duty.* Boston, 1677.

————. *Returning unto God the Great Concernment of a Covenant People.* Boston, 1680.

————. *Seasonable Meditations both for Winter and Summer.* Boston, 1712.

————. *Seasonable Testimony to Good Order.* Boston, 1720.

————. *A Sermon Concerning Obedience and Resignation to the Will of God in Everything.* Boston, 1714.

————. *Sermon Occasioned by the Execution.* Boston and Salem, 1686.

————. *Sermons Wherein those Eight Characters . . . Commonly Called the Beatitudes.* Boston, 1718.

————. *Several Reasons Proving that Inoculating or Transplanting the Small Pox, is a Lawful Practice.* Boston, 1721.

————. *Several Sermons Wherein is Showed That Jesus Christ is a Mighty Saviour.* Boston, 1715.

————. *Solemn Advice to Young Men.* Boston, 1695.

————. *Some further Account of the Small Pox Inoculated.* Boston, 1722.

————. *Some Important Truths about Conversion.* London, 1674.

————. *Some Remarks on a Late Sermon . . . by George Keith.* Boston, 1702.

————. *Some Remarks on a Pretended Answer.* Boston, 1713.

————. *Soul-Saving Gospel Truths.* Boston, 1703.

————. *Successu Evangelij Apud Indios in Nova-Anglia.* London, 1688.

————. *The Surest Way to the Greatest Honour.* Boston, 1699.

————. *A Testimony Against Several Prophane and Superstitious Customs.* London, 1687.

————. *Testimony Finished.* In Cotton Mather, *Elijah's Mantle.* Boston, 1722.

————. *The Times of Men are in the Hand of God.* Boston, 1675.

————. To the Reader. In Thomas Thacher, *A Fast of God's Chusing.* Boston, 1678.

————. To the Reader. In Nehemiah Walter, *Plain Discourse Concerning the Wonderfulness of Christ.* Boston, 1713.

————. *Two Plain and Practical Discourses.* London, 1699.

————. *The Voice of God in Stormy Winds.* Boston, 1704.

————. *The Wicked Man's Portion.* Boston, 1675.

————. *Wo to Drunkards.* Cambridge, 1673.

Mather, Increase, et al., *Account of the Reasons.* Boston, 1720.

Mather, Increase. Last Will and Testament. *New England Historical and Genealogical Register*, 5 (1851): 445–447.

Mather, Richard. *A Farewel Exhortation to the Church and People of Dorchester*. Cambridge, 1657.

———. Last Will and Testament. *New England Historical and Genealogical Register* 20 (1866): 248–255.

———. and Jonathan Mitchell. *Defense of the Answer and Arguments of the Synod*. Cambridge, 1664.

Mather, Samuel (1626–1671). *The Figures or Types of the Old Testament*. Dublin, 1683; London, 1705. Edited by Mason I. Lowance, Jr. New York: Johnson Reprint Corp., 1969.

Mather, Samuel (1674–1733). *Memoirs of the Life of the Late Reverend Increase Mather, D.D.*. London, 1725.

Mather, Samuel (1706–1785). *The Life of the Very Reverend and Learned Cotton Mather*. Boston, 1729.

Mather Papers. MHS, *Collections*, 4th ser., 8 (1866).

Murdock, Kenneth B., ed., "Increase Mather's Expenses as Colonial Agent." In CSM, *Publications*, 27 (1932): 200–204.

Newton, Isaac. *Sir Isaac Newton's Mathematical Principles*. Translated and edited by Florian Cajori. 2 vols. Berkeley: University of California Press, 1934, 1962.

Norton, John. *Abel Being Dead, Yet Speaketh; or the Life and Death of . . . John Cotton*. London, 1658.

———. *The Answer to the Whole Set of Questions of the Celebrated Mr. William Apollonius*. Translated by Douglas Horton. Cambridge: Harvard University Press, 1958.

Quick, John. *The Young Man's Claim Unto the Sacrament of the Lords-Supper*. Boston, 1700.

Richardson, John. *1670. An Almanac*. Cambridge, 1670.

Rowlandson, Mary. *The Sovereignty and Goodness of God . . . A Narrative of the Captivity and Restauration of Mrs. Mary Rowlandson*. Cambridge, 1682. Reprinted in Richard Slotkin and James K. Folson, *So Dreadfull a Judgment: Puritan Responses to King Philip's War, 1676–1677*. Middletown, Conn.: Wesleyan University Press, 1978.

Sewall, Samuel. *Diary of Samuel Sewall, 1674–1729*. Edited by M. Halsey Thomas. 2 vols. N.Y.: Farrar, Straus and Giroux, 1973.

Shepard, Thomas. *God's Plot: the Paradoxes of Puritan Piety, Being the Autobiography and Journal of Thomas Shepard*. Edited by Michael McGiffert. Amherst: University of Massachusetts Press, 1972.

Sherman, John. *1674. An Almanac*. Cambridge, 1674.

———. *1676. An Almanac*. Cambridge, 1676.

———. *1677. An Almanac*. Cambridge, 1677.

Shurtleff, Nathaniel B., ed. *Records of the Company and Governor of the Massachusetts Bay in New England*. 5 vols. Boston, 1853–1854.

Slotkin, Richard and James K. Folsom. *So Dreadfull a Judgment: Puritan Responses to King Philip's War, 1676–1677*. Middletown, Conn.: Wesleyan University Press, 1978.

Stoddard, Solomon. *The Doctrine of Instituted Churches Explained and Proved from the Word of God*. London, 1700.

——. *Guide to Christ*. Boston, 1714.

——. *The Inexcusableness of Neglecting the Worship of God*. Boston, 1708.

——. *The Safety of Appearing at the Day of Judgement*. Boston, 1687.

Suffolk County, Massachusetts. *Records of the County Court, 1671–1680*. CSM, *Publications*, 29–30 (1933).

Thorpe, Francis Newton, ed. *The Federal and State Constitutions, Colonial Charters, and Other Organic Laws of . . . the United States of America*. 7 vols. Washington: Government Printing Office, 1909.

Torrey, Samuel. *An Exhortation unto Reformation*. Cambridge, 1674.

Toxan, Robert N. and Alfred T. S. Goodrick, eds. *Edward Randolph; Including His Letters and Official Papers. . . .* 7 vols. Boston: Prince Society, 1898–1909.

Tully, John. *An Almanac*. Boston and Cambridge, 1687–1691.

Walker, Williston. *Creeds and Platforms of Congregationalism*. New York: Scribner's Sons, 1893. Boston: Pilgrim Press, 1960.

Whitmore, William H., ed., *The Andros Tracts*. 3 vols. Boston: Prince Society, 1868–1874.

Willard, Samuel. *The Character of a Good Ruler*. Boston, 1694.

——. *Ne Sutor Ultra Crepidam. Or Brief Animadversions Upon the New-England Anabaptists Late Fallacious Narrative*. Boston, 1681.

Wise, John. *The Church's Quarrel Espoused*. New York, 1713. Edited by George A. Cook. Gainesville, Fla.: Scholars' Facsimiles and Reprints, 1966.

——. *A Vindication of the Government of New-England Churches*. Boston, 1717. Edited by Perry Miller. Gainesville, Fla.: Scholars' Facsimiles and Reprints, 1958.

Wood, William. *New Englands Prospect*. London, 1634. Facsimile reprint in *The English Experience*. Number 68. New York: Da Capo Press, 1968.

IV. PRINTED SECONDARY SOURCES

Auerbach, Erich. *Scenes from the Drama of European Literature*. New York: Meridian, 1959.

Backus, Isaac. *Church History of New England from 1620 to 1804*. Philadelphia, 1853.

Beal, Otho T. "Cotton Mather's Early 'Curiosa Americana' and the Boston Philosophical Society of 1683." *William and Mary Quarterly* 3 ser., 18 (1961): 360–372.

Belknap, Jeremy. *The History of New Hampshire*. 2 vols. Dover, N.H., 1812, 1831; New York: Johnson Reprint, 1970.

Bercovitch, Sacvan. *The American Jeremiad*. Madison, Wisc.: University of Wisconsin Press, 1978.

Bolleine, Geneviève. *Les Almanaches Populairs Aux XVIIᵉ et XVIIIᵉ Siècles*. Paris: Mouton, 1969.

Bosco, Ronald A. "Lectures at the Pillory: the Early American Execution Sermons." *American Quarterly* 30, pt. 2 (1978): 156–176.

Boston, Museum of Fine Arts. *New England Begins: The Seventeenth Century*. Prepared by Jonathan L. Fairbanks and Robert F. Trent. 3 vols. Boston: Museum of Fine Arts, 1982.

Boyer, Paul and Stephen Nissenbaum. *Salem Possessed: The Social Origins of Witchcraft*. Cambridge: Harvard University Press, 1974.

Breen, T. H. *The Character of the Good Ruler: Puritan Political Ideas in New England, 1630–1730.* New Haven: Yale University Press, 1970.

Bremer, Francis J. "Increase Mather's Friends: The Transatlantic Congregational Network of the Seventeenth Century." AAS, *Proceedings* 94, pt. 1 (1984): 59–96.

———. *The Puritan Experiment: New England Society from Bradford to Edwards.* New York: St. Martin's Press, 1976.

Bridenbaugh, Carl. *Cities in the Wilderness: the First Century of Urban Life in America, 1625–1742.* Ronald Series in History. New York: Ronald Press, 1938.

Brumm, Ursula. *American Thought and Religious Typology.* New Brunswick, N.J.: Rutgers University Press, 1970.

Burg, Richard Bary. *Richard Mather of Dorchester.* Louisville: University of Kentucky Press, 1976.

Burke, Peter. *Popular Culture in Early Modern Europe.* London: Temple Smith, 1978.

Cadbury, Henry J. "Harvard College Library and the Libraries of the Mathers." AAS, *Proceedings,* n.s., 50 (1940): 20–48.

Calder, Isabel M. *The New Haven Colony.* New Haven: Yale University Press, 1934.

Caldwell, Patricia. *The Puritan Conversion Narrative. The Beginnings of American Expression.* Cambridge: Cambridge University Press, 1983.

Chapman, Clayton H. "Life and Influence of Reverend Benjamin Colman, D.D." Ph.D. diss., Boston University, 1947.

Cohen, I. Bernard. "The *Compendium Physicae* of Charles Morton." *Isis,* 33 (1942): 659–660.

Cook, George Allen. *John Wise, Early American Democrat.* New York: Columbia University Press, 1952.

Cragg, G. R. *From Puritanism to the Age of Reason: a Study in Religious Thought within the Church of England, 1660–1700.* Cambridge: Cambridge University Press, 1966.

Dalton, John Vasmar. "Ministers, Metaphors, and the New England Wilderness, 1650–1700." Ph.D. diss., University of New Hampshire, 1981.

Damerall, David Odell. "Modernization of Massachusetts: the Transformation of Public Attitudes and Institutions, 1689–1715." Ph.D. diss., University of Texas at Austin, 1981.

Davis, Thomas M. and Jeff Jeske. "Solomon Stoddard's 'Arguments' Concerning Admission to the Lord's Supper." AAS, *Proceedings* 86, pt. 1 (1876): 75–111.

Demos, John Putnam. *Entertaining Satan: Witchcraft and Culture of Early New England.* New York: Oxford University Press, 1982.

Demos, John. "Notes on Life in Plymouth Colony." *William and Mary Quarterly* 3rd ser., 22 (1965): 264–286.

Dobree, Bonamy. *English Literature in the Eighteenth Century.* Oxford History of English Literature, vol. 7. New York: Oxford University Press, 1959.

Drake, Samuel G. "Pedigree of the Family of Mather." In Cotton Mather, *Magnalia Christi Americana,* Edited by Samuel G. Drake. Hartford, Conn., 1853.

Elliott, Emory. *The Power and the Pulpit in Puritan New England.* Princeton: Princeton University Press, 1975.

Emerson, Everett and Mason I. Lowance, Jr. "Increase Mather's Confutation of Solomon Stoddard's Observations Respecting the Lord's Supper, 1680." AAS, *Proceedings* 83, pt. 1 (1973): 29–66.

Fiering, Norman. "The First American Enlightenment: Tillotson, Leverett, and

Philosophical Anglicanism." *New England Quarterly* 54 (1981): 307–344.

———. *Moral Philosophy at Seventeenth-Century Harvard. A Discipline in Transition.* Chapel Hill: University of North Carolina Press for the Institute of Early American History and Culture, 1981.

Fleming, Sandford. *Children and Puritanism. The Place of Children in the Life and Thought of the New England Churches, 1620–1847.* New Haven: Yale University Press, 1933.

Foster, Stephen. "English Puritanism and the Progress of New England Institutions, 1630–1660." In *Saints and Revolutionaries, Essays on Early American History.* Edited by David D. Hall, John M. Murrin, and Thad W. Tate. N.Y.: Norton, 1984.

Giles, Charles Burke. "Benjamin Colman: A Study of the Movement Toward Reasonable Religion in the Seventeenth Century." Ph.D. diss., University of California at Los Angeles, 1963.

Gilsdorf, Aletha. "The Puritan Apocalypse: New England Eschatology in the Seventeenth Century." Ph.D. diss., Yale University, 1965.

Goulding, James A. "The Controversy Between Solomon Stoddard and the Mathers: Western versus Eastern Massachusetts Congregationalism." Ph.D. diss., Claremont Graduate School, 1971.

Green, Samuel Abbott. *John Foster, the Earliest American Engraver and First Boston Printer.* Boston: Massachusetts Historical Society, 1909.

Greenough, Chester Noyes. "John Dunton's Letters from New England." CSM, *Publications,* 14 (1913): 213–257.

Greven, Philip J., Jr. *Four Generations: Population, Land, and Family in Colonial Andover, Massachusetts.* Ithaca: Cornell University Press, 1970.

Gura, Philip F. *A Glimpse of Sion's Glory. Puritan Radicalism in New England.* Middletown, Conn.: Wesleyan University Press, 1984.

Haffenden, Philip. *New England and the English Nation, 1689–1713.* Oxford: Clarendon Press, 1974.

Hall, David D. *The Faithful Shepherd: A History of the New England Ministry in the Seventeenth Century.* Chapel Hill: University of North Carolina Press for the Institute of Early American History and Culture, 1972.

———. "On Native Ground." AAS, *Proceedings* 93, pt. 2 (1983): 316–336.

———. "Understanding the Puritans." In *The State of American History.* Edited by Herbert J. Bass. Chicago: Quadrangle Books, 1970.

Hall, Michael G. *Edward Randolph and the American Colonies, 1676–1703.* Chapel Hill: University of North Carolina Press for the Institute of Early American History and Culture, 1960.

———. "Introduction of Modern Science into Seventeenth-Century New England: Increase Mather." *Ithaca* 26 VIII–2 IX, 261–264. Paris: Hermann, 1962.

———, and Lawrence H. Leder and Michael G. Kammen. *The Glorious Revolution in America.* Chapel Hill: University of North Carolina Press for the Institute of Early American History and Culture, 1964.

———, and William L. Joyce. "Three Manuscripts of Increase Mather." AAS, *Proceedings* 86, pt. 1 (1976): 113–123.

——— and ———. "The Half-Way Covenant of 1662: Some New Evidence." AAS, *Proceedings* 87, pt. 1 (1977): 97–110.

Haller, William. *The Rise of Puritanism.* New York: Columbia University Press, 1938; Harper and Row Torchbook, 1957.

Hambrick-Stowe, Charles E. *The Practice of Piety. Puritan Devotional Discipline in Seventeenth-Century New England.* Chapel Hill: University of North Carolina Press for the Institute of Early American History and Culture, 1982.

Hill, Christopher. *Puritanism and Revolution: Studies in Interpretation of the English Revolution of the Seventeenth Century.* New York: Schocken, 1964.

Hill, Hamilton A. *History of the Old South Church (Third Church) Boston, 1669–1884.* 2 vols. Boston: Houghton-Mifflin, 1890.

Holifield, Brooks. *The Covenant Sealed: the Development of Puritan Sacramental Theology in Old and New England, 1570–1720.* New Haven: Yale University Press, 1974.

————. "On Toleration in Massachusetts." *Church History* 38, no. 2 (June, 1969): 188–197.

Holman, Richard B. "John Foster's Woodcut Map of New England." *PAGA: Printing and Graphic Arts* 8 (1960): 53–92.

Illick, Joseph E. "Child-Rearing in Seventeenth-Century England and America." In *The History of Childhood.* Lloyd de Mause, ed. New York: Psychohistory Press, 1974.

Johnson, Richard R. *Adjustment to Empire: the New England Colonies, 1675–1715.* New Brunswick, N.J.: Rutgers University Press: 1981.

Jones, James W. *The Shattered Synthesis: New England Puritanism Before the Great Awakening.* New Haven: Yale University Press, 1973.

Jones, R. Tudur. *Congregationalism in England, 1662–1962.* London: Independent Press, 1962.

Joyce, William L. "Note on Increase Mather's Observations Respecting the Lord's Supper." AAS, *Proceedings* 83, pt. 2 (1973): 343–344.

Kellaway, William. *The New England Company, 1649–1776.* London: Longmans Green, 1961.

Keller, Karl. "Edward Taylor and the Mathers." *Moderna Språk* 72, no. 2 (1978), 119–135.

Kimball, Everett. *The Public Life of Joseph Dudley.* Harvard Historical Studies, vol. 15. New York: Longmans Green, 1911.

Langdon, George D., Jr. *Pilgrim Colony: A History of New Plymouth, 1620–1691.* New Haven: Yale University Press, 1966.

Leach, Douglas Edward. *Flintlock and Tomahawk: New England in King Philip's War.* New York: Norton, 1958.

Leverenz, David. *The Language of Puritan Feeling. An Exploration in Literature, Psychology, and Social History.* New Brunswick, N.J.: Rutgers University Press, 1980.

Levin, David. *Cotton Mather: The Young Life of the Lord's Remembrancer, 1663–1703.* Cambridge: Harvard University Press, 1978.

————. "Did the Mathers Disagree about the Salem Witchcraft Trials?" AAS, *Proceedings* 95, pt. 1 (1985): 19–37.

Lewis, Theodore B. "Land Speculation and the Dudley Council of 1688." *William and Mary Quarterly* 3rd ser., 31 (1974): 255–272.

————. "Sir Edmund Andros's Hearing before the Lords of Trade and Plantations, April 17, 1690." AAS, *Proceedings* 88, pt. 2 (1974): 241–250.

Littlefield, George Emery. *Early Boston Booksellers*. Boston: Club of Odd Volumes, 1900.

——. *The Early Massachusetts Press, 1638–1711*. 2 vols. Boston: Club of Odd Volumes, 1907.

Lockridge, Kenneth. *A New England Town: The First Hundred Years*. New York: Norton, 1970.

Lovejoy, David S. *The Glorious Revolution in America*. New York: Harper and Row, 1972.

Lowance, Mason I., Jr. *Increase Mather*. Twayne's United States Authors Series. New York: Twayne, 1974.

——. *The Language of Canaan. Metaphor and Symbol in New England from the Puritans to the Transcendentalists*. Cambridge: Harvard University Press, 1980.

—— and David Watters. "Increase Mather's 'New Jerusalem': Millennialism in Late Seventeenth-Century New England." AAS, *Proceedings* 87, pt. 2 (1978): 343–361.

Lucas, Paul. "'An Appeal to the Learned': the Mind of Solomon Stoddard." *William and Mary Quarterly* 3rd ser., 30 (1973): 257–292.

——. *Valley of Discord: Church and Society along the Connecticut River, 1636–1725*. Hanover, N.H.: University Press of New England, 1976.

McLoughlin, William G. *New England Dissent, 1630–1833. Baptists and the Separation of Church and State*. Cambridge: Harvard University Press, 1971.

Matthews, A. G. *Calamy Revised, Being a Revision of Edmund Calamy's Account of the Ministers and Others Ejected and Silenced, 1660–1662*. Oxford: Clarendon Press, 1934.

Merton, Robert K. *Social Theory and Social Structure*. New York: Free Press, 1968.

Middlekauf, Robert. *The Mathers. Three Generations of Puritan Intellectuals*. New York: Oxford University Press, 1971.

Miller, Perry. *Errand into the Wilderness*. Cambridge: Harvard University Press, 1956; New York: Harper and Row, 1964.

——. *The New England Mind: From Colony to Province*. Cambridge: Harvard University Press, 1953.

——. "Solomon Stoddard, 1643–1729." *Harvard Theological Review* 34 (1941): 277–320.

—— and Thomas H. Johnson. *The Puritans*. 2 vols. New York: Harper and Row Torchbook, 1963.

Morgan, Edmund S. *American Slavery, American Freedom*. New York: Norton, 1975.

——, ed., *The Founding of Massachusetts*. New York: Bobbs Merrill, 1964.

——. *The Puritan Family. Religion and Domestic Relations in Seventeenth-Century New England*. Revised edition. New York: Harper and Row Torchbook, 1956.

——. *Visible Saints. The History of a Puritan Idea*. New York: New York University Press, 1963.

Morison, Samuel Eliot. *Harvard College in the Seventeenth Century*. 2 vols. Cambridge: Harvard University Press, 1936.

——. "The Harvard School of Astronomy in the Seventeenth Century." *New England Quarterly* 7 (1934): 3–7.

Murdock, Kenneth B. "Clio in the Wilderness: History and Biography in Puritan New England." *Church History* 24 (1955): 221–228. Reprinted in *Early American Literature* 6 (1972): 201–219.

————. *Increase Mather, The Foremost American Puritan*. Cambridge: Harvard University Press, 1925.

————. *Literature and Theology in Colonial New England*. Cambridge: Harvard University Press, 1949.

————. *The Portraits of Increase Mather*. Cleveland: W. G. Mather, 1924.

Nelsen, Anne Kusener. "King Philip's War and the Hubbard-Mather Rivalry." *William and Mary Quarterly*, 3rd ser., 27 (October 1970): 615–629.

Ornstein, Martha. *The Rôle of the Scientific Societies in the Seventeenth Century*. New York: Columbia University, 1913.

Parrington, Vernon Louis. *Main Currents in American Thought*. Vol. 1, *The Colonial Mind*. New York: Harcourt, Brace, 1930.

Petit, Norman. *The Heart Prepared: Grace and Conversion in Puritan Spiritual Life*. New Haven: Yale University Press, 1966.

Plumstead, A. W., ed. *The Wall and the Garden*. *Selected Massachusetts Election Sermons, 1670–1775*. Minneapolis: University of Minnesota Press, 1968.

Pope, Robert. *The Half-Way Covenant: Church Membership in Puritan New England*. Princeton: Princeton University Press, 1969.

Quincy, Josiah. *History of Harvard University*. 2 vols. Cambridge: J. Owen, 1840.

Reed, Susan Martha. *Church and State in Massachusetts, 1691–1740*. Urbana: University of Illinois Press, 1914.

Robbins, Chandler. *A History of the Second Church, or Old North in Boston*. Boston: The Society, 1852.

Roper, Stephen J. "The Early History of the Paul Revere House." In *Architecture in Colonial Massachusetts*, CSM, *Publications* 51 (1979): 3–21.

Rutman, Darrett B. *Winthrop's Boston: Portrait of a Puritan Town, 1630–1649*. Chapel Hill: University of North Carolina Press for the Institute of Early American History and Culture, 1965.

Sachse, William L. "Harvard Men in England, 1642–1714." CSM, *Publications* 35 (1951): 119–144.

Scholem, Gershom. *Sabbatai Sevi. The Mystical Messiah, 1626–1676*. Princeton: Princeton University Press, 1973.

Shea, Daniel B. *Spiritual Autobiography in Early America*. Princeton: Princeton University Press, 1968.

Shipton, Clifford K. *Biographical Sketches of those who Attended Harvard College. Sibley's Harvard Graduates*. Vols. 4–7. Cambridge: Harvard University Press, 1933–1945.

Shurtleff, Nathaniel B. *Topographical and Historical Description of Boston*. 3rd edition. Boston, 1890.

Sibley, J. L. *Biographical Sketches of Graduates of Harvard University*. 3 vols. Cambridge: MHS, 1873–1885.

Silverman, Kenneth. *The Life and Times of Cotton Mather*. New York: Harper and Row, 1984.

————. "A Note on the Date of Cotton Mather's Visitation by an Angel." *Early American Literature*, 15 (1980): 82–86.

Simmons, Richard C. "The Massachusetts Charter of 1691." In *Contrast and Connection: Bicentennial Essays in Anglo-American History*. Edited by H. C. Allen and Roger Thompson. London, 1976.

————. "Studies in the Massachusetts Franchise, 1631–1691." Ph.D. diss., University of California at Berkeley, 1965.

Sosin, J. M. *English America and the Restoration Monarchy of Charles II*. Lincoln: University of Nebraska Press, 1980.

————. *English America and the Revolution of 1689*. Lincoln: University of Nebraska Press, 1982.

Stannard, David E. *The Puritan Way of Death: a Study in Religion, Culture and Social Change*. New York: Oxford University Press, 1977.

Starkey, Marion L. *The Devil in Massachusetts: a Modern Enquiry into the Salem Witch Trials*. New York: Knopf, 1949; Garden City, N.Y.: Doubleday Anchor Book, 1969.

Stearns, Raymond Phineas. *Science in the British Colonies of America*. Chicago: University of Illinois Press, 1970.

Stowell, Marion Barber. *Early American Almanacs: the Colonial Weekday Bible*. New York: B. Franklin, 1977.

Thomas, Isaiah. *The History of Printing in America*. 2 vols. AAS, *Transactions and Collections* Vols. 5–6. New York: 1874.

Tichi, Celia. "Spiritual Biography and the 'Lord's Remembrancers'." *William and Mary Quarterly* 3rd ser., 28 (1971): 64–85.

Toon, Peter, ed. *Puritans, the Millennium and the Future of Israel: Puritan Eschatology, 1600–1660: a Collection of Essays*. Cambridge, Eng.: James Clarke, 1970.

Torrey, Clarence Almon. *New England Marriages Prior to 1700*. Baltimore: Genealogical Publishing Company, 1985.

Toulouse, Teresa. *The Art of Prophesying. New England Sermons and the Shaping of Belief*. Athens, Ga.: University of Georgia Press, 1987.

Turell, Ebenezer. *Life and Character of the Reverend Benjamin Colman, D.D.* Boston, 1749. Gainesville, Fla.: Scholars' Facsimiles and Reprints, 1972.

Tuttle, Julius H. "The Libraries of the Mathers." AAS, *Proceedings*, n.s. 20 (1910): 269–356.

Tuveson, Ernest Lee. *Redeemer Nation: the Idea of America's Millennial Role*. Chicago: University of Chicago Press, 1968.

Van de Wetering, Maxine. "Moralizing in Puritan Natural Science: Mysteriousness in Earthquake Sermons." *Journal of the History of Ideas* 43 (1982): 417–438.

Van Dyken, Seymour. *Samuel Willard, 1640–1707*. Grand Rapids, Mich.: Erdman, 1972.

Vaughan, Alden T. and Francis J. Bremer, eds. *Puritan New England; Essays on Religion, Society and Culture*. New York: St. Martin's Press, 1977.

Walsh, James P. "Solomon Stoddard's Open Communion: a Reexamination." *New England Quarterly* 43 (March 1970): 97–114.

Weber, Max. *The Protestant Ethic and the Spirit of Capitalism*. Translated by Talcott Parsons. New York: Scribner's Sons, 1930, 1958.

Weis, Frederick L. "Check List of the Portraits in the Library of the American Antiquarian Society." AAS, *Proceedings* 56, pt. 1 (1946): 55–128.

Willey, Basil. *Seventeenth Century Background. Studies in the Thought of the Age in Relation to Poetry and Religion*. London: 1934; Garden City, N.Y.: Doubleday Anchor Books, 1953.

Wroth, Lawrence and Marion W. Adams. *American Woodcuts and Engravings, 1670–1800*. Providence, R.I.: John Carter Library Associates, 1956.

Youngs, J. William T., Jr. *God's Messengers. Religious Leadership in Colonial New England, 1700–1750.* Baltimore: The Johns Hopkins University Press, 1976.

Ziff, Larzer. *Puritanism in America. New Culture in a New World.* New York: Viking, 1973.

Index

Page numbers in *italics* refer to illustrations or captions.

OTHER BOOKS BY MICHAEL G. HALL

Edward Randolph and the American Colonies, 1676–1703

EDITED BY MICHAEL G. HALL

Autobiography of Increase Mather

The Glorious Revolution in America
(WITH LAWRENCE H. LEDER AND MICHAEL G. KAMMEN)

Science and Society in the United States
(WITH DAVID D. VAN TASSEL)

ABOUT THE AUTHOR

Michael G. Hall is professor of history at the University of Texas at Austin, where he has taught since 1959 and served as chairman from 1976 to 1980. He is the editor of Increase Mather's autobiography and the author of *Edward Randolph and the American Colonies, 1676–1703*. A graduate of Princeton University (B.A. 1949) and Johns Hopkins University (Ph.D. 1956), he was a senior Fulbright lecturer at Quaid-i-Azam University in Islamabad, Pakistan, in 1985. Hall lives in Austin, Texas.

ABOUT THE BOOK

This book was composed on the Mergenthaler Linotron 202 in Garamond No. 3. Garamond was introduced in America by ATF in 1919, when their cutting, based on the caracteres de l'Universite of the Imprimerie Nationale, appeared. Many other versions were made by the English and American Linotype and Monotype, by Intertype, Ludlow, and the Stempel Foundry. It has been adapted for phototypesetting, CRT typesetting and laser typesetting.

The book was composed by G&S Typesetters, Inc. of Austin, Texas and designed and produced by Kachergis Book Design, Pittsboro, North Carolina.

WESLEYAN UNIVERSITY PRESS, 1988